CW01546075

Love Magic Power Danger Bliss

Love Magic Power Danger Bliss

YOKO ONO
and the
Avant-Garde
Diaspora

PAUL MORLEY

faber

First published in 2026
by Faber & Faber Ltd
The Bindery, 51 Hatton Garden
London EC1N 8HN

Typeset by Typo•glyphix, Burton-on-Trent, DE14 3HE
Printed and bound by CPI Group (UK) Ltd, Croydon, CR0 4YY

A CIP record for this book
is available from the British Library

ISBN 978–0–571–37924–8

MIX
Paper | Supporting
responsible forestry
FSC® C013604

Printed and bound in the UK on FSC® certified paper in line with our continuing
commitment to ethical business practices, sustainability and the environment.
For further information see faber.co.uk/environmental-policy

Our authorised representative in the EU for product safety is
Easy Access System Europe, Mustamäe tee 50, 10621 Tallinn, Estonia
gpsr.requests@easproject.com

2 4 6 8 10 9 7 5 3 1

'Art doesn't interest me. Only artists interest me.'
Marcel Duchamp

'Anything is possible – even conceptual art.'
John Cage

e.s.p.

Contents

I.

If you believe Yoko Ono was your favourite Beatle
explain why in book form.

II.

1. Write a book based on a true story.
2. What was Yoko Ono doing before 7 November 1967?
3. Embroider.

III.

Vitriol.

IV.

Strategy.

V.

Begin anywhere.

This is a book about Yoko Ono, and some other artists she met and worked with, taking on the avant-garde and collectively planning a future. John Lennon will not be mentioned. This is her world, and we can't let all of that other business blot out the light.

On the other hand, it would be silly to pretend that you can write a book about Yoko Ono without ever getting to John Lennon. There, it's already been done. Twice. On the first page. Johnandyoko, oh Yoko, bottoms, bed-ins, and all that etc.

Maybe that's it. So you know where you are, just in case you started wondering. It's that Yoko, and from now on, it's all Yoko.

Then again . . . Did Yoko Ono actually exist before John Lennon? Is she born – named, known and notorious – only after John Lennon and all his raging energy flows into her life? She first came across him in an art gallery in London in 1966, when they were fashionable places to be seen if you were a pop star, or any kind of entertainer. She was taking her art seriously, he wasn't in the mood to. She was the more experimental, he was more the performer. They could easily have looked past each other and never met.

She was the Yoko Ono best known in 1960/1 for the short series of events and activities she organised in her cold-water Lower Manhattan loft with the experimental composer La Monte Young. They were initiating a new kind of scene, but every participant was an individual, not interested in being part of a movement or a follower.

She was the Yoko Ono best known in 1962 for displaying works in the process of realisation in obscure underground art galleries, the Yoko Ono whose paintings came in the form of instructions.

The Yoko Ono inviting others to participate in a long-running artistic process exploring the relationship between mind and things that for a while looked like it might only have an audience of hundreds. The Yoko

Ono who was different at different times. The Yoko Ono as a social agent dividing the world into two groups more than any other artist: those who understood avant-garde art and those who not only didn't understand avant-garde art, but actively disliked it and could not see a place for it in the grand scheme of things. The Yoko Ono who had three husbands, each one helping her become herself in different ways.

Or the Yoko Ono who turned her fame and fortune into an extended absurdist performance. The Yoko Ono who often felt like just screaming into the void.

The Yoko Ono who was accused of making her third marriage strange and unlovely and infecting her husband with slapdash extremism, breaking up his supremely popular and beloved group, and dragging him over to the dark side, ruining his innocence.

The John Lennon who was never widely accused of disrupting her momentum, pulling her away from her place, breaking up the group she was in and dropping her into tabloid hell.

This is a book about Yoko Ono in which it's another John, the philosopher-musician John Cage, who helps her become an artist, sometimes by following through on some of his ideas, sometimes by breaking away from his thinking and continuing with her own. He helps her understand things she understood her whole life, but in a new way.

She first came across the genial, devious John Cage in the late 1950s in a classroom in New York, where he was teaching a few stray dissidents how to think conceptually in the area of art and music. He did this mostly through urging his students to experiment with their lives – to try out different lives – and develop strategies for coping, because if you were avant-garde, you were a kind of deserter, you were hiding in the woods. It might be a lonely life, spent mostly as a fugitive lurking in the margins. And if it wasn't a lonely life, you'd still have a lot to deal with.

When John Cage first smiled at her after one of his talks, she thought, I know exactly what he means. We are links in a chain. We are all a necessary part of an important search, for which there is no end. Being an artist is as much about building a higher awareness as it is about making things.

3

Then, when she put on the first night's musical and artistic activity at the Chambers Street loft, in front of a handful of curious onlookers, John Cage was there, and so was the elusive, vital Marcel Duchamp, who, rumour had it at the time, had revolutionised art – and as we can see more clearly, and darkly, in the twenty-first century, in one way or another, because facts can be distorted, revolutionised the lives we all lead. He had certainly inspired John Cage to see that art, and music, may be discovered everywhere.

When Duchamp first smiled at Yoko, it was just a glance, a nod, a gesture, but simply that he was in the same room as her, sharing a moment, obliquely approving her movements, was all the advice she needed. Anything is possible, even turning your life into a work of art.

The rest was up to her.

Here's Yoko Ono, introducing herself. I'm a spirit in the world. I'm a woman. I'm a human being. I have agency. I have a voice. I don't give a fuck. I'm violent in my desire for peace. I go with the flow. I'm valued. I'm not valued. I'm beautiful. I'm a cruel joke. I'm talking to anyone who will listen and those who won't. I am the avant-garde. I am beyond the avant-garde. I'm alone. I'm not the only one. Fuck you. I'm not going to disappear.

The Yoko Ono who for many just appeared out of some kind of fog in about 1967. There she was, an unknown from an unknown country. For some, where she had come from was somewhere not worth knowing and she was here purely in order to declare war on the order of things, so as to bother people who decided she didn't belong where she ended up. It would be best all in all if she just went back to wherever it was she had come from and was never heard of again. She deeply troubled people, for being so different, for thinking and seeing and hearing things differently, for, so it seemed, breaking the world, and breaking promises she'd never even made.

The Yoko Ono who has only just started.

The Yoko Ono who knew without art there is only fiction. Without art there is only order. Without art there is no way forward. Without art nothing happens next. Without art everything is forgotten.

The Yoko Ono starring in a history of avant-garde art, perception, sound and language as viewed through the life, style and experiences, through the dreams, actions, objects, the terrors, disasters and traumas, the marriages, collaborations and close calls, the influences, inspirations, the masking and unmasking of Yoko Ono.

The Yoko Ono who was the first avant-garde artist many had any knowledge of, who, for some, took the whole weight of the perceived silliness of the avant-garde on her shoulders, as though she was the only representative.

The Yoko Ono longing for magical transformation.

The Yoko Ono continually on the hunt for a new home, always finding new comrades and challenges and collaborators. Discovering new life, new ways of being after a series of traumas – violence, exile, separation, miscarriage, cultural limbo, populist and patronising hatred that was all at once racist, sexist, misogynistic, a monument to ignorance and insensitivity. The devastating violent loss of a partner, soulmate, playmate, other half, and the afterlife of that partnership, a new exile, with all of the assimilation of the previous traumas, which also were magnified and constantly emphasised by a constant hardening of the mainstream coverage of her.

The Yoko Ono claiming equal rights as a female artist to selfishness and artistic self-obsession generally the province of men.

The Yoko Ono whose very existence was an act of rebellion.

The Yoko Ono who focused on realities and worlds that some people just didn't want to see.

The Yoko Ono who was once asked, 'What do you think will be your legacy?' – and she sighed, 'They're going to make it up anyway, but I hope they are a bit kinder to me than they are now.' 'They' were those who were always fighting her, for some crime against humanity, or something. 'They' wanted her dead, sometimes it seemed simply for breathing, or perhaps because she talked about breathing being important, precious, something. 'Now' could have been any time after the mid- to later sixties and the early part of the twenty-first century, after which there was a change in the air, as she was gradually blown into a different part of history. She didn't believe in legacy, she said, and if her work is inspirational and encouraging and joyful after she dies, that's beautiful, and she would be thankful. If not, she can't complain, that's fine too.

The Yoko Ono who dealt in her own calm, subversive way with being lied about and summarily dismissed as part of some long-running international trolling campaign to keep her quiet and even remove her from sight, because her art was sinister and pointless, because the assumption was she was tricking everyone to get some attention.

The Yoko Ono who more or less before anyone else or around the same time as a handful of others thinking of the same thing put language on the wall of a gallery and left things open, so a passing viewer could complete the thought and develop the idea, for real, using their own instincts, the power of their own imagination, or not.

The Yoko Ono who was in favour of intangible ideas and the conceptual above material aspects, and what they might reveal about ourselves and the world around us, how ideas could transform thought and in that way change the world, or propose the possibility of a world that can be changed.

The Yoko Ono who wanted people to understand her perspective on a variety of subjects, for no other reason than that if she managed to express herself, to get something out of her system, to surprise herself, get to know herself, explore the impossible, complete some emotional circuit, it became a form of protection, which she needed in a world that threatened her in all sorts of ways, from apocalyptic to just plain mean, scary and prejudiced. Life could be wild in the worst sense of the word, as though it was just about to tip over into an abyss, and believing that the world was a better place because she was in it, working things out, leaving little clues to whoever might be looking her way, gave her some peace.

The Yoko Ono exploring a lack of concrete identity status decades before that would even begin to make sense to a wider culture.

The Yoko Ono who was blamed for how she was misunderstood, because obviously it was her fault that she was suspected of foul play.

The Yoko Ono who sometimes felt frightened of being Yoko Ono. It ended up being a lot to take on.

The Yoko Ono who was 'mindful' and meditative decades before it became a worldwide digitally distributed lifestyle mantra, regularly issuing brief comments, recommendations and suggestions in order to influence behaviour or change a mind or two or point out something she was thinking that others might like to try, or not. As relentless often lone campaigner, constant whimsical recorder and collector of everyday activities and feelings ranging from the banal to the profound, habitual designer of all kinds of self-portraits and random confessions, seeing art in everything she did, saw, documented and captioned, the permanent presenter of herself in everyday life, she imagined a world that eventually everyone would live in, for better or worse.

The Yoko Ono who decided, as one or two had before her, and a few at the same time in the paranoid, xenophobic America of the 1950s, to make something based on the quality or distinction of her thoughts that appeared to belong in the art world, but only by accident or coincidence or because there was nowhere else for it to belong.

The Yoko Ono who once said: 'The job of an artist is not to destroy but to change the value of things . . . in order to change the value of things, you've got to know about life and the situation of the world.'

The Yoko Ono who waged battle against the heroic and exclusively male legend of the avant-garde, which never went down well, combined with her refusal to view mass culture with suspicion.

The Yoko Ono who prepared people for understanding simply how to inhabit the earth, on a planet that if it managed to survive would always be a very strange place to live.

The Yoko as lightning rod where what you think of her says more about you than her.

The Yoko Ono who even when she was running a multi-million-dollar business and curating the legacy of a legend never abandoned the avant-garde world that had been her salvation, and sometimes her ruin. A no-nonsense uncompromising avant-garde artist, she nonetheless had the background to manage money and family reputation without being overwhelmed.

The Yoko Ono who said, 'I was a rebel even in the avant-garde.'

The Yoko Ono who finds herself, like it was always meant to be, in a barely lit chilly room, somewhere a little off-kilter, in a city always building itself up to be more than a city, with three master avant-garde titans, all up to something at various stages of their life. It was as if just by being together they had made up a space that was at the centre of the world, and not just their world, and also at the edge of the world, where they liked to be, all the better to make sense of things, and indulge their passions and obsessions. There were a few others in the room as well, the kind that like to make connections one way or another and find space to move and think, but notably these three obsessives, John Cage, Marcel Duchamp and George Maciunas, deep in an avant-garde state of mind – not necessarily wondering what the avant-garde was, or, if it was anything, where it came from. They were all in their own way committed to building the new, curious about ideas and the execution of ideas. They found themselves together in this room at the centre of things and in the middle of nowhere because of Yoko Ono, and her obsessions, which shared certain characteristics with theirs. She was in her mid- to late twenties, the most obscure she would ever be, destined in some ways to remain unknown. She had something to say, and something to show, about how to go forward, and how things as fragile as a thought, a dream, a legend can go on and on.

The Yoko Ono who is always here in spirit even when she seems to go missing.

The original military term 'avant-garde' slipped across into an artistic context around 1825, 108 years before Yoko Ono was born, when various factors including revolution and industrialisation were creating a traumatic break with the past as conceived and controlled by monarchy, aristocrats, academics and Christianity. It started to be used in an artistic context when there was a greater sense of a history of art, of a sequential series of developments and movements leading to the emergence of 'the modern', sometime during the three major revolutions in France ending with the February Revolution in 1848.

A follower of the early nineteenth-century French political theorist, pioneering socialist thinker and idiosyncratic aristocratic social reformer Henri de Saint-Simon, the mathematician and banker Olinde Rodrigues, finessing and organising Saint-Simon's own illuminating but sometimes erratic thinking, drew parallels between that agile, mobile part of an army that goes into battle ahead of the rest and the artists trying out new artistic forms, to reflect changing times and new technological and psychological demands.

Rodrigues connected the especially skilled independent advanced guard scouting the terrain ahead and contacting the enemy with artists who are the first to discover and distribute new ideas and use non-conformist techniques to break new ground, discover new paths and recklessly seek adventure, sometimes for its own sake. Artists should serve as a vanguard for the people, moving ahead of the more practical scientists and industrialists in order to map out progress and social possibility before anyone else, to introduce things never seen or done or even thought by anyone else.

There was also the idea, as with the military avant-garde heading out into unknown territory, that the avant-garde artist didn't necessarily know where they were going, but they were the first ones to get there. They exposed themselves to greater risks from the enemy, who were all around them ready to pounce – or not even there and completely indifferent, posing imagined, existential threats – but they possessed greater strategic and tactical advantages if they surprised an unprepared enemy.

Saint-Simon himself was often the first to get somewhere and wrong-foot the enemy, those who angrily disagreed with him, as he worked out what a new society was going to look like in the aftermath of tumultuous times and how the transformation of society is always accompanied by a significant transformation of knowledge. He had made money during the first French Revolution, shapeshifting and changing his name to avoid the guillotine or exile, fought on the American side in the War of Independence in the 1780s, and lost his fortune and lavish lifestyle in the early 1800s, living in near-poverty for the last twenty years of his life.

He mentored and collaborated with the philosopher Auguste Comte, who is seen as the original social scientist and founder of sociology. Together they coined the term positivism, which viewed social reality through the filter of science and scientific principles. Positivism set controlled limits which were at the opposite end of the spectrum to limitless artistic avant-garde thinking, but which could include procedural, experimental elements.

Seeking ways to reconstruct society after the French Revolution and the dangers of a new Napoleonic monarchy, Saint-Simon's many-sided ideology was mostly optimistically directed towards the future. His romantic utopian view of the transformative benefits of industry and industrialisation (a word he coined) meant he considered the Industrial Revolution to be more significant than the French Revolution, as a potential way of making life better for all people, and raising the living standards of the lower classes. Saint-Simon audaciously envisioned a total scientific transformation of Western civilisation, believing in positivism as a new philosophy for the educated and at the same time a religion for the masses. Visionary industrialisation controlled by scientific guidance would mean that poverty, war and class struggles would disappear.

11

Wherever his restless curiosity took him, Saint-Simon's work, at a decisive point in European intellectual history, was always based in hope for a better world that was somewhere between naive and knowing, between the sentimental and the organisational. His aim as a proto-futurist, as much as a proto-socialist, proto-technocrat, proto-sociologist and ultimately proto-avant-garde impresario, was to develop things that are valuable to life.

Always looking for new ways to analyse new circumstances, Saint-Simon had himself used the term 'avant-garde' in a non-military sense in 1808, when he had described how the English had been for a while humanity's avant-garde – *le poste d'avant-garde l'humanité*. Perhaps he had come across revolutionary eighteenth-century journals such as *L'Avant-Garde de l'Armée des Pyrénées-Orientales*, a mouthpiece of a French revolutionary army describing radical and dangerous military operations in the fight against the kingdom of Spain. The journal's opinions about given problems and solutions and diaries containing attitudes, prejudices and reactions were printed that articulated the revolutionary mentality at its most intensely philosophical, loosening the idea that the 'avant-garde' was purely a description of a military unit. It could reach beyond military circles and become part of a different campaign.

'Avant-garde' could also suggest certain kinds of thinking, of behaviour, and a sense that the truly committed are dedicated to drawing attention to their every activities and utterances in a way the more moderate and less ambitious aren't interested in doing. An avant-garde expressing brand-new feelings as unprecedented situations reveal themselves, and expressing responses to given dilemmas and disputes, is therapeutic, strategic and enlightening all at once, in both practical and mystical ways.

Saint-Simon understood how a new world was forming as the industrial age developed that required new disciplines and techniques, and he believed that the social power of the arts meant that artists would be among the leaders of a new understanding of society alongside scientists, engineers and industrialists. Artists would supply the glorious visions that industry could now introduce into the world, glamorising, publicising and illuminating the directions being planned for society by its new rulers. A peaceful new social order would be based on equality for all, with no difference between classes or the sexes.

Rodrigues – as a collaborator and disciple of Saint-Simon, a devout Saint-Simonist continuing his efforts – was committed to clarifying and distributing his assorted, sometimes imprecise and unformed ideas, and wrote in an 1824 text based on a dialogue with Saint-Simon, '*L'Artiste, le savant et l'industriel*':

> We artists will serve you as an avant-garde, the power of the arts is most immediate and fastest; when we want to spread new ideas we inscribe them on marble or canvas; we popularise them by poetry and singing; we use the ode, the song, the story and the novel; the dramatic scene is open to us and it is here especially that we exert an electric and victorious influence. What a magnificent destiny for the arts is that of exercising a positive power over society, a true priestly function and of marching in the vanguard of all the intellectual faculties.

Rodrigues' reshaping and elaboration of Saint-Simon's utopian pacific principles – the idea that a golden age was ahead of us, not behind us – and his development of socialist ideas meant from the very beginning there was an affinity between the artistic avant-garde and social revolutionaries, and a link between creativity and aggression.

Both the artistic revolutionary and the political revolutionary believed that the fundamental truth about reality and the world around us is that it is something we make, and can make and remake in many different ways. It can be willed into existence. Both believed in the power of the imagination to invent and design reality itself, and always with the idea this would be positive and progressive, a constant invention of a brave new world whatever challenges and changes occurred politically, technologically and economically. Both recognised the power of the individual to cause things to happen.

13

The Yoko Ono producing, piece by piece, action after action, a vast array of poetic, absurd and utopian revolutionary thinking as though using a machine that manufactured mind expansion.

The Yoko who once said, 'In a way, I created a power as an outsider. I mean, being an outsider is an incredible power, actually. I always think that you should never be in the centre. Centre is a blind spot because you can't see anybody. You are being seen, but you can't see anybody.'

Art could be a celebration, a complement or completion of the essential consciousness-altering virtues of revolution, a signpost, often an abstract prediction or endorsement of change to come, or a vague, dreamlike recommendation of the changes that should happen for the sake of civilisation, equality and socially beneficial progress.

In a less directly revolutionary sense it could guarantee the constant presence of living myths and maintain magic in an increasingly mechanised and brutalised society. In any new utopian government, artists of all types as fanciful lawmakers, as surreal rule makers, as inspirational aesthetic enthusiasts, would be essential militant leaders supplying society's moral compass and generating a poetic revolution of daily life and living.

'What better destiny for the arts,' wrote Rodrigues, 'than to exert upon society a positive power, a true priesthood, and to leap ahead of all the intellectual faculties at the time of their greatest development!'

Positivism followed through on the poet Shelley's belief that 'poets are the unacknowledged legislators of the world'. Artists should be leaders, fighters, hunters, preachers, prophets and propagandists as well as dreamers, philosophers, designers, social tacticians, stylists, writers and illusionists. By imagining the artist as something other than just a creator of images, shapes, melodies, stories and theatre, and setting them on a battlefield of ideas fighting for souls, the unlikely union of Saint-Simon and his ghost writer Rodrigues had produced an avant-garde event, a prediction of energy to come, a making up of an extra element of reality.

They made something up out of their imagination, came to some sort of conclusion, saw where things were heading because of what had come before, and hoped others would follow. You couldn't hold what they had done; it didn't represent anything that already existed in the world. It was an indefinite instruction, a performance in text form, a sculpture made out of thought, a fantasy influencing reality itself. The avant-garde existed, a wide variety of behaviour and activity began, once the banner had been waved that announced, 'this is the avant-garde' and 'it is what it means'.

Saint-Simon once said that his life had been a series of experiments, and this also anticipated the idea of an artistic avant-garde where you live your life as a work of art, being a constantly active player in your own life, creating your life, and thus yourself, in much the same way as a painter paints a painting or a poet writes a poem. Art and life intertwine. Nothing Saint-Simon did necessarily endures, as an object or a book, but his experiments in expressing and passing on new experiences of reality have changed the world. To some extent they have become *the* world now that everyone can experiment daily with their appearance and the endlessly published and broadcast content of their life, creating reality in their own image(s).

Some concluded Saint-Simon was imagining a conceptual space outside politics that could be governed by the kind of untethered thinking and apolitical detachment that artists specialised in. The inconsistencies in his thinking – such as championing the working class but never calling for a revolution, for fear of the violence – didn't put off potential followers, but seemed to inspire them, or to invite opportunists and imposters of various shapes and sizes.

Dogmatic, hardcore followers envisaged an emergent new church with its own commandments, demanding complete obedience, setting Saint-Simon up as messiah. The twentieth-century French social theorist and historian of ideas Michel Foucault traced a line from Saint-Simon's version of a future society to Adolf Hitler. Then again, showing how the doctrine of Saint-Simon, imagining a world where no difficulties exist, headed in many different directions, one of the more practical, if controversial inheritors of Saint-Simon's social idealism and his role as a utopian architect was Baron Haussmann. His radical two-decade redevelopment and remodelling of Paris starting in 1855 for another Saint-Simon believer, Napoleon III, introduced the city's distinctive wide boulevards and grand parks, following 'the cult of the beautiful, of the good, of great things'. Modern Paris, a city of dreams, was one destination of the experimental thinking of Saint-Simon: thought, imagination, willpower helping the future take shape.

Some radical artists and writers in 1830s Paris explored what the enlightening Saint-Simon instructions could mean as they spread beyond their renegade aristocratic roots, including the writer and working-class activist Claire Démar, one of the leaders of a combative women's section of Saint-Simonianism when feminism was known as 'the emancipation of female thought'. At the time it was a particularly lonely, frustrating life demanding liberation and freedom of expression for women, and Démar would become known as a feminist martyr after ending her own life in 1834 aged around thirty-four, two years after writing the pamphlet *A Woman's Appeal to the People for the Enfranchisement of Women*. She described it as 'a gauntlet thrown into the arena', demanding for women 'liberty without bounds', and as a fiercely articulate, outraged manifesto it became the avant-garde origin of feminist thought, already anticipating struggles, social events and crises to come.

The Yoko Ono making herself up as a female creator of obscure disruptive artworks in a male-dominated world, moving wherever the culture moved before it actually moved there.

The Yoko Ono who waged battle against the so-called heroic and exclusively male legend of the avant-garde, which never went down well, combined with her refusal to view mass culture with suspicion.

The Yoko Ono living through and after a time when psychoanalysis, wars, social changes and inevitable reaction against nineteenth-

16

century habits of mind meant a revolution in art, which was often art about art, and so on, and which also meant a sexual revolution.

The Yoko Ono who once wrote that 'we should keep going until the whole female race is freed'.

Yoko Ono was born on a Saturday at her great-grandmother's imposing estate overlooking the city of Tokyo, drifting off into the distance below them towards Tokyo Bay and the Pacific Ocean. It was the early morning of 18 February 1933, and overnight there had been a heavy, patient snowfall. A nurse ceremonially pulled back the curtains to show her mother the magical change that had happened to the city, harmonising with the arrival of her daughter.

Tokyo was covered in white, as far as the eye could see, in stark contrast to the cloudless blue sky overhead, which seemed to float serenely in time and space, holding reality, and humanity, in place, surely forever. A descendant of a ninth-century emperor of Japan, Yoko – the name chosen by her wealthy and well-connected parents, Eisuke Ono and Isoko Yasuda – meant 'Ocean Child'.

Eisuke's deep-thinking aristocratic grandfather Atsusho Saisho had no sons but was devoted to his daughter Tsuroko, who studied English and music at a Protestant school where she converted to Christianity. Tsuroko married Eijiro, a poor descendant from a family of famous samurai warriors who had lost their privileges in the radical late nineteenth-century emergence of a modern Japan, as the isolated country began to look to the West for security and company and, ultimately, power.

To make a comfortable living, Eijiro decided to go into business, and after studying at the Tokyo Imperial University he joined the Bank of Japan in 1890, eventually becoming president of the Japan Industrial Bank, a major part of the origins of Japanese capitalism. Eisuke, Yoko's father, was the third son of Tsuroko and Eijiro, and even though he earned degrees in mathematics and economics at Tokyo University and spoke fluent English and French, his real passion was music. His dream was to become a pianist, and the classically trained Russian-born musician wife of an older brother gave him lessons.

He became quite proficient, and would perform at Karuizawa, a pleasing, scenic resort at the foot of the still-active Mount Asama eighty miles north-west of Tokyo founded by missionaries in the late nineteenth century, favoured as an enchanting retreat by the Japanese social elite. Among those who would see Eisuke perform was his future wife, Yoko's mother, who was attracted by his charm and good looks. (Later, Yoko would visit the still-popular resort with her own family, especially in the late 1970s, needing an escape from a life crowded with the disorienting consequences of an unlikely fame and an unwelcome notoriety.)

Isoko's family was extremely wealthy: her industrialist grandfather Zenjiro Yasuda founded one of the industrial and financial conglomerates that along with Mitsui and Mitsubishi controlled the Japanese economy until the end of the Second World War. One of Japan's major philanthropists, he was assassinated in 1921 at his country home by a member of the far-right anti-capitalist 'Righteousness Corps of the Divine Land', who claimed he was attempting to rid Japan of corrupt businessmen, and was particularly irritated that Yasuda refused to donate money to his group.

Concerned that Isoko – their eighth child – had fallen for an unreliable and impractical Christian musician, Isoko's Buddhist parents permitted a marriage on the condition that Eisuke joined his in-laws' banking firm instead of following a whimsical, irresponsible musical career. They had been cut out of Yasuda's will before his assassination, but had their own banking connections and – even though they were exiled from his fortune – could count on the mighty Yasuda reputation.

Eisuke took a position at the government-sponsored Yokohama Special Foreign Exchange Bank, a predecessor of the Bank of Tokyo, and moved into his wife's family estate, his dreams of a successful musical future quickly fading. In choosing Eisuke with his artistic temperament, Isoko had demonstrated her own animated, independent thinking, and a spirit of a relative defiance inside her conservative family, but she still enjoyed the security of the family home and money. Behind the scenes, she knew her own mind.

Yoko would describe her mother as being a *modan gara*, abbreviated to *moga*, a form of avant-garde feminist making waves in contemporary magazines for their Western-influenced lifestyle choices. They were young, fashion-conscious Japanese women who emerged after the First World War, representing a disruptive, new, forward-looking, relatively liberated woman, shaking off rigid state-mandated expectations of the 'good wife and wise mother' that traditionally limited women to managing the home, serving their husband and running the family. They challenged the Japanese status quo with blatantly Westernised energy appropriated from American movies, or were simply developing their own militant, self-motivated cosmopolitan trends that coincided with new female thinking and fashions in Europe and America in the 1920s.

Eisuke had been transferred to his bank's San Francisco office a few weeks before Yoko was born, and didn't see his daughter until August 1935, when her mother joined her husband in California. Yoko was already walking, talking and in her own way performing, more a lively sidekick to a confident, demanding *moga* than the mute child of a traditional Japanese wife.

Home life as a toddler was mostly spent on her own, living a dry, hemmed-in and usually completely silent aristocratic life, looked after by servants, maids and tutors. They became an audience for her, and she discovered performing and performance by dancing on her own among the flowers and trees as the family maid occasionally checked her whereabouts. Most of the time she would be entertaining herself, lost in her own world. While her father was working in America, her busy, enterprising mother was distant from Yoko's everyday reality, wrapped up in her own interests and friends, and pursuing lightly shocking *moga* activities such as smoking, drinking cocktails and dancing.

Used to finding her own fun by daydreaming inside her isolated home while her mother relished her freedoms, Yoko found herself brightly skipping around San Francisco, once she was released into America – dressed like Shirley Temple, curious about her new surroundings. Later

20

she'd look at home movies taken of her at the time by this affluent, unorthodox family. She'd see a father reluctantly stuck inside the banking business who didn't look too delighted by her presence and exuberance as she had her first exciting taste of America marvelling at the Golden Gate Bridge, the other side of the Pacific Ocean from Tokyo, reaching out towards the soaring sky and freedom.

In April 1937 she returned to Japan with her mother and a younger brother, Keisuke, born a few months earlier. A few weeks later conflict began between an ambitiously imperialist Japan seeking materials to fuel its growing industries and an impoverished, divided China. The US disapproved of this Japanese aggression but there was no official punishment, just the beginning of a period of poor relations between the two countries that would erupt in four years' time when the Imperial Japanese Navy Air Service audaciously bombed the American naval port of Pearl Harbor on Oahu Island in Hawaii, the peak of its military strength, which had been growing during the 1930s.

As anti-Japanese sentiment grew in America, Yoko's father remained there while she started school back in Japan. He worked in the Manhattan branch of his bank, and during her first visit to New York in 1940, Yoko went to public school on Long Island.

The Ono family got caught up in increasingly dangerous collisions between countries fighting for territorial and political space. Relationships between America and Japan worsened as both competed for Asian natural resources, with Japan moving towards being the dominant imperial power in Asia, and America maintaining isolationist distance from the faraway war in Europe.

Warily watching Japan's aggressive movements, but still hoping to negotiate, America cut off access to its oil and tightened other restrictions. In early 1941, as tension between the two nations increased, Isoko and her two children sailed back to Japan, just before Yoko's father was transferred to the Hanoi branch of his bank. Eight weeks before the Japanese surprised America with their sudden November attack on Pearl Harbor, inflicting considerable destruction and shock, Yoko's sister

Setsuko was born into a Japan finding itself immediately at war with America, which had formed a military alliance with China.

While their father was incarcerated in a concentration camp in Hanoi as Japanese troops invaded Vietnam – the consequences of which sowed the seeds of the Vietnam War – their mother shielded Yoko, Keisuke and Setsuko as best she could from an increasingly vicious war and its direct effects on Tokyo. Eventually, absolute horror and an unprecedented hell on earth was hurled at the city, fuelled by American frustration at Japanese military stubbornness and accumulating revenge-fury that Japan had outrageously violated American territory. This was going to be ultimate payback for the affront of Pearl Harbor, even if the targets in this case were civilians.

Months in the planning, it was the first time in history that a transoceanic bombing raid was attempted. Just after midnight on 10 March 1945, 279 massive, low-flying Boeing B-29 Superfortresses firebombed the city, dropping 2,000 tons of incendiary bombs in 142 minutes which released napalm – gasoline jelly – as they fell, years before the word became notorious during the Vietnam War. The intention was to start uncontrollable fires, indiscriminately destroying most of the specifically targeted eastern parts of the city, where 750,000 people lived inside typical Japanese, very vulnerable, wooden homes.

As soon as the first bombs were released, instantly bursting into flames on impact, the early pathfinder B-29s retreated, leaving their target lit up below for the next waves of bombers in the shape of a monstrous blazing X, wantonly making a mockery of civilised behaviour. One hundred thousand civilians were estimated to have been slaughtered in this drastic American attempt to break Japanese morale and force a surrender, a million were left homeless, and 250,000 businesses, shops and homes were incinerated. The searing heat sucked the oxygen out of the air so those who weren't burnt to death were asphyxiated; liquified glass was blown into the air by the firestorm, then hailed down on the helpless civilians, melting into their hair and skin. It was one of the most brutally destructive acts of war in history. The Japanese called it the 'Night of the Black Snow'.

Yoko's mother, baby sister and younger brother were removed from the horror of the heinous attack to which the Americans gave the innocuous-sounding codename Meetinghouse. They were safely locked inside a special bunker under their home in an area of Japan outside the bombers' main target. Yoko was ill, weak from a high temperature, paralysed with fear, and stayed in her room in a less exposed part of the house.

Eventually, she awoke from a fever inside a house that seemed abandoned to a world on fire. She stared out of her window at the terrible, twisted, smoking hellscape that Tokyo had become, a city blown to bits that would burn for days after the raid. It was as though the sun had fallen out of the sky and crashed into Tokyo. She innocently assumed this was a natural thing to happen in the world, part of some weird natural cycle: that sometimes the world abruptly bursts into flames and hungrily obliterates souls, flesh, objects, everything familiar – but she knew deep down that all was not as it should be, and nothing would be the same again. When her mother rushed into her room and held her tight, she could see it in her face.

The sheer tornadic devastation and the charred, piled-high corpses that took weeks to dispose of were a living horror. Over the next few days, other cities and their vulnerable populations – people who lived, learned, dreamed, imagined, invented, loved, explored – were being assaulted in a similarly ferocious and unforgiving manner. At the time it seemed there could be nothing worse than these incendiary but relatively conventional air raids, that this tragic form of massacring was the ultimate limit of war. These lethal new raids decimated cities, killed 330,000 more and injured nearly half a million. Somehow, though, it wasn't to be the end of the infernal punishment. There was still the whole course of history to be completely mutilated and reality itself to be ferociously reshuffled, the whole world cast into new fates.

For those who experienced it and somehow survived the relentless, exhausting savagery, it would always be difficult to talk about. You would want one way or another to recognise and keep alive the significance of what was lost and those who suffered that night, to never lose the feeling that one set of human beings could make life so dark and desolate for another set of human beings, but there were no words. If there were the words, they could only scratch the surface.

From then on, throughout her life, even if everything got less and less magical, however mad and cynical and unforgiving her surroundings, Yoko would never stop wishing. Wishing for something was a way of holding on to hope when all seemed lost. The simple, sweet demand for peace, the wishing for a better world, can seem the only weapon you have to fight the kind of pure evil and suffering that smashed into the world itself during the Second World War.

Sometimes it might seem that your talk of the need for peace and your gentle, disconnected wishing for an end to war has become a little repetitive, naive and simplistic over time, especially when such nightmarish violence gets safely slotted into manageable history, competing with other atrocities for occasional attention, or gets packaged up and neutralised as movie or TV history.

Yoko was used to wishing as a form of power, from the times, as a child, she would be taken to the temple, where she would write out a wish on a fragile piece of paper, tying it in around the branch of a tree. You could wish for anything you desired, as long as your wish didn't harm anyone else. Noble-looking trees in the courtyards of temples would be filled with people's wishes, a form of prayer, which from a distance would resemble flowers. There was something magical about the sight of all the wishes, created with the quiet unbroken hope that the gods, or whatever higher force you believed in, one day, somehow, would receive the messages, and know exactly how to respond.

Certain nineteenth-century artists, on their own search for greater truth, began to articulate the beginnings of an avant-garde rationale. The French Romantic artist Eugène Delacroix and powerful and unwavering Realist Gustave Courbet took up the Saint-Simonian idea of the intense, provocative modern artist becoming a part of an elite system of schemers and dreamers that ran society. They explored a merger between politics and art, between art and life, but, for all their zeal and aggressive style and uncompromising anti-market sensibility, they effectively stayed safely inside a protected bohemian sector of the capitalist-supported artistic network. This wasn't yet an avant-garde intent on using art and ideas as a weapon to overthrow bourgeois values and/or radically break free of settled and restrictive artistic traditions. Saint-Simon's instruction needed to travel outside France, to find interpretation in Germany, Russia and Italy at the turn of the twentieth century to add dynamism to the select French radicals forcing themselves on the future.

Courbet considered that the radical artist should positively challenge the ruling forces of society and take inspiration for their work from their anger and frustration with the methods of the regulatory establishment. They should approach the task of confronting with verve those they believed held back the masses, keeping them locked inside dispiriting and limited versions of society. The artist had often been the eccentric, independent, romantic outsider developing new art forms, pleasing the eye, but there had not necessarily been a connection between radical painting style and widespread, socially impactful progressive ideals. And those artists who were progressive idealistic thinkers didn't automatically produce innovative, unprecedented new art.

Nineteenth-century rebel artists still dealing with relative realism like Courbet and the so-called early French Impressionists changing the nature of painting in a pioneering, vanguard fashion later in the nineteenth

25

century were not avant-garde in the subversive sense we would come to understand – mocking, playful, ironic, destructive or self-destructive, explicitly alienated, using art as an abstract or even more explicitly militant protest against the status quo. They were still making pictures, perhaps finding more extreme, flamboyant methods of expressing reality, but a dislocation was materialising where inevitable contemporary art, that which was being made at the time and was therefore modern and intellectually restless even if linked to traditional art history, was becoming more what we would recognise as avant-garde.

The earliest known reference for the idea of an artistic avant-garde comes from *De la mission de l'art et du rôle des artistes* by Gabriel-Désiré Laverdant, a follower of the utopian social reformer Charles Fourier, written three years before the 1848 Revolution in France, railing against the conservatism of art institutions and art history, promoting art as the forerunner of the most advanced tendencies. It was still subordinate to the political, but able to agitate for change through the production of revolutionary propaganda. 'To know whether art worthily fulfils its proper mission to initiate, whether the artist is truly avant-garde, one must know where Humanity is going . . .'

The bold, exploratory artist, scouting ahead along with the innovative poets and novelists of the time, making full creative use of the tension between a wild, lost, revolutionary Paris and Haussmann's cleansing ruthlessness, was beginning to make critical, satirical and self-conscious comments on the nature of art within the art itself, on its role and context, on its form and style, on its ultimate meaning and purpose.

Artists started to cause offence with their pictures by stepping outside what was seen as the immediate, the only concern of the artist and their art – a generally decided-upon version of beauty, truth and realism. It wasn't as such a directly revolutionary gesture in a social or political sense, a blatant protest against old-fashioned thinking, but a more iconoclastic, even whimsical assault on the cautious and the conservative. This insertion of mischievous, irreverent messages inside the paintings, the breaking open of tradition by putting things into a painting that seemed chronologically or aesthetically inappropriate, was the beginning of an artistic avant-garde separating itself from the more obviously warring avant-garde of political revolution.

It was the beginning of artistic life moving outside the frame itself, beyond the canvas, and ultimately outside the gallery or museum. The DNA of the avant-garde's emergence out of revolutionary impulse still existed, but there was an early split in the idea of avant-garde art so that there would also be a more roguish, prankish, insolent and high-spirited side. Avant-garde could be either, or both, deadly serious and facetious, even farcical – and it would be gelastic and unpredictable enough that its militant side could include more capricious elements and its impetuous, impudent side could possess social motives and political underpinning. Sneaking through and around, the result of an inevitably lively, roaming spirit, pulling it all together, or pulling it all apart, there would appear elements of mysticism. It was avant-garde; everything started to overlap.

Some artists yearning for an audience, for attention of any kind, used the extreme unexpectedness and even unpleasantness of their work to create a reaction rooted in shock – even disgust. Some got attention when they didn't necessarily go looking for it because their ideas were so novel, unsettling or apparently deranged. All this again fed into a general understanding of what avant-garde meant: difficult, uncompromising, distant, desperate, unhelpful, ugly, boring, unskilled, noisy, tuneless, obscure, a deliberately niche operation.

The Yoko Ono who was surprised to discover that people were sceptical that what she did could be termed art, and concluded her only intention was to bore, repulse, annoy, fool, anger and defy them.

Edouard Manet connected the Realism of Courbet with the Impressionism of Monet, while formally belonging to neither movement. He rejected traditional artistic sensibility by including images of contemporary life and people usually ignored by French society, alongside the expected, comfortable religious and allegorical iconography. His paintings didn't militantly break with the past – they still seemed inspired by Titian – but were at the same time definitely modern in attitude.

In an 1863 painting, *Le Déjeuner sur l'herbe*, he set an image of a nude woman making direct eye contact with the viewer, outstaring them, sitting in the park alongside fully clothed men, a disruptive combination of subjects and styles, an apparently timeless evocation mixed with modern expressions and clothing, painted with a suspect energy and lack of expected, natural smoothness. The artist was up to something – was it a provocative joke, a mistake, youthful clumsiness? – and these early signs of an artist producing a painting as a comment on what it was to be an artist, what it was to be living in the world, someone noting the ultimate artificiality of art, were so advanced that few could see the irony or understand the conceptual sophistication.

It was offensive enough that Manet's paintings utilised unusual perspectives, fast, loose and unfinished brushstrokes, a strange flatness, enigmatic arrangements, dishevelled figures, an unprecedented immediacy, a bold passion for women and fashion, let alone that he was adding personal sensibility, enthusiasms and editorialising attitude to his work. He was not just being an artist and capturing scenes, but expressing awareness of the idea he was an artist, and painting people who were not doing anything in particular other than being in a painting. When he painted someone it was with full awareness that he was playing with the view of his subject(s) and the view of the spectator looking at the painting, but also with his own view, how he decided to tell the story.

Influential on the Impressionists who were about to make their leap forward, Manet was no instant success, financially or critically, in an art world still favouring idyllic landscapes, impossible goddesses, dead, decorative still lifes and dramatic war scenes, technically sublime but lacking dynamism. 'They are raining insults upon me,' he wrote to his friend, the poet Charles Baudelaire. 'Something must be wrong.'

Baudelaire didn't think there was, but if Manet was wrong, he was the right kind of wrong – here was the artist he was looking for, one who could see and communicate the tumultuous quality of contemporary life. He relished how Manet captured the exciting transience of the new Paris and the compelling unnaturalness of urban life with the maturity and sentimentality of a classical painting.

What was 'wrong' was that Manet wasn't afraid to fight the establishment, especially when they rejected his paintings because they seemed to mock and vulgarise their notion of fine art even as they followed, however approximately, some of the classic rules. The mix of the delicate and the raucous was almost blasphemous.

His participation in the pleasure-seeking possibilities of the new Paris that was being seen, for better or worse, as the centre of the world also placed him in settings where other factors were influencing his art, not just other art, and an accumulated history of art. Fashion, gossip, writers and the latest trends all played a part in his painting. He was also fully up to date with popular turns of phrases of the time, and knew all about the concept of the *blague*, the put-on, the wind-up, a pet child of the revolutions that hadn't been stripped of its volatile energy. A *blagueur*, the early adopters of the word in a new context said, was a jovial imposter – a distinctively melancholy liar.

It was Manet's artful application of the dark arts of *blague* and how its facetiousness, parodies and repartee sneaked from the shadows into his paintings that led him to be labelled not just a prime antecedent of modernism, but also a signpost towards an avant-garde that placed art and life together in the everyday and broke away from centuries of art practice while still linking arms with it.

The use of *blague* in the 1870s to denote an intellectual exercise represented how a post-military avant-garde spirit was revealing itself – through the freedom of artists, writers, musicians in Paris bringing into their work a new form of biting wit, and an ironic, liberating distance from the smothering morals and expectations of traditional society. The *blague* came out of the cafes, cabaret and burlesque clubs and informal gatherings of non-conformists scattered around the new Paris, hungrily seeking illumination and new experiences, and represented the thinking of a new caste of dreamers, transgressors, prophets, technicians, lovers, collaborators and proto-conceptualists – and practical jokers with atti-tude – finding spaces to function outside the insidious controlling reach of the Church, politics and the establishment.

The avant-garde found its first venues, by its very nature, on the margins of any modernised centre; its members were rogue planners of the future looking for a balance between Haussmann's grand regenerating hygiene and the crowded, revolutionary wild old soul of Paris that had been lost in the rush to move forward and calm an agitated population.

The Baudelairean modernists looked for remnants of the past left behind by Haussmann's gutting of the dirty old city, searching for a lively lingering anarchic spirit. They found it in a bohemian network of bars, halls and cafes that acted as though the old Paris had not been demolished but had found its way to the future. Revelry and the search for dissonant joy and sundry shenanigans happened under the cover of night as audience and performers intermingled, on the hunt for the life and soul of whatever next, in whatever form.

Those attending these undercover meetings were searching for differ-ence, for a way of escaping the crowd, of not following the obvious next move, of making the chaotic vertigo of the present come to a stop, or move in a sudden, energising new direction. They were looking for places of reflection, for ways of losing themselves in the city, so that they might find their city, a new city that might eventually replace the old city, or at least become part of its magical residue.

They were looking for traces of a time before – or after – the city was colonised by the ordinary and the banal, for traces of an exciting city before – or after – too much order and too much 'system', too much process, eradicated spontaneity and negotiated pseudo-freedom. They were hunting, in a way, for ghosts, ancestors and spirits, and locating them in places that only a very few, by temperament and inclination, are interested in going: places that draw people to them precisely because they are of interest only to a select, daring type.

Those bohemian places might not necessarily be an intended part of Haussmann's Paris, but they were an essential part of a modern, fully functioning Paris where there was space for the forbidden and forward-thinking. They were where modern Paris manifested itself in the minds of those moving ahead of the crowd for their own urgent, desperate reasons: places where they could change shape at will, find new routes and directions, and create communities and groups from a constantly changing set of unconventional personalities resisting classification. It was an underground scene, a social machine for the production of ideas, events, art, entertainment, pleasure, trends, and an almost simultaneous mockery of those same things, as though to ward off the seriousness that led to the stultifying status quo favoured by the establishment.

The culture of *blague* thrived in this underground. In 1878, it found a home at the Cercle des Hydropathes held in a cafe on the corner of rue Cajas and boulevard Saint-Michel, a semi-private weekly literary meeting organised by the poet and journalist Emile Goudeau of idiosyncratic artists, poets, revellers, actors, political idealists and students. He hoped his small anti-academic movement would 'penetrate the brains of those young students destined to join the ranks of the haute bourgeoise with their notions of art and poetry'. Hopefully, those who became part of the elite with little understanding of the arts would receive a crash-course education in its more rebellious elements.

The quickly popular literary circle gathered to recite poetry and debate literary ideas, and published its own journal, a random collection of proto-modernist poems, unfinished short stories, various political demands and a scattering of sly, knowing, often bawdy and self-referential jokes. They were named for the hell of it after those who liked water, or hated water, or perhaps had feet made of water. An editorial, opening up the idea of the artistic manifesto, outlining intentions to encourage freedom and open-mindedness, for an audience that will like some performances and hate others, and some who were in the mood to love and hate, begins with an opening line that could be included in any avant-garde manifesto from Futurism to Fluxus:

31

The doctrine of the hydropathes consists in not having one.

Various associates in this new kind of forum for art came up with something previously unheard of – jokes, as part of an overall artwork – that very quickly issued challenges about how extreme a work of art or a piece of music could be while still being a work of art or a piece of music. There was much laughter at the preposterousness of these tongue-in-cheek antics, although one or two artists and musicians took the gags as serious clues about the future of art.

The groups and ensembles and collaborators multiplied and interbred, their art becoming more numerous and, despite itself, more complex and artful. The Hydropathes lasted a couple of raucous, joyful years before various members, viewing shapeshifting as a natural part of their approach to things, moved over to the Chat Noir, a cafe started in November 1881 by the would-be artist, raconteur and theatre worker Rodolphe Salis for his artist friends. He inaugurated what he called a 'cabaret' – French for tavern or inn – presenting the evening's entertainment as a menu of delights offering a variety of performances from madcap sketches to pre-cinema shadow plays.

The cabaret invited the original makers of the Cercle des Hydropathes to create their own weekly satirical four-page *Chat Noir* journal, which refracted the edgy, disreputable cabaret performances in text form, adding jokes, satire, wordplay, caricature, silly rants and a healthy amount of poking fun at the bourgeoisie, perpetual scourge of both common sense and the healthy necessities of nonsense.

If Paris was the centre of the world, the Hydropathes and Salis blithely claimed that the club's part of the world, the hilly Montmartre to the city's north, was the centre of Paris, and therefore the cradle of humanity. It was a ridiculous thing to claim, but it was also not necessarily completely far out. Montmartre was becoming a site for the feverish underground – a glorious underworld – of a border-blurring collaboration between artists, writers, composers, performers, humorists, rebels and unclassifiable, trouble-making free spirits, and an important location for the growing multidisciplinary body of new forms of art. Pimps and petty criminals lurked in the shadows, adding to the edgy, fluctuant glamour and took care of various goods, energies and shady talents that supplied extra inspiration and welcome derangement of the senses.

The journal made up its own mythology, and was as much publicity for itself, its performers and poets and the perverse pleasures of Montmartre as it was a celebration of how much potential joy and freedom there was when you worked and played outside official control. How exhilarating it was breaking the tidy, insipid middle-class grip on both art and entertainment, its reliance on the fundamentally commercial principle of the 'masterpiece' and the canonising of the individual genius. The Chat Noir became an early example of alternative ways to organise cultural consumption and distribute artistic energy.

The cafe attracted a wide audience both for its dramatic artistic cabaret and for its lively, sometimes shocking journal, marketing a resplendent entrance to a paradise that featured access to intoxication and eroticism as well as irrational flashes of novel artistic potential, offbeat music and trickster craziness. Eventually the crooked energy and its tenacious distillation of a culture of *blague* spread throughout Europe, the Chat Noir trend quickly spreading to high society, the template for future establishments – although it was too self-consciously artistic, politically jarring and spikily bohemian for British taste.

British music hall and vaudeville might have had their own version of meta-theatrical antics but lacked the shattered fragments of fine art or any savage attacks on establishment power structures to add shock value to the fun and games, and definitely lacked a political consciousness.

In Munich at the turn of the century, an anti-authoritarian political cabaret group, the Eleven Executioners, anarchic inheritors of the Chat Noir experience, who performed in private to bypass ever-watchful censorship, presented performances that mixed insolent comedy songs, satirical ballads, recitals, puppet dramas, theatrical presentation and literary shams.

One of the Eleven Executioners' co-founders was Marya Delvard, who would perform as a chilling, transgressive, extremely thin femme fatale wearing full-length black dresses, with a painted white face and black-rimmed eyes under a single spotlight, prefiguring Marlene Dietrich and beyond that Nico, Siouxsie Sioux and Grace Jones, and, a regular guest, the mighty Frank Wedekind, whose abrasive, moralising gothic rebel ballads, sung to a rigorously strummed dislocated guitar, were early signs of the German cabaret style later finessed by Bertolt Brecht and Kurt Weill.

Wedekind was to Brecht what Woody Guthrie was to Dylan: Brecht took over Wedekind's 'dry metallic voice', what he called his 'eyes like a gloomy owl' and his austere, riveting appearance. He headed into a fiercely challenging new world wearing countercultural armour he had borrowed from Frank and skilfully adapted and developed. The Eleven Executioners had ceased operations in 1903 after a couple of hectic, mischievous years, but its mystery and notoriety, intensely represented by Wedekind, channelled through Brecht's revolutionary theatre, had a massive impact.

The invigorating, pre-First World War German abstraction of French cabaret was where the cultural avant-garde could experiment with form and performance, and a more politically critical reflection of social, critical and intellectual unrest. Cabaret was a performance laboratory that created a space where high art and popular culture could coexist, and the idea of art for a mass audience become a reality.

The Yoko Ono landing from somewhere in time with her sly, insignificant-seeming provocations, or outrageous dares, who would have seemed as alien and incomprehensible as something from the outer reaches of space.

The Yoko Ono who wondered, 'Why paint the tomato? Just leave it as it is.'

Fearing another uncontrollable killing spree, a quick, vicious reprisal of America's monstrous, somehow gleeful vandalism, thousands of utterly powerless city dwellers escaped Tokyo as quickly as possible. Families of a similar status and class to the Onos fled to the secluded, pastoral resort village of Karuizawa, where they were used to escaping for peace and quiet. Ono's mother thought that was too obvious or even too indulgent a place to seek sanctuary, with its inappropriate association with rest and recreation. It might become an easy target for pitiless enemy fire.

She had her own resistance to the worst habits of the upper class, which she had been born into, and then, to some extent, expelled from by her grandfather. Under the circumstances, with no word from her husband, who was last heard from while imprisoned in Hanoi, who might even be dead, she preferred anonymity in the less accessible countryside, out of the way not only of the terrors of Tokyo, but also of an elite crowd all fleeing in the same direction, drawing attention to themselves. She had another direction in mind, another early lesson for Yoko. Go against the grain, choose your own way.

Isoko rented a farmhouse in an isolated rural village surely distant enough from any sudden, furious, fire-breathing air raids, accompanied by the last member of her staff still alive and not conscripted into the military. The move backfired, as the locals treated her and her family, with their single servant, symbolising untold riches, as an example of exactly that upper-class exodus she herself was trying to avoid. Whatever criminal horror rich Tokyo people were steering clear of, they were still rich Tokyo people, in some ways responsible, with their worldly power-mad greed and ambitions, for the ruthless barbarity reducing the country to ash from the outside.

In fact, they had some of the characteristics of those American out-siders determined to ruin Japan. There was something American and alien about the twelve-year-old Yoko, definitely changed by spending time in American cities with a father who had been head of the Yasuda bank, content to live side by side with the enemy.

Stuck in a limbo between persecution in America for being Japanese and persecution in Japan for being American, already adrift from a fixed, stable position as a half-Buddhist and half-Christian, Yoko found herself an outsider among outsiders. Neither one thing or another, from somewhere other than here wherever she found herself, she was now a city girl used to certain privileges stranded in the hostile wild, with a desperate mother and a father who was neither dead nor alive.

When Yoko arrived in the countryside, the first thing she missed in an endless landscape of featureless wheatfields was the carefully arranged colourful flowers in her mother's rose garden in Tokyo, which now lingered in the memory like a long-lost and irreplaceable paradise. Such rich, soothing colour was something she had left behind along with the rest of her life. Maybe she would never see it again, forget what it even was unless she held on to her memories of her mother's flowers in her dreams, found a way of passing those memories into the real world, as fantasies, as things she made up to add her version of colour, of beauty, to the world. Beauty became something to fight for, to keep alive in her imagination.

Overhead, ominous bombing planes flew on their way to attack some terribly exposed large city, or maybe return from what victors would describe as a successful raid, gloating and roaring high in the sky. This, and the extraordinary violence that the distant planes signified, an irrational violence that now seemed to be part of Japanese society, because the country started wars, became normal, part of some insidious faraway world that had nothing to do with them, and yet ruled their lives. Over the horizon, the war carried on, tearing apart everything they knew, and they had to deal with it in their own way, wondering why people wanted to annihilate each other.

Sometimes Yoko would walk by herself across empty fields to a patch of mulberry bushes where she would gather as many berries as she could for something to eat. If she stayed late searching for the fruit, the sun would start to set, and the shadows lengthened around her. Racing back to her family across the fields before it got dark, it seemed as though ghosts – the ghosts of the Tokyo dead, or the ghostly trails of crazed American invaders – were chasing her all the way back home.

With her mother, she was compelled to sell treasured family possessions from a wheelbarrow for food, but even the fact they owned things of value set her up as a pampered child of the monied class while all around them there were locals so hungry they were dying in nearby fields, as they desperately hunted for edible mushrooms.

She still relied on her precious daydreams to help the days pass, even though her circumstances were very different from when she lived among staff, with the boredom you can feel when you have everything you need and yet something is missing. Now she had nothing, and the past and future had gone missing, the present was hanging on by a thread, the boredom was streaked with fear, apprehension and despair, and she had younger siblings, even more scared and bewildered than she was, to care for.

With her younger brother Keisuke, holding on to each other in a neutral forever place caught between life and death as if they were the same thing, she'd lie on a bed in their temporary – maybe even permanent – home, miles from their once-upon-a-time home. They stared up through a small window in the roof at the sky, the one thing that stayed the same and never changed, static and dynamic, a reassuring constant even as lightning struck and clouds rolled and the sun shone and the sun disappeared.

Sometimes all she could trust was the sky. Sometimes it seemed it was all that was left of the world, safely intact above the mess and mayhem, a counterforce to the bloodlust, something directly connected to the imagination. The sky was not something that just goes away and dies in a mad, manmade moment.

The sky was calling her, she listened to the sky, the sky was showing her she wasn't alone. As desolate and frightening as things were, she could still see the beautiful sky, the sky that had greeted her when she was born, and somehow made her feel that everything would change for the better.

The stars could still come out at night, the sky was a blank piece of paper waiting to receive instructions, it was a container of consciousness, where everyone on earth eventually ends up. The sky was her introduction to abstraction, an image of something that was like nothing on earth.

There was something she wanted to explain, to her brother, to herself, but she knew she wasn't ready yet. She would have to live long enough to know what today was like.

She was always gazing at the landscape and she was always in the landscape.

For the moment, her mind was blank, a map of absence. Her crying became music to her ears.

Starving – she would later say she looked like a little ghost – Yoko and her brother swapped remembered items of food they could only dream about, each visualising a menu of possibility. If her brother wanted ice cream, they would stare at the sky and imagine eating ice cream. Her brother would smile and lick his lips, as though the unreal menus they exchanged 'in the air' were more real than the old reality that had fallen away around her, into unremitting bleakness.

Later in life she would think of their conceptual dinner as her first work of art, the creation of a helpful, consoling and inspiring dream-world that didn't oppose the world of reality but that could organise and explore a shared reality just like science and technology. She instinctively understood that in a world being smashed to pieces, its traditions ripped apart, she needed to invent new rituals to keep hold of her sanity. She was already beginning to fight for truth, to develop her own ideas about what truth was, a truth she wanted to know by any means necessary, even if it meant making things up, and trusting what she decided to trust.

Everything was in her head, which sometimes seemed filled with death, near and far. She became a teenager, as lonely as she would ever be, apart from when she felt lonelier because the whole world seemed to be watching, and she'd had more than enough of death, people disappearing through no fault of their own, falling into the dark where there was no sky, and no way out.

The Chat Noir led to the rise of the pleasure-seeking, provocative German cabaret of the Weimar Republic that prospered during a time of political and economic crises. It was also a preview of Dada as pure farce, basic cheek, vicious protest, carnivalesque gesture, but still madly wondering what the purpose of art was, who was it for, and why it was usually so contained and controlled inside boring buildings and boring minds.

Never fixed to one place or one group, one assembly of activists who'd slipped between the Hydropathes and various cabaret venues, exploring what happened when you blurred art and comedy, music and drama, liberty and humour and song and spoof, was formed into the Incohérents by the writer, publisher and Hydropathe Jules Lévy. The Incohérents were the ultimate ironic oppositional gang to the solemn, joyless academic movements of the late nineteenth century with their preposterous airs and graces and arbitrarily assigned rules.

Inside all the hectic jesting there were notes of necessarily camouflaged seriousness. They were fighting the serious-mindedness and dreary good taste of the art world and the stagnation it caused, and wanted to break that earnestness apart through humour, but they were serious about their mission.

Their dark relish for laughter and rule breaking was known as *fumisme*, from an article written by the Hydropathe Georges Fragerolle in 1880 about the value of the hoax. Fragerolle was a regular pianist at the Chat Noir, composing its unflappable, impertinent incidental music with Erik Satie, and he provided a manifesto for *fumisme* which described it as being a lesser or cruder but not less useful form of wit: 'To be considered a wit it is sometimes enough to be an ass in a lion's skin; to be a *fumiste* it is often required to be a lion in an ass's skin.'

There was a discreetly formalised strategy in *fumisme*'s puerile, antisocial lack of decency and order designed to undermine the hypocrisy and pomposity – and 'good taste' – of society, to 'cut open the smug sky under which we live'. (*Fumisme* appeared like smoke from the Hydropathic Society, or vice versa, and as a prototypical anti-art performance, an early attempt to dismantle the borders between art and life, it could also refer to joker, skiver, phony, sceptic or crackpot, and, forty years later, dada.)

With Svengali instincts, Lévy sensed there was a feeling that art had run out of ideas in a world dominated by distracting scientific discoveries and relentless social innovation, that it was losing its place as a significant cause of good things being made to happen in the world.

His outlaw plan for a regeneration of inspiring energy was enshrined in an anti-Salon exhibition marketed as 'an unusual evening' featuring 'drawings by people who can't draw' – reacting to the view of some that modern painters, such as the Impressionists, actually couldn't paint. Art should be for all, and when it's for all, it won't lose its relevance.

The 'undrawings' attracted the sort of artists and curious onlookers who would find relief from art establishment strictness in such haywire irreverence. Hundreds turned up at Lévy's tiny home on Saturday 2 October 1882 for his next exhibition, with the tantalising title *Arts Incohérents*, including Manet, Renoir, Pissarro and Wagner.

A few decades later the exhibition would have been called 'a happening' and much of the activity would have been described as performance art, many of the works as installations. In 1882, it was a joyously conceived, fly-by-night assault on inflexible establishment sensibilities, on authority and control, featuring an arousing selection of ephemeral 'incoherent' pieces made from a variety of materials and dangerously subversive non-traditional media. The extended ridicule of high art, endlessly held up to scorn, ended up generating exciting mad hybrids, each one setting off in an expectant, confident direction towards an unknown avant-garde destination.

Unprecedented collaborative efforts and a sculpture made of bread and cheese were displayed alongside a canvas painted all black by the poet Paul Bilhaud, and a silent march for the funeral of 'a famous deaf man', essentially a piece of music that contained no sound at all. Decades later the idea of a monochrome canvas or a silent piece of music would become significant conceptual landmarks rather than quirky, isolated tomfoolery.

The future of art was coming to life in public venues, creating itself through audience participation and delirious social communing. Over the next few years of shows and the occasional masked ball, Incohérent occasions presented photographs juxtaposing incongruous imagery in ways that suggested there actually could be photos of a dream, a cow painted in the colours of the French flag, a pair of trousers entitled 'The Eiffel Tower', and in 1887 Eugène Bataille, better known as Arthur Sapeck, an artist famous for walking the streets with his head painted blue to remove negative thoughts, depicted Leonardo da Vinci's Mona Lisa smoking a pipe – an image which materialised out of *fumisme*, and so involved both manipulation and wordplay – probably while sinking a few gins in a Montmartre inn with Paul Verlaine.

A masterpiece was casually undermined, its seriousness disfigured, its reputation redirected. The Incohérents had taken control of that which was deemed beyond control, claiming power for themselves. They were taking over, waving their homemade flag of hostility and sabotage to invisible, non-existent future Cubists, Dadaists, Surrealists, situationists, conceptualists, pop artists, Black Panthers, Vienna Actionists, cartoon-ists, talk-show hosts, punks, advertising agencies, graffitists, social media impresarios and agitators and hip-hop tycoons.

Like these non-existent protesters, desperados and ideological guerrillas in a possible future, Incohérent militants were often anonymous or pseud-onymous, and one of the Incohérents, possibly the painter and illustrator Henri de Toulouse-Lautrec, capturing the dark, sordid side of fin-de-siècle Parisian glamour and the cabaret scenes from the inside, went by the name Dada.

Perhaps he accidentally stumbled on the delightful-sounding word meaning hobbyhorse the way a few years later a poet did, needing a word to describe a group of artists leaning towards remaining unnameable;

maybe he slipped the word into an unmarked envelope passed from artist to artist until, in dire need of assistance, it was time to open it, fifteen years after Toulouse-Lautrec died.

Perhaps, best of all, it was a curious coincidence.

Boredom, they cried, is the enemy of incoherence. 'It would seem to me', one of their type wrote, that in front of Michelangelo's *Moses*, the true artist of today should say, 'I would like to do something else.' They weren't looking for permission or approval to do something else. It was all there for the taking. All works were accepted, it was explained, except for the serious or the obscene. Any tinkering or manipulating of iconic art and the appropriation of previous ideas was welcome, as long as it made the audience laugh and questioned the rights of the elite with all their laws and reasons to be the sole arbiters of taste.

Garishly countercultural more than strategically ideological and ground-breaking, the Incohérents produced performative seances that conjured up ghosts of the future, which disappeared after a cackle or two in a puff of smoke as if that was that, and on to the next wacky punch-line, the next punch in the face.

Some of the jokes, which in hindsight had as much potential power as any of the later jokes that rewired the history of art, appeared at the wrong time in the wrong place, as though a Miles Davis materialised before Louis Armstrong in nineteenth-century Tokyo. The theoretical implications of the jokes would be followed through later, when viewers didn't just laugh at the joke and then move on to the next one but understood the deeper, stranger reasons for the joke, when similar ones were made in what turned out to be the right time and the right place, as though a glitch in the soft machine of time, space and history had been fixed.

After a decade of their naughty, chic and scurrilous art parties, their anarchistic agitation, the Incohérents ran out of steam, or ran out of luck. Some were suspicious of their motives, and saw through some of their tricks. Lévy was accused of using the Incohérents to promote his own inter-ests and, worse, of taking himself seriously, the radical self-inventor now appearing to be nothing other than a brazen conman peddling gimmicks and exploiting his artists as though they were merely displays in a freak-show. The showman had nothing new to show.

There were also pale fraudulent cash-in copies of what had begun so irresistibly revelling in its own glorious fraudulence, rapidly diluting the brand. The press lost interest as the novelty waned, and the once-amusing ideas about blank canvases, defaced Mona Lisas and silent music seemed tame and old-fashioned, the idea that anything could now be considered art and the overall institutional critique doing nothing to revitalise the power and purpose of art.

By the early 1890s, the Incohérent art movement was being ignored, a victim of an early hard rule of the materialising pop culture, and the social media it would ultimately feed, that the latest thing is quickly replaced by another latest thing, and if your entire value is you being the latest thing, with no greater dimension, you are left alone with no laughter, and no fun, and nowhere to go. The 'likes' dried up, the numbers plummeted, the followers moved on, the technology was updated.

Lévy's attack on art had failed to land any lethal blows, and elsewhere art history was carrying on more or less as it always had, in the hands of the same breed of self-appointed officials, gatekeepers, entrepreneurs and taste-makers. The usual protected academic salons were still in charge of commerce, patronage and criticism.

The Incohérents and their infectious disdain for respectability quickly became a myth, a lost legend. Thousands of Incohérent pieces disappeared as though they never existed, getting an afterlife only as a minor part of the history of the belle époque Montmartre cabaret, and as an obscure, frivolous-seeming part of a conventional art timeline that connected Manet's art and ensuing Impressionism with the modernism and associated, increasingly fracturing art developments of the twentieth century.

One piece that survived was by the arch humorist and ingenious problem solver Alphonse Allais, who edited the weekly journal *Le Chat Noir* and had been responsible for the blank music score and a series of coloured rectangles inspired by poet Paul Bilhaud's painting of a black

43

square. This may or may not have been on Kazimir Malevich's mind when he produced, as prank or prayer, the terrifying or teasing Cubo-Futurist *Black Square* in 1915, an entirely different creation of alleged anti-art, a different sort of aesthetic crime. 'This is not art,' Malevich said. 'It is something else.' (Earlier black square precedents included the occult-leaning astrologer-physicist Robert Fludd's 1617 black square representing the universe before there was anything, and Laurence Sterne's insertion of a black page into his 1759 novel *The Life and Opinions of Tristram Shandy, Gentleman*, at a point where the narrator Tristram is at an unusual loss for words – possibly mocking the black rectangles printed on pages in mourning books.)

Bilhaud was a colleague and drinking partner of Allais in another lively offshoot of the Hydropathes and Chat Noir associates that fed into the Incohérents, the Salon of Untethered Art. In his collected works, titled for April fool's day, he called his colour series 'magnificent plates', and red was titled with deadpan aplomb *Tomatoes Being Harvested by Apoplectic Cardinals on the Shores of the Red Sea*, white was *Anaemic Girls Making Their First Communion in Snowy Weather*, and green was *Some Pimps, Known as Green Backs, on Their Bellies in the Grass, Drinking Absinthe*. Colour wasn't being used to represent something else, it was the something else, an end in itself.

The plain colours needed the addition of the funny titles, and cheeky solemn decorative frames, to generate meaning; to some extent the titles were the main component, or at least completed the work, finished the hoax, story or taunt, even the beauty, sending ghostly traces into the future to search for likely places to land and seep into art history as if landing from another planet.

Allais was a derivative, engaging chancer smuggling himself into a wider money-making scam, making use of a quick wit, or he was an example of an individual genius with something prophetic on his wide-ranging mind that contradicted the essential democratic spirit of the art jokers. Mostly he was both, with the added avant-garde authenticity of debt, numerous love affairs, a troubled marriage and enthusiastic but self-destructive heavy drinking with a side-line as an inspired cocktail-making expert.

The radical Oulipo poets of the 1960s honoured him as an 'anticipatory plagiarist' for his irrepressible imagination and scientific love of wordplay. As thinker, storyteller and inventor, a specialist in appreciating how the performance of everyday life could constitute works of art, he was certainly an inspiration for the proto-Surrealist writer, absinthe-soaked Montmartre regular, actor and puppeteer Alfred Jarry, who nimbly patrolled the unstable borders between the late nineteenth-century avant-garde and the emerging modernist movements of the early twentieth century. Allais's influence on Jarry rebounded forward via the modernist champion Guillaume Apollinaire and Surrealist saint and disappointed Dadaist André Breton, who included him in his famous *Anthology of Black Humour*, and on to Jorge Luis Borges and Italo Calvino.

Allais was an artist-colleague and Incohérent Chat Noir-based friend of Erik Satie, whom he nicknamed Esoterik Satie, and — curious coincidence — they were born in the same street in Honfleur, a port on the Normandy coast. A critic at the time described Satie as a 'musical Allais', and in that sense the absurdist wit and subversive whimsy of Allais still live on today, because the music of Satie does, familiar and uncanny at the same time. The atmosphere of spiritual effort it creates never dates; it timelessly lives beside the world.

Allais is a strange ghost in the music, which does strange things to truth and reality, and whenever you hear Satie, with his wild, forlorn desire to put things in the right order, against all odds, you are also in the company of Allais, who otherwise, quite happily, would disappear into the shadows at the edge of time, a fabulous mind completely lost to us.

Yoko's life seemed over before it had even properly begun, as though she had never even existed. She'd ended up so near to death it seemed there was no coming back, which would also, eventually, once her life had begun, and became something known to a few and then more than a few, make her seem beyond weird. It was like she'd disappeared into the shadows at the edge of the woods, near the ghost-ridden mulberry bushes, and slipped from an uncertain unsettled earth into the underworld, and never quite returned to reality even as she lived and made what she could of her accidental life.

She'd learnt the hard way, although it actually came to her quite easily, that the dead and the living were not so separate. They found themselves on earth at the same time, separated by visions and illusions. Which made her feel calm, and left her absolutely knowing she needed to love life, however long it lasted, and once she'd survived, she must commit herself to it, and what it felt like, its electric essence.

Oh, she whispered to herself, who in the hell set things up like this, like it was the end of everything. They must be stopped.

Elsewhere, close by, real, raw history and a traumatic change in the very idea of humanity was still ahead, approaching fast without mercy. The firebombing was not the end, a final action. It was a prelude to the final action, which seemed beyond final. It was a dreadful warning.

The route to the instantaneous nuclear attacks on Hiroshima and Naga-saki on 6 and 9 August 1945, each requiring just one modified B-29 bomber, the first time nuclear weapons had been detonated in combat, began with the firebombing of Tokyo, with the decision made that the deadpan, barbaric mass extermination of hundreds of thousands of civilians in a few history-collapsing seconds was now an accepted element of modern warfare.

In a blinding flash the atomic bombs finished off the inexplicable and obscene work that the firebombing had begun, not necessarily immediately killing more individuals than the firebombing, which had generated huge populations of unlived futures, but unleashing a deeper, darker series of philosophical, physical and psychological aftershocks that would reverberate through human time.

Six days later, at noon on 15 August, the Japanese surrendered. The Second World War had ended and a new nightmare had begun, with America and its mixed-up partners thrusting ahead on course to determine the immediate direction of the post-war world, as if they alone could control the sky and bend everything to their will.

Only magicians, perhaps, or artists, poets or musicians, if they thought about it hard enough, could take back control of reality. Even just imagining they could take control might be enough. This contemplation, this play-acting, that Yoko did at the time to console her brother and herself, and then later in her life, wasn't some idle bourgeois luxury, a whimsical indulgence. It was a fight to survive, to be optimistic when you were overwhelmed by despair and panic, a way of believing there could still be hope for the future in every action you made, however small. You weren't only demonstrating this to yourself. You were showing everyone, in theory, that however dark things get, however much reality is shredded, however close the end of everything seems, there is still a way to hold on to hope.

Twenty-five years after the Incohérents and fifteen years after Munich's Eleven Executioners, the Cabaret Voltaire in Zurich appeared on 5 February 1916, in the middle of what had become a world war, under the name Künstlerkneipe Voltaire, the Voltaire Artists' Pub. An unassuming rented bar with a small stage and seating for about fifty people, it was opened by the poet, nightclub pianist and mystical anarchist Hugo Ball and poet and cabaret performer Emmy Hennings. The curious first mob of stop-at-nothing exciters that turned up included twenty-year-old Romanian Tristan Tzara, his friend the painter Marcel Janco and the sculptor Jean Arp. By the end of the first evening the bar was overcrowded with a rogues' gallery of disaffected refugee artists taking advantage of Swiss neutrality – students, poets and nascent revolutionaries finding their idea of a good time as the world, weaponised beyond the imagination, teetered on the brink of disaster.

A night's angry, giddy show would include staccato bursts of dance mostly to display crude, confrontational and symbolically key handmade masks, Cubist costumes, improvised comedy sketches, rhythmical noise-music and vocal chants, and spoken-word recitals ranging from nonsense poetry, readings of Rimbaud, Jarry, Laforgue and Apollinaire, to rousing manifestos, often backed by the loud, steady beat of a drum. If the drumming stopped, perhaps the world would too, so the drum kept thumping.

The mobile, manic performances were co-ordinated by outcasts and exiles who found something they needed, or didn't even know they needed, that they couldn't get anywhere else. They demanded participatory response from the audience, also finding something they needed or didn't know they needed, and placed one thing – noise, word, movement – next to another even if it didn't seem to belong, or they let things happen at the same time. The shows and devious displays evolved into

48

the structures, gestures and collisions of Dada, which had been there on the opening night only in spirit. Within weeks, Dada made it into itself, falling into a name, if only so it could be carried through history. As soon as it had a name, it started beautifully to fall apart, as though some celestial physician had determined it only had a few years to live, best make the most of it, nothing lasts forever, especially pure invention.

The prototype French cabaret style, its heightened, haphazard combination of delight, deception and disruption turned into a potential alternative performance space for art now being stretched into uncanny, adaptable, even violent and grotesque new shapes and guises.

The French parodies, distortions and transformations of art had led to a borderless art movement reacting strongly to the ugly, inhuman impact of the First World War, dropping a bomb on art itself made up of nonsense, lies, fury, pranks, ridicule, disgust, doubt, parody, cunning, shit, intellect and Dada. A few months of barely recorded, mostly rumoured Cabaret Voltaire pandemonium, part of a drive to find purpose and unity amid chaos, barrelled into novel forms of art and a whole host of new techniques. 'A fusion not only of all arts,' wrote Ball, 'but of all regenerative ideas.' 'Explosions of elective imbecility,' announced Tzara.

If Europe had lost its grip on reality, Dada came to the rescue, all puns blazing, adding haywire footnotes to the mind-bending, world-shaking theories of Freud, Marx and Einstein, given licence to roam off the page and off its rocker by the atonal storms, or post-atonal entertainments, of Schoenberg, the silent black-and-white movies forever held on the cusp of the sound revolution, the shattered words of Rimbaud and Cubism's carving up of shape, form and flesh.

Dada by its very nature instantly came in many shapes and sizes – positive and negative, divine and diabolical, catastrophic and utopian, primitive and subtle, male and female, madcap French theatrical and feisty German radical, New York and beyond – all of it targeting and encapsulating the accelerating fluctuations of modern experience.

The world was in a state of confusion, and Dada threw itself into the confusion, because nothing could be more absurd than the abhorrent

Great War, which needed some explaining. Sometimes that explanation involved nailing a stuffed monkey to the wall and calling it Cézanne. And how to explain, or explore the impact, of a fast and furious modern media, and the emerging industrial age of science and technology, that threatened to herd people into total obedience or turn them into machines?

The Dadaists who described themselves as Dada – acting out somewhere between being a disease and an abolition of logic – released information about their antic activism through print, manifestos, letters, poetry, posters, leaflets, entertainment and collaborative provocations. They made it clear that Dada meant nothing, it believed art was shit, it was a piece of tomfoolery from the void, it wanted peace through dynamism, and obliged no one to follow what they were doing. It was best that 'professors' from the future didn't try and sort it all out and summarise it in a couple of weak-kneed paragraphs, reduce it to its component elements, or explain it as part of the complacency, ignorance and simplification – and fear – they were trying to avoid, destroy, abuse.

In another future before Dada, Dada by any other name, before the fantastical industrial abstraction of the post-Revolution Russian Constructivist artist-engineers, there were the Italian Futurists, led, financed and driven by the red-blooded, high-powered, failed lawyer, extreme poet and pen pal of Hugo Ball, Filippo Marinetti. The Futurists manfully and mentally charged into the modern technological world of cars, trains, machinery and electrical dynamism, crying out for an aggressively revolutionary art that would reflect and mobilise this noise and violence.

Falling out of the sky in 1908, ringleader Marinetti set out his demands with a thunderous manifesto, a dramatic, questioning call to action through the power of rhetoric in times of uncertainty, becoming the quintessential modernist affectation. This was a time when, without a manifesto, it seemed impossible to conceive the future. This was a time when manifestos urging imperative change and the complete and utter revolutionary renewal of all aspects of life, including the destruction of museums, opera and libraries, were printed on the front page of Parisian newspapers. Manifestos were part of the news.

It was through words and a love of twisted typography, in small self-produced magazines and manifestos to emphasise and project their mood, confidence and vision, that the Futurists, as with the early pre-modernists, advocated and advanced their art. The words were where the art, which was often temporary and gone in a flash, was sent out into the world, taking on power, creating an assault on lethargy and indifference, focusing minds, winning over new converts.

The Futurists began as a literary movement, and their rapidly evolving visual art seemed an intense Italian counterpoint to Cubism, but their manifestos talked of change coming to music, poetry, cinema, theatre, advertising, architecture and design. Their call for the glorification of war, and the combination of poetry readings and disorderly art exhibitions with speeches keen on inciting riots, inspired the Cabaret Voltaire evenings using outrageous statements and love of violence as abstract methods of ending the disgusting status quo.

Futurism splintered into different directions – forward into the strategies of pre-revolutionary Russian Futurists, crazily into the arms of Italian fascism, taking as sincere and practical the fiery, demolishing rhetoric and belief in war as the highest art form, and deep into the minds and methods of Dada.

For Dada, that cleansing, rejecting love of the new and scattershot forward movement was done through art, and what that could become, rather than through war, and what that destroyed. Marinetti said, 'Get to work with all your heart, resolute on being bolder, crazier, more advanced, incomprehensible and grotesque than anyone else. I urge you to be a madman.' To those who would be Dada that seemed a sign that it was time for Dada, time to take it out onto the streets, shouting their slogans, banging their drums, pulling their faces, marching from the dawn of time into the future.

Everything that follows, including Surrealism, which had its own perception-altering time as the avant-garde place to be up until the Second World War, carries with it Dada, is an offshoot of Dada, with its use of the media as an artistic tool, the necessary deadpan and deviant humour that showed itself in different ways from Surrealism to pop art, and the resolute juxtaposition of phantasmagorical images and cryptic messages that reached into the imagery of Hollywood, television, advertising, the internet and social media, deep into the everyday life that Dada and its offspring, including Surrealism, where Dada went to dream, were so keen on infiltrating.

Having survived the war, on returning as part of a fractured family to an exhausted Tokyo, Yoko now had to survive the aftermath, which also involved surviving the pressure of being a Yasuda/Ono, and the fixed expectation of becoming successful, and beautiful, on inherited terms appropriate to her gender and social position, not her own, which she was forced to work out for herself.

It turned out survival itself was a talent, and she sensed that the chances of survival increased with each new thing she learnt and each new idea she had. She was a war child, conspiring against the adults who may have suffered the war but were also those who permitted it, working out who she could trust, those she could find who would never lead her towards such ruin and dread.

Before the war, her mother had sent Yoko to the exclusive Christian school, run by the Mitsui family, which she had attended herself, but wasn't impressed – perhaps because one of Yoko's homework assignments as a five-year-old was to listen carefully to the noises around her, whether the ticking of a clock, the dripping of a tap or the tweeting of birds, and turn them into musical notes, or perhaps because there wasn't more of that form of teaching.

Isoko then enrolled Yoko at the Gakushuin early school, near the Imperial Palace – the Peeresses' (girls') division of the Peers' School, established in the mid-nineteenth century to educate the children of the social elite, open only to those with relatives in the imperial family or the House of Peers, made up of hereditary aristocrats and limited members appointed by the emperor, modelled on the British House of Lords.

When Yoko returned to the Gakushuin middle school after the war, the traditional elite rules for attendance were already relaxing in a new Japan being marshalled and reorganised as surrendering losers by the American victors. Yoko's schoolmates at the boys' school included Emperor

Hirohito's two sons: the future emperor, Akihito, and his younger brother, Yoshi, who was quite taken with the unusual and refreshing energy of Yoko, which had been so alienating to the country people during her wartime exile. The emperor and his immediate family were still allowed to retain their titles as the peerage and all other titles were eradicated.

In the girls' school, there were plenty of imported so-called high-class European subjects and Protestant teaching mixed in with a gentle, 'feminine' curriculum with Buddhist Japanese calligraphy, flower arranging, poetry and painting. As a young teenager, Yoko studied musical theory, taking a class in Italian opera. Opera was a relatively new art in Japan, with the country only becoming acquainted with European classical music during the beginning of the twentieth century, in the early years of Japan's post-isolationist modernisation.

The country opened its mind to Western trade, culture and musical ideas, determined to make up for lost time. Wagner was a particular favourite, the starting point of an acceptance of opera, not least because of Japan's alliance with Germany during the Second World War and the composer's nationalist spirit. After the war, during the occupation, Japan opened up more fully to Western influence and opera started to take hold.

In the late 1940s opera was still a rare, mysterious sound for the Japanese. Young Yoko was taken more with the uncanny power of the singing than the music, the orchestra or the stories. She wasn't interested in performing opera, but took seriously the study of how the voice could create enough resonance to fill an entire theatre and how professional singers projected their voice enough to sing over a full orchestra. She remembers intensively training her voice like an athlete, dreaming of being able to do what she wanted with her voice, whatever kind of music she was singing. She developed a sophisticated vocal technique mixing strength and delicacy, even if she would never sing the typical lyrical music expected of those learning this way.

Yoko's formal post-war musical study, grounding her in technique, was influenced by her father's love of music and his early hope that she might become a musician, because, for love, he was forced to stop. Her mother played the traditional Japanese lute-like, three-string *samisen*, which dates back to the fifteenth and sixteenth century, with a sound that seemed to be connected with an old-world Japan. It was pretty and evocative but lacked the transformative urgency Yoko was instinctively looking for. After her time trapped in war-ravaged Japan, the quaint instrument didn't help her see a way forward, or help find ways to repair a world that had been ripped apart.

The teenager pulled away from her mother's expectation of her becoming a progressive woman relative only to the Japanese times, fitting into the role of a mild social rebel but ultimately safely sewn inside the rigid Japanese society. After what Yoko had been through, the past crashing around her, everything had to be exceptionally new, and even involve the danger she had become used to, and what she was learning at school was more she would reject rather than meekly follow. The world didn't need to be put back together as it had been before the chaos; it needed total reconstruction.

The Yoko Ono who at school would be reprimanded by her teachers for wearing black top and trousers and not the school uniform, separating herself from the herd from a young age without really thinking about it.

She learnt enough basic music technique for there to be much to reject when she started to develop her own unclassifiable musical thinking, reacting against Western classical convention while Japanese society was beginning to study it as a way to be accepted by the rest of the world. After the centuries of self-imposed isolation and its abortive, impulsive mid-twentieth-century attempt to modernise through militaristic aggression, Japan was now looking to modernise in a way that didn't appeal to Yoko. There was something outside this decorative and superficial 'modern' that she was craving.

Her father also expected her to be 'modern' and artistic in a docile, conservative, female manner, leaving the real work – counting and thinking, managing and judging, ordering and dictating – to the men. His plans for Yoko were naturally businesslike and disappointed even as he encouraged her feelings for music and drama. Her hands were too small for her to continue as a pianist, leading to sleepless nights as she willed them to grow larger. Instead of lowering her expectations, perhaps becoming a music tutor or a kindergarten teacher, his dreary realism pushed her to think of becoming something else, something other, something she couldn't yet articulate.

The interest in composition she expressed, if professional piano playing was apparently physically beyond her, was far too wild a notion for her father, who made his point by asking his daughter to name one single successful female composer. For him the conversation was closed when she failed to; for her, the fact she couldn't think of anyone was the beginning of her work, not the end. Her work also began when her mother, considered a beauty in her circle, considered Yoko merely 'handsome', like a boy, rather than a striking extension of her own very acceptable looks.

This made Yoko consider new strategies, part of how she built herself, as reality collapsed around her and time seemed to stop. It was a time of uncertainty, homelessness, fear of famine, damaged transportation networks and social unrest, which also meant, among the young, a desire for change, for there to be an outright denunciation of the horrors of war and a necessary support for pacifism.

What her parents told Yoko about how her unsatisfactory skills and unsavoury behaviour would limit her future potential, she made into a new talent. As she approached eighteen and the early 1950s, this coincided with emerging pockets of Japanese renewal, especially among the young, where a shattered, confused and demoralised post-surrender mentality was being replaced by optimism and hope. Japan had entered a state of ideological crisis, haunted by all sorts of demons from its recent past and ghosts from its pre-modern history. A need for new energy and ideas and the end of Japanese authoritarian rule were generating an unprecedented form of freedom and open-mindedness, and an intellectual radicalism appeared in high schools and universities throughout the country.

Yoko started at Gakushuin University in 1952, the year it opened its philosophy department, having successfully negotiated with the General Headquarters of the Allied Powers that this former aristocratic college could continue as a private university, no longer under the jurisdiction of the Ministry of the Imperial Household. Yoko was its first female philosophy student, seeking ideological alternatives and clues about the life of the mind, and a role and cultural identity beyond the restrictive, corroded realms of family and nationalism.

Up until 1952, and the end of their seven-year rule, American forces occupying Japan had censored artistic expression and independent-minded publications, especially mentions or memories of the atomic bomb, intending to suppress freedom of expression. This actually enabled greater artistic freedom among new Japanese artists and thinkers than was possible under the previous regime. Japan was an occupied country, but there was also a feeling of liberation – it was being controlled by outside forces, which led to natural youthful rebellion against the captors, but also thinking about how they would now control themselves from within, without repeating the mistakes of the past.

Students alive to new political and social ideas felt a responsibility to help heal the damage and lead the social and moral reconstruction happening around them. Artists felt that the destiny of the country should be in their hands, and that this self-recovery should be achieved by pushing against traditionalism.

As a student, Yoko thrived in a space where new intellectual movements were constantly arriving from around the world as Japan's radical youth caught up with pre-revolutionary Russian literature, including Tolstoy and Dostoevsky, and outside philosophical trends from Marxism to atheistic existentialism, ideas spilling over into numerous pro-democratic left-wing magazines.

The war, and the two hell-bringing bombs that ended it with ferocity, fire and oblivion, had definitively proved to a broken youth that if you obediently followed a religion or a strict political outlook as a belief system, you were believing in an authority that doesn't really exist as anything other than a deliberately planned social structure, a way of organising people and taking away their ability to think for themselves.

You might as well believe in something you make up for yourself; you might as well create your own meaning in life rather than accept meaning created for you. Think for yourself. You first of all exist, as nothing, and then you find yourself in the world at a particular time in history. You accelerate into reality, and then begin to define yourself. You can be what you make of yourself, pushing yourself towards the future, aware of what you are doing. Responsibility for your own existence rests on your own shoulders, but also responsibility for every-one. As Sartre said in 1946, 'In fashioning myself, I fashion everyone.'

As well as any official, still relatively nationalist and increasingly patri-archal moves to rebuild Japan's economy and raise living standards, various undefined underground scenes flourished, symbolising the excitement there was in general for being rescued as individuals and com-munities by new ideas and liberal thought. The country was filled with people who had grown up on chaos, relishing the emergent transitional state of things as an opportunity for experiment and radical thinking, and the chance to work out how to develop useful, progressive ways of thinking and planning the future for themselves.

What had been made clear in the preceding few years was that there was no such thing as normal, and it was hard to find anything to cling on to, and the solutions to the basic problems of existence, of coping with absurdity, needed to come from positive, new and even strange, wonder-ful and outrageous thinking.

Yoko, in choosing philosophy, was studying independent thinking – because it claimed to answer the so-called big questions: what is truth, what is happiness, what is good, what are the rules of life – and Marx had said it was the task of philosophy to change the world. She was studying herself, examining and defying received wisdom, and creating a new emotional and intellectual environment for herself to operate inside, that took her outside of her country, her family, her history and her gender and deep inside her mind.

She was exposed to the enormously challenging twentieth-century philosophical discipline phenomenology, the study of how things materialise or present themselves through first-person experience and/or consciousness, taking in the French existentialists' insights into the mystery of life, the German philosopher Martin Heidegger's definition of phenomenology ('to let that which shows itself be seen from itself in the very way in which it shows itself from itself') and his teacher Edmund Husserl's theory of knowledge and meaning.

With its affinity to the groundless ground of East Asian thinking, which made it alluring to left-leaning post-devastation mid-century Japanese scholars also examining existentialism as they looked for a new way of living, there were of course more questions than answers, but not necessarily the clichéd philosophical ones. Phenomenology asked less obvious questions: what is the secret place like in the world of the child, what is the first smile of the newborn like, what is it like to be bored, what is it like to experience the sublime through images?

It didn't take Yoko long to realise that to study philosophy, to take it seriously in an academic way, was in a sense a contradiction in terms, or at least that the process of learning would lead her into another cul-de-sac, or another abyss – and she was trying to escape an abyss; to get out of the hopeless, useless space she found herself in, not go round in circles looking for an ultimate explanation for existence. Maybe she learnt within a few weeks, with some help from a fashionable existentialist or two, that it is important to take responsibility for our own lives, and if we avoid false situations and accept our condition, we establish purpose – even happiness – in the face of absurdity. It was enough to realise that, after a few intense lessons, it was time to move on from philosophy, even if in many ways she never stopped being a student of philosophy.

Maybe she noticed that all these competitive male philosophers had not produced, after centuries, any collective convergence to the truth on the big questions of philosophy. It might be a pleasure running rings around the pointlessness of everything, in continually refining various arguments and insights, but it didn't help her with where she was at the time.

As Ludwig Wittgenstein said, philosophy is not a theory, an abstract academic exercise, but an activity, and in a way it is also an art form and/or a spiritual path, and studying it in a formal setting was as pointless as engaging with the mind of God, which, even if it existed, had to be interpreted and therefore completely made up, using stories, rules and regulations.

There was naturally philosophy in her home country as well, far away from the dense metaphysical scheming of the European philosophers. There is a fundamental and unique element of centuries-old Japanese culture, *mono no aware* (aw-are-ee), that would have drifted via Japanese Buddhism and various traditional and family rituals into Yoko's life, and was felt more deeply after experiencing death and destruction coming so close to her during the war.

Indian Buddhism arrived in Japan in the sixth century via China and Korea, unfolding in new directions and gathering new messages and meanings as it travelled through scattered communities. Zen emerged in the twelfth and thirteenth century: Buddhism with elements of Japanese Shintoism. Shintoism's pragmatic respect for living things and sensitivity to the world's energies was mixed with Zen's spiritual belief in the transient nature of the environment and everything that exists within it.

The evolving combination of understanding and accepting the uncertainty and impermanence of life, and the appreciation of how everything forms and changes infinitely, was defined as the *mono no aware* concept by the eighteenth-century Shinto scholar, philosopher and poet Motoori Norinaga. A nationalist resolve at the time was committed to removing all outside influences from Japan, but by then Buddhism was so ingrained in Japanese culture that it was not considered 'outside' and something to be banished.

Yoko's artworks were often motivated by a desire to understand, and communicate, *mono no aware*. It would have been a constant factor in her thinking, whatever other philosophies, ideas and theories, and artistic currents she was exposed to. It explains her sensitivity to ephemera, to what is mysterious in even the most ordinary object, the pleasure she took in pursuits that were made to vanish. Deep impressions could be produced by small, apparently trivial moments and events.

A hard thing to grasp in English, *mono no aware* typically translates as 'the pathos of things', more subtly as a 'sensitivity to things', and suggests how all objects have their own power to stimulate feelings of impermanence, the inevitability of change and the beauty of transience. Things are beautiful precisely because they won't be here forever. *Mono no aware* causes, or is caused by, a range of emotions. Melancholia, fragility, sensitivity are not negative things in a Japanese context.

Everything in life must disappear one day, and you have no control of this reality, which evokes sadness and sorrow, but also a sense of peace and lightness. Acceptance of impermanence and the passing of things becomes an aesthetic sensibility, a state of mind that savours and understands this ephemerality. The sorrow at loss and the end of things that are precious and loved comes with an exquisite feeling of joy and gratitude that we had the chance to experience something wonderful, however fleetingly. Temporal things must fade away so that they have the power to enthral and move us in the first place. If they were permanent and ever present they would mean nothing. Experiencing *mono no aware* means savouring life and living more deeply.

The brief annual bloom in Japan of cherry blossom became the main symbol of *mono no aware*. As quickly as the radiant pink petals arrive, they are carried away by the wind: the branches are stripped of colour. The beauty is intensified by the fact it only lasts a few days. In the same way, a fading sound is considered more lovely in its tantalising elusiveness than a clearly heard one.

Basho, the revered seventeenth-century master of the haiku, walking through nature at the crossroads between the real and the unreal, between sad and happy, between an astonishment at being alive and a gentle melancholy at its necessary briefness, wrote: 'Summer grasses – the only remains of warrior dreams.' Japanese mythology was never built around stories with a happy-ever-after mentality.

The Yoko Ono who understood that beauty was not external, but already in the mind.

Some gossip suggests that one or two of freaky philosopher Alphonse Allais's quips, inventions and objects made direct contact with one Marcel Duchamp, who was born in 1887 as the Parisian art resistance was at its liveliest. He was a resident seventeen years later with his brother Gaston, maybe rifling through its recent art history or visiting the right cafes and shops and coming across words and failing local memories of the eccentric aesthetic ne'er-do-well Allais, as he worked out what kind of artist he was going to be. So eccentric was Allais that he imagined a world where paper would become scarce and you would transfer magazines and books onto tiny squares of film which you would project on the wall, and the necromobile or corpsecar, which cremated a dead person on the way to the cemetery, producing the fuel to power the vehicle. There was also a long-lost object made by Allais that was dramatically unveiled in 2021 alongside other Incohérent pieces found in a trunk, an incredible find considering the rarity of original Incohérent art: a piece of frayed green cloth, the curtain from a cab suspended from a wooden pole, formally presented with no additional manipulation, as a work of art made in the 1880s, that suggested Allais had miraculously reached the momentous idea of the readymade decades before Duchamp. Given a title – 'Pimps Still in the Prime of Life and Lying Face Down in the Grass Drink Absinthe' – the piece of cloth was ripped out of context and made into a work of art, with a very different ritualistic presence in the world.

It seemed someone – and therefore obviously others, less able or willing to add elements of mischievous mythmaking to their findings – had realised this before Duchamp. He had only followed previous farcical and facetious footsteps, not got there on his own, but by following roughly mapped out routes and signposts.

Later it turned out the green cloth with its all-important clarifying or disconcerting title – actually taken from Allais's green rectangle – was a modern-day hoax, a readymade equivalent of the Turin Shroud, enough of a swindle to perhaps make Duchamp briefly grin in his grave. It intended to echo the nature of Allais and company's mostly forgotten mischief-making devilry, and perhaps gently explore why Duchamp's methods, decisions and questions about the very nature of art and authorship achieved a kind of immortality, and his obscure antecedents turned to dust, or fell into dustier parts of the library.

A work of art was always made by taking other items and objects and rearranging them into something else. Duchamp decreed those other things didn't have to be paint, brush, canvas, clay, marble, chisel, instruments, sound, words; they were whatever you found around you. You grabbed something, anything, anywhere, found a way to put it into a gallery or exhibition, surrounded by a certain inbuilt aura and established hoo-ha, which certified the object, however mundane or unlikely, as a formal work of art. And any rejection of the object, or argument that it was not a work of art, or anger that art was not a place for such nonsense, then became the work of art, so even if it hadn't been one, it now was.

Maybe Duchamp was aware all along of the Incohérents and their antecedents, rivals and allies, and couldn't resist a little similar trickery when there was more of a twentieth-century time and place for it by adding a moustache and goatee to the *Mona Lisa*, an act of homage to the ignored underdog as much as a sly, shrewd comment on the painting's deadly revered status.

Reversing time as part of his effortless skill at disrupting or disguising reality, he made Eugène Bataille's smoking *Mona Lisa* seem the kitsch, immature, later rip-off, and his (*actually* later) mix of reproduction and originality, joker and genius, vandalism and throwaway quick thinking the most influential twentieth-century work of art, not least because it wasn't first shown in an exhibition or sent through the usual commercial channels. It appeared in a little-known Dada magazine, as if merely a mildly witty illustration, and then slowly released its occult powers over the next few decades, gaining attention, like all his most famous works, not because of what it was but because of what others decided it was. Duchamp supplied the initial nudge, and then the subsequent nudges never stopped.

Duchamp's choice of the facial hair rather than a pipe propels his interference, with its more devious mixing of genders, into another world, and its title – with some French wordplay involving apparently random letters that, when said aloud, seemed to say, 'there is fire down below,' or 'she is hot in the arse' – takes it into the future.

He'd turned sniggering mockery of a masterpiece, or a cheap postcard of the painting he found in a shop into its own masterpiece of mockery that simultaneously elevated and undermined itself. With a little knowing touch here and there he made a bewitching, already world-famous Renaissance representation of ideal feminine beauty into a risqué, scandalous analysis of androgyny, and by turning the *Mona Lisa* into a man cast a slight, furtive glance in the direction of Leonardo da Vinci's alleged homosexuality. Also, in some part of the self-built multiverse Duchamp was moving through, he was paying homage to Leonardo as an earlier advocate of art as idea, of the mind for the mind, which is where it begins and ends, for all the fuss in between.

Duchamp was not so much the missing link between Da Vinci and Dada. Dada was the missing link between Da Vinci and Duchamp. He would not stay stuck in Dada time when the time came for Dada to make way for the softer, dream-pierced Surrealism, but drifted effortlessly alongside Surrealism during its pre-war imperial phase, before elegantly dematerialising, knowing full well the fixed penalties for being associated too closely with one particular movement, trend or tribe.

It was such acts that made some consider whether he was deliberately pursuing modernist *blague* in an attempt to escape being considered merely a minor, if technically gifted, painter who, ambitiously looking to join the new, had briefly flirted with Cubism, Fauvism, Impressionism and proto-Surrealism before moving into less formal areas. He peaked as a conventional if 'approved' avant-garde painter in 1912 when he was roaming similar territory to the Cubists and therefore the Italian

Futurists and produced, as part of a short exploratory series, *Nude Descending a Staircase No. 2.*

Along with three other Duchamp paintings, this was part of the controversial and significant 1913 Armory Show travelling from New York to Chicago and Boston that helped introduce the idea of European modern art to America, even as his paintings seemed at the extreme end of what was already seen as extreme. Duchamp was shown alongside the likes of Picasso and Matisse – all troubling to an extent, to the elite and their mainstream minds, but there was something more troubling and even devious and uncouth about Duchamp.

His *Staircase* lacked vibrant colour and even, it seemed, a staircase, or anything that seemed to be up or down, left or right. A prize was offered to those who could locate the nude among all the jagged, blurred lines, and helpful newspapers provided clues about which way was up and where left and right was in what was called 'a snapshot of a nightmare'.

For Duchamp it wasn't a painting of a woman, nude or otherwise. The title wasn't intended to take you into the picture, but out of yourself, and hopefully out of your mind. It was a painting of the process of thinking about something. He was painting the imagination, an incredibly complex mystery-generator of possibilities, other times and other perspectives he was trying to get inside.

Duchamp was already moving beyond painting, seeing it as diagrams of an idea, as interesting to him as a comb or nail. He was already thinking of using ideas that would better describe an idea. Painting was not something he thought should fill a lifetime's enquiry, and with the Armory paintings he had both summarised Cubism and seen through it. Any more of the same would be dreadful repetition.

Duchamp arrived in New York two years later, fleeing French conscription, by which time he had already all but left behind anything that would seem connected to what he called 'retinal art' – as in, painterly. He wasn't a Cubist. He wasn't anything, apart from what he thought he was, which he would contemplate at length over the next few decades from a position of delectable self-ruling inscrutability. 'The *Nude* painting' was referred to, known in certain art circles, as curiosity or outrage, a definite change in circumstances for better or worse, but not yet the name Duchamp. The name would arrive gradually, appearing inevitably, as the twentieth century, all that art and war and other increasingly transmitted fuss, became more itself.

The Yoko Ono producing, piece by piece, action after action, a vast array of poetic, absurd and utopian revolutionary thinking as though using a machine that manufactured mind expansion.

The Yoko who once said, 'In a way, I created a power as an outsider. I mean, being an outsider is an incredible power, actually. I always think that you should never be in the centre. Centre is a blind spot because you can't see anybody. You are being seen, but you can't see anybody.'

The Yoko Ono who was once told by Marcel Duchamp in some small nondescript room when she asked about how to deal with the confusion and derision that greeted her art, how to cope with alienating the audience she was hoping to reach, 'There is no solution to the problem because there is no problem.'

As a teenage schoolgirl living in Tokyo in the late 1940s, Yoko had been an avid film buff. After another school day, hiding any signs of her prim school uniform, she would sneak into a movie theatre with friends instead of going straight home. Some of her friends loved the many American films imported during the occupation, the ones starring Jimmy Stewart and Katharine Hepburn, Bob Hope and Bing Crosby, Doris Day and Rock Hudson, but she preferred French films, the ones that made her feel more intellectual, the ones more evocatively an escape from the uncertainty of occupation-era Japan.

A particular favourite was Marcel Carné's 1945 tragic romantic epic *Les Enfants du Paradis* (*The Children of Paradise*), filmed during the German occupation and released shortly after France's liberation. It was based on a vivid, melancholy Oscar-nominated script by the iconoclastic Surrealist poet, lyricist and screenwriter Jacques Prévert, who styled himself as an artisan looking to entertain and at the same time elevate his audience. He filled his extravagantly literary script, a cinematic equivalent of Henry James' 'loose baggy monster' novels, with dramatic transmutations, unexpected revelations, coded meanings, messy misunderstandings, earthy glamour, clichés twisted into transcendence, and a cast of thousands – hucksters, thieves, scoundrels and drifters making themselves at home in dives, dens and nightclubs, all used as much as anything as hiding places. Artists and performers mix madly with beggars, criminals, informers and villains. An early trailer described it as the French *Gone with the Wind*. Set in 1828, in a seamy, dreamlike Paris filled with a variety of ragged, unsavoury street entertainers, it features a mysterious, beautiful, fiercely intelligent actress filmed at one point naked in a bath, covered by water, symbolising the naked truth.

She was being romantically chased by a mime, an actor, a sly, cutthroat philanderer and writer and an aristocrat, all fatefully smitten with her, led to their ruin by a classic sensual, mostly mute, cinematic femme fatale designed for male desires, but also an elusive, enigmatic, inaccessible proto-feminist.

At one point, the actress is arrested, accused of stealing the watch of a wealthy passer-by. Eventually released, even though she's not necessarily innocent – part of a random relish for recklessness – she is told by the police she is free to go. 'Fine, I love freedom,' she says, a line with particular resonance at the end of the Second World War, part of a film tumultuously celebrating any attempts, in the midst of improbable chaos and social pandemonium, to create something magical.

The film moves stylistically up through the theatrical ranks – beginning with basic mime, leading to lively melodrama and higher up to a sophisticated rendition of *Othello*. Everyone is, in the Shakespearean sense, always on stage, existing in various overlapping theatrical worlds, acting and concealing, pretending and make-believing, playing their part, resigned to their fate, their inevitable destiny, in a way following predictable patterns and strange orders and stage directions, trapped by ritual, but fighting all the way to stand out, to be someone and something different. They are fitting into pre-existing roles and the costumes that come with them, but also trying to find a new role, a new way forward – being anyone, whatever role you found yourself playing, and being yourself, making up your own identity.

Children of Paradise, with all its colliding colours, characters and mesmerising confusion, landed in 1940s Tokyo like something both from another century and from outer space. It brought with it, amid its multi-layered investigation of a society in full disorienting flow, a history of theatre and related media, including film – this is a film about theatre, and also a film about film. Novelty, it says, is as old as the world, and never loses its charm.

The film reveals the origin of French pantomime as a silent response to censorship imposed by the government, which feared an uprising by the poor if they heard subversive onstage words. The establishment, as always, didn't want ordinary people getting any ideas in their head. Actors were stopped from uttering a single word from the stage, forced to communicate instead through expression and gesture, using body language to transmit information and meaning and, ultimately, the ideas in their head.

The film's title came from the top gallery, the gods, in the rougher Parisian theatres in the 1840s – the cheapest seats, the paradise occupied by the poor, 'the children', who sat there, rowdy and unpredictable, the noise they made possibly a sign of their easily pleased ignorance, possibly, more dangerously, of their ultimately discerning need to know.

Seeing this film became a surreal, mind-blowing education in the purpose of performance, rooted, via the exuberant imaginations of writer and director, in rituals embedded in human history, myth and psychology, in fertility dramas.

Paris, a Paris of the mind, and myth upon myth, had, somehow, as promised by some, across time and space, on the other side of the threat of the destruction of the world, become a young Tokyo girl's education: a place for indulging the senses and engaging the intellect. Whatever she was learning in school – the usual sums, the common legacies, the normal ways – was blown apart by seeing a film like this explode all around her, opening up worlds waiting for her out there.

It would have been a surreal, energising, seductively forbidden experience seeing it, without the permission of grown-ups, in a part of town parents would warn against, doing something expected more of boys, in a small 1940s Tokyo *meigaza*, but the Surrealism of *Children of Paradise* is set in a world and time where Surrealism itself was still sixty, seventy years ahead.

Surrealism spiralled more directly into Yoko's mind through films she watched on the sly, with school badge hidden, cut off from Tokyo's limbo state by the protean, mischievous modernist, radical socialite and avant-garde high priest Jean Cocteau. He celebrated and mingled with Cubists and Futurists, Surrealists and Dadaists, while inevitably denying he was one or the other, seeing himself as a do-it-yourself amateur craftsman and self-taught artisan making 'tables' where anyone interested could sit and conduct seances, and come to their own understanding of his work.

Cocteau was painted as an intense, vain young poet by his friend Amedeo Modigliani in the spring of 1916, when Paris was at the centre of the creative cosmos. He paid for the portrait, but never collected it. As an abstract promoter and publicist Cocteau's clients ranged from Proust to Picasso, Satie to Stravinsky, Diaghilev to Piaf, Sartre to de Beauvoir. His restless multifaceted experiments as poet, photographer, essayist, dramatist, sculptor, animator and designer explored elegantly disordered dream-worlds rendered most intensely in his film-making. For him, film-making was an art – *the* modern art – not an industry, as he decided it was in America, but the most poetic way of expressing the mysterious and eternal in the everyday and investigating and playing with the thin membrane between the here and now and other worlds.

Beginning in 1932, looking back to Chaplin and Méliès and forward to the French new wave, to Bergman, Warhol, David Lynch and del Toro, Cocteau described his avant-garde first film and one of the first real surreal films, *The Blood of a Poet*, as a 'realistic documentary of unreal events'. He wanted to make the unreal seem real. The mystery of how you make a film became part of the film, which is about how you are a poet and more or less why, and, fantastically, what it looks like.

Yoko saw Cocteau's first full-length feature, the opulent, audacious 1946 film *Beauty and the Beast*, based on the 1756 fairy tale, another film made at the end of the Second World War in a shattered, anguished France, wounded like Tokyo. It was produced under challenging conditions with a limited budget. In it, Cocteau takes the viewer as far away as possible from the realities and challenges of the time. It's in shadowy expressionist black and white, but the deep, ecstatic cinematic black and white that can seem more intense and bewitching than real-world colour.

The original tale as old as time was viewed by Cocteau as an Anglo-Saxon horror story, a weird tale, opening with written instructions to watch it – very much a provocative, primal and suggestive even sexual adult adaptation – with the faith and open-minded wonderment of a child, who still believes a thousand simple things they should take into adulthood. The instruction ends with what Cocteau calls four truly magic words, the open sesame of childhood – Once upon a time – followed by the off-screen cry of 'ACTION', because this is a film, a film about a story as well as a film telling a story, something real made about something unreal, the making up of a desired reality using carefully created images and fake surfaces.

Yoko would then have seen something supernatural-seeming and subtly unsettling, a dream of a dream, the cinema of a painter who was also a poet, a poet who was also an illusionist, a complex over-the-top lather of emotions, visions, slow motion, special effects, reversed action, erotic displacements, coded messages, extravagant costumes, visual metaphors, endless transitions and, of course, the smoke and mirrors – doorways into other states and places – generated by someone who appreciated how cinema emerged from the magic lantern entertainments presented at nineteenth-century circuses and funfairs. The other side of Surrealism from the beginning of cinema, Cocteau sets us inside a castle located beyond space and time where bodies and minds and logic seem to float.

Candelabras are held by disembodied living hands. Statues come alive. Shadows move independently. Beds make themselves. A rose has the power to influence emotions. Love conquers all. Loveliness and beauty exist amid the ordinary and ugly. However bad things are, there is no cause for fear. Ugliness will vanish with time. You too can fly off through the clouds with your lover. Optimism will never die. If you are willing to believe me I will show you wonderful things.

It all makes more sense than a reality careering out of control; it is more comforting, especially in devastated post-war Japan with its uncertain future. It's also a film that makes sense to those suffering under foreign occupation – Cocteau uses *Beauty and the Beast* to represent breaking free of the occupier's evil hold, something yet to happen in 1940s Japan. The Beast was still in full view.

There's little dialogue that needs translating, so it's as connected to the wordless visual and visceral purity of the silent movie as anything by Kubrick. And an artist with avant-garde sensibilities and a faith in the unfamiliar and new ways of seeing and feeling can make something, for obscure, oblique, autobiographical purposes, that can reach into people's hearts.

Yoko also mentions seeing and being infected by Cocteau's 1950 film *Orpheus*, in which the Greek myth is transferred to contemporary beatnik Left Bank Paris, another of his enchanting, poetic films using deceptively simple special effects, clever cuts, trick shots, scintillating symbolism, secret forces, strange encounters, evocative atmosphere and bewitching smoke and mirrors to achieve an almost direct translation of a dream, of a haunted inner world. It's another magical film about movie magic and you enter it as if it doesn't matter if you ever come out again.

Cocteau, the lover of mirrors, of reflections, uses the myth of a death-confronting trip to the underworld and back to tell a story reflecting his own interests, obsessions and inspirations about searching for new inspiration and experimenting with form and style to reinvent yourself, to come back from obscurity and creative uncertainty.

It's an absurdist psycho-dramatic adventure story referencing Hollywood detectives, Orson Welles and James Dean as much as Greek myths and Surrealist enterprise, its arty black clothing anticipating the New York Beats and the informal uniforms of early pop singers.

Most Surrealists attempting to continue what they were before the war seemed quaint and old-fashioned; their dreams had been melted down and made merely decorative by the war, with its ultimate take on Surrealist distortion. Cocteau, viewed with suspicion by the pre-war hard-core Surrealists for repeating and diluting occult Surrealist ideals for his own ends, for tending his own reputation, proved more resilient. What was considered aesthetic cheating and cheapening by purists, his energetic ability to detect and process the latest trends as dandy and cultural critic, helped him continue to shapeshift – enough to form a link between early twentieth-century French artistic thinking and the new recuperative thinking of existentialism and the new wave.

He kept a thread going between turn-of-the-century surreal theatre pioneer Guillaume Apollinaire and the revolutionary stream-of-consciousness films of Jean-Luc Godard, both as infatuated as Cocteau with the multi-sensory borders where fantasy becomes reality and reality fantasy, each finding their own form and style appropriate to time and place.

In Orpheus, Yoko glimpsed through Cocteau's vivid veil the early stirrings of the sights and sounds and glamour of pop culture consumed and guided by the increasingly liberated post-war teenager. A moody, ageing but legendary proto-pop-star poet losing inspiration and facing artistic death is adored by screaming girls and envied and despised by an assortment of rivals jealous of his fame and acclaim for simply refurbishing the style and voice of others. Younger poets aim to replace him. It's the natural order of things; you're in, you're out, you're hip, you're square, you're alive, you're dead. You're here. You're gone. You were never really here.

The poet, becoming romantically tangled with a beautiful woman representing Death, attempts to bring his pregnant dead wife back to the world of the living, as with the original Greek myth, in which the musician sings such sad songs after his wife dies that the gods suggest going to the underworld and using his music to persuade Hades to send his wife back to him. Hades agrees, but Orpheus mustn't look at her until they are back with the living. Checking she is with him as they leave the underworld, he looks at her and loses her for ever.

Cocteau, in the modern world, adds motorbikes and a Rolls-Royce and a police investigation. Cocteau's Orpheus, turned from the original into a modern artist, an adored celebrity, is accused of plagiarising the poetry of a younger poet. A car radio broadcasts cryptic messages like 'silence goes faster backwards', 'a single glass of water lights up the world' and 'the bird sings with its fingers'. This Orpheus is on the hunt for artistic immortality, and sees signs in these messages, these instructions – to be interpreted as you like, perhaps as offering help about how to travel between dimensions, the way Death comes to him via a mirror, the underworld's Surrealism materialising in the land of the living, or as clues to enriching his poetry and extending his success. And with Death on his side, he can achieve immortality.

Who knows what Yoko made of this mystery about mysteries, this film of memories, living legends and dead idols, as it entered her mind and reached into her dreams, this thing that resembled a dream and somehow summarised life, and the death you see revealing itself over time in mirrors, sharing the secret of all secrets? Maybe she had been asleep while it played and did indeed dream it. Maybe it was something she didn't need to understand, to which she could just experience an emotional response, accepting its representation of the intrigues of the universe at face value.

Maybe, among all the maybes of a life, of a film about a life, it made her consider being an artist, the kind of artist who, like Cocteau, viewed the things he made as simply machines for generating meanings – the kind of artist who keeps coming alive through their work, the kind always searching for inspiration.

After seeing Cocteau's *Orpheus*, especially if you're at your most open to somewhere and something new, you'll never be the same again. You might lose track of what was going on. A moment an action a kiss a fight a might make you lose yourself completely, and/or drive yourself into yourself. You might not remember much of its detail, which was never entirely clear in the first place – this mix of Death and dying, truth and lies, falling into and out of a realm that previously only sleep and dreams had led you to – but you never forget that you've seen it, what Cocteau called a petrified fountain of thought.

You might remember only the strange messages coming through on the radio, from the underworld, or the memories of an invented dead poet, or your own memories. You might see that each of the messages is itself like a work of art, making your mind go in many different directions at once. A few words of suggestion, of direction, are themselves as much an idea as a painting, a sculpture or a piece of music. An image followed by another image and then another in a certain order can take your breath away or emphasise the everyday miracle that lies within ordinary things, seen from a particular angle, as if it really happened, and at the same time never did.

Yoko discovered that she liked being disturbed by oddly spiritual beings like Cocteau, the poet as liar who always spoke the truth, and although 'disturbing others' wasn't necessarily an occupation, it was something she decided she could do as well. She had found something that she wanted to get closer and closer to – not necessarily making films, but exploring the relationship between art and life, imagination and reality, illusion and truth. She discovered that she tended to identify with characters that were in the wrong, up to no good, fallen from grace, escaping from something.

She would come to agree with Cocteau when he said, 'What the public criticises in you, cultivate. It is you.'

She looked in the mirror(s) that Cocteau held up to the world and saw herself. What could she do with all this? What was to become of her? What next?

As Duchamp's post-painting work branched out towards the apparent gestures of the jester, but revealed something more considered than just the jokes and hoaxes of a conniving non-artist, there was some anxiety among establishment forces that perhaps he was gaining access to something dangerously alluring beyond the usual realm of the non-sensical easily dismissed non-artist. This tension between seeming an emperor with no clothes and yet also possibly some sort of authentic magician tapping into the secret, long-lost power of images, words, objects and numbers, a genuine discoverer and not a scamming pre-tender, reflected the feeling most people have about modern art, a mixture of suspicion and grudging admiration. Or maybe just a mixture of suspicion and irritation.

His first, partial readymade, fusing two ordinary objects, made with some delight in 1913, was a bicycle wheel he paraded upside down on a mass-produced wooden stool, fixed together so the wheel could still spin. When he spun the wheel, the spokes would blur, which he said was like watching the flickering flames of a fire, which helped ideas form in his mind.

He had been fascinated by the question of how to represent movement in art, and here he bypassed all that skill, insight and trickery he was impatient with in painting, and just created something that moved, in real space and time.

Bringing this completely novel idea into existence, and treating it both seriously and with a sense of emotional indifference, utilised a new kind of skill, insight and trickery, and carved out a place where a shape shift-ing, unprecedented artist could operate. It didn't matter at all that the original wheel he made was lost, and the next one, and that it lived on in the mind or in myth, or through various authorised copies, some by Duchamp himself, some not; it was a part of this new way of creating something and then letting it take on a life of its own without having to conform with the old, steady definition of art and the usual patterns.

The Yoko Ono who sought answers by asking questions that had no obvious answers, who challenged herself to never do the same thing twice even when she was doing the same thing twice.

The Yoko Ono who, as a survival mechanism to ward off imaginary and real terrors and assault on her being, assembled a life of art which had as one of its subjects the art of living.

The Yoko Ono whose art, in the words of Marshall McLuhan, took on the role of indispensable perceptual training rather than the role of a privileged diet for the elite.

The Yoko Ono who made art from 'this is what I am feeling', 'this is how I feel', 'a fundamental feeling to explore and express and a sense that consciousness begins with feeling not thinking'.

Duchamp apparently went to *blague* extremes when in 1917 he anonymously presented a white porcelain urinal, set on its back and signed by R. Mutt, to the Society of Independent Artists in New York, which had claimed that as an unjuried society it rejected elitist French classification and would accept any entrant who paid the six-dollar fee – but then impatiently rejected the urinal as not being close to worthy of consideration. They considered it an elaborate, even immoral con, some stupid joke about pissing all over art. It was plagiarism. It was the vulgar work of a charlatan, a mindless, insensitive saboteur. It was a plain piece of plumbing, separated from its actual usefulness, an insult to their intelligence.

As a member of the society's board, who had been testing their resolve, Duchamp resigned when they failed the test he had set them, and proved they were precisely the conservative organisation he didn't want to be part of.

He hadn't gone completely rogue – or *blague* – because in titling the object *Fountain*, he had turned it into something else. There was enchantment there as well. There was confusion. There was a reaction. There was controversy. There was, one way or another, emotion. It released all the power an authentic work of art did, where magical worlds collided, with puzzling, liberating added extras. An artistic intervention had been made.

Concept was now more important than object. All previous assumptions were destroyed. As with God, you had to believe it was art for it to exist as art. And Duchamp wasn't admitting whether he believed or not; he was simply wondering aloud. The question alone was a new work of art, and a full-page photograph of *Fountain* in volume 2 of the Dada publication *The Blind Man* by pioneering art photographer and avant-garde advocate Alfred Stieglitz framed it as though it was already an iconic object, helping it become one. Stieglitz showed it for a short while in the 291 Gallery on Park Lane that he managed, before it was disposed of: his image in *The Blind Man* is the only record of its original existence. After all, it didn't come off an assembly line.

The editorial accompanying the photograph, outraged at the outrage the humble sculpture had caused, was headlined 'Buddha in the Bathroom' – which was what Louise Norton, the wife of another French exile, the experimental composer Edgard Varèse, called it, also playfully and seriously making a connection between the porcelain's erotic curves and the long, round nude ladies of Cézanne.

The editorial defending the merits of the piece – it was chosen, it was thought about, it generated new thoughts – and criticising the censorship was written by the editors of *The Blind Man* itself – Beatrice Wood, Henri-Pierre Roche and Duchamp. The essay, therefore, could have been signed Richard Mutt, like *Fountain*, and was itself part of the work of art, along with its deliberate disappearance.

The legend grew as modern media grew, relying on such scandals, antics, hypes and mysteries, and the new opportunities to help make something exist that hadn't before and inform people about something and, in one way or another, provoke them, even if they had no direct experience of it. Even if a work didn't exist, or was never finished, it still had inward significance.

The Yoko Ono who said, 'I think it is possible to see a chair as it is . . . But when you burn the chair, you suddenly realize that the chair in your head does not disappear.'

thirteen · creation

The choice was ultimately made for Yoko that she had to leave university and philosophy because her father, who had returned from his mysterious exile in an enemy prison, proud and reserved and carrying on as though little had happened in the lead-up to the surrender of Japan, returned to America to continue work as a bank manager for what was now the New York branch of the Bank of Tokyo. In the post-war years, the bank was described as a 'New Bank for a Reborn Japan', shouldering part of the task of revitalising the peacetime Japanese economy.

Not even the war, miserable imprisonment and profound post-war turbulence could shake his ties to the bank, and the power of money, and Yoko with her brother, sister and mother joined him in the pretty, affluent suburb of Scarsdale in Westchester County, twenty-four miles north of New York City, popular with the wealthy Japanese who settled in the New York area.

Yoko, the war still under her skin, feeling her way forward as an outsider in Japan, an outsider in America and increasingly an outsider in her family, still enjoyed the insider privileges of being the daughter of a wealthy banker. Continuing what had become an idiosyncratic education in Tokyo, she was enrolled in Sarah Lawrence College, a private liberal arts school, six miles from Scarsdale.

It was originally set up in 1926 as a college dedicated to instructing women in the arts and humanities, with a record for experimental educational programmes based in productive leisure aiming to 'recognise the total personality of the student as the educational unit rather than to isolate her intellectual development . . . All education must be self-education and it proceeds best when there is readiness to learn.' Founder William Lawrence, a real-estate mogul, opened the college in Bronxville, New York, in honour of his wife Sarah, and died months before it opened in 1928.

Yoko spent three slow, nourishing years there studying – or more accurately circling, absorbing, sifting – poetry, literature and musical composition, largely left to her own devices at a place that encouraged their students to push at the limitations of their favourite subjects.

One of her professors was the Scottish poet Alastair Reid, who possessed an amused, humorous take on life and nature. He had some poems published in the *New Yorker*, and in 1953 a book, *To Lighten My House*, as someone who became a poet when he had the 'dazzling realisation of all that seemed to be magically compressed into the word weather'. Reid was lean, tall, with an exotic-seeming Scottish burr; many of the students quickly found his lectures, and him, irresistible.

Yoko started to consider the idea of becoming a poet, and a life spent in an abstract buffer zone of contemplation and self-preservation. This close proximity to a wry, witty, real-life published poet, fresh from wartime Britain, passing on his unspoilt astonishment at the beauty and power of words and what they can do on a page, mostly just having great fun with words, made her think – what would that be like? The idea of creating a world that could exist outside or even inside the world that does exist . . .

She dated a boy who would later go out with Sylvia Plath – he noticed Yoko at a Sarah Lawrence dance, where she was clearly something different from the other girls, intense with a gentle, faraway stare, comfortable being on her own but nervous with obscure American rituals. Their almost instantly deep conversation contained an admission that when the war seemed to have destroyed all joy, she had once tried to commit suicide. He let her down gently, and moved on to Plath, who seemed a little lighter.

At Sarah Lawrence, where students fancied themselves as different, even avant-garde, happy to take risks, Yoko as a provisional poet craving the unconventional stability of pure originality was drawn to classes exploring experimental developments in music, movement and writing.

The deep, dense, enticingly revelatory adventures of the early twentieth-century twelve-tone music composed by Schoenberg,

Webern and Berg that still seemed from the future suited her desire to discover the surprising and relatively unexplored. It sounded nothing like anything she had heard in Japan, which helped her make up a country in her mind only she belonged to, the kind of country no one would want to destroy. This was music that was now up to thirty, forty years old. Where had this music gone next? Where had ideas like this gone next? Where can it take me?

Elsewhere, around the time she was hearing Schoenberg and those he influenced, enthralled by his radiant logic, and as she ended her teens, there were writers and artists dealing with the post-apocalyptic anxiety she had encountered in the aftermath of Hiroshima, dealing with profound crisis, looking for choice, meaning and direction, for a way forward, a way of escaping the poisonous influences of the past few decades, for signs, however desperate, that all is not lost.

There was Samuel Beckett's *Waiting for Godot*, with its austere stage setting: a rough country road, a pile of earth and a bare, ugly tree, above them only sky, and two characters in constant pain, not sure why they have been put on earth, speaking words that are jumbled and fragmented, searching for a way of rising above their futile existence, endlessly waiting – a fundamental condition of life – as the sun and moon come and go and time dilates and where they are stays exactly the same. It was Hell, but it was also life.

There had been Robert Rauschenberg's *White Paintings*, five sets of different numbers of panels of basic white house paint arranged in a square, where the only detail was the shadows of those looking at the painting, or reflections of the room they were in. The almost literal blank canvas could be an alien artefact never touched by human thing, a hypersensitive mirrored machine for detecting how many people were looking at it, the weather outside or whatever dust or stray particles might fall on them. Onlookers would pay more attention at what they were, and weren't, looking at, causing it to become a work of art, perhaps leading to a special awareness, or they would dismiss it as not being a work of art, an inconsequential hoax, whatever any expert or curator said, and pay no attention.

Just in case he was implying that the *White Paintings* were the only answer to some question or another, maybe to what makes a painting a painting, Rauschenberg created a series of black paintings that are also on the edge of being collages, made up of dense black paint and layers of newspaper. He wanted his paintings, he said, to create complexity without revealing anything.

There was Jean-Paul Sartre's monumental 1952 tribute to Jean Genet, *Saint Genet: Actor and Martyr*, a stunning study of self-mythologising artistic creation and the artistic obsession of someone who identified with the poor and oppressed but also with the rebels who challenged social and political hierarchies. It is a biography that is not a biography if you consider that a biography should simply be a chronological collection of facts. Facts have their importance, but they can also be where a biography comes to grief. As Virginia Woolf wrote, the best method is to separate the two kinds of truth: let the biographer print the facts fully, completely, accurately, the known facts without comment, then let them write the life as fiction.

In this 1952, aged nineteen, on the cusp between a Japan that had fallen away and a nebulous foreign place that needed to be filled in and made into something, Yoko was already beginning to make theories about how her life should be lived with the ardour of a discoverer, already frustrated at smashing against other people's prejudices, with the idea that she would always have to live in the shadows of men following the straight lines of history.

Every day, too, there was something inside her that made her toss aside her theories, and force herself to remake them as something new. She was living an obscure life, and maybe always would, feeling an outsider even though she was on the inside of a renowned family. However much her father seemed on the inside of the world of money, she started to turn some of her memories, which were also part of her theories, into stories, which were mostly told using wispy, whispering outlines of drawings, made using smeared charcoal.

She wrote about the time she was evacuated in northern Japan, far too north for roses to grow like they had in her mother's pretty, well-tended

Tokyo garden, and remembered how in order to change a disappointing, even dangerous reality, she would dream things up in an effort to change reality. She imagined she could see, even smell, a single white rose, an impossible sign of a beauty adrift in a time of war, and refused to accept that it did not exist, even though no one else could see it. It disappeared when she tried to get close, but it reappeared in her dreams.

A passing stranger who happened to be called John said that he could see it as well, either to make her feel better and less alone amid darkness and fear, or because he really did see it.

The first known creative marks of a playful, meditative and self-referential minimalist whose every gesture was a form of memoir mixed with charged fantasy, who used art to make up a life, to fill in the blanks, to constantly begin again, to heal wounds, 'The Invisible Flower' is a secretive Yoko Ono origin story combining evocative images, hazy self-portrait and brief, almost mystical lines of text.

Something, or someone, that is invisible can be seen, or sensed, by another person, who understands that all is not what it seems, and it takes imagination to believe in something when no one else does. The rose might not be there, but to believe that it is, when everything seems broken and doomed, is a sign of hope, a sign that things can change however helpless you feel, a sign that you can still dream. You can trust that even if time doesn't actually exist, you will be alive in the future. There is no rose, but there can be a rose, and by remembering it, and turning it into a story, or a drawing, there is a rose – in the lost past, and in the near future. A memory can one way or another be permanent. A rose is a rose even when it isn't. The drawing of a rose that never was but now exists is a promise of resurrection. What we believe in will eventually happen.

It's 1952, and there are hints, in the sparse charcoal impressions gracefully pulled around the white paper, of an awareness of, or an instinctive sympathising with, Abstract Expressionism, from someone who grew up surrounded by the Japanese calligraphy that the American Abstract Expressionists had been inspired by. The story of the beautiful invisible flower that only Yoko can see – and the mysterious character called Smelty John with his sweet faith in hope and love, in peace and quiet – drifts across the border of existentialism.

The black scratches, inky smudges and flamboyant swoops, the meandering flow of realisation, the outcome of a mysterious delirium, the creation of airy entanglements, her hair floating in the ocean wind, are like gentle Jackson Pollock; the text, the captions, discreetly champion the infinite power of poetry and therefore the importance of free speech as a vehicle for transformation.

It's 1952, and Yoko is beginning to make her choices, already with a desire to leave traces of her existence, however obscure, already interested in life's mysteries, such as growth, eroticism, procreation and death. She's looking back to her childhood, where she was invisible, stuck in time, surrounded by chaos and death, but also beyond, to a new life, and unexpected change in a universe that is always moving, always in flux. Human existence is as brief as the life of a rose that hardly anyone ever noticed. What was there to fear from taking chances with your life?

Duchamp was sixty-seven when there was a first French public exhibition of his collected work, in 1954, as his ideas and philosophical challenges increasingly made more sense after the atrocious negative space of the Second World War, and a need for fresh thinking, for radical breaks with a broken past. A first monograph appeared five years later, a first retrospective in a Californian museum was in 1963. Duchamp's name was now better known, and once the momentum had picked up, and there was pop art, pop music and popular culture all craving influence, precedent and daring, untapped resources, the momentum couldn't stop. As an obscure artist, in secret, he had been the prophet of the changes in art, and over time he would become acknowledged as the prophet of the changes in art. For decades of his life he was barely visible; afterwards he would be called the most influential artist of the twentieth century, the one who changed the world of art.

Making sure he was directing the history of himself that would eventually be out of control, he would occasionally do interviews revealing, a little out of elusive, secretive character, some of his thinking; in 1956, he said: 'I believe that Art is the only form of activity in which man, as man, shows himself to be a true individual who is capable of going beyond the animal state. Art is an outlet toward regions which are not ruled by space and time.'

Even as he seemed to have stopped making art, or creating pieces that could be called art, deep in the world of privacy he had constructed around his name, yet with increasing visible presence as his profile and influence revealed itself, he was up to something. This 'something' would somehow underline his alleged status as retired, cultishly treasured art legend as much as undermine it.

From 1946, for twenty years, in relative hiding as the Second World War receded, and the avant-garde-streaked counterculture formed around him, he worked on something in total privacy, building one of those uncanny, untouchable visual, psychological and philosophical dramas that resemble nothing else that anyone had ever thought of or somehow made.

It didn't fit into any art movement, and it didn't fit into any of his self-made scenes, predictions, themes, digressions, obsessions, retreats, other than that it was of itself in its own time and place, concerned with desire, play, magic, wonder, mind, body, fear, violence, strangeness and what to all intents and purposes is making decisions about human nature. In that sense, it gives another fastidious, enigmatic glimpse into a mind acutely aware of its own unnerving and unfathomable workings, and its own even deeper, darker, astonishing out-of-reach corners.

In a minuscule room in his small home on West 14th Street, New York, which he acquired in 1942 having moved from France after the fall of Paris – arranging his travel by posing as a cheese salesman – and kept until his death, Duchamp secretly constructed, using items found on neighbourhood walks and drives into the country, what is as much a being, a complex new life form, as an object. If we use language associated with art, *Étant donnés* (*Given*) – its shortened title – is a combination of performance art, film, video, installation, diorama, collage, blueprint, photography, sculpture, self-portrait, happening, tableau, stage set and work on paper. It's also a peep show, a kind of trap, and by being his last major artwork, it became his conclusion to art. There was something about it that seemed as much late nineteenth-century as it did post-Surrealist, as much medieval as postmodern, a missing link between the uncanny magic of raw Dada and the almost tongue-in-cheek eeriness of early artificial intelligence artwork.

Like a dream, it cannot be captured by being photographed or filmed, and it is wrong – although vaguely, politely accurate – to suggest it is as it seems to be some sort of landscape fixed behind an ancient-seeming brick-framed wooden door viewable through two ragged peepholes where a partially seen nude woman, or lifelike doll, is arranged like a murder victim on a bed of dead leaves and twigs, her hairless crotch facing the viewer.

There is an antique gas lamp held by the woman illuminating a representation of cotton clouds, dense trees and a flickering toy-town waterfall spun from see-through glue made to seem far off in the distance. These settings, visions and possibilities are part of what *Étant donnés* appears to be, echoing nothing but its own aura, its own abominable isolated wildness, Duchamp caught in the act of being Duchamp, even if it can't exactly be proved, as he moves through the shadows of his own thoughts to carve something out of space and time that is an irrational image of itself.

It's a three-dimensional description of something yet to exist, or of a form of life that is long extinct. As he was working on it, as if in another time, on another planet, contemporary art action and art superstars and counter-reformers collaging real objects into their paintings paraded nearby in New York, art and artists tending to their own public personas who did what they did because of what he did.

The slowness, the lonely length of time it took to develop, was as much as anything the point of the work, as was the fact it evolved during the last years of his life, not to be finished, but simply thought about, studied for, prepared. It would be exactly what he wanted it to be as part of his legacy, the secretive last work of an arcane, crafty thinker who spent his days revealing nothing about everything and everything about nothing, endlessly fascinated by things he did and didn't understand.

Or maybe the full esoteric title was the point, disclosing and screening the unknown essence it was and wasn't experiencing: *Étant donnés: 1° la chute d'eau, 2° le gaz d'éclairage . . .* (*Given: 1. The Waterfall, 2. The Illuminating Gas . . .*). Or maybe the point was that this meticulously assembled mystery about mystery conceived by someone keen on outwitting the deadening institutionalisation of art had a final resting place in one of America's largest museums, the Philadelphia Museum of Art, in a windowless room next to a space containing the parallel universe of his dirty, broken, conceptual sculptural meta-painting *Large Glass* – a crude, cosmic, opaque and transparent contraption, an alien craft he made sure was cemented into the floor to guard against removal into a dingy forgotten storeroom, kept close to other examples of Duchamp's thinking and given wider context by his last 'secret' work.

If *Étant donnés* resembled nothing he had ever done before, and could have existed at any point during his life, it was also the latest deviant, carefully controlled variation on everything he had ever done before, where everything led to something that began before, during and after his *Three Stoppages* from 1913/14 and his 1919 alteration of the *Mona Lisa*. The *Stoppages* were the connection between his paintings and his readymades. They still used canvas, relying on chance for their appearance: he dropped three metre-long pieces of string from a height of one metre – a measurement, an abstract invention in itself, conceived during the French Revolution – and recorded the outline in pencil on a painted canvas but also on glass and wood, to create different shapes.

The standard one-metre length had become something individual; a unit of measurement had become conceptual. A straight line, Duchamp noted, had been changed into a curved line, without losing its identity as a measurement, but introducing an element of doubt that would now exist for ever. You could drop the string a thousand times and never repeat the pattern.

He found the title for this series, the French for 'invisible mending', walking past a shop sign advertising sewing material. Further inside such a shop were more signs of what came next, after playing with the readymade idea of the metre, and manipulating the readymade material that was the piece of string, and turning a piece of household equipment into something that could be exhibited almost simply through the power of the mind in an art gallery. Three dimensions were the beginning of other dimensions, if you knew how to get there, and had a sense to perceive them.

Étant donnés was a folding in of this early discovery and all his other indicative actions, a sombre, neutral civic setting for his last laugh, the day of reckoning, the conclusive checkmate never formally actioned.

Wrecking, or refining, artistic standards, criticising, or accepting, art as commodity, questioning the actual realness of even such a realistic portrait, opening up all of space and time to what lies beyond art that you only look at, Duchamp's *Mona Lisa* placed him in 1919 at the beginning of an aesthetic conceptual avant-garde, which he had been circling since he manipulated the metres of his *Stoppages*, and which fifty years later he was still circling, and toying with, and remeasuring.

It is also achieved immediately, as far as the avant-garde could go, so even though it liberates artists over the next century to head as far out into the unknown as they liked, as long as they hold their nerve, keep a straight face or refuse to sacrifice their soul, however far they go, whatever they think, however rich they get, however critical and original their work, they can never go beyond Duchamp, whether the merry moustache he stuck on history or his eerie peepholes that opened onto eternity as conceived through the workings of the mind.

It would still take courage, audacity and deep, dark wit to go as far as he did, but however far out artists went, even if they were funnier, smarter, more outrageous, more innovative, more modern, more advanced, even if they deviated into music, fame, theatre, film, gaming, the mainstream, the internet, Duchamp would be lurking or wandering or taking forty winks or sighing nearby.

He would be there in the far-out as a shadow or a ghost or a spiral of water or a wall or a mound of sand or a comedian or a celebrity or a fly on a mirror or more than one person or a can of soup or a bus ticket or a pile of bricks or someone else or a crumpled-up piece of paper or a blood cell or a staged game of chess or a bottom or a sad endless electronic drone or a haunting photograph or a meme. But he would always be there.

Even as the world slides into the meta-universe, into a world splitting into worlds and regions that helplessly watched the emergence of artificial intelligence as a kind of playful error-strewn God-like creator, or its exact solemn opposite, toying with art history as with everything else, all its surfaces, assumptions and patterns, Duchamp is still there, having somehow seen it all coming, this disconcerting post-human appropriation and deconstruction of art's place in human history, this shredding and lunatic recombining of art, reality and human history.

You couldn't draw on a goatee and improve or profoundly remake anything produced by Duchamp, which was sometimes just a perception, or an illusion, or a passing thought, or a pile of prepared dust, or a change of mind, or an abstract auditing of the uncanny, or years of doing very little, even if you felt you'd worked out his secrets, or matched his subterfuge, or apparently escaped his influence. Whatever he produced, however sublime, complex, pretty or ephemeral, there was already the moustache and goatee metaphorically, or in code, built in.

He was the beginning of the avant-garde and he was the end, even though he made it clear there need be no end, there could be no end. There would always be something else, something new, even if it was only the inevitable and/or shocking result of what had gone before with the addition of what was yet to come, depending on when you were born, and the technology you were born into, and enslaved to.

In 1919, gently taking the *Mona Lisa* apart and putting it back together again, perhaps playing along with the roguish Dadaists scampering nearby, deciding art was an archaic construct and/or anything he wanted it to be, he couldn't resist a little wink to those who came before, appropriating *him*, sensing his coming, preparing the way, setting the scene, following him even before he was born, as he passed through a network of influence on the way to what seemed beyond influence, to what hadn't been thought of before, at least with his radiant self-awareness: the Renaissance intensity of Lucas Cranach the Elder, because like the most rootless, severe avant-garde composer, Duchamp needed to go into the far depths of untrammelled, under-developed pre-classical to begin again; the hyperbolic doubt of René Descartes; the laughter and energy of Allais and the Montmartre cartoonists; the wonderland and looking glass of Lewis Carroll; the sexual spoofs, strange plays and pataphysics of Alfred Jarry; Raymond Roussel's use of chance procedures and carefully arranged layers of arbitrariness in *Locus Solus* and *Impressions of Africa* reaching what Duchamp called 'the absolute height of unusualness'; Roussel's punning sentences, his stories-within-stories, his lack of consciousness of himself as an avant-garde or difficult artist, his belief that anything can be invented, the furtive hints of a history of art that was yet to happen, a constant sense that there is always something anomalous and tantalising just beyond the horizon, and it's just a matter of how, if and when you get there. And, of course, if you *want* to get there . . . maybe everyone gets there in the end, it's just some get there quicker and with more delight than others, and then keep moving, even if sometimes you don't seem to be moving at all, because there's nothing more there.

And then Duchamp died, just one of those things you could see coming and yet was out of the blue, at his home in the comfortable suburb of Neuilly-sur-Seine west of Paris in the very early morning hours of 2 October 1968, after a pleasant day writing letters, discussing chess and death with a friend, drinking wine, eating dinner with his wife Teeny (the former wife of Henri Matisse's son) and close friend the experimental photographer Man Ray, and strolling to a local bookshop.

After browsing at the shop, he bought volume 3 of *Tout Allais*, a compendium of Allais's journalism, and a few hours later died suddenly, as if by chance, while reading a passage and, Teeny says, quietly chuckling to himself. Not long after he died, Man Ray, who had taken a photograph of Marcel Proust on his deathbed, took a photograph of the gone, calm Duchamp on his, a final sublime collaboration, an uncanny afterthought, the last swapping of mental and visual ideas between two great nonconformist accomplices whose friendship began in 1915 as a game of netless tennis, a way of communicating when neither of them spoke the other's language.

Alphonse Allais can also take some of the credit, for being there, close to the end, at the spellbinding intersection between everything and nothing, having written something playful, gently enjoyed by someone who believed that being playful was the only form of fun possible in a world that wasn't always much fun.

And when the end comes, and you lose, as you will, despite all your best efforts, and best moves, and whatever cunning and anger you've mustered, it is best to lose graciously, having done whatever turned out to be your duty. We are part of nature, whose order we obey, even when we've got a few things to say about that, to put into words, or whatever you've got to hand.

Perhaps Allais was telling Duchamp, from wherever he was, what was coming, and it made a great deal of sense, and he got the joke, and he understood it, he could always see it coming, he was ready, made for this moment, and he knew what death was. He'd put it into his creations, along with all that life.

For as long as the game lasted, life was alive with near-infinite possibilities. Towards the end, there are few moves left, and even fewer pieces, which only increases the challenge even as options run out. And when it's over, it's nothing in the end. 'Life is like a game of chess,' wrote Schopenhauer: 'we draw up a plan, but it remains dependent on what the game, and if life fate, sees fit to do.'

Death was something ineffable, forever unfolding just beyond the horizon. It was when, having once self-identified as a breather, a *respirateur*, because breathing was everything, each one a lost, lonely, work of art, a constant euphoria, a move into the next world, and more life, he stopped breathing.

It was when and where he was once and for all liberated from his past, where at last the mystery of art was explained, or better still, left open to interpretation, because there are no answers, no meaning, *sub specie aeternitatis*, and perhaps he would come back in the next life as a mote of dust floating in an antique bookshop, a tin of mackerel fillets, a love affair, a foraging bumble bee, a magical sunset, a ghostly algorithm, or something to be completed by others, or . . .

An album, perhaps, one released about a month after Duchamp died, a record by him and her, her and him, east and west, from one heavenly city to another, from one place to no place, one musician producing an artist, one artist directing a musician, a unity of opposites, one some kind of self-christened Christ, the other some kind of Philistine courtesan of unholy persistence and devilish conceit, rising suddenly from darkness, who had personal charm, mental ability, self-command and nerve, one giving the other something they do not have, both determined to live well their own way, a record presenting the sound of falling in love, two warriors, worlds apart, had for each other, the sound of imagine this or imagine that, the sound of two descendants of the naive, busy and fantastical socialist-capitalist conceptualist

Henri de Saint-Simon, the sound of 'this is music if we say it is', the sound of laziness as a philosophy, the sound of putting yourself in the line of fire, because you just can't help yourself, the sound of things getting very intense, the sound of two lives being completely reorganised, adjustments will have to be made, the sound of repeating the same things over and over and over, for love to continue and be gradually different, the otherworldly and this-worldly sound of a record entitled *Unfinished Music No. 1: Two Virgins*, or not . . .

Everything comes into focus, if only for a moment. Yoko is already using words carefully, as though she has already worked out how many words she will use during her life, and it will be a long life, so a few words at a time, building up a picture of dissent, despair and desire. Words that carry with them more than words.

There is a piece of something – work, art, self-consciousness, self-soothing ritual – Yoko Ono made perhaps in 1953, because it is not precisely recorded, and there is no one watching, no one paying attention, she is on her own, even if surrounded by the power and accumulating interconnectedness of America. The thing she thinks is named as a piece: it is called, then or later, 'Secret Piece', and in that sense, it is her Opus 1, and the very beginning of many of the pieces – of thinking, creation, writing, therapy – that will be called 'pieces'.

This first piece represents a prescient transition between a traditional score, written out on music manuscript paper even though it is only one repeated base note, and a short description instruction how to 'perform' or play a piece of music. It was too basic for it to require being written out as a conventional score, but also had its own sophisticated intentions that were limited by writing it out as a score, which couldn't include the parts that would properly reproduce what Yoko had in her mind when she thought of what sounds she was looking for. It couldn't include natural sounds, emotional intensity, the imagination itself and the dream-world, or any accidental moments and incidents that Yoko was intending to be a central ingredient of the piece.

It wasn't a piece of music that could only be played by trained musicians in some ways restricted, by their training and even their instrument, from adding their own energy and dreams to the piece. Yoko wanted to issue some guidelines to what she had in mind, not write out a piece of music that would then be slavishly followed by musicians and only musicians.

97

She was thinking of something that could be 'read' by anyone, as if their instrument was the imagination, their mind. She wanted to somehow use some words and suggestions that could be turned into a story by whoever came across them. Ideas were more important than rhythm or melodies. The conventional written score as the central essence, almost the guardian, of music was becoming outmoded by electronic equipment, the word of mouth of folk and the blues, recording studios and improvisation. Yoko was among those imagining a form of score that would fit into this new world, where music was being generated by mood, instinct, influence, atmosphere, acoustics and imagination.

At the time, she was struggling to find the language to express what she was feeling, a unique emotional urgency after feeling she was being erased, and the text she started to use, which was both a poetic distillation and something else, which wasn't really seen as art but felt like it to her, helped her reach for some sort of reassurance. Regular language wasn't enough, and these instructions, essentially to herself, to achieve some nurturing calm, were one way of working out what her new self was, and how she decided what she could do with this new identity, how she could keep refining and revising it so that whatever happened to her, it would never be taken away from her.

The lines, layout and technical etiquette of a musical manuscript did not help her communicate her wishes and make herself new. A small poetic sentence or two, written out as an instruction to follow roughly, to see where it led, made more sense to her as she looked to rebuild the world, not merely make do with what was left of it. What 'Secret Piece' shared with a conventional music score was that it needed participation to come into existence in the real world. The piece of paper with notes on only becomes something real when it is played by a musician. Yoko's art would only exist when her instructions were acted upon, when someone – including herself – was inspired enough to carry out its orders.

The repeated note and the old-fashioned music paper, with a description of how to play the piece, and the performance direction – 'with the accompaniment of birds singing at dawn' – were replaced by words without a score, and replaced with more choice, of note and of instrument. 'Secret Piece' became: decide on one note that you want to play. Play it with the following accompaniment:

The woods from 5 a.m. to 8 a.m. in summer.

This was now an instruction, an invitation to act, to try something, to exercise the imagination, whether making sound, or thinking, doing, believing, feeling, imagining something; the work of art was something you created for yourself based on the story, the wish, the actions, the moods of someone else. The idea was based on the musical score – where you followed the guidance of another to produce a piece of music – but they quickly became ways of mapping out and recommending possible options for new kinds of behaviour and approaches to life and living.

Yoko's art was meant to be realised, and over time that realisation would change, and be finished off again and again as time and the world changed.

Even if an individual didn't finish it off, the 'no finishing it off' was a form of finishing it off. It was as far as she wanted to go, under the circumstances, given the conditions. The simple unadorned text she used in these instructions came out of the allusive stories and short poems, themselves influenced by Zen parables, Surrealist imagery and her own feverish post-war dreams, that she was contributing to the Sarah Lawrence College school newspaper *The Campus* in the last few months she attended classes.

With these 'instructions', these transitory abstract musical scores made up of words and proposals, Yoko was asking, in a sly, minimal way, for something new to happen, without forcing it, without fixing it in time and space, without connecting it to a ruined world. Others individually and/or part of new post-war artistic groups and scenes were coming to similar open-ended conclusions, based on different influences, desires and life stories, but Yoko came to them from her own direction. What they shared was the idea that a work of art need not be confined to a gallery or exhibition space, and it could be an experience, an event, an image as much as it could be an object.

She was indirectly connected to atomised new international avant-garde scenes searching for new forms of expression and demanding change and positive progress as part of a process of recovery and renewal, but also part of her own world, still in shock, resisting feeling forced to follow the direction of others even if she sometimes found herself heading the same way.

One of her tutors at Sarah Lawrence was the forty-six-year-old Hungarian composer and pianist André Singer, who had set Walt Whitman to music, corresponded with Edgard Varèse, written songs in Vienna in the 1930s that were banned by the Nazis, and written a comic opera based on Alfred Jarry's *Ubu Roi*. He'd been on his own restless, mischievous journey through the turbulent twentieth century, jumping from city to city and finding artistic treasure and pleasure, and tension, amid the cafes, bars, dead-end streets, endless wars, dispute and savage conflicts.

With a traveller's experience and an immigrant's uneasiness, adjusting his character place to place, he noticed how Yoko enhanced her Japaneseness while in America – imagining she built up her Americanness in Japan – intrigued, sometimes inspired by the subtle, or sometimes abrasive, disconnection this would cause around her. She didn't go out of her way to fit in, and she wasn't very talkative, but acted like she was fitting in even as she was noticeably, even self-consciously, an outsider.

She was interested in sound and words, especially when it became the kind of music and poetry that seemed to annoy or upset or actually hurt most of her contemporaries, but she resisted being guided towards becoming something and someone in particular. She took things seriously but didn't seem to want to be anything, except perhaps someone who found herself interesting, as interesting as the things she found interesting. She was secretive, working things out at her own pace, but for all her inwardness and distance, she seemed an empathiser of extraordinary powers.

This made her one of the more enigmatic students Singer taught, and he noted how she seemed to spend a lot of time in her own head, presumably building worlds where borders between music and language naturally disintegrated.

Yoko was on her way somewhere, even if it wasn't clear where. Where she ended up going was not far from her school in New York State, if measured in miles. Measured in other ways – by ideas, and ideals, by the number of artists, activists and freedom seekers rapidly forging new kinds of connections between esoteric reckoning and transformational creativity, discovering on the fly how to invent the future, make it take shape so they could fit into it – it was on the other side of the world.

Singer knew that she was likely to find out where that was by continuing her education more informally in the less familiar parts of Manhattan, where he knew she could find like-minded thinkers, nomads, refugees and exiles, scattered, various and gregarious, but also contained and intensely intermingling inside a few densely packed square miles, also on their way somewhere, some of whom had a better idea where that was than he did.

Global conflicts and the people they shed seemed to culminate in these few square miles, in a city that reflected like no other in ways both painful and spirited the origins and backgrounds of its inhabitants. New York, which seemed in some ways to have it all, reflected the tensions and elemental aspirations of the world in a dynamic and fervent manner.

Even at a school with such a commitment to multidisciplinary work, she didn't necessarily need a teacher but a co-conspirator, or a gang of them, living a life of art, music, gatherings and artist-run galleries, the sort of spaces where ideas were found, swapped, developed, turned into something else.

Downtown Manhattan in the 1950s was a place where the aura, mutiny and future-facing speed of 1890s Montmartre seemed to have been fed into some impossible metaphysical machine and emerged – the other side of psychoanalysis, electricity, motor travel, cinema, tyranny and atom bombs – from the warren of old shops, slums, semi-derelict buildings, lofts and basements in the area below 14th Street: an area where the rules of the old world were being discarded and new ways of thinking applied. New technologies were being tried, entrepreneurial individualism, critical reflection and sexual freedom developed, with a general consensus that the production of the new is perpetually open-ended and adaptable.

Singer recommended she go and have a look and listen at what was happening there, indicating there was a direct link between Schoenberg and one of the more intriguing, provocative composers and teachers, who like Yoko always seemed to be practising art whatever they were doing: it was on his mind in some form morning, noon and night, even if he didn't think of it as art, with his background in Dada and admiration for Duchamp, his yearning for salvation. He was called John, like the character in her story who, like her, saw something no one else could see, which, even if it wasn't real, became real through the act of imagining.

This John had been making, and unmaking, music since more or less the year Yoko was born, and he was now in his early forties. In the late 1930s and early 1940s, reacting against a history of classical music and the European canon that was mostly, even when it was at its most experimental, 'an endless arrangement of old sounds', he preferred rhythm to harmony, uncertainty to virtuosity, ambient abstraction above instrumental busy-ness. He was escaping the traditional, sentimental and exhausted business of musical scores, to the point of regularly drifting through found sound and secret new systems into near and actual silence.

As wars raged all over, adding terrible, destructive volume to the noise of the world, he rebelled against what he called his training as a sentimental American to fight for noise, to be hard-hitting, to celebrate bigness, the sort that was now destroying the entire world. He decided to use only quiet sounds and small, intimate gestures. This was his protest against violence, his undemonstrative, even unemotional way of awakening a listener to the horrors and devastation spread around the planet. 'Quiet sounds were like loneliness, or love, or friendship.' Because his music was not being explicitly influenced by other music, or only by music that hadn't been, or it responded to music from mostly unexplored parts of the world, it was something outside music even when it delicately, or chaotically, resembled music.

Talking about this John, Singer seemed to be describing someone who was somehow reading her mind, a mind that was still making itself up. Maybe he was describing a ghost, or a prophet who understood that clairvoyance is not for the faint-hearted or the weak-willed . . . or, for some, a monster, a charlatan.

Her teacher didn't say it in so many words but effectively he was saying, track down someone called John Cage, you'll find him talking somewhere, making a noise and/or circling silence, he'll show you a few things, whether you agree with him or not. And he'll prefer it if you don't exactly agree with him and have other ideas about ideas.

It was the kind of advice Yoko was looking for. Head for the unknown, head away from your family and its own internal prejudices towards a vision of the future, towards recreational mystics and philosophical scoundrels, towards a spirit of anything is possible, where you can breathe the air of ideas, especially if you get there by using public transport.

The Yoko Ono passing on a message from Wittgenstein that only by thinking more crazily than philosophers can you solve their problems.

In Japan after the war, as things slowly returned to some kind of order, artists started to feel their way forward into new territory, working out how to move from blackened nightmare into post-surrender light.

Artists with avant-garde sympathies reacted to the thinking that safe and escapist conservative art, acting as if nothing had happened, would help heal deep psychic wounds. Fukuzawa Ichiro of the Nihon Avant-Garde Artists' Club faced up to the horror, devastation and uncertainty by working extreme, unfiltered violence into his work. Artist turned soldier Furusawa Iwami returned in 1946 from wartime imprisonment to find his house and paintings bombed into ashes.

His formally Surrealist pre-war paintings which led to him being nick-named Japan's Dalí were transformed into disturbing, surreal refractions of suffering and chaos; it seemed madness to ignore the impact the last few years had on fragile minds and especially vulnerable bodies. Painting representative and figurative images, however abstracted, seemed disappointingly normal in what was now clearly an ugly, horribly topsy-turvy world. The nation was in shock, and it needed the apparently shocking to galvanise it, to rediscover its soul.

Two years after the Americans handed power back to the Japanese, a more adventurous, bitterly anxious artistic renewal was clarified in 1954 – the beginning of a seven-year first phase – by a loose collective of energised freedom seekers called Gutai – *gu* from the Japanese word for concrete and *tai* from tool.

Gutai began relatively paint-based, but as part of their stretching of the imagination and their extending of art's boundaries, its members burst beyond paint, taking it with them into new places, but messing with its nature, then going where it couldn't go, into the ephemeral and performative, into film, performance, sound, light, air, and sometimes making a glorious mess to move beyond the horrors of war.

104

Based in Osaka, separating it from the usual Tokyo-centred art world – let alone Paris or New York – and giving it driven, less dogmatic and protective regional dynamism, generating more experimental space, the group was founded by high-energy painter Jiro Yoshihara, who assumed leadership duties and informally vetted potential associates, which led to the group comprising around fifty mostly male members.

Gutai was determined to open up Japanese art to the new in whatever form it could, and not just Japanese new, but in its view new unlike anything ever seen or heard before. This determination to achieve extreme novelty and in Gutai's words to 'go beyond the borders of existing art' was now an avant-garde tradition – the idea that art only changes through convictions strong enough to change society.

Avant-garde now had traditions, even as it had become a range of schools, styles and offshoots, but these traditions were built on the principles that there would always be the need for artists on the margins facing up to different times, circumstantial pressures and forms of elitism that needed opposition.

By the end of the 1930s, the idea of the avant-garde was already being co-opted by the mainstream, absorbed into the system as it merged into the canonical art history it set out to resist and change. After the war, in shadowy places inside countries like Japan with their own severe social and cultural problems, avant-garde ideas could have the potency and power they'd had in early twentieth-century Europe.

A furiously anti-traditional movement would still be necessary, and what seemed typically avant-garde, a dream of a purer, fairer future, still connected to revolutionary politics, a form of revolt that announced and defined itself as revolt, wasn't necessarily a sign of loss of vitality.

Gutai's volatile purification demonstrated there was still plenty of light and life in avant-garde strategies involving both the work itself and the methods used to reach a wider world, and helped recover the early twentieth-century avant-garde momentum that had stalled during the obliterating war.

The movement made use of an ethereal, near-lost national sensibility that when mixed into the unavoidable door-opening avant-garde energies defined in the first decades of the twentieth century would create a Zen Futurism. It was a new kind of Dada but not Dada, posting messages and communicating feeling as much as exhibiting artworks, another more interactive warrior form of the surreal, a more playful, gleeful Abstract Expressionism and its rioting on the wall. It was articulating a mutant revolution all of its own, unique to post-nuclear Japanese circumstances and wider psychic sensitivities, even as it inevitably echoed the radical essence of other movements.

The Yoko Ono who said, 'Leap before you look.'

Artists and art activists came before them with the radical attitude and extreme energy they would have explored anyway, and Gutai shared a similar approach with the Abstract Expressionists to the idea of painting as theatre, as action, as performance, the kind of spontaneous expressive energy that led to the happenings materialising in New York at the end of the 1950s, where audiences became incorporated into the experience. Despite the precedents and the contemporary parallels, by virtue of their location and cultural pressure, their particular need to use art as a survival mechanism, Gutai were as new as anything.

The idea of the happening, the live event as art, was coincidentally explored in Japan a few years earlier by artists using their body as part of their material and materials as part of their body, and celebrating their uncompromising individuality as their contribution to social reconstruction, a symbolic part of the struggle for freedom felt more deeply in a country that had suffered a nuclear attack. In a country deeply faithful to the orderly idea of art as two-dimensional painting on a flat surface, these whimsical antics had their own internal violence, but a violence that attacked, mocked, deliberately offended and provoked the rigid mindset that led to war.

Gutai member Atsuko Tanaka was born in Osaka in 1932, a year before Yoko Ono, making them almost the same age when the American occupation of Japan ended. One stayed where she was to find herself, one was moved elsewhere, both taken by oblique external forces beyond their control. Both discovered a similar creative desire to work out their place in a transformed world unpredictably transitioning between war-torn and urgently prosperous through and with art when a sense of self was being destabilised, and needed reimagining. Tanaka's disorienting, disoriented paintings of colliding, interlocking shapes, circles and splashes had a vivid, kinetic connection to Gutai hero Jackson Pollock; they were blueprints of movement, the explosive energy playfully sculpted from paint motivated by nervy post-war uncertainty and a need to respond, to generate control. They weren't paintings; they were events. Events that leapt outside the frame.

It was Tanaka's tangled, exuberantly eerie *Electric Dress*, a hybrid of the past – a traditional kimono – and the future – a world lit up by electricity – of human fragility and cyborg strength, of hope and fear, that seemed to crash with sudden force into art never seen before, anywhere, let alone Japan. Evolving out of a work where Tanaka peeled away the layers of a larger-than-life paper dress to reveal a leotard fitted with blinking lights, it drew connections between electrical wiring and the physiological systems that make up the human body.

It was first exhibited – first worn in public – in 1956, in an unsettled, newly interconnected Japan of increasing population, rapid industrial development, unprecedented commercialisation, advertising signs, crowded transport, the Americanised commodification of the female body. Beautiful and alien, futuristic and unwieldy, the dress symbolised this modern strange new country where the reborn city streets began fizzing with chaos and light, and it sketched out a future of constant tension between threatened tradition and a dependence on technology, between the individual and mechanisation, between opportunity and invaded privacy, between outside coercion and untouchable dreams. The dress needs the body, but the body is overwhelmed by the dress, just as the city needs people but ultimately dominates them.

It was also a performance piece, a development of Bauhaus theatrical workshops exploring the relationship between sound, space and light, between painting and dance, ritual and spontaneity, and a volatile fem-inised link between the urgent, madcap theatricality of the Futurists and Dadaists and what within a few years would become named as performance art.

It was art you could wear, art that turned you into art, an intimately personal reflection of Japan's unavoidable post-war engagement with exciting, intimidating, mysterious new machinery. Paint and colour on flat surfaces had become a pulsating circuit of cascading wires and fizzing neon light bulbs, each one painted by hand.

Electric Dress exists because it is worn, but completely covers the wearer, becomes a costume and a mask, a magical disguise, a self-designed armoured outfit, illuminating and concealing, and includes genuine danger and potential violence – when the electricity was turned on, bringing it to life, there would be a real threat of electrocution or being severely burnt.

Its weight alone – fifty kilos – gave it a certain power, and meant it needed to be hung from the ceiling so Tanaka could remain inside for long periods of time. The weighed-down human in the middle of all this is plugged into a wider network and all on her own, connected and isolated. The artist has put herself on show, but separated herself from any audience. She's close enough to touch, but you cannot reach her behind the heat, light and dangling electrical cables creeping up her body.

You needed to have a sense of humour to think of it, you needed to have been paying close attention to what was happening around you as a country turned almost to ash was anxiously, desperately modernised, and also courage and commitment to complete the piece by stepping inside the contraption and becoming it, losing yourself as you find yourself somewhere else. It took a new kind of spirit to essentially be asking the question, by building it and being consumed by it, by being effectively trapped inside your own imagination, your own enterprise – what were you turning into?

The Gutai solution to eliminating the horrors of war and bringing life back to a country that had seen its life almost completely destroyed was to bring life to the art they made, optimistically looking for unusual beauty in ruins, in cracked surfaces, in decay, distress and disaster, in physical action, in unexpected materials.

As well as encasing themselves in tangled wires and flashing lights, Gutai artists would shoot paint out of cannons at a canvas, wrestle in mud, hang from the ceiling while painting, burst through rice-paper screens, decorate their body with objects. They pushed their bodies to extremes in an artistic setting as a way of protesting how war destroyed bodies, and brutally collapsed the future, often by destroying the past, replacing progress with a void.

The first phase of Gutai by necessity involved finding new sites for art, outside the galleries and museums, which were too rarefied, settled and imperial to deal with what the world had become. Gutai artists sent their art out into the streets, into subway stations, onto parkland, finding new kinds of playground for their art, an interaction with the environment, which acknowledged what the Dadaists had said, that if art could be anything, it could be shown, displayed, performed and shared anywhere.

Anticipating Gutai, which issued its intense, rousing foundational manifesto in 1955, with its essential anti-law laws and its uncompromising self-conscious demand for total originality and pure creativity, there were early, more obscure signs of a Japanese avant-garde making tentative moves to imagine a new Japanese reality by inventing the new music and art that would accompany it.

Founded formally in Tokyo in 1951 after a few years of conversation and intermittent speculation, the anti-establishment, anti-academic Experimental Workshop – Jikken Kōbō – explored unusual, often self-taught artistic processes and deliberately fragmented and protean forms of art. Its members' tendency towards the untrained and unorthodox contributed to a greater willingness to break rules and boundaries, usually by never knowing they were there in the first place, and if they did, not allowing them to limit their explorations. The group reacted to the ambiguities of Japan as a nuclear-scarred semi-colonised nation temporarily caught in limbo between American jurisdiction and a free Japan, symbolising an urgent need for entertainment, culture and freedom of expression that broke free of the wrecked Japanese past, and the past in general.

The fourteen young, diverse members in Jikken Kōbō included composers experimenting with electronics and *musique concrète* using found sound such as Tōru Takemitsu as well as five visual artists, a lighting designer, an engineer, a pianist and a poet/music critic, Kuniharu Akiyama, known for his studies of the French avant-garde prophet sending reserved musical signals and elevated conceptual clues forward in time, Erik Satie.

Jikken Kōbō rejected Japanese traditions that had directly led to hypernationalism and a brutal war and felt its way towards avant-garde pre-war European art from Schoenberg and Webern to Dada and Bauhaus and emerging American extensions and deviations. These influences, the members' individual transdisciplinary interests including ballet, found objects, painting, sound, recitals, theory and readings, and their particular, peculiar post-war situation led to a natural instinct for combining different art forms with the added element of non-traditional spaces, which emphasised and enhanced the liberating newness of their work.

Their vision of a total art and a provisional media art collaboratively mixing their particular technical and artistic talents was progressive, not only locally but internationally, too: it was an energised development of the pre-war avant-garde, intensified by the nuclear shadow over Japan, forming an oblique link between the European avant-garde, which was relocating after the war in and around New York, and what it was becoming in the city as it commingled with emergent technology and the inventive, hyperactive new language of popular culture.

Part of Jikken Kōbō's site-specific elaboration of avant-garde art was its role in the swift post-war rise of Japanese commercialised technology and early ways of using tape machines, radios and television in the making of art. These artists were immediately adept at incorporating advanced audiovisual technology into their art and music performances, and one of their fusions of sound and vision, the first example of a synchronised audio slideshow in 1953, was co-ordinated by technicians and 'auto-slide' equipment provided by Tokyo Tsushin Kogyo, or TTK – the Tokyo Tele-communications Corporation.

TTK began business in 1946 working from the third floor of a bombed-out department store as a radio repair shop, before moving on to employ transistors mostly used for military application to create the first pocket radio for mass consumers, a radio that didn't need an electric cord so you could carry it around with you, untethering entertainment for the individual. They had branded the radio with the letters Sony, a made-up word easy to pronounce in any language mixing *sonus*, the Latin for sound, and 'sonny', American slang for a smart and cute young boy. The new company felt the name represented a small group of ener-getic, optimistic youthful people committed to innovation.

The collaboration between a technology company working from a real workshop feeling its way towards new electronic product and a pioneer-ing arts collective utilising a virtual workshop to propel art and music beyond art and music was payment in kind for musical collages on tape that Takemitsu composed for TTK using their relatively lightweight, shrewdly designed home tape recorders.

TTK needed musicians and artistic technicians to demonstrate and also help develop their new inventions, and the alliance between TTK and the Jikken Kōbō, led to artists and musicians employing new tech-nology to open up video art and experimental film, finding radical ways to use economical and portable audiovisual equipment.

Sony products would play an important part in avant-garde art, with Jikken Kōbō associates, solo and in various configurations, unhindered by academic caution, quick to see how new reproduction technologies would lead to new creative possibilities and introduce new artistic dimen-sions. Technology helped create a new national space for artistic and social adventure, outside of the traditional 'Japan' that was proving diffi-cult, that then became part of a new international Japan.

111

Tōru Takemitsu was born in 1930, and after early years in Japanese-occupied north-east China, then known as Manchuria, he returned to Tokyo to live with his aunt, who taught the national insrrument of Japan, the *koto*. His almost allergic aversion to Japanese music developed as the consequences of war, both personal and general, overwhelmed his young life and infected reality. In his imagination, the jazz his father loved, like Kid Ory and the Creole band, made sense and moved him more than the traditional Japanese music that, for all its calm and delicacy, seemed a soundtrack to turbulence and disruption.

Japanese music reminded him of the war. When he decided at fifteen to become a composer, as a means of combining the practical and the mystical, inspired by Western music he heard on radio broadcasts and precious fragile records from during and just after the war, he considered himself a Western composer as an act of rebellion and a way of discovering non-Japanese influences.

The music that found its way to him while he felt buried under the sound of bombs and military aggression suggested there was beauty and humanity out there, and it could be communicated, kept alive, through music. He made up music in his mind using a piece of paper with a drawing of a keyboard on it – his family's house had been destroyed twice, and the possibility of a real instrument was as distant as owning a time machine. At first it was music that only he could hear, sounds lost in his mind. Eventually it would move into the world, taking his mind with it.

At the time, there was no solo instrumental tradition in Japanese music. Hearing a solo piano piece on the radio by the nineteenth-century French Romantic composer and pianist César Franck was one of Takemitsu's most important musical discoveries, making him realise that such thinking, seemingly forbidden in Japan, was out in the world, normal and enticing. He was hearing the previously banned in different spaces. When he was fourteen, working in an underground military provisions base, he heard Josephine Baker singing the luminously romantic Parisian cabaret song 'Parlez-moi d'amour' being illicitly played on a wind-up record player using a piece of diligently sharpened bamboo as a needle. In these dreary surroundings at the end of a terrible, claustrophobic war, he could think of nothing outside the song, sung in a language he didn't understand, the depth of emotion shutting out all distractions. He surrendered himself to the music, a perfect expression of romantic desire heard as a kind of forbidden fruit, adding a sense of danger. He was seduced by an illicit-seeming musical act of seduction, and another revelatory listening experience, what he called the 'splendid quality' of prohibited Western music. All his music throughout his life to some extent was written trying to recapture and represent this almost religious experience, recreating the sense he had after the shattering violence of the war that music was the only thing that was left of human grace.

When he was twenty he wrote a piece for solo piano that could be heard, but wasn't by many, being too delicate to break out of the shadows; the poetic timelessness and otherness that would eventually become an essential Takemitsu element made it sound at the time strange and uncomfortable outside of a small community of enthusiasts. One critic dismissed it as 'not even music'; another described its apparent vagueness and hesitancy as a kind of 'pre-music'. It didn't fit into any known patterns of either Japanese or Western music.

Collaborating with Jikken Kōbō, Takemitsu wrote an essay on Paul Klee and music, 'Ad Marginem', exploring the relationship between music and visual art, the closeness between ears and eyes. When he heard sound, he saw visions, the intensity of his early visceral experiences of music meaning music powerfully activated his imagination. His first musical teacher, the radio, continued to teach him in the early 1950s when, weakened by tuberculosis, he spent hours listening to classical music being played on American Forces Radio, deepening his love for the dreaminess of Claude Debussy, music that had reacted against dominating Germanic force in much the same way he resisted unhealthy Germanic influence on Japanese culture during the war.

Debussy replaced the radio as a main teacher. Another spiritual patron was the Workshop's founder Shūzō Takiguchi, a poet and a Surrealist conscious of inhabiting a post-nuclear, post-apocalyptic, proto-postmodern society searching for liberating new forms of performance. He could see no reason why you couldn't combine music, visual art and literature as a new experimental form of activity.

Being part of the Workshop collective with its interest in multimedia events and unorthodox performance settings pushed Takemitsu the art activist further into avant-garde territory. He wasn't necessarily chasing some kind of elusive east–west hybrid, even if one way or another a protean blend of the two indirectly emerged as he set sail for an unknown destination. If there was any sort of hybrid that emerged, it was between his positions of the Japanese composer and the avant-gardist. These were his east and west, his opposite, his contradictions that he would set out to resolve, or relish: the sound designer understanding the radical artistic potential of new media and the musician.

On one side, moving on from Edgard Varèse and his 'non-musical' music working with rhythms, frequencies and intensities, he constructed tape, electronic and concrete music that broke free of the score, or invented new kinds of instructional scores. These had carefully conceived abstract, literary titles that emphasised their unmoored, speculative nature: 'Flame', 'Condition of Love', 'Relief Static', 'Vocalism'.

On another side, he wrote more formally titled, conventionally notated music using straightforward instruments, if often eccentrically assembled. Elsewhere, emphasising his difference, connected to the flexibility and versatility encouraged by the shapeshifting nature of Jikken Kōbō, he produced incidental music for radio dramas, television, advertisements and commercial film which began in the early 1950s, and continued even after he became internationally known for his 'serious' concert work – more than ninety film soundtracks, from Kurosawa to Hollywood, demonstrating an ability to move through a variety of different worlds and other-worlds, still chasing the feeling of hearing for the first time raw, splendid, in-the-moment jazz, or a divine love song, or a transcendent Debussy, an antiquated but cosmic Wagner.

For Takemitsu, there was no difference between one and the other, between the so-called high and the so-called low, and work in one sphere would continually influence work in the other. It was a rare enterprising response of a contemporary classical musician to the novel demands and opportunities created by the new formats and expectations of popular culture. Pop music would become a legitimate area for experiment.

Takemitsu's experiments with the human voice in radio dramas such as 'Vocalism A.I.' in 1955 featured a male and a female voice stretching and manipulating the two syllables of the Japanese word for 'love'. Takemitsu would add electronic sound transformation to the voices, an early example of using technology to transform the human voice, anticipating the post-Kraftwerk musical world of combining human voice and electronica, the emotional and the virtual.

At this stage, in Workshop minds, there was no border between classical and pop, between art and entertainment, between painting and poetry – everything coalesced, and any focus, any sorting out of the elements into a new, more formal order, could wait while they worked out where they were and what might come next.

In 1958 Takemitsu discovered someone who, for a few years, was simply a whispered rumour. He heard about John Cage, a teacher teaching a new kind of subject about how music could go beyond music, now based in New York – the same tightly packed streets and underground spaces in Lower Manhattan that Yoko was curiously patrolling. The Los Angeles-born, increasingly nomadic Cage became Takemitsu's spiritual guide to a Japan he'd travelled as far away from as he could, but which was inside him after all, immovable, instructional, waiting, a Japan that John Cage had, himself, made up.

The Yoko Ono who, when confronted by an unexpected turn of events says, oh, well, I expected this.

The Yoko Ono speaking for herself, that it's not where you take things from, it's where you take things to.

John Cage once asked a Surrealist friend how history came to be written, and he was told, 'You have to invent it.' He lived the sort of life that seemed invented, however you tell it, as the fluid story of a genius and absurdist, philosopher and fantasist, hedonist and theorist, revolutionary and charmer, Futurist and trickster – perhaps because he made sure after the fact that it would seem he was always making it up as he went along, and always starting from scratch.

His father John Milton, an eccentric inventor, amateur scientist and wilful romantic reluctant to take no for an answer, sought practical, idealistic solutions to various modern problems of varying degrees of urgency – from early colour television to travelling through space without fuel, thus demonstrating Einstein was wrong, and from prototype homeopathic medicine to seeing through fog. His madcap plans for the military use of a submarine led to bankruptcy, although along the way he did break the world record for the number of hours spent under water. The story made the front page of the papers, with Cage's cheerful father being greeted by his chic-looking mother, Crete.

His less fantastical but stylish, witty, hard-boiled and depressive mother was a *Los Angeles Times* editor and journalist. Using a deliberately dry, almost deadpan prose that would influence Cage's later writings, she wrote hundreds of pieces covering speakers giving self-improvement talks on art, politics and social issues in the city's numerous study clubs, instilling in Cage a love for individuals and communities sharing information and knowledge to improve the quality of life and explore diverse lifestyles.

116

His dad's early experiments with radio caught his attention, and at twelve, in 1924, an already enterprising John Jr, a Tenderfoot in the Boy Scouts, had the idea of a radio show centred around Scouts. He hosted his own gentle, freeform local radio show, which involved live piano, trumpet and trombone playing, local clergy giving inspirational talks and Scouts talking about tying knots and building fires.

He grew up an only child in an optimistic, forward-looking and even kooky Los Angeles that had all the idiosyncratic and freaky ingredients to become a home to Hollywood. It was a city on the make that liked to show off and to seek out curious, quasi-mystical new trends, attractions and cults, however calculated some of them were to snare the unwary and suggestible. Mass automobile ownership boomed. California was getting ready to sell the rest of the world a utopian, free-wheeling spirit of experimentalism – the self-consciously sunny side of the avant-garde – that would eventually feed into the popular culture that with the help of West Coast technology would reshape reality.

Cage enrolled as a theology major at the open-minded liberal arts college Pomona in Claremont, ostensibly to become a Methodist minister like his paternal grandfather, but his eventual ambition to become some kind of writer was undermined by what he found to be the underwhelming ordinariness of the environment. The other students mostly seemed to be all thinking the same way and reading the same books, all of which they were told to do, which provoked him to do the opposite. The bright, likeable teenage student comfortably loyal to conventional religion and middle-class comforts quickly became restless and a little brittle, and he lost touch for a while with the religious thoughts and spirituality at the heart of his family. When he arrived at the college he listed his interests as swimming, riding and tennis. By the second year they were the less wholesome sleeping, talking and stealing.

A Portuguese art professor introduced him to the ideas of a then extremely mysterious, almost mythical Marcel Duchamp, which made complete sense to this new, idle but intense novice. The enigmatic experimental Californian composer Henry Cowell performed in the college's brand-new hall in 1929, bringing with him his most modern technique of banging the piano with his fists and arms, and plucking and attacking with fingernails the piano strings, using all of the piano, inside and out, as the percussion instrument it essentially was.

There were suggestions in some of the rowdy, early jazz piano that there was a different sign of life inside the instrument, and on two pieces in the early 1920s, Maurice Ravel required a piano with paper woven between the strings to recreate the sound of a rare nineteenth-century luteal, a mechanism mounted onto a grand piano that could change its tone and timbres.

In his late teens, Cage spent time in Europe, searching for something between nothing in particular and his version of a musical holy grail. His first thought on hearing the mysterious music of Erik Satie was the same daydreamy but sincere feeling he had when he first saw modern painting: I could make something like that.

To earn money during the Depression required thinking up new things to sell that might tap into the city's craving for progress and innovation, however tenuous. Cage had few practical skills apart from an intense, growing enthusiasm about his new passions, and decided here was something he could trade in. He gave lectures about modern art and music to local housewives, going from door to door to introduce himself and his set of lectures, ten for $2.50, making a virtue of his informal, inquisitive and unthreatening approach. He learnt about that week's subject as he went along, deciding to do Dalí on a Monday, reading up through the week, ready to speak with his newly learned knowledge on a Friday. As he planned his lectures, he taught himself about modern art, and listened to a lot of new music.

As he mixed and occasionally mated with Los Angeles spirits spending most of their time engaged with artistic pursuits, inspired by conversations and contacts to improvise songs with words taken from Gertrude Stein, he moved closer to considering himself a composer, an occupation that could still allow for wandering with no fixed obligations.

Henry Cowell, playing some of Cage's early pieces and learning of Cage's interest in Schoenberg's radical organising methods of making twentieth-century music immediately modern, recommended he prepare for possibly studying with the New York-based Schoenberg by taking classes in New York with a former Schoenberg pupil, Adolph Weiss. Weiss made it clear that to be taught by Schoenberg, you must already have attained a certain level of sophistication.

The classes ended when it got back to Weiss that Cage felt the only thing he had learnt from Schoenberg's prized pupil was how to drink Manhattans. It might not necessarily have been a complaint. He was more likely to complain about his own shortcomings; his music was starting to sound organised, but, he accepted, did not sound very nice to listen to. A piece written in 1934, 'Six Short Inventions for Seven Instruments', was still loyal to standard European classical instruments – flute, cello, clarinet, trumpet, two violas and violin – but already rejecting expected classical traditions, especially predictable climaxes and transitions.

All of this ad hoc apprenticeship, even with the glitches and misdirection, seemed to fall into place in Cage's own version of space and time as it was meant to be. He moved closer to the most prestigious of pioneers, Schoenberg, just as Schoenberg, in 1934, who had recently turned sixty, moved from New York to Los Angeles having failed to find a full-time paying position on the East Coast.

Cage's studies with Schoenberg became the most important thing in his life. Schoenberg was musically descended from Brahms and Wagner, but his quest was to take music beyond them, developing new structures for music, and in doing so throw out the key system and initiated atonality, which he felt had outgrown their use.

Cage loved the audacity of the achievement, the theatrical-seeming entering into the promised land of non-tonality, the writing of what even relatively open-minded local critics called 'the strangest music I have ever heard', with the less sympathetic dismissing it as 'deranged'. Schoenberg, the terrible atonalist, was the devil himself, which naturally attracted the wilful Cage.

119

Schoenberg maintained that all music that is the product of a creative mind is new, and music without ideas is useless. To be understood, every true work of art has to be thought about, otherwise it has no inherent life. Cage had found his guru.

He would write that when he first asked Schoenberg for lessons, Schoenberg – who, with German bluntness and a little problem speaking a nuanced English, always went straight to the point, tending to warn students his lessons might stop them ever writing music – told him he couldn't afford the fees. Cage said, well, I don't have any money anyway. Schoenberg, making enough from professional musicians, intrigued by Cage's wide-eyed confidence and insatiable intellectual curiosity, and perhaps a little hoodwinked by some prime LA flimflam, replied he would teach Cage for free if he promised to dedicate his entire life to music. Cage knew enough by now to say he would, which naturally led to his thinking that most things in life were, in one way or another, music.

He would effectively dedicate his life to music, wherever his mind strayed, which was another way of saying he dedicated his life to life. Over forty years after, as he told it, promising to devote his life to composing music, he said that he was still composing music not necessarily because he felt a great need, but because he had promised Schoenberg that he would.

(On the other hand, in a different, poorer story, with less mythical resonance, Cage banded together with a handful of other intrepid young students to take lessons from Schoenberg as a group and split the fee.)

An awestruck Cage, 'tingling and active in every direction', first joined a course on analysis that Schoenberg was giving on 18 March 1935 for local music teachers and professors keen to uncover his secrets and absorb some of his tremendous knowledge, or at least earn some extra credits so they might increase their salary.

Everyone, including himself, seemed dull and out of their depth as the great innovator and giant musical brain with a hint of the tyrant dived deep into the complex mechanics of works by Bach and Brahms and his own Third String Quartet. Schoenberg was like a God speaking a language few would ever understand. He once complained that teaching many of his American students was as though 'Einstein was having to teach mathematics in a secondary school'.

Cage was surprised that Schoenberg, this avant-garde Kaiser, first demanded that you master traditional techniques before you could start moving to any radical, revolutionary stage. Modernism and the twelve-note system was not a random, slapdash breaking away from the classical form: it first of all required a reverence for the classics. You weren't mindlessly destroying; you were strategically continuing momentum.

Cage felt after two years with Schoenberg that he was no nearer actually learning how to compose in an original way. He didn't seem to be creating anything specifically requested by Schoenberg, only completing exercises and repeating theory. Anything he wrote that he showed his teacher never seemed to impress him, and any comments he made regarding the work of his fellow students were snootily dismissed.

Schoenberg was in fact not teaching composition, and not interested in pretending to encourage his pupils that he could turn them into composers if they didn't already have the instinct and commitment necessary. If they needed encouragement, he would discourage them. They must need to compose above all else. He could prepare the way by taking them through a history of music and an exploration of musical literature with his own unique insight; he could train them to present their own thoughts, arouse their sense of expression; but essentially they were on their own. If they had no ideas, and nothing to say, they could never be composers, however technically gifted they were. And without technical understanding, no matter how interesting and inventive their ideas, the music would sound basic and unconvincing.

His two most famous students spent years with him finding the correct balance between rigorous hard-earned technique and original ideas – Berg, already musically skilled, then spent seven years training with him, and Webern, already grounded in counterpoint and harmony, studied with him for six years. Only then could they start the real work. Cage didn't have the time or inclination to hang around.

Schoenberg was particularly suspicious of those who came to him expecting to be taught how to become a musical modernist, as if there was some kind of short cut. Henry Cowell said that Schoenberg was concerned that Cage was more interested in his philosophy than acquiring his musical technique. Cage was definitely seeking the Schoenberg who said things such as 'I disagree with everything' and 'If it is art it is not for all and if it is for all it is not art' rather than the austere, unplayful-seeming musical disciplinarian.

Schoenberg told Cage that without an understanding of harmony he would never be able to write music. Like his father, he was some kind of idiosyncratic, problem-solving inventor, possibly a genius, but as a composer without a proper understanding of technique he would come to a wall and never be able to break through it.

Cage knew he was at best average when it came to harmony and all that came with it, in the same way he realised early on he was not destined to be a strong performing musician. He knew in both cases he needed to find a way around his limitations as player or composer, and make a virtue out of them by having to think harder about what it was he could be better than average at. In the end he found that the only thing he could be great at was being one of a kind.

First, he had to deal with the brick wall Schoenberg had placed in front of him, blocking off a future in music, or perhaps challenging him to find a future in music. He reports that he then told Schoenberg, as if his teacher had become his straight man in the time they spent working each other out, that he would spend the rest of his life devoted to banging his head against that wall. Schoenberg wished him luck.

It was all too eighteenth- and nineteenth-century for Cage, who was in too much of a hurry, and whose path if it started with Bach led to Satie and then Duchamp and Varèse, Mondrian and Breton, electric wires and automobiles, the radio and sundry Eastern philosophies. And if it led to Schoenberg it really followed the paths that led away from him.

In the early 1900s, Schoenberg might have anticipated that his new compositional systems would ensure another century of German musical supremacy and German heroes, but he hadn't allowed for the Wild West emergence of eccentric, self-determining American originals piecing and collaging together their own histories and systems and ignoring scholarly techniques.

Henry Cowell, influenced musically by his Irish background, Icelandic and Indian folk music and Japanese instruments as much as the poetry of William Blake and Marinetti's Futurists, showed Cage how to seek new ways to write new music without resorting to old-fashioned means. In New York in 1934, Cage attended Cowell's classes exploring folk music from around the world and non-Western music – Music of the World's People, Primitive and Folk Origins of Music, Music Systems of the World – and Cowell's desire to live in 'the whole world of music' and his reverence for non-Western music struck Cage as a better way of going backward, towards the neglected and mysterious, in order to go forward. It was about other people thinking – communion with everyone – rather than the usual select few.

Schoenberg was teaching Cage how to be an autodidact, how to think of every possibility when writing and thinking, and in his own way he was teaching him everything he knew, which Cage, in his own way, was taking and processing and using to become his kind of composer, which involved inventing new kinds of instruments, and new ways of using traditional instruments.

Schoenberg was clearing Cage's mind, creating space for him to move into, where he could explore everything he wanted to, which meant getting as close to everything as he could get, and then, almost as an afterthought, spreading the gospel.

As a teacher himself Cage would say that the last thing he wanted was to turn out a tribe of Cageian imitators, blindly copying his sounds, systems and thinking, and it was the same with Schoenberg. A sign of his success would be that any genuinely new kind of composer he taught would be absolutely nothing like him. And Cage was nothing like Schoenberg, but wouldn't have been who he was without Schoenberg.

The Yoko Ono starting out looking for a new language to speak because the one she had didn't communicate enough.

Another more informal teacher, the German American animator and film-maker Oskar Fischinger, whose hypnotic combination of experimental film and music was one of the inspirations for Walt Disney's *Fantasia*, had encouraged Cage to explore the relationship between sound and image, music and technology, and between sound and object. Research for his inventor father into new entertainment technologies, his assisting Fischinger on filming and editing a stop-motion animation intermingled with his Schoenberg studies, Luigi Russolo's Futurist *Art of Noises* and the influence of what Varèse was calling 'organised sound' inspired a compositional movement away from concert instruments to making music using percussion.

This took Cage away from the predictable sound of the usual classical musical instruments towards the idea of using noise within a compositional system. Schoenberg broke free of tonality, and Cage was breaking free of the idea that musical instruments were the only source of sound used in composition.

Fischinger told Cage that 'everything in the world has its own spirit which can be released by making it vibrate'. Every sound in the world was worthy of attention. Intrigued, Cage began using anything he could hit as a percussion instrument, to push his music away from instruments and therefore away from sounding familiar even if the structure was intensely novel. He banged, scraped, rubbed kitchen utensils, metal sheets, ornaments, tin pans, iron pipes, wheel rims, blocks of wood, and the brick wall in front of him wobbled a little.

Percussion was his revolution, and he was influenced by Cowell and Varèse in terms of structuring according to time rather than pitch, and by

Schoenberg with essential compositional discipline, how to use very few instruments but produce a substantial sound, and the need for musical structures however extreme.

He also, like Schoenberg, moved into teaching to find a steady income, assisting his Aunt Phoebe, who had taught him as a youngster how to sight read, and was now the elementary musical supervisor at UCLA. She was teaching a course, Musical Accompaniments for Rhythmic Expression, and he would perform as an accompanist for the dance students, which allowed him to experiment in an informal setting with his percussive compositions. The dancers assumed he was banging and slapping arbitrarily but he was working on a new kind of music writing.

Because he was working with dances, rhythm was key, and he would teach percussion courses, using skills inherited from his father to invent a water gong that could be heard under water for an aquatic ballet choreographed by swimming students. He had found his own world where he could explore idiosyncratic, novel musical ideas at his own pace with no academic or commercial pressure.

When his wife Xenia worked in a large Santa Monica mansion as an apprentice bookbinder with other apprentices, he would organise them during their spare time into a makeshift percussion ensemble. He used random pieces of junk and metal and any likely-looking objects lying around, which saved money on any real instruments he couldn't really afford, and worked and rehearsed these non-musicians as though they were professional musicians. He was forced to use them because the idea of a percussion ensemble playing original music was considered a joke, and no professional percussionist was interested in his peculiar idea, but using untrained percussionists allowed him greater freedom to try things the professionals would have resisted.

Always looking for new sounds, devising his own tools as part of his search for new systems, he would mix the large and small found objects from coffee cans and jawbones to anvils and washtubs he used for his percussion ensemble with conventional cymbals, bells, maracas, tamtams, sleighbells, rattles and the more exotic type of percussion from

125

China, Turkey, Japan and Brazil he had access to when he taught or which he collected using donations from family and friends.

Sometimes a new percussive object could be found on the shelf in a hardware store or rusting in the junkyards that he explored with Xenia, just needing some cleaning and waxing to become an effective sound-creating object no more or less weird an invention than a saxophone or piano. Cage discovered and repurposed brake drums, a metal bowl with a hole at its apex that was a humble, practical part of an early car's braking system which the brake pads pushed against, causing friction to stop the vehicle.

He homed in on the one-piece Ford Model T brake drums from the 1910s and 1920s, which made super-resonant, penetrating sound somewhere between a tam-tam and an anvil when hit with a hand-held metal-headed hammer – an equivalent of Trinidadian steel bands using discarded oil barrels. The search for a new sound-music produced something that was both ancient and modern, combining natural and supernatural sound, the urban environment and something intangibly other.

Cage moved up and down the Pacific coast from school to school, job to job, building his percussion arsenal, and writing percussion pieces, becoming a composer by leading and writing for his unique percussion ensemble. It was not the sort of music that could be recreated by anyone else, existing somewhere between avant-garde novelty music and unpublished incidental sounds written specifically for the movement of the human body, music following movement following music, which sometimes left periods of silence, as the body adopted another position, or steadied itself.

The ingenious ultra-modernist composer, poet, painter and also pupil of Cowell and Schoenberg, Lou Harrison, introduced Cage to educator and choreographer Bonnie Bird, the head of the dance department at the Cornish School in Seattle and a member of the Martha Graham Dance Company, and recommended him as the accompanist for Bird's modern dance course.

It was a place of heightened awareness of poetry, literature, avant-garde music – Bird would stage productions based on works by Jean Cocteau and W. B. Yeats, with abstract music played by Harrison. The school had been set up by its founder Nelly Cornish for its students to never specialise but study everything that was offered. Cage thrived in its lively interactive environment, and his percussion music was perfect for modern dance.

It was not necessarily a composition that confirmed Cage's arrival as a composer, outside the niche, mostly local areas he had been working in. Like any good avant-gardist craving revolution rather than evolution, he came up with a manifesto, his first major musical statement, which he read at an arts conference in 1940.

The Future of Music: Credo outlined how his intellectual and aesthetic infatuation with percussion was a route to the sounds he imagined being created electronically, the ultimate way to leave behind the restrictions of the nineteenth century and generate a new universe of sound with an emphasis on texture and timbre. *Credo* effectively ends with him requesting something that wouldn't exist for at least a decade – an electronic recording studio, dedicated to electronic sound production, what he called a centre of experimental music. He moved closer to his dream of sourceless-seeming uncanny sound by merging his love for the potential of percussion with his original instrument, the piano itself, which he would turn into its own centre of experimental music.

Three works mixing mathematical permutation and individual improvisation and various materials from 1939–41 using the title *Construction* were a significant part of Cage's percussion pieces for dance, originally performed by Cage's troupe of what he called literate amateurs that included his wife Xenia and one of Bird's dance students, Merce Cunningham.

Concentrating on percussion and making it the centre of his music as opposed to being a supporting element or a backdrop allowed him to find his own style, somewhere few other composers have tried. When Cage began working on new pieces for percussion ensembles, around

1935, there were perhaps three that already existed: Varèse's *Ionisation*, Lou Harrison's *Fugue for Percussion* and William Russell's *Three Dance Movements*. Over the next five years Cage extended the range to nearly fifty, expanding his original almost madcap intentions to combine Schoenberg and improvised hot jazz.

The percussion works echoed Schoenberg's mathematical system as well as introducing an architectural element, everything Cage had passed through, influence, borrowing and suggestion piling up into a whole new method of using performance and music and combining the two, so there is also an echo of how Henry Cowell extended the sound of the piano by banging on it to create sound clusters and reaching inside the instrument to manipulate potential sound.

Cage also used what Cowell and occasionally he had called 'string piano' on the first of his *Imaginary Landscapes* in 1939, which has entered music history as the first piece of electroacoustic music ever composed, and what Cage described as a landscape from the future. 'You use technology as if to take you off the ground and like Alice you go through the looking glass.'

Cornish had created the first course on radio technology in America, and had its own radio studio equipped with the latest broadcasting and recording gear. Finding himself, as was often the case, in the right place at the right time, Cage started experimenting with using electrical sounds in a musical way.

He used abstract radio and recording frequencies as percussive elements along with the manipulating of the strings inside the piano, and wrote the piece to be specifically heard as a recording. When Bonnie Bird used it for a six-minute dance piece representing disembodied body parts, the choreography creating the illusion of floating heads and hands was performed to the recording made in the studio next door to the dance theatre, not a live version.

The Cages were part of the quartet that performed it, along with experimental composer Doris Dennison, who had studied the Dalcroze eurythmic method of rhythmical movement linking the ear, mind and body, and student Margaret Jansen. They were like a Dadaist variation of a jazz quartet, using the sensible name Cage Percussion Players. Looking like a proto-psychedelic pop group who supported the Soft Machine in 1967, they could easily have been called the Metaphysical Bohemians.

Imaginary Landscape sounded eerily, sometimes funnily futuristic, moving fast and slow and seeming large and small simultaneously and unlike any music being written or played at the time, although cinema audiences were used to the screeches, shivers, plucks, whistles and unnerving atmospheric interference in the context of a film, and the sounds were intended to be otherworldly to combine with the fragmented otherness of the dancers.

Within months of his first *Constructions* and *Landscapes*, echoing his own endless appetite for what happens next, Cage was taking Cowell's 'string piano' that he had absorbed into his percussion pieces somewhere else. In a way he altered the sound of the piano he was using more as a piece of percussion by the way he would take certain influences and ideas that stimulated him and alter them to suit his own needs, or react to a situation created in the busy cross-fertilising artistic environment he was in that needed an original solution. He was still inventing, but as well as inventing contraptions and uncovering unprecedented sound sources, he was also inventing new moods, and new structural and sonic possibilities.

Enhanced percussion – not necessarily just hitting and stroking but 'the liberation of all audible sound from the limitations of musical prejudice' – was the first stage on his travels towards the unlimited freedom of electronic music that hadn't yet been realised, but which he knew would be. His next discovery, the anomalous transition between his open-ended percussion and the electronics to come, involved a preparing of the piano, releasing different sonic possibilities. Cowell's string piano became Cage's more dynamic, versatile and in the end historic and better-branded prepared piano.

The Yoko Ono learning that in ordinary life most activities, if not all, start with an idea. 'I have an idea.' 'It all started when I thought of . . .'

As Cage moved along the West Coast chasing work and collaborators and accumulating an array of influences and oblique antecedents, he applied to be in the music section of the Works Progress Administration: the New Deal agency set up by President Franklin D. Roosevelt during the Depression to employ the millions of skilled and unskilled workers desperately needing jobs in various public works projects. The WPA hired more than ten thousand artists to create works of art across America – murals, theatre, writing, design, the arts and music – not only as part of the attempt to stimulate the economy but also in the middle of demoralising times to project a distinct American experience and capture the soul of people, to counteract the rising nationalism and politicisation of art around the world, especially in Russia and Germany.

Obscure, struggling artists such as Willem de Kooning and Jackson Pollock could think of themselves as working, professional artists for the first time, able to make a direct, significant contribution to American life without having to rely on private sponsorship, the market or elite institutions. For Roosevelt, the arts were a crucial element of a positive democratic society, and freeing artists to do their work, and even reach an audience as part of a general community spirit, had the side effect of maintaining unconventional artistic energy and encouraging the idea that art had an abstract, spiritual value, a greater, life-changing purpose, during the most difficult of times. Employment and better living standards, the building of roads, bridges, schools and public structures were absolutely vital, but so too were art, literature, photography and music, even if their value was sometimes elusive or negligible.

Cage's application for music work was rejected because it was decided by the processing board that he was not a musician. He had told them he worked with sounds and used percussion instruments, but percussion wasn't considered music. He was offered work in the recreation department as a group leader, keeping spirits high and alleviating stress by encouraging exercise, socialising and the learning of new skills.

Naturally, his role as recreation leader, working in schools and hospitals, taking it all very seriously and cheerfully entertaining children with made-up games – on one occasion, when he needed to keep quiet in a hospital setting, getting his class to dance to silence, what he called rhythm in space – fed into his thinking as the musician it was said he wasn't. He was in fact quite happy to take on board that, officially speaking, he wasn't a musician. He was something else, and it was up to him to work out what that was.

His experimental thinking was influenced by this desire to absorb people in ideas and come up with solutions – inventions all in the mind – to particular problems. He thought up the prepared piano out of necessity or accident or both. He happened to be the only accompaniment available when Syvilla Fort, a twenty-two-year-old Black dancer/choreographer in Bonnie Bird's class at Cornish, needed some music for a dance she was working on. After Fort was rejected by several ballet schools in Seattle from the age of five, her mother had gathered a group of Black children and hired white ballet students to teach them, leading to Cornish giving Syvilla a scholarship in 1935.

She stayed for five years, and for her graduate recital she had been working on an original dance piece called 'Bacchanale' that was due in a few days. Still looking for the right kind of music, she explained to Cage about her Caribbean and African influences, and how she was striving for a combination of African and modern Western movement.

Cage had already found in his collaborations with Bird's classically trained but progressively minded group of dancers that percussion worked best accompanying movement that in looking to be truly modern incorporated ideas from non-Western dance, and therefore non-Western music.

131

Fort, expecting something obviously rhythmic, asked Cage for some sounds on a Tuesday, with the performance scheduled for the Thursday.

The Cornish Theater where Fort was performing was small and had no space in the wings and no pit for instruments and musicians, so a selection from Cage's growing percussion collection would have taken up all the space she had to move in. There was a grand piano in front of the stage, and at first Cage tried some sort of African tone rows, part Schoenberg, part his sense of an African rhythm, influenced by Charles Ives's pioneering experiments with polyrhythms and the memories of the children he had worked and played with in San Francisco.

Failing to produce any sounds that satisfied him and that seemed to be appropriate for the rhythms he wanted, he ever-optimistically concluded that it wasn't his ideas that were wrong but the piano itself as it usually sounded. He decided, remembering Cowell's tinkering with the piano, to find a way of changing it.

Observing and in his own way understanding Fort's elastic Afro-modernist movement and rhythmical urgency, as free as the latest jazz, but as precise as Satie, he set out to modify the sound the piano produced to resemble African and Cuban instruments he had heard Cowell play in his music from around the world classes. In Cage's history-shaping telling, the sound he was looking for came to him by careful manipulation of the strings inside the piano, using fibrous weatherstripping inserted between strings and carefully positioned nuts, bolts and screws to achieve the exotic vibrations and non-specific otherness he believed matched Fort's deft, energised movement.

According to Bird, the clipped, deadened metallic sound came to him accidentally when a piece of metal pipe fell onto the strings as he played with them, suggesting the direction to head with various objects that pushed and pulled the piano's sound and its clear classical pitches into new, unexpected, percussively sonic places. He could also change the sound created by one of his preparations by using the soft pedal, so something resonant could become more muted, the rattling, humming timbres more complicated and mysterious.

The result was a combination of progressive Black dance movement and a breakthrough in experimental minimal music, one triggering the other to give the history of modern non-classical dance and the history of music in general a considerable push into the future.

Cage had no direction outside optimism and ambition, and was just trying to discover what the next day would bring, hoping, under the increasingly dark circumstances, as Depression slid into America's involvement in an ominous world war, that there was a next day. He was trying out living, and art, or whatever you wanted to call it, was an experimental station where you could make your various attempts.

For now, the trick, the genius, with the piano was just a perfect, quietly astonishing way conceived under time pressure of representing a vibrant percussive rhythm using the European piano, and preparing the piano using the screws, nuts and bolts, and later rubbers, twigs and paper turned the instrument into visual poetry. Pierre Boulez would later note that one way or another, for whatever reason, Cage had transformed the piano into an African sanza, an ancient thumb piano used across the continent in generational storytelling and ceremonial rituals, with a sound intended to project into the heavens and attract spirits to earth.

This transformation was either magical, or the act of an irrepressible trickster breaking some kind of cultural prime directive. He wasn't criticising the piano as such; he was just turning it into something else, or what in a way it always was.

Hearing it now, in an approximation of what it would have sounded like at the time, its textural approach to structuring the dynamics of sound and establishing and maintaining determined rhythm anticipates how music would be multi-tracked recordings using electronic methods; it's an acoustic blueprint of programmed electronic music.

For a couple of years, the prepared piano could have become an obsolete relic from the past, occasionally resurrected by a curious composer or experimentalist seeking an unusual sound. If the electronics Cage was confidently expecting had arrived earlier maybe 'Bacchanale' would have been the end of the burrowing inside the piano and manipulating its sound.

He returned to his percussion collection and, interacting with choreography to extend his compositions, started to teach courses on percussion as an accompaniment to dance. His attempts to set up a centre for experimental music failed to win any financial support from business or educational institutions, but in autumn 1941 he moved to Chicago to teach a class in sound experiments as a faculty member of the new School of Design set up by László Moholy-Nagy.

Hungarian modernist, innovative thinker, radical stage designer and Dada-inspired visual artist, Moholy-Nagy had been a professor at the Bauhaus school of art and design in Berlin between 1923 and 1928; the Nazis later shut down what they saw as a dangerous avant-garde centre in 1933.

Moholy-Nagy's Chicago New Bauhaus was his version of a sequel to Bauhaus, with an ambitious, utopian, socially idealistic cross-disciplinary fusion of art, design, architecture, sound and new technology and a belief that it should have a social purpose. Fellow Bauhaus members Ludwig Mies van der Rohe and artist Josef Albers were also involved, as were the Americans painter Mark Tobey, architect Buckminster Fuller and the microtonal composer and instrument builder Harry Partch, all of them placing emphasis on the process of education rather than specific results or qualifications. It was an exhilarating place for Cage, run by one of his spiritual mentors – one of the first artists to create art mechanically with an unshakable belief in the future – and filled with thinkers sharing his own verve and optimism so that it could feel like a repository for the world's wisdom, which meant for two years he was distracted, and there was no real development of the prepared piano.

There was also America declaring war on Germany, Italy and Japan, after the Japanese attack on Pearl Harbor. Cage was exempt from service under the hardship to descendants rule – his wife Xenia walked with a limp since contracting tuberculosis as a child – and he was helping his still energetic shapeshifting father on some top-secret research for the navy. For Cage, looking for what he might find in the oddest, strangest, most isolated spaces between art and thinking, between music and knowing, was his contribution to the war, his way of building something new and nourishing, however slight or even invisible, while the whole world seemed threatened. As always, he needed to find the right people with the right minds seeing things only they could see over the horizon to help him save the world, or at least keep it civilised, in a quiet, distant, sometimes dreamlike way.

Cage brought to Chicago his vast three-hundred-piece percussion arsenal, but when he was teaching and demonstrating his conventional and unconventional instruments, the banging, scraping and jangling made too much noise, and speaking as a responsible administrator, Moholy-Nagy asked him to teach theory only.

There was no money for his real dream, his experimental music centre and recording studio, and a chance to work full-time in sound production at CBS – making soundtracks for radio programmes, as a conceptual relative of the Orson Welles of the radio artwork *The War of the Worlds* – came to nothing. Cage was continually drawn to the radio industry, the home of the latest advances in audio technology, but his ambition to make the combination of random sound a new kind of orchestra generating immersive soundtracks proved completely impractical, technologically and financially; his ideas would be more practical decades later, especially in film.

Still looking for a role, a form of sound that was all his own, he was invited to stay in New York by a friend of Moholy-Nagy, the Surrealist and prime Dadaist founder, painter and poet Max Ernst. He had fled Nazi persecution and moved to New York in the early 1940s, where he had met and married the radically flamboyant art lover/patron and avid collector of Dada and Surrealism, Peggy Guggenheim. At thirteen, she had lost her father, who went down with the *Titanic* in 1912, which led to a rebellious rule-breaking, art-buying lifestyle achieved if nothing else to break out of a sheltered childhood and irritate her family.

New York was a significant reset for Ernst, who had been at the heart of the Parisian avant-garde since moving to Paris in 1922, and it seemed to the thirty-year-old Cage – busy, ever hopeful, but still not earning a steady income – a place where he and Xenia might finally find their fortune, or at least what they needed to live comfortably. They arrived with no money, and couldn't afford to transport Cage's inspired but unwieldy percussion collection, but had enough credentials to find themselves with almost instant access to artists and thinkers exiled from a war-ravaged Europe. They were immediately part of New York's growing bohemian society.

Cage and Xenia stayed for a while in Hale House, the East 51st Street home of Ernst and Guggenheim, two eccentric enigmas enjoying each other's company for as long as they weren't bored with each other. The house had become a meeting place for modernist artists escaping a threatened Europe, where their progressive presence, however abstract or theoretical, and evolving identities were in themselves a dangerous, shapeshifting threat to the Nazis. As well as Ernst, there was Piet Mondrian, Joseph Cornell, David Hare, all featuring in the short-lived but intensely influential and architecturally vibrant Art of this Century Gallery Guggenheim opened in two old tailor shops on 57th Street in November 1942, a gallery as much a work of art as what it displayed, with Ernst and Mondrian as 'acquisitions advisors'. The pre-war European avant-gardists Paul Klee and Marc Chagall avidly interacted with the emerging American Abstract Expressionists like Pollock and Rothko, to some extent quickly eclipsing their Surrealist antecedents with a more urgent-seeming and definitely more fashionable contemporary vigour.

Guggenheim understood completely the responsibility, even savage irony, of opening a gallery dedicated to what some dismissed as frivolous, indulgent non-realistic art at a time 'when people are fighting for their lives and freedom. This undertaking will serve its purpose only if it succeeds in serving the future instead of recording the past.' Even if it seemed inaccessible and irrelevant – although Guggenheim was committed to presenting challenging abstract art as though it was completely accessible and natural, and as much entertainment as scarily strange – avant-garde art was an absolutely central part of the tumultuous international battle against totalitarian repression and censorship.

Within days of being in New York, Cage also met Marcel Duchamp for the first time, recently arrived from Nazi-occupied France, inevitably elegantly and inscrutably located at the centre of Guggenheim's ever-changing circle of guides, friends, artists, intellectuals and visionaries.

It was Duchamp who suggested to Guggenheim after she had opened her gallery that, as one of the very few female gallery owners of the time, she should have an all-female show. Her *31 Women* exhibition – which utilised – as well as Guggenheim – Ernst, Duchamp and André Breton and other men as part of a European-style jury selecting the artists intending to disrupt a male-dominated field – featured artists from sixteen countries, including Frida Kahlo, Leonora Carrington, Méret Oppenheim, Buffie Johnson, Sophie Taeuber-Arp, Muriel Levy, Valentine Hugo and Leonor Fini. There was a clothed self-portrait by the well-known vaudevillian stripper and writer Gypsy Rose Lee, and a delicate mobile sculpture by Xenia Cage, representing those in the exhibition whose work was usually overshadowed by the reputations of their male partners and husbands, and whose vital contributions to the men's discoveries and enthusiasms were ignored.

The exhibition also introduced Max Ernst to his next, younger wife, the Surrealist artist Dorothea Tanning, provoking Guggenheim to joke she should have made it thirty women. Georgia O'Keeffe declined to take part, uncomfortable with being so irrelevantly identified, locked up like some kind of freak, as a 'woman painter'.

The exhibition intended to show that where there were male artists up to something new there were also female artists with their own strategies and breakthroughs, often viewed more as supporters, muses and sponsors of their artistic partners, but the advance publicity for the gallery's next monthly exhibition, part of a regular series Guggenheim established, based around her energised new star Jackson Pollock, relegated the 'women painters' to charming but irrelevant status, and a possibly permanent, shadowy exile.

Critical (male) response veered between lurid condescension and straightforward alarm that women considered they were useful for anything other than making babies and looking after men; if they had artistic dreams, their only hope was being at the side of tragic, damaged men at artistic work, ensuring they were in the right frame of mind to be important.

After the critically damned ludicrous personal expressions of the delusionary thirty-one, and a handful of sales, the post-Picasso early drip bursts of energy in Pollock's one-man show a few weeks later led to a relieved exaggeration of his revolutionary qualities. Guggenheim, of course, according to the cliché-loving sensationalist press, was no pioneering Svengali with an eye on art's future, just a bored socialite looking for excuses to spend money and throw parties.

Seeing something in Cage, if only his ability to find himself in the right place at the right time, sharing similar hope for the future as her favourite artists and writers, Guggenheim had agreed to pay for his percussion to be shipped to New York, so that he could give a concert at the opening of the Art of this Century gallery. His eagerness had also led to him organising a concert at the Museum of Modern Art. An incensed Guggenheim told him at dinner that she was cancelling his appearance at her new gallery, and therefore not paying for his equipment to be brought to New York.

Cage was so upset he charged into a spare room next to his at the back of the house and burst into tears. While he raged, a quiet, halting, accented voice from the shadows suddenly asked him why he was so upset. It was Marcel Duchamp, sitting in a rocking chair, as though that in the end was his actual profession, to peacefully smoke a cigar and offer sage advice to any passing person in distress.

Cage told him what had happened. Duchamp nodded but didn't say a word. Cage, though, immediately felt better, and stopped crying. There was silence, and Cage felt himself thinking about things in a new positive way. In the silence, Duchamp had somehow made him feel important. He had somehow made him think that you can only lose what you cling to. The two of them sat there for a while, doing nothing.

The Yoko Ono who was never afraid of the irrational imagination.

Yoko dropped out before graduating from Sarah Lawrence, unable to resist the pull of nearby New York, where a progressive artistic action was actually in motion, and there were obscure but fertile communities randomly receiving strange, cryptic signals travelling across time and place from pre-war avant-garde Europe and adding their own transformative, trouble-making and site-specific additions and interpretations.

The qualifications required to join these official and unofficial communities were to some extent demonstrating that you understood what they were doing and spoke their language, which you could effectively do by simply turning up, expressing interest and finding useful ways to join in. Yoko also had the additional qualifications of seeming to belong nowhere, and not being unnerved by this. A new place, new to her, built on nothing that was poisonous and aggressive, could give her confidence, and a sense of security. She could work out for herself where she was and where she was going, and first of all, she moved somewhere filled with others looking for the new, the new to them.

She needed a place to go, and all things considered she was in luck; there wasn't far to go to find herself where she could make up herself. She picked up her bag, and off she went. Yoko Ono arrives shrouded in invisibility on secretive high alert knowing no one in a mid-1950s New York where, in an intense, interconnected downtown, there was a considerable attack by artists, sculptors, musicians, actors, poets, dancers and film-makers on post-war American middlebrow sensibilities and the sky-scraping flash imperiousness of the city itself from what was an underground position.

America was easing into its position as leader of the world, with New York as its financial and social capital and the United Nations setting up its headquarters there. Uptown was the most twentieth-century, gold, shiny and modern, its light and glass surfaces reflecting the future.

Midtown Manhattan became the centre of the American music industry: within a few streets from the UN, RCA, Columbia and Decca, and numerous studios and publishers, made the city their home, a place where the action was, with its own spectacular soundtrack reacting to every shift in New York's mood.

Further downtown, you could still see and smell the nineteenth century, which brought with it an elusive, formless wildness. Civilisation was round the corner, but you didn't necessarily know which corner took you there. Some corners took you into a stubborn, broken unknown where familiar history had only made it in fits and starts.

There were smaller streets and grungy nooks and crannies, a patch-work crazy quilt of low-slung buildings, abandoned commercial buildings, working-class tenements and cheap rentals packed between two rivers used to connecting time and space as well as ocean and land. Lower Manhattan with Greenwich Village melting into the East Village was historically a first stop for new immigrants, and in this rougher, evolving collection of neighbourhoods outside of the buoyant and arrogant empire-building and elevation of the American Dream, a collection of malcontents, drifters, interlopers, musical geniuses, vagabonds, actors, Beats and bohemians were carving out space where they could thrive.

Thinking through in their own way what needed to change in the middle of all this persuasive but possibly traumatising American Dream national confidence, they were obliquely making New York a new avant-garde capital, and setting up underground scenes and off-grid communities that would grow into the counterculture of the 1960s. They took at face value the idea that in a truly great country, if that's what it was becoming, anything and everything was possible, including the interaction of art and life, and the agile, empathetic subversion of routine and the ordinary.

If before the war Paris was seen as the centre of the Western art world, the centre had shifted to New York, and a scene emerging from the downtown rubble and its cheap rundown spaces that was all New York energy and power, skipping over Dada's naughtiness and nihilism back to considering the sanctity of paint, and the canvas, taking cues from Surrealism about how painting could go deep into the subconscious.

What became Abstract Expressionism, insular approaches to painting building up since the American Depression and exploding after the war, aggressively seized the spotlight from a depleted, emptied Paris, in a location almost designed to house the kind of innovative frenzy and freed technique of a group of artists loosely connected if only by time and place. They were desperate to get something out of their system and take on the system, and fight for a kind of beauty that made up for the world chaos of the preceding few years.

New York's artistic post-war rebuilding involved an intense, unsentimental nostalgia for what was happening in avant-garde art before the necessary anti-war furies of Dada and in the less fanciful areas of the oddly more conventional Surrealism, often delivered by canvas. The Abstract Expressionists went back to paint, to painters, so they could go forward, surging into an imagined space where Picasso, Manet, Monet, Cézanne and Matisse were heading before the mind games and game playing of Duchamp and company.

There was continuation of the 'retinal art' Duchamp despised, but with a Dada element that it was the actual act of painting that was more important than what the painting looked like. The painting was an after-effect, an after-image, an impression of the effort and thinking it took to make the painting. It was not necessarily art about anything other than itself and what it should, and could be, and ultimately what it would become once it took its place in the passing of time and a changing of cultural perspective.

In the brushes in the hands in the minds of Franz Kline, Jackson Pollock, Robert Motherwell, Mark Rothko, Dorothy Dehner, Clyfford Still, Willem de Kooning, Sari Dienes, with their own crazed, heroic origin stories, an American avant-garde emerged in New York, the monumental, epic and triumphant widening the scale of art, keeping up with the size and new confidence of America as everything was transformed

141

and transcending the mysterious European influence that once seemed so enigmatic and intimidating.

After the concentration camps and the nuclear bombs, the once-dramatic gestures and processes of European Surrealism seemed somehow quaint and insipid; abstract art needed something more dynamic, more concrete and intense, more personal and emotional, and that came with the American attitude to the intangible, stripped of the Freud, of the fantasy, and paintings that reflected the skyscrapers, the traffic and forward noise of the new New York, and ultimately the skyrocketing money and competition – as originally obscure, neglected, reviled paintings that some said anyone could make became valuable rare assets, prized luxury commodities, glittering symbols of high capitalism.

Mad visual rantings and wanton brushstrokes became treasure. Whatever bitter glory and utopian vision had been released into the world in the back of beyond eventually became controlled by money, as though on some measuring scale, avant-garde striving for freedom articulated as pieces of art initially revered by idealists and mavericks symbolised the insulated freedom captured by the bizarrely, rudely wealthy.

Before the many millions and the institutionalised transformation of artistic rebirth into iconic consumer items disappearing into billionaire mansions and retreats, for this new American avant-garde made up of big thinking and heavy lifting, a certain local sort of pissed-off determination, this defiant modification of Surrealist freedoms, the canvas was a place for action, for performance. The influence of these artists would be as spontaneous, adventurous performers digging into and exposing their feelings rather than painters representing, or analysing, or rearranging outside objects, concentrating only on appearance, and the style and substance of the appearance. They weren't copying nature or recording information about how people looked and moved, they were screaming, or whispering, or dancing at the edges of the oblivion the world had just about missed crashing into.

They were painting the imagination, under all sorts of stresses and strains, and this meant more to other exploratory artists, musicians, poets, film-makers and thinkers than it did to the wider mainstream public, even as the leading figures including Jackson Pollock achieved a kind of notoriety that made them celebrities, initially in their own world, among interconnected friends and neighbours, within a few streets, and eventually as independent-minded icons of the rebellious spirit that entered the DNA of popular culture.

European modernists and miscellaneous progressives moved to New York to escape war and repression, looking for safe spaces, and a place where the artists had the energy and idealism to take art, and life itself, forward. They all found themselves in a small, cheap area of New York, people drawn from around the world as well as around the country to where the action was, to where the rebuilding of nerve, morale, imagination was centralised and to a social circle that made use of Lower Manhattan as a small town of connected experimental spirits rather than part of a vertical city, a vertiginous social experiment that had become the capital of the world.

It's an electric small town Jack Kerouac writes about in *The Subterraneans*, where he creates a grungy, cramped, smoky bar, the Black Mask, based on real bars where the New York New School poets and painters and students from Judith Malina's and Julian Beck's experimental Living Theatre meet up to drink beer, gossip, swap notes, chase dreams, affairs and lovers, and hunt aesthetic perfection, talking about everything with nervous intelligence.

The Black Mask was a blend of the literary bar, the San Remo, and the artists' bar, the Cedar Tavern, and the likes of Miles Davis, Montgomery Clift, William Burroughs, Dylan Thomas, James Baldwin, Gore Vidal and Tennessee Williams would mix with Barbara Guest, Gregory Corso, Frank O'Hara and John Ashbery – the latter two noticing the language of Cage more than his music – who'd write poems, so the myth goes, while the adversarial painters argued in drunken free flow, testing all sorts of limits. (No one painted, said O'Hara, while the writers argued.)

Yoko disappears into the big busy city at the centre of the new world, arriving with little money and no connections, and finds herself in a fast-moving small town somewhere between dishevelled and magical, a subculture of like-minded souls, where there's a lot of thinking and playing and making the fantastic going on, a lot of coming and going, a lot of learning.

Just around the next corner, down a side street, there's someone bringing something strange and brilliant into the world that wasn't there before and insisting on freedom. Over the road, sometimes in clear view, the modern world was forming, too permissive and outrageously liberated for some, too far-fetched for some to see, but for those who could see, and believe, it could only lead to no good.

Sometimes around the corner in some basement or at the top of a low-slung building they're bringing something in the shape of a painting made of juicy, shattered paint, sometimes they're bringing performance out of how they study themselves, some are bringing a little *blague* to proceedings, they're announcing a list of priorities, or playing jazz that's trying to reach the realm of Buck Rogers, and there's someone thinking to himself he's not going to write a poem until he's in the right mood. They're bringing wild dreams of a new beginning into theatres, clubs, bars, classrooms and galleries. It seems like a good place to become yourself.

Sometimes they're bringing something that could easily have come from Japan, because one way or another, alongside the perversely all-American Abstract Expressionism, where art broke up with the more radical, roaming reimagining of Dada for a while, there were signs of other people from places bringing in the otherworldly, the not-America that would become part of America, and you might turn a corner and hear someone say: 'Technical knowledge is not enough. One must transcend techniques so that the art becomes an artless art, growing out of the subconscious.'

You'd walk into a room at the end of an echoey corridor and everyone there seemed to come from somewhere else, so it was a room full of strangers finding themselves together, and the first words you heard were: 'The truth of Zen, just a little bit of it, is what turns one's humdrum life, a life of monotonous, uninspiring commonplaces, into one of art, full of genuine inner creativity.'

Yoko blinked and breathed in the air. She looked and listened. It seemed like a good place to become yourself. From Japan, dust to dust, and at the same time, from a place in the world that hadn't got a name, and maybe never would, and now, by chance, from a city full of ways forward if you found yourself in a certain room with a certain sort of person.

Cage had nothing, so anything was possible. And he had the contacts he had made and the ones that he was making, the ones he was choosing to make, as though in the end he was who he knew and collaborated with, and he now had New York, with its own version of Europe, of the history of twentieth-century art, of Duchamp, settling inside a few streets that therefore contained universes.

Cage decided that having no money, and none of his percussion, and now no affiliation with any kind of institution, and a marriage that was drifting into being nothing like a marriage, was 'exhilarating'. (Xenia would soon start work assisting Duchamp in the planning and making of meticulous miniature models of sixty-nine of his artworks, contained inside portable galleries.)

It was a kind of freedom, opening the way forward, promising new life. He was backed into a corner, and he invented a way out, a combination of the odd little things he had discovered while he worked out what he was going to do in his life, and the odd little things he came across mixing with the people he met along the way. After losing their comfortable place at the Guggenheim home, they camped out in various places around Greenwich Village, including for a few weeks at the home of the academic and explorer of mythic traditions Joseph Campbell, an old Carmel friend of Xenia's, and his wife, the dancer Jean Erdman, a member of the Martha Graham Dance Company.

Cage returned to preparing the piano as a way of going forward, creating his more mobile version of a percussion section. A professional relationship with the dancer Merce Cunningham, still dancing with Martha Graham, which began briefly at Cornish, and became something deeper in Chicago, was to become a place where work and play and romance and sex would become a new kind of invented collaboration, built of love and inspiration and sometimes desperation and always passion and erotic energy.

146

Merce arrived in New York. There were still collaborations featuring Cage, Cunningham and Xenia, but Cage and Xenia stopped living together. It was as though percussion provided the thrilling, tempestuous, constantly evolving soundtrack to the ten years of John and Xenia as they travelled the country, and then the prepared piano was the searching, speculative soundtrack to the intense, passionate coming together of John and Merce, the sound of the beginning of a personal and artistic relationship that would last for the rest of their lives.

Cage's percussive period largely existed in the build-up to America's entry into the Second World War, the pulsing and propulsion, crashing and banging, the collaborative effervescence, the combination of movement and noise forming a soundtrack to immense, unpredictable change.

The prepared piano, a calmer, softer, isolated abstraction of percussion, represented Cage's anxiety and apprehension during the war, and the intimate, personal change in his life as his marriage came to an end; he said that he decided to use quiet sounds, pings, thuds and shivers, because in times of uncertainty there seemed no truth, no good, in anything big in society. 'Quiet sounds were like love, of loneliness, or friendship. Permanent, I thought, values, independent at least from *Life*, *Time* and Coca-Cola.'

On 'Primitive', written in 1942, he extended the range and potential of the prepared piano, moving away from what he had called the 'primitive, almost barbaric' stop-start 'Bacchanale' towards deeper, richer, more resonant sound, using the altered piano to explore a hyper-real zone between the orthodox beauty of the traditionally used piano and the vivid action of his enhanced percussion, learning how to make melody materialise from a percussive approach. The prepared piano was becoming more multi-dimensionally musical, a fluid, lyrical combination of sounds from imaginary instruments mingling with the still-existing unprepared instrument so that, after careful selection and positioning of objects and materials around and inside the strings, which becomes a defining element in the overall composition, one player now controls a kind of rudimentary music synthesiser.

147

He can summon up ghostly guitars, drums made of glass, distorted lutes, metallic attack, wooden clicks, bruised gamelans, fractured violins, echoes of jazz riffs to come, whispering cellos, essentially producing an intimate, alternative memory of classical music, dissolving its clichés and routines, rewiring the volume. Cage's favourite music, as he once said, was always what he hadn't heard yet.

To generate a barrage of bangs and a shivery sprinkle of meditative sounds Cage didn't need the percussion instruments and objects he carefully found and collected; he just needed a bag of items that he then placed with some consideration and discipline inside a grand piano, which in some ways becomes less grand, and in other ways grander, and more beautiful and enigmatic.

The changeover between Xenia and Merce to some extent happened in public, in April 1944 at New York's Theatre Studio on West 16th Street, or at least there is a performance where the percussion ensemble has disappeared and the evolving prepared piano is how Cage now creates sound and rhythm. Merce Cunningham makes his solo debut in concert in April 1944, encouraged by Cage, and it is also the first joint recital given by Cage with Cunningham as a new kind of collaboration putting together music and movement without one dominating the other.

The minimal, jarring and gentle pieces he had written for prepared piano showed how much Cage had discovered since 'Primitive' about how varied the preparations of the piano could be. The titles alone said a lot about how anomalous these pieces were – 'Roots of an Unfocus', 'Tossed as It Is Untroubled', 'The Unavailable Memory of' and the tormented, emotional 'Perilous Night', a twelve-minute piece in six movements each with its own rhythmic structure.

The score to 'Perilous Night' includes Cage's first concrete definition of the prepared piano: 'Mutes of various materials are placed (in a grand piano) between the strings of the keys used, thus affecting transformations of the piano sounds with respect to all their characteristics.' It took its title from an epic Arthurian legend about a night of danger recommended to Cage by Joseph Campbell, and Cage with an unusual biographical literalness described it as capturing a sleepless night caught between the unsettling loneliness of ending a life with Xenia and the forbidden-seeming excitement of beginning a very different kind of life with Cunningham.

The prepared piano was Cage's main instrument until the end of the 1940s, while he still concentrated on dance composition, writing for dance recitals and dance dramas and dancers including Cunningham, but also created new structural, spatial and vivid music. As his writing for prepared piano became more ambitious, it moved towards a radiant emotional neutrality. He had been concerned that the soulful, confessional pieces he wrote while breaking up with Xenia were mostly reviewed as though they were merely random sounds, either pretty or pointless depending on your musical taste. To some they were so odd-sounding and unfamiliar they seemed comic. What could he communicate through music, if not his feelings?

His thinking, perhaps. His methods. His choices. The compositions became less intentionally personal and more about themselves and their own timing, about the nature of sound, about their own place in their own world, part of a desire to understand the purpose of music. And for him, seeking the purpose of music meant seeking his purpose in life. When he wasn't sure of this purpose, he needed to take control. To take control, he needed to plan. He needed a plan to know his purpose.

Campbell and another one of Cage's friends – and ultimately advisors – the Indian musician and preservationist Gita Sarabhai gave him reading recommendations – the polyglot philosopher and progressive Indian historian of art and culture Ananda Coomaraswamy's *The Dance of Shiva; Essays on Indian Art and Culture* and *The Transformation of Nature in Art*, the gospel of the great Indian saint Sri Ramakrishna – which took him a year to read, and where he learnt that all religions are the same, like a huge lake with different parts having different flavours and called by different names – Carl Jung's *The Integration of Personality* and Aldous Huxley's *The Perennial Philosophy*.

Whatever calming effect this reading – and Sarabhai's revelatory suggestion that the purpose of music was to make the mind receptive to the spiritual aspects of living – had on his mental state, it started to have an effect on his music, and to make sense in terms of how he assembled his compositions for prepared piano.

He'd read about the Hindu aesthetic theory of *rasa* in *The Dance of Shiva*, the *rasa* being the dominant emotional theme or character awakened in the listener or spectator by an artwork, a feeling that cannot be put into words. *Rasa* appealed to Cage, disillusioned with the idea of clearly communicating his feelings, because it concluded that the essential element of a piece of theatre, music or poetry can only be implied, not objectively described.

Fundamental human feelings such as joy, laughter, sadness, anger, hate, heroism and wonder are abstracted into the eight *rasa*s – love, humour, compassion, fury, the heroic, fear, disgust, wonder – which inspires such a state of serenity and satisfaction that strong, violent emotions are calmed down. The four bright emotions and the four dark emotions all lead to a ninth *rasa*, tranquillity.

The aesthetic theory of *rasa* with tranquillity at the centre, the 'endless now' he loved about the music of Satie, and everything he had learnt in the practical and imaginative preparing of a piano since 'Bacchanale', were reflected in the incandescent timing of 1947's 'Music for Marcel Duchamp', which itself drifts towards the majestic deftness of the *Sonatas and Interludes* collection. He worked on it between 1946 and 1948 on a Steinway baby grand, while entering the intense romance of his relationship with Merce Cunningham, using the periods he was alone to immerse himself in the preparations required to create the sounds he was looking for.

He found that by avoiding bringing expression in his music he could be 'overwhelmingly expressive'. The secret to beauty, he decided, was inexpressivity. He could put as much information and intensity as he had put into longer pieces into pieces that lasted for two to four minutes, twenty of which when combined would amount to a relatively monumental, quietly epic and epically quiet seventy minutes, not broken into fragments but put together as a continual piece, an unhurried accumulation of inner coherence guiding the listener towards a new kind of purposefulness. Existing in its own anomalous, hyper-modified prepared world, almost unrepeatable in terms of how the piano must be set up in order to recreate this particularly prepared world, *Sonatas and Interludes* also exists in a traditional classical history that Schoenberg would appreciate.

As well as being the ultimate reflection of Cage's invention of an altered, reimagined piano, a magic box making ancient and modern noises in an ethereal space he's accidentally encountered and then controlled somewhere between the acoustic and the electronic, it also connects with a familiar history of solo piano inspiration that begins with Bach and moves on through Beethoven and Schubert, Schumann and Chopin to Ravel, Debussy, Satie, Schoenberg, Bartók, Ives and Messiaen. It could be seen as Cage definitively being the Cage of legend, absorbing influences abstract and scientific, technical and ephemeral as he wanders from task to task through a self-engineered distant reality, but also Cage still being the student of Schoenberg.

Sonatas and Interludes becomes the summation of Cage's compositional procedures since the early 1930s, a balancing act between acknowledging the system and 'official' cultural standards, while also wanting to get outside the system and reject those standards. It simultaneously fills time and empties it, organises space and disorganises it. It's within sight of tradition, of what has been, but it has the same relationship to what has happened as Cage's modified solo piano music has to previous solo piano music. He disrupts the history in the same way he disrupts the sound of the piano.

Sonatas and Interludes comprises sixteen delicate, deft sonatas and four freer, fancier interludes, precise, shimmering bell-like sounds from the West, toneless wooden drums from the East, faint, lingering echoes of the Enlightenment, dreamy hopes for a kind, uplifting space-age future, dances and lullabies, energy and decay, spectacle and secrecy, an ever-cascading flow of events intimately connected. The piano became a mystical mechanical music box.

Cage never completely lost an allegiance to compositionally induced continuity but the consequence of his inventions, the constant temptation, more or less reached with the completion of his most conventional masterpiece, is to explore what lies beyond continuity, where anything can happen by allowing anything to happen, and whatever happens next is what is going to happen next, expected, and a surprise.

As something trying to make sense of an extremely altered world, and of the overriding weirdness of consciousness, it is also one of the great post-war works of art, withdrawing into the self, into the unknown, drawing with it through a few years of chaos and trauma pre-war avant-garde techniques, tactics and tendencies. It places into suspended animation all those turbulent, art- and world-changing movements, provocations and mannerisms to protect them on a dangerous journey through a menacing, threatening reality. It's as if he is smuggling through a vast irrational wasteland in his piano-turned-time-machine some precious last-of-their-kind seeds, waiting for the time to be right so that he can plant them, and see them grow. His response to the horrors and destruction of the war was quiet and intimate but in its own way aggressive and necessary, an avant-garde serenity; he extended the borders of beauty, and let that be an answer to extreme belligerent violence.

Having created the perfect music for his latest invention, the perfect ending, Cage moved on, as if annoyed or embarrassed he had, perhaps tugged too much by the lessons of Schoenberg, created one of those 'frightening masterpieces' in Western music that he derided for their oppressive archival and institutional presence. It was, though, a lonely kind of 'masterpiece' that required hours of preparing for the piano to get close to being in the correctly engineered altered state to capture the instrument's shadowy, perpetually one-off otherness.

He matter-of-factly set off towards chance, a by-product of the randomness built into some of the preparing of the piano – the observation and commemoration of natural events, a responding to the experience of being where he found himself in life, in performance, a music on the outside of music, or deep inside it. There was enough unpredictable change and flexibility in the chance happenings to take him through the rest of his life, enough moments, incidents and natural events happening around him to come across, observe and put into some kind of unbound and often unattended space.

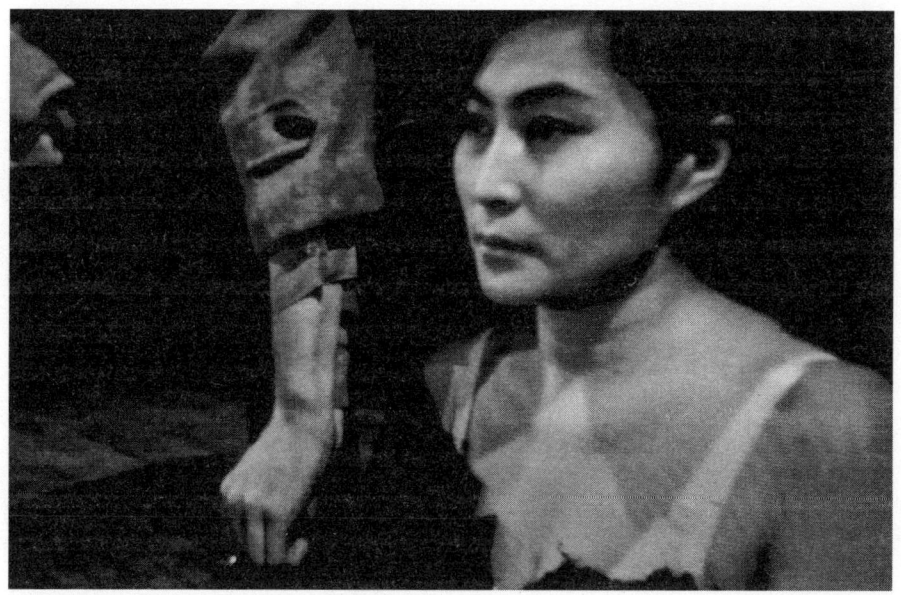

Yoko Ono, Cut Piece, Dusseldorf 1965. There was a long silence between one person coming on the stage to cut away her clothing and the next person. Yoko said this silence was a fantastic, beautiful music. Alamy / IMAGO / Klaus W. Schmidt

Cage transfers the idea of using melodies made up of vastly different sounds and tones to his 1949 string quartet in four parts, which leads him to finding melodies in an increasingly accidental way, abandoning any final reliance on the intentional. The prepared piano had shown him the way out, and after that, the way out always led to other ways out.

His final preparations in 1952, for 'Two Pastorales', are partial, and he's lost interest in the quiet, restful movement he circled and recircled on the *Sonatas and Interludes*, and the *rasa* fascination has become an obsession with Zen, another Eastern construction. In the same year, the brief atmospheric silences between the prepared piano's resonant thuds, shudders and pings will soon be extended to become a whole piece that studies silence from the viewpoint that there can be no such thing. A short solo piano piece written in April 1952, 'Waiting' acts as a preview. It begins with sixteen bars of silence lasting over a minute – the performer and the listener waiting for something to happen – and then a few spaced-out and hesitant notes, before ending with silence. Almost, but not quite, a final sketch.

Silence has its own rhythm, is its own structures, and allows all sorts of sounds to exist inside its apparent emptiness, so if presented ritualistically, within a certain prepared setting, with the suggestion of a beginning, middle and end, it becomes something else, and it becomes music, which now becomes silence.

The silent piece, '4'33"', written for any instrument or combination of instruments, was first publicly performed using a non-prepared piano, as was 'Music of Changes', premiered on the very first day of 1952 in a concert also featuring music by Pierre Boulez and Morton Feldman, written using a new method, another change in system, with a title explaining this. It was the ultimate example of Cage using music, essentially a distraction, to remove distractions, so that listening to it becomes a meditation without an object.

When starting to study Zen Buddhism in the late 1940s, finding a connection with the Christian mysticism he flirted with in the early 1930s, he had been given a copy of the I Ching – the Book of Changes, the ancient Chinese book of wisdom – by Christian Woolf, who had been studying with Cage and advancing his own take on the prepared piano. Woolf along with Morton Feldman, Earle Brown and the pianist and composer David Tudor – whom Cage would use to give a voice, a presence, perversely an expression, to his ideas about silence and randomness and the removal of self-expression – became known in 1952 as the New York School.

They each had their own direction, but where they connected was a commitment to imagining a progressive American music severing as much as possible any connection with European modernism. They were the musical New York School shadowing and being shadowed by the New York School of painters including De Kooning, Rothko, Pollock and Guston and at the abstract edges Jasper Johns and Robert Rauschenberg; at the same time, there was the New York School of poets including John Ashbery, Kenneth Koch, Alice Notley, Barbara Guest, and around the enchanted beatnik edges William Burroughs, Jack Kerouac and Allen Ginsberg, looking for a bigger bang.

They shared the same sense of displacement, forced to make new connections and find financial support, trying out new ways of living, finding a place within the city that offered great opportunities and stimulating uncertainty, and ultimately mutually intertwined inter-art collaborations and the kind of friendships that Cage and the others thrived on.

It was seeing Rauschenberg's blank *White Paintings* and the way they reflected the room they were in, creating shadows by chance, using basic house paint applied with a roller, with no content, no positive, no image, paintings that just seemed to have appeared in the world pure and alive without any human interference, that led to Cage's '4'33"'. He felt that music should keep up with the latest development in the visual arts, that the *White Paintings* made him pay attention more than usual, and therefore he wanted to make up a piece of music that did the same thing.

Cage set out to make silence by building up three movements of silence using the I Ching and some Tarot cards to work out duration and tempo, and handed David Tudor a score, which effectively asked him to sit still and listen for the amount of time it said the piece lasted, which required three extended rests.

Cage wrote a brief statement to accompany a 1953 showing of the *White Paintings*, and the text could also go with the silent piece and where his thinking was at the time. The text could also mean the opposite, or be a reply to those who thought the apparent non-painting and the apparent non-music were some sort of hoax, a fraud, a scandal, a waste of everyone's time. 'To whom; no subject, no image, no taste, no beauty, no message, no talent, no technique, no why, no idea, no intention, no art, no object, no feeling, no black, no white, no and.' He had called the *White* work 'a mirror of the air', not empty of form at all, and it clarified the ideas he had been playing with for a piece of uninterrupted silence. '4'33"' is a spiritual experience more than a musical experience, and yet somehow connected more directly to Bach and medieval chants than it seems, hymn-like in its purity.

Cage had come across the I Ching a decade before, but it now seemed to offer an infinite extension of his experience with *rasa*, and a new way of abstracting and remaking musical conventions and extending the principles of abdicating his memory, taste and preconceptions. For his purposes – the pursuit of what he called purposeful purposelessness – random numbers were just as useful as logic.

This was the big new change first explored in the 'Music of Changes', another invention of a personal, one-off system, his own discipline, but so flexible and, for him, so useful, in overcoming what he saw as the obstacles to achieving the purest, freest results, often producing sounds that were beyond his control, once he had thought of an idea. Chance operations immediately spawned indeterminacy, where the composer produces a set of rules for a performer to operate within, making their own random choices, meaning that the piece is never played the same way twice.

Cage the composer would use the I Ching for the rest of his life, chance replacing the prepared piano as his 'instrument', where he could make all the changes to a potential piece of music, its sound, rhythm, duration, tempo, structure, instrumental grouping, in his mind, asking questions of the I Ching, which he used as a random-number generator to compile sequences and instructions. He no longer needed a bag of household items and a few hours painstakingly attending to the inside of a grand piano. He just needed, essentially, to toss an I Ching coin, roll the dice, which was a form of proto-computing, a way of overcoming habit and creating unforeseen intersections between ideas and energies.

Henry Cowell had mentioned to Cage that 'Music of Changes' still betrayed signs of Cage's personal 'taste', his ego, which pushed him to create 'Imaginary Landscape Number 4' using twelve radios and twenty-four performers, with each performer tuning or adjusting the radio using scripted cues supplied by I Ching but relying completely on what was being broadcast on the radios at the time of the performance, even if it was silence or static interference.

The combination of the constant fulfilment of how to replace music itself with his very own version of music and post-war technological advances also meant that in a busy 1952 he initiated a project for the 'making of music directly on magnetic tape'. He was noting how far the electronic music he knew was approaching had gone, a couple of years after the French sonic explorers Pierre Henry and Pierre Schaeffer had called their experiments with the 'image' of sound at the studios of French national radio *musique concrète*. As with Rauschenberg's *White Paintings*, Cage was concerned that something was happening that he was outside of – or worse, behind.

Henry and Schaeffer spliced together unpitched found sounds – a collection of natural and artificial noises recorded on tape was juxtaposed, overlaid, fragmented, enlarged, dissected to create seething sonic collages. This was what Cage had seen coming in 1937 when he wrote, applying a term first used by Varèse, 'If the word "music" is sacred and reserved for eighteenth- and nineteenth-century instruments, we can substitute a more meaningful term: organisation of sound.'

The first piece in Cage's magnetic tape project was 'Imaginary Landscape Number 5', composed for a dance piece by Jean Erdman, the final instalment in the *Imaginary* series which involved the piecing together of material sampled from forty-two different records, mostly jazz, so that where Number 4 used radios, Number 5 used records, cutting up tape recordings of the records and using the I Ching to work out what order they would be assembled. The follow-up, more explicitly in the realm of *musique concrète*, which Cage had been working towards before it had a name, was 'Williams Mix', one of the first ever compositions to be generated electronically.

The silent piece opened up a brief space for the accidental emergence of whatever noise was occurring while Tudor sat at the piano, but 'Williams Mix' was a vast and elaborate Joycean compilation of a variety of natural and artificial sounds and noises – approximately the same length as '4'33"' but the very opposite of quiet and empty.

Both transcended any Schoenberg-like conflict between the tonal and the atonal – they played with form and content in a way that was influenced more by Dadaism than musical history, or, if musically, by the provocative, trickster Dada mind of Satie and his experiments with the perception of music and a love of absurdist-generated scandal that bloomed in Paris in the 1920s.

To construct 'Williams Mix', Cage used the electronic and studio-engineering expertise and Greenwich Village studio of Louis and Bebe Barron, who in 1948 had received a rare tape recorder as a wedding gift from a German friend. Both pianists and composers, they set up the only recording studio around Lower Manhattan, relishing the company of young, restless artists, poets, actors and musicians, and experimented with generating electronic sounds using radio-testing equipment.

In 1956 they would create the first totally electronic soundtrack for a commercial film: the abstract, unmusical and enchantingly unnerving sound effects they pieced together in musical form were perfect for the ambitious science-fiction space-travel fable *Forbidden Planet*, set in a 1950s American dream of the twenty-third century. Their soundtrack wasn't seen as being music by the American Federation of Musicians, threatened by their synthetic manipulations of sound, so the Barrons were credited as contributing 'electronic tonalities'.

With his long-term interest in the rapidly developing technical systems of radio and the sound effects of radio programmes which had led to his belief that electronics would be the future of music, creating film soundtracks could have been where Cage headed professionally. He had too many ideas about too many things to settle down in one area, and after *Forbidden Planet* the Barrons themselves suffered exactly the kind of typecasting as merely wacky, oddball, kooky that Cage spent his life resisting. The film industry assumed they were only good for creating weird-sounding sound effects for niche science-fiction adventures, and they never wrote another film score.

With Cage's instructions and guidance as he prepared for 'Williams Mix', the Barrons created an extensive library of sounds, a realisation of Luigi Russolo's imaginary sonic classification for his 1913 *Art of Noises*, which could now become a reality.

Hundreds of sounds were captured from their fastidious field recordings, separated into six categories specified by Cage – city sounds, country sounds, electronic noises, manually produced human sounds, sounds made by wind including songs, and smaller, subtle noises like the striking of a match requiring amplification to be mixed with the other sounds. Sounds were also sorted by their predictability or unpredictability, and by frequency, volume and timbre.

The mix used randomly generated choices, with three thousand pieces of tape drawn onto a 192-page score which becomes like a dressmaker's pattern for the cutting and splicing of the tape intended for eight magnetic tapes played simultaneously. As the Western classical music Cage was

161

determined to outstrip and outwit relied on ancient symbols of notation to ensure the continuing identical performance of a piece, he was developing new scoring systems that would never lead to exact recreations, and new graphic forms of transmitting instructions and signals to musicians and performers, even to the point of impossibility. It took a year to make the montage, along with the Barrons, and regular associates Morton Feldman, David Tudor and Earle Brown.

It was defiantly impractical, a deadpan, screwball combination of exercise, research and curiosity, satisfying a desire to know if any of it was possible, a quick-witted, technically exact conceptual performance reflecting both a love of becoming absorbed in a task for the sake of it and a drive to extend the range of sound so that music could match the metamorphosis of modern life and living.

Such efforts also led to new thinking, and for Cage one immediate result of 'Williams Mix' was an appreciation of how a sound begins, continues and dies away, and how a combination of sounds at various stages of beginning, continuing and dying away creates a new kind of music. In a way, he was experimenting with multi-track recording and the capturing, editing and controlling of sound before there was such a thing as multi-track recording. He was producing a 'mix', selecting one set of sounds from endless possible sets of sounds, long before there were the increasingly complex multi-track music mixes.

On both the near-empty '4'33"' and the crowded, antic 'Williams Mix' the silent piece is as much about noise as the noisy piece, which is as much about silence as the silent piece.

Somewhere in between these two masterpieces indifferent to the idea of masterpieces, in his transformative 1952 there is also 'Water Music', maybe more of a subversive, indifferent masterpiece, where water is not only the theme, as it would be in classical music from Handel to Debussy, but also part of the composition, which is also a performance, a calculation, a meditation and a vaudevillian visual drama.

It is Cage the tricky ritualist, the divine dilettante and the spiritual joker, and when Cage himself performed it as 'Water Walk' on an NBC

162

game show, *I've Got a Secret*, in 1960 as a kind of Dadaist variety act, the audience saw a line-up of instruments that included a grand piano but also an iron pipe, a watering can, a rubber duck, a food mixer, a vase of flowers, ice cubes, five radios and a bathtub. It seemed something you should laugh at, and the audience did, not realising these were Cage's carefully chosen instruments, rooted in his old percussion collection. The host was concerned that this revered if obscure modern composer might be insulted, but Cage was not at all put out. Better laughter than tears, he said.

'I consider music the production of sound,' Cage announced with a gently mischievous smile, having been introduced as possibly the most controversial composer in the world. 'And since in this piece which you will hear I produce sound, I will call it music.' The opaque avant-garde temporarily blurred with jaunty mass entertainment, an oblique hint of things to come in the art world as popular culture and its associated events and opportunities became something for the contemporary artist to manipulate, appropriate and fold into their thinking.

The Yoko Ono who never stopped to think: is this art? Is this music? It was obvious. This is art! This is music!

The Yoko Ono who believed that art and experience are built on continuous moments of touching the unknown.

In the same month in 1952 as he wrote, or built, or imagined, or delivered '4'33"' Cage, as evolving independent-minded mixture of teacher, artist, theorist, composer, illusionist, curator, provocateur, performer and collaborator, organised a 'theatrical event' at Black Mountain College, the independent, relentlessly experimental arts institution in a magical location in rural North Carolina. Its central doctrine – received directly from the Bauhaus but with a less rigorously professional approach – was the notion that knowledge is acquired through play, direct experience and social interaction.

Black Mountain was founded in 1933 at the height of the American Great Depression and the rise of fascism in Germany, at the peak of progressive educational philosophy. Cage first visited in 1948, and became a faculty member, part of a group of working artists mixing up art and life – and work, as even the most esteemed visiting artist, the most respected genius, was expected to contribute to the day-to-day chores. While on garbage duty, Robert Rauschenberg and his artist wife Susan Weil would gather discarded rubbish which became part of his three-dimensional *Combine* paintings, pieces of collaged reality, what he called a collaboration with materials.

An unusual-for-the-time co-ed enterprise following Oxbridge ideas of tutorials and independent study driven by academic freedom, the community committed in the darkest of times to utopian spirit, ideas and vision, putting art at the centre of the universe, focusing on discussion and process, making the college the ultimate art school, essentially run

164

by artists setting out no particular goals other than self-discovery and learning by doing and finding out. The advisory board included John Dewey, Walter Gropius, Carl Jung, Franz Kline and Albert Einstein. Visiting artists and full-time teachers influenced each other as much as the students with their dreams of a better world achieved through music, painting, design, dance and architecture.

The first complete performance of the gently mighty *Sonatas and Interludes* was at the college in April 1948 on a small stage with a basic piano in front of fewer than a hundred of the students and teachers. Cage and Cunningham had been invited by the director of the art department, modernist maestro Josef Albers, who had transplanted the courses he'd taught at the Bauhaus in design and drawing and set up a course in colour that would influence students such as Rauschenberg. It was Albers seeing ahead who once said, 'We do not always create "works of art", but rather experiments; it is not our ambition to fill museums: we are gathering experience.'

Cage was invited back later in the summer, and he organised a five-day festival dedicated to his latest fascination, the then obscure-to-the-point-of-folkloric Erik Satie. Half-hour after-dinner concerts featured a talk defending Satie, essentially for his sly, dry rejection of the Germanic structural logic that Schoenberg for all his radicalism had inherited from Beethoven. Beethoven, explained Cage the angelic-seeming heretic, was in error because of his faith in harmony, whereas Satie was correct for seeing the core basis of music as being duration, little buckets of time that you fill with sound and/or silence.

In August 1952, returning to Black Mountain College for the summer, he extended the performative nature of 'Water Music' and organised an evening's collaborative activity making use of the various experimental talents of other artists and performers. Eventually it would be given the name 'Theatre Piece No. 1', existing in parallel with the multimedia presentations of Jikken Kōbō in Japan combining apparently unrelated forms of performance and the finding of new ways to look at and experience art.

165

The events took place in the college dining hall, with an audience Cage had placed into four triangles around an informal square-shaped performing area, each section facing the others, with a different view of what was happening. There was no front of the stage, there was no centre of proceedings, just a general sense of encouraging everyone to think across boundaries, to find their own action to concentrate on.

Cage stood on a stepladder in the centre of this space featuring Rauschenberg's *White Paintings* hanging from the ceiling and delivered various lectures exploring purposeful purposelessness and the relation of music to Zen Buddhism. Sometimes he wouldn't say anything. Merce Cunningham and friends danced around various pathways that opened up around and through performers and audience while Cage talked, David Tudor played the piano, literary theorist, influential poet and Black Mountain rector Charles Olson and innovative Black Mountain teacher, poet and potter Mary Caroline Richards read poetry, a movie was shown, Edith Piaf records were played at double speed and dogs ran around excitedly barking.

Cage structured the performance following timings he had created using chance methods, in that sense designing, or allowing, as he was at the time with his music, formless unity within a structural form. The duration was the length of his talk; inside that one limitation, that necessary lifespan, was a joyous collision of the unlimited, the unbound, a profusion of expression, a Dadaist unfastening of rules and reason.

It was a convivial, collective effort, this networked interaction of thought and idea, this simultaneous connection and collection of individual knowledge, technique and personality, but it was also pure Cage, a summary of his loose, driven, casual, optimistic and utopian dream of collective and individual usefulness, a theatrical demonstration of why he loved Black Mountain College so much and its celebration of shared learning. His mind was buzzing with dreams, projects, puzzles, questions, answers, possibilities and desires, and the evening, a mobile X-ray of his whimsical, entrepreneurial, speculating, emancipatory, endlessly malleable imagination, became known as the first happening.

It was reading Antonin Artaud's *The Theatre and Its Double* in 1952 that had given him the idea of a 'theatre without literature', which became the theatre piece. There could still be words and poetry, but there could also be anything else, even everything else. Theatre takes place all the time, wherever one is, he said in 1954, and art simply facilitates persuading one that this is the case.

Cage's 1952, with its notorious silent piece that ultimately made the most historic noise, its absurdist water show and one-night-only prototype happening, happened to follow the year of Schoenberg's death. He died in July 1951, a few days after David Tudor had debuted 'Book 1' of *Music of Changes*, where Cage's use of chance definitively left behind any of the sort of rigorous systems he had pursued following his time with Schoenberg. He kept pointing music in new directions, one after the other, breaking out of systems that – however modernist – could still be linked with traditional processes.

It was as though he had waited for the ailing last days and the death of his true, or largely imagined, teacher before he abandoned the sort of musical frameworks Schoenberg would appreciate, even as they involved experimenting with instrumental groupings and even mechanically interfering with and diminishing the expressive range of the piano.

He stayed true to his vow to Schoenberg that he would dedicate his life to composing, and even as his compositions veered further and further into becoming artworks and performances that used sound as their material, he could still be placed in a post-serial avant-garde classical lineage that in 1951 included Shostakovich, Stravinsky, Messiaen, Boulez, Varèse, Ligeti, Hindemith, Stockhausen, Milton Babbitt, Elliott Carter and Luciano Berio.

After 1952, released from certain informal obligations to his mentor, Cage, and the theories of Cage the intellectually generous inventor, educator, craftsman, collector, children's entertainer, jester, preacher, absurdist and self-made expert at inventively exploiting the connections between people and places, broke away from that small elite crowd of cultish, recalcitrant musical mavericks on a mission. He wasn't continuing where music had been; he was imagining a completely new conception of music that incorporated an Americanisation of Satie, Zen and Duchamp.

He discovered post-musical ways to go it alone that would not just lead to more experimental, dissonant, deep-listening, minimalist, electronic, modern and postmodern music – all the way through remixes to deep-fake mishmashes and AI extrapolations – but would also contaminate post-war contemporary art and lead to happenings, installations, conceptual art, performance art, pop art, sound art, video art and beyond.

Much of this influence and direction came via the impact his methods of dramatising artistic practices had on the early whispers of mischievous madcap inter-art movement, with the chaos and characters of 1950s Lower Manhattan a creatively congested urban counterpoint to Black Mountain, filled with makeshift galleries, cafes, bars, clubs, concert venues, cold-water walk-ups and, at the centre of it all, the Arts Club on East 8th Street, opened in 1951. Members-only, and as much as possible artists-only, escaping the confines of their studios, with no pictures on the walls, it hosted various intellectual pursuits and art talks as though they were as much a social, hedonistic activity as smoking, drinking and dancing.

The discussions were no longer about what was happening in Paris before the war, but what was happening in heady, unreal New York now that the local Abstract Expressionists and experimental musicians were setting the pace, and places like the Club were creating their own space and inventing a new kind of collectivity, which somehow liberated individuality, where John Cage always seemed to be present.

Cage started variations on the amorphous classes he ran at Black Mountain, teaching experimental music at New York's New School for Social Research in Greenwich Village, founded in 1919. Early lectures at the New School were given by Bertrand Russell and John Maynard Keynes and members of Freud's inner circle, and during the 1930s it was filled with refugee academics fleeing Nazi Germany. Avant-garde artists got the message from the Nazis early, realising they would not be able to function as creative thinkers or even as free-thinking human beings.

Cage had been introduced to the School in 1950 by faculty member Henry Cowell, initially to take part in performances and debates, and between 1956 and 1960 he too became a faculty member. It was the sort of non-aligned sanctuary for abstract and radical intellectual thinking Cage relished, especially for the way it viewed the free exchange of progressive ideas as integral to maintaining sanity in a politically chaotic world regularly assailed by war and dispute. Artists attended to learn about esoteric ideas and philosophies outside art itself, and after the war, it seemed that the combination of the German professors, the defeat of fascism and progressive American idealism could illuminate all the darkness in culture and the psyche.

Cage's participation at the New School, especially when he was more guest speaker, curator and performer rather than running specific courses, was as though the intense concentration of performance information and artistic speculation presented in the 'Theatre Piece' were talked through in front of a few highly motivated and uniquely qualified art activists. They were looking for the same socio-historical evidence and experience Cage had accumulated over the past twenty years as he launched constant and ingenious assaults on traditional forms.

He never taught as such. His classes were all part of his overall investigation into sound–stage–vision and theatre, media and art, and he liked it when everyone in the classroom was as involved as he was. Everyone's opinion was as important as his. His classes, with usually no more than eight to twelve in attendance, were what he called 'lively situations', planned to a point, but mostly in a way that leads to the unplanned. Ultimately, the connection, and disconnection, between the planned and the unplanned was exactly what he was teaching, or at least pondering at length.

Yoko continued being curious, seeking things out that made her more curious, and increasingly free, and ready for whatever action made sense. Within months of searching through the streets, cafes and venues of Lower Manhattan coming across diverse coalescing art forms influencing each other as various branches of the New York School became the de facto leaders of the local avant-garde, Yoko Ono met someone else who had left Japan not necessarily because there was no developing avant-garde scene, but because one way or another, for family, or learning and new experience, New York called.

The vibrant New York nexus of art scenes was made up of like-minded friends as much as anything else, creating a mingling of disciplines, an interaction of ideas. Even at the edges, trying to find a way in, a place for yourself, you could feel part of the scene, and the scenes within scenes. You could form your own scene, a personal scene, maybe just a couple of you, feeling part of something bold, new and amazing, even if you were no one, and in some ways at the background of nowhere.

Yoko was soon friends with a Japanese musician and composer friend of Tōru Takemitsu who had moved to New York in 1954 knowing it was a lively place but knowing none of the details of how deeply social and creatively active the overlapping art scenes were. Brought up by musician parents encouraging an interest in classical music, he'd been fascinated with America, and American music, and played as a jazz pianist in American camps in Japan after the Second World War, now that Japan had lifted the ban on jazz, along with Western popular and classical music.

Toshi Ichiyanagi found twelve-tone composing increasingly old-fashioned and irrelevant when he studied it during three years at Juilliard music school, looking for a new direction. In 1956 he came across Yoko, just a couple of weeks younger than he was, and they liked the way the other thought, the friends they were making and the venues and cafes they visited. They became a guide for each other as they navigated New York, Toshi from the point of view of a contemporary composer influenced by Webern and Stravinsky, Yoko as something she couldn't quite pin down herself, which sounded incredibly vague to her parents – a poet using very few words interested in mixing sound, image, performance and philosophy, so she said, or rather, didn't really say, just hinted at.

After the twelve-tone cul-de-sac he found at Juilliard, Toshi went looking for John Cage, just as Takemitsu and others had, the composer who had seen beyond and outside serialism and even beyond composition, sensing that here were answers he was looking for to the questions he had about musical time and space. He'd heard about Cage's lectures at the New Music School and listened to whatever live Cage music he could at a time when it seemed more rumour than reality, feeling that here was someone making intriguing connections consciously or not between the sparse, isolated musical events, the quiet noise, of Webern and the sequestered, resonant emptiness of traditional Japanese art and music, the *mono no aware* that seemed to have been destroyed by the violence of war. He felt the art, anti-art and non-art of the post-war Japanese avant-garde could only go so far, and that the centre of avant-garde thinking was now in a village-sized set of interlocking streets strangely making itself a home inside New York City.

There was something about how the charming, even slightly cheeky West Coast adventurer and wanderer John Cage – telling wonderful stories essentially about the imagination, about what comes after, drawled with a mischievous twinkle – was speaking about a way of approaching art, life and music, even eating, sleeping and breathing. It all seemed to have a little Japanese tilt, the genial succumbing to an alternative, mystifying realm. Cage was a hint of Japan, of home, the home that is in the mind as much as anything.

Yoko and Toshi first came across each other at classes in Zen Buddhism which Cage also attended that were being given by the charismatic Buddhist scholar, Daisetz Teitaro Suzuki, born in 1870 and the author of works such as *Essays in Zen Buddhism*, *The Manual of Zen Buddhism*, *Zen Buddhism and Its Influence on Japanese Culture* and *Living by Zen*. He had become famous for helping introduce Zen Buddhism to America at a time when links were being made between the flights of Abstract Expressionism and meditative Asian writing, and had become Cage's latest guide, after he'd drifted along the surfaces of Hinduism and Indian spiritual traditions and discovered personal decision-making uses for the I Ching.

After the war, detailed books on Japanese culture previously impossible to get were being stocked in the bookshops lining 4th Street, helping correct (to a point) lazy stereotypes about the country and its history, influencing a wide variety of artists, musicians and writers to take into their work the meditative, the mysterious, the non-linear and the non-rational.

Yoko and Toshi came to the lectures from one direction, curious at hearing how a hidden sense of Japan was being presented in this part of the world, and to whom, and Cage came from another, always interested in unfamiliar new ways of life that could help him as he continued his search for his own way of life. He shared a concept absolutely fundamental to Asian culture, a sense of lineage, a way of transmitting forms, spirit and knowledge from mind to mind.

Suzuki distilled his ideas into a series of mid-1950s lectures at Columbia University. Cage, Toshi and Yoko heard the complexities and simplicities of Zen poetically explored through the expert English Suzuki developed when spending time in America at the beginning of the twentieth century. Suzuki's lectures started in the university's Department of Religion, but didn't quite belong there, and after moving to other places where they didn't quite belong, they settled on the seventh floor of Philosophy Hall, where they didn't quite belong, but where they stayed.

Imagine that in a classroom on the seventh floor, a small, colourless collaborative space filled with a few restless like-minded spirits, Toshi found himself sitting next to a small, reserved woman from his home country hiding behind masses of dark hair hoping it made her invisible.

172

She was the only woman in the room, the only other Japanese person there, which made him think about what kind of boldness she possessed. She never smiled, not that he noticed at the time, as if her brain was suffering from infinite thoughts.

When they were more of a couple, and he was, perhaps, someone to trust, the smile often broke through, a quick, vivid smile that contained so much but gave nothing away. She explained that when she was a child, her parents told her it was vulgar for a young woman to smile. It was hard to fight free of this forbidding early training even if you eventually made an escape from their influence.

Years later, when she was being widely, terrifyingly noticed as a cold celebrity oddity, as something of a discordant intruder, the ultimate, dangerously transgressive older 'other' woman, her occasional, fleeting, smile of delight, still suppressed by memories of her parents, was interpreted as an arrogant half-smile, a smirk. It was as if she felt above everyone else, fancying herself as enigmatic and special as the *Mona Lisa*, her sly smile barely hiding another world where everything is dark and ugly, filled with tears and loneliness. The smile of someone keeping secrets, judging you.

Toshi liked her; he wasn't exactly unreserved himself, and had his own secrets. She reminded him of home and his artistic friends, but she also made him think about the strange city he was now in, and how things were happening there that could only happen there but were also somehow reflecting the outside world.

That two exiles from Japan had found themselves in this room listening to this fellow countryman say these things must mean they had something in common, even if it was only that they had both been intrigued by the visit of Suzuki, the moods, memories and *mono no aware* he brought with him, and for reasons of their own wanted to hear him in person, and see where that led, if anywhere. There is no such thing as coincidence, he thought, she thought, they thought.

Perhaps she was a singer, or an artist, grieving for something – or waiting for something – he couldn't quite work out. She listened intently to Japanese thoughts turned into English, to a Japan mind bringing Japan to her new home, and sensed next to her someone else listening intently, someone who would join her as she familiarised herself with her new world, which contained so many attempts to create a new world. It meant there was still some Japan with her as she entered the local avant-garde, but a Japan that was also attracted to the avant-garde. As they encountered the unfamiliar, they supported each other, at least intellectually and emotionally.

Suzuki's influence in making the tantalising obscurities of Zen Buddhism known to the more open-minded Americans was immense, leading to an American Zen boom in the 1950s and 1960s, beginning in New York, felt in the deviant rhythms and time-stamped reasoning of Beat writers, even as critics suggested this was mainly because Suzuki spoke English and therefore effectively diminished pure Zen, producing a kind of diluted, paradoxically egocentric version. His was the fashionable celebrity version, a trivial self-help gimmick; the cheap paperback versions of his books made him a spiritual hero but possibly a fake one, with too easy an access to sudden spiritual enlightenment. Even the fact he wrote so many books and delivered so many lectures to explain the unadorned simplicities of Zen was itself a sin, as he admitted.

For Cage, Zen was more than a fad. It was sensing sublime atmosphere, a tempting new clear pathway, the serious playing with something called Zen that attracted and enlivened him, and influenced and elevated his own individual interpretation of Zen as it combined with his interpretations of art and music. That there could be no definitive Zen seemed a core Zen belief, so it felt misplaced to complain about one person's way of explaining what it may or may not be.

Suzuki Zen was not necessarily a strict, narrowed-down Buddhist ritual but was the spirit of all philosophies and religions in one place – even as it opposed the idea it was a dogmatic religion or philosophy – which particularly appealed to Cage, and the Beats and New York poets, with their own post-war distrust of doctrines and institutional practices, their own search for new forms and visions. Against a backdrop of violence and continuing unpredictable international tension, Suzuki presented himself as a beacon of light, taking on the responsibility of transmuting the hopelessness of nihility into the tranquillity of emptiness.

Whatever it was that Cage took from Suzuki, it made sense, except when it didn't, which brought its own wonders, and it changed his way of living and working, and making music, and there could be no feeling he was receiving something 'wrong' or turning it into something 'wrong'. He'd had his music described to him by more formal musicians as 'wrong', and as far as he was concerned, it was right, and so was Suzuki Zen and how it became Cage Zen.

Suzuki spoke very quietly during his three-hour lectures, said Cage; sometimes his words were drowned out by the sound of a passing airplane or blasts of downtown traffic, and one or two listeners dozed off. Cage would not immediately understand what was being said, and sometimes the meaning, or some useful approximation, would only dawn on him weeks later, when he was doing some chores, or in the woods picking mushrooms, suddenly hitting him in the solar plexus.

The meaning was along the lines of: there is no centre to anything, just a series of interpenetrating centres we come to from constantly shifting directions. You turn your eyes and minds away from the earth, look at the stars in the sky, and then look back at the earth in a new way, which could make a change to our mundane human existence. There was a need in the exhausted post-war era to discover some form of salvation, an antidote, that went beyond economic rebuilding, to the severe distortions of the modern age. Everything had been destroyed, so search for something pure and beyond limits.

Suzuki was advocating a transformation of human consciousness, which seemed extraordinarily tempting at such a dark time, and it appeared entirely refreshing to Cage because it came to him as an 'Eastern' enterprise, even as Suzuki took it beyond 'Easternness' so it wasn't limited to the East, with an otherness that made the concept of a global counterculture, different ways of being and seeing, seem suddenly attainable.

175

Yoko's parents believed their daughter's stubborn flirtation with the cheap dives, smoky lairs, messy art clubs and untrustworthy-seeming intellectual deviants of Lower Manhattan was a childish phase, something she needed to get out of her system, and she would surely soon return to their normal way of doing things and their modest, realistic version of her future.

They worried that the poor, extremely obscure twenty-three-year-old avant-garde composer with limited prospects she was now attached to was trying to exploit her for the family wealth, or perhaps to take her further into the murkier side of forbidden independence. Their reaction to the couple pushed them into a young marriage, and in the end, it pushed Yoko further into a world they found completely mysterious and even dangerous, and very definitely not for a young girl, used to different ways, and part of a different culture. Their elopement was a kind of artwork.

Artist and artist inevitably together experiencing art and living life, and vice versa, were a constant part of the avant-garde enterprise, doubling commitment and strength, intensifying each other's passions, seeing and feeling and learning through the other's eyes, ultimately protecting each other from suspicious outside scorn and aggressions. If you were looking for inspirational and visionary female representation in art, for the female leaders and innovators, they were usually hidden off to one side, somehow lesser beings, lacking the anger, the chaotic dedication of the men, and if they did have the anger and commitment, they were dismissed as hysterical or temperamental. You tended to find them as part of a couple, grabbing as much light as possible from what was shining on their partners, working in the shadows.

There were art couples and marriages of minds everywhere at the time, like drawing like, other captivating other, creativity framing love, adding unconventional fairytale romance, and associated emotional turbulence, jealousy and despair and fights for control; behind them there were Virginia and Leonard Woolf, Man Ray and Lee Miller, Emmy Hennings and Hugo Ball, Jacqueline Lamba and André Breton, Sophie Taeuber-Arp and Jean Arp, Wassily Kandinsky and Gabriele Münter, Georgia

O'Keeffe and Alfred Stieglitz, Edgard and Louise Varèse, Kay Sage and Yves Tanguy, Pablo Picasso and Dora Maar, Gala and Salvador Dalí, Aleksandr Rodchenko and Varvara Stepanova, Diego Rivera and Frida Kahlo, and in the next Lower Manhattan street, maybe next to them in some gallery or cafe or even classroom, Willem and Elaine de Kooning, Anni and Josef Albers, Jackson Pollock and Lee Krasner – 'You're a damned good woman painter,' said Jackson on first seeing a Krasner painting – Max Ernst and Dorothea Tanning, after Max Ernst and Peggy Guggenheim, Jasper Johns and Robert Rauschenberg, and John Cage and Xenia Cage, and then John Cage and Merce Cunningham – 'I do the cooking and Merce does the dishes.'

On the horizon Sylvia Plath and Ted Hughes, Mary Bauermeister and Karlheinz Stockhausen, Jean-Claude and Christo, Alison Knowles and Dick Higgins, Sara Seagull and Larry Miller, Shigeko Kubota and Nam June Paik, Niki de Saint Phalle and Jean Tinguely, Peter Blake and Jann Haworth, Gilbert and George – 'It was love at first sight' – Patti Smith and Robert Mapplethorpe, Kim Deal and Thurston Moore, Björk and Matthew Barney. These relationships were artistic adventures and sites for numerous dramas, for anxiety and harmony, for love and dreams, for the impact of each other's art, as much as any sort of traditional domestic and romantic arrangement.

For better or worse Yoko would always be part of an art couple, small, mobile partnerships exchanging energy, concepts, passion, obsessions, trauma, ultimately disaster, an expert when things were functioning at their best in developing her own independent identity, supporting the ideas of another and in turn having her ideas. She was a very separate thinker who while chasing equality and revolutionary focus perfected artistic togetherness, attempting to escape a world where women with minds of their own were safely considered girlfriends, wives, muses, dilet-tantes, assistants, groupies or mere distractions.

It was the thinking of Suzuki mingling with Cage's thinking that made Cage seem a little Japanese to Yoko and Toshi – but a Japanese that was made different because of how it mixed with Cage's interests and impulses.

Cage represented an interest among Western intellectuals in the elements of Japanese tradition that Japanese avant-garde intellectuals were denying or dismissing along with the nationalistic ideologies and tendency to conform that had led to the war.

Yoko and Toshi would not have taken these thoughts so directly from a Japanese philosopher, but warmed to them when they were filtered through the curious, social, evolving mind of John Cage, who saw nothing wrong with redefining and redirecting Asian philosophy by passing it through a Western prism with his American optimism and joyful existentialism. Something deep in their soul reconnected with the values of a desirable, spiritual East that had survived devastating and numbing destruction and seemed to be a key element in the making up of the future.

One way or another Zen Buddhism had been materialising in Cage's mind since 1936, when as he collected his haphazard compilation of influences from wherever and whenever he heard a lecture called 'Zen Buddhism and Dada', by his friend the American novelist and Eastern religion authority Nancy Wilson Ross at the Cornish School in Seattle. The lecture made a connection between the wisdom traditions of Zen and the deviant sanity of Dada, which made sense to Cage because, as he said, neither was a fixed tangible, both embraced absurdity to various degrees, both involved generating a kind of constant euphoria, each was in a constant state of change, and in different times and places they invigorated action.

Perhaps at some stage in the future, once other co-ordinates and connections had been made, and discoveries and decisions, there might be some movement or scene or collection of personalities and energies in one particular time and place that finds a way to put Zen with Dada to make whatever occurs when Zen and Dada are somehow put together.

Cage, assimilating and adapting Zen Buddhist thought, encouraged his core students to take further his ideas of using chance and randomness in their work to resist the pressure of personal taste, of being hemmed in by their likes and dislikes. He explained that using chance could set him off down paths he would never have thought of if he hadn't, one way or another, asked the universe for directions.

The Yoko Ono thinking that her favourite unrealised project was the one that would come to her tomorrow.

The Yoko Ono saying don't be cynical. Cynicism is death.

It was Cage's way of starting from zero, which appealed to artists and musicians looking to begin again, seeking a new social order as a reaction to the senseless carnage of the Second World War and the greed and temptations of capitalism.

Cage recommended removing artistic choice to bypass a restrictive reliance on any aesthetic judgement, to free creative activity from intentional subjectivity, indecisive doubt and assumed 'tasteful' shaping of ideas. He proposed allowing random events to happen inside a basic, preconceived controlling system. Chance was a discipline that allowed anything to happen, tapping into any facet of an unpredictable and manifold universe. It was a way of escaping the artificial, the inauthentic and inherited, of imagining a radical newness based on the universe's natural resources.

Cage's students paying attention to how he hoped artists and musicians would pay attention to the universe tended to be those who had already come to the idea of following chance based on their own influences and instincts and desires for radical possibilities, with their own belief in synchronicity and predestined expressions. They came to his classes because he was the world-leading expert in placing randomness at the centre of all he did, not to copy his methods but to find ways to place randomness at the centre of what they did. Some, like George Brecht and Jackson Mac Low, had already begun using chance; others, like Allan Kaprow, Dick Higgins and Al Hansen, quickly followed. Cage's creative DNA, a customised version of Zen developed since the late 1940s, was passed on to a younger generation of artists with their own individual attraction to the mind of Zen and the multiple methods and modes of Dada.

Cage's classes needed no entry requirements – apart from the desire to attend, and the time to do it – and there were no examinations. They featured him setting challenging puzzles and creating what were almost circus situations, the setting of scenes, conceptual frameworks, following on from his multi-sensory Black Mountain avant-garde music hall, prompting his students to see what happened once they had thought of something, and set it in motion.

Cage, who taught an attitude rather than a straight curriculum, talked about Zen, told some anecdotes, cryptically narrated off the top of his head a hidden history of music, touching on nothing obvious. He talked about ways of inventing musical notation systems using symbolic structures so that someone who knew nothing about music could make certain sounds that happened as they happened, with or without a version of a conductor that could be soft and loud and last a certain amount of time.

You could apply this approach to any art form, whether you were a complete primitive or had some prior knowledge and technique, and produce a film or a painting or a sculpture or some kind of performance that came out of your imagination. For Cage, any previous experience or technique interfered with the purity of the result.

Cage had become a fluid link – time-ghosted by Japan's Jikken Kōbō – between Dada's Cabaret Voltaire and the happening 'art for the five senses' that was perfectly placed to become incorporated into the popularisation of an anything-goes approach to pop and culture in the 1960s. (Stretching it further, because of course why not, he could also be seen as a multi-dimensional, culture-sampling link between Renaissance Rome as the city underwent massive reconstruction funded by

180

Florentine wealth and the street-art/hip-hop scenes of New York in the 1970s and 1980s, responding to decay, urban industrialisation, crime and financial crisis.)

It was the student Kaprow who came up with the idea of calling his take on the artist-arranged participative events that Cage had built in his own image happenings. Happenings, because once you decide to do something, something just happens to happen. Other words used as well included situations, and events. An early manifesto included on a flyer began: we have things to do. 'The long shadow of Michelangelo and Dante is only a shadow after all. We are adventurers. We are busy dreaming.'

Kaprow wasn't a musician so didn't initially think Cage's classes were relevant to him. He went on a mushroom hunt with Cage and a couple of mutual friends and Cage students – mushrooms obsessed Cage, as though they came before music in some cosmic alphabet of revelation – and he asked Cage for advice on the sound he wanted to use in his post-Pollock and De Kooning performative paintings. Cage suggested he come along to one of his classes, which happened to be examining recording, editing and tape looping.

Intrigued at how almost visually abstract sound could be, Kaprow went to more classes, and in response to Cage's weekly homework assignment, to create a piece of work, he started to create room-sized collages in the style of Rauschenberg's *Combines*, with added timed but non-linear theatrical elements including sound, light, speech and random spontaneous actions presented by a procession of performers, a general manipulation of environment and everyday events and the active involvement of the audience, as suggested by Cage. The happenings were an American action painting turned into a form of real life; he 'widened the concept of theatre to include them'.

Kaprow's 'homework', the low-budget *18 Happenings in 6 Parts*, opened at the Reuben Gallery, a decrepit second-floor loft space in New York in October 1959, in front of an audience given some guidance how to follow proceedings – including that they would sit in various chairs, and there would be no curtain call. The no-smoking evening consisted of

181

eighteen performances split into three parts where the actions happened simultaneously.

Another artist who dropped in on Cage's classes, Jim Dine, took the idea of happenings and assemblages into pop art, something else emerging in Lower Manhattan from the different approaches of different artists.

A happening, said Kaprow, could end up being like slipping on a banana skin, or going to heaven. It was always a gamble, whether you would experience pratfalls and skid marks or revelation and bliss, and sometimes the two states of mind were very close indeed.

Happenings became such a hit – by the early sixties becoming everyday fashionable slang, making it into films, ads and pop music – that Kaprow, trapped inside the label, a cousin of 'groovy', wished he could disown it. It was too late; the crude, adventurous stirrings of marginal, anarchistic avant-garde actions were already being used as fuel by demanding pop culture to promote novelty, coolness and fresh, perversely audience-pleasing way-out entertainment.

Free for a few, brief moments, the original happeners, experiencing and expressing pure liberty, in their beginning, seen by very few, were already facing their end – for some, fame as successful, compliant radicals; for others, the obscurity of the losers finding strange triumph in loss, at best being left to their adventures in splendid isolation. Happenings were a state of mind, and Kaprow knew the deal almost as soon as he thought of the idea, and saw it actually happen; those who were actually there at the event would become like the sea monsters of the past or the flying saucers of yesterday. 'For as the new myth grows on its own, without reference to anything in particular, the artist may achieve a beautiful privacy, famed for something purely imaginary while free to explore something nobody will notice.'

Yoko was also tuned into this Zen–Dada-inspired randomness, coming to similar conclusions as she immersed herself in the liberating American-scale avant-garde energy of Lower Manhattan and those she found committed to implicitly reactivating the radical ideas of Dada in a new setting. Dada had started being active in and after the First World War, and this replenished New York re-enactment was post-Second World War, with its enemy a new form of Cold War ideological rigidity and a battle for truth. There was optimism for the future and belief in progress, but never baldly stated, represented by the music, poetry, literature, theatre, art and fashion, and at the same time there were nagging fears about nuclear war and the real or imagined enemies of communism.

The student Brecht called this way of behaving in a way that turned nothing into something, believing that art and music was everything that happens, not just the look and the sound, an 'event score'. It was considered the most durable innovation resulting from Cage's teaching, perhaps a by-product of taking notes as Cage talked about making music that left things to chance, notes about music that could be made without needing a score. This music was written down in a different way, so that the music wasn't improvised, but it wasn't specific. The notes taken from Cage's experimental pursuit of a new way of explaining how to play a piece of music that had its own identity and sense of place, offering suggestions about how to musically frame everyday actions, became the event score.

Language led to performance, allowing a concept to be expressed, which didn't have to be musical. At the same time, with more of an elusive, *mono no aware* sensibility than Brecht, Yoko had also been writing down a few words of what she called instructions that imagined an action or artwork that someone else could read and then follow. These texts were initially for herself, but she realised that the instructions could be for anyone, and become a kind of artistic collaboration. There was 'Secret Piece' and then in 1955 'Lighting Piece' – light a match and then watch it go out, originally a method for calming her nerves when she was feeling agitated, becoming over time a written instruction, coming to life between the mind and the world.

Brecht and Yoko, before and after Cage, were beginning to discover that language could be in itself an art object, as well as a short, cryptic script leading to various forms of mental and physical performances.

In the late 1950s, this combination of imagining new art and music, talking about it, and setting extreme pieces of homework that turned into events, performances and accidental content – proto-happenings abandoning fixed form – was coalescing namelessly and spontaneously into what became set by 1961, in some ways, more or less, as Fluxus.

What was being studied, what Cage was teaching, involving discipline, serendipity, enterprise, sound, self-alteration, focused mindfulness and thinking outside thought were the abstract lessons that enabled an amorphous, abstractly aligned collection of artists, introverts and extroverts, dissidents, dramatists, dreamers, oddballs and subversives to create a scene that was all at once in the shadows of Dada, beyond Dada and nothing Dada at all.

Yoko never studied directly with Cage, unlike her new husband, who participated more formally and regularly in the New School for Social Research classes. She was there at the edges, quietly attending some lectures, close to all the gossip, discussions and experimental procedures, keeping her distance but keeping an eye on proceedings and keeping up. She couldn't bring herself to belong to anything – a movement, a class, a collective – in case it trapped her, echoing the threatening structural fixedness she found herself in at the end of the war. In her marriage with Toshi, at least at first, she could still find the space to be on her own, but she was still wary of anything, however loose and liberating, that reminded her of the dogmas and expectations she was escaping.

She was part of the milieu surrounding Cage that eventually gathered as a collective, but even as she was connected to the leading activists, and had her own ambitions to be at the centre of things, she was also a loner, on the hunt for her own space, and her own friends and collaborators, her own learning about who she was, where she found herself, and how she wanted to transform herself.

Her late 1950s were spent on her own, sharing a life at home and in various venues with Toshi, and circulating among those heading towards becoming a movement, and the development of performance art, the product of the experimenting in Cage's class and quickly beyond with written instructions for events, interventions and performances, essentially exchanges between artist and audience, theatre using language in a different way.

The new art she was experiencing, not necessarily in galleries but in performance spaces, where art and life became one, gave her hope, helped her work out her own emotional and aesthetic co-ordinates, and seemed to be the start of a new life cycle. Art was the one pure thing capable of effecting the transformation of human beings, and she found herself surrounded by art and artists interested in working out how to achieve that transformation and get it noticed.

The Yoko Ono relishing how everyone was influencing everyone else.

Before John Cage, musically in general, and for Yoko in particular, there was the secular German American-Jewish émigré musician Stefan Wolpe, at the time considered a less esteemed, less notorious and much more directly political teacher and composer than Cage. The nineteenth century was still tugging at Wolpe's shoulder, even as he was looking forward as much as Cage.

At eighteen, in 1920, Wolpe was mixing with the Berlin Dada group as it picked up the pieces of a world in ruin, and witnessing gloriously chaotic action performances by the loosely connected, unfettered multi-disciplinary Dada illusionist Kurt Schwitters setting to music his deviant love and/or lust musical prose poem, words as sound before meaning, 'An Anna Blume'. Wolpe dived deep into the alluring, somehow sensible post-tonal strangeness of Schoenberg and Scriabin; each note, each bar was a key opening a new door to another idea, and some other music.

He was a friend of Kurt Weill, and they were both part of the early 1920s Novembergruppe, eagerly performing the latest modernist pieces by Bartók, Stravinsky and Hindemith. They were both students of the vision-ary traditionalist, virtuoso pianist and free-thinking musical philosopher Ferruccio Busoni, author in 1907 of the poetic, prescient manifesto on the future of classical music, 'Sketch of a New Aesthetic'.

Varèse, Sibelius and Schoenberg had been pupils of the elusive, charis-matic Busoni, challenged by his ideas about a conceptual and formal reinvention of the essence of music itself and his commitment to creating transcendent sound free of rules, dogma and fear. If there was turn-of-the-century despair that the great classical golden age had come to an end, Busoni imagined with near-psychic insight what might come next. He abstractly anticipated or demanded at the beginning of the twentieth century, still under the shadow of the nineteenth, all of the advancements that would be made during the coming century by the disruption of tonality, electronic technology and brave modernist and postmodernist minds teasing or tearing apart classical dogmas.

Busoni didn't reflect his innovative ideas about the potential for musical renewal in his own music, perhaps concerned he was too wedded to conservative techniques, and too old – he was born in 1866 – but passed them through his students. Being faithful to his more radical ideas meant they quickly shed his view that you should fuse all past musical experiments with new forms and sonorities.

Busoni, with his interdisciplinary ideas of alternative ways to make music, exploring spatialised sound and montage forms, became a significant mentor to Wolpe, whom he encouraged to make his own rules and follow his own path. His sensing where the future, and not just the future of art, was taking shape encouraged Wolpe to connect with the emphatically non-authoritarian Bauhaus, where modern art was taught by great artists, continually investigating the interaction between various art forms.

Wolpe studied art and colour theory at the Bauhaus under Paul Klee and the Swiss expressionist and revolutionary educator Johannes Itten, making Schwitters-inspired collages from objects found in the street, cigarette butts, nails and dead birds, seeing the connection with how a post-Dada Erik Satie made musical collages from a combination of found sounds – typewriter, foghorn, milk bottles – and melodies borrowed from music hall, silent-film scores and early jazz.

Wolpe was the only professional musician to study directly at the Bauhaus, and his time there influenced his interest in the interplay of vision and sound, and his belief that music and art should have a social use – after joining the Communist Party as the Nazis deformed Germany, he would write anti-fascist songs for trade unions, mass rallies and political cabarets, paralleling Weill's work in activist musical theatre with Brecht, and as dense and intense as his classical music would be, it was always composed with a sense of purpose.

Over a period of about eighteen months, Wolpe had six or so one-on-one lessons with Busoni, and he said he remembered every single word. Busoni and Schwitters, two great teachers and energisers engaged in philosophy more than entrenched academic theory, led to Wolpe as another great teacher and energiser, as Schoenberg and Cowell had led to Cage, who would eventually lead, to a point, to the endgame of everything.

The Wolpes and Yoko first met in 1957, when Stefan and his third wife the poet Hilda Morley started inviting her to their apartment in the Upper West Side for tea, and sometimes an incredibly exotic espresso, with lemon rind casually dropped into it.

She loved their company, the way they fitted together, the way Hilda calmed his nerves, how Stefan was so full of life and you never quite knew what he was going to do next, making all sorts of magical connections between the verbal, the visual and the musical. She thought as a one-time student of serialism that his music was complex, precise and beautiful: 'I don't know any other composer of the time who represented atonal music so brilliantly.'

Where did the Wolpes find Yoko? Walking alone in Central Park in a different realm from Greenwich Village, staring at the sky, wondering about the sort of people who lived nearby, with a view that made the park seem like an enchanting wonderland in the middle of all the city's noise and movement? At some recital of modern music Yoko had gone to with Toshi – a musician they admired – featuring the obscure extraordinary music of Morton Feldman or Earle Brown, or Cage and Wolpe themselves?

Or did they come across her in a student cafe on MacDougal Street as she made a fifteen-cent coffee last a few hours, intrigued by this young Japanese woman with long thick black hair tangled in a thousand strands, reading a book of poetry – let's say, for the sake of biography, the pacifist, educational reformer and pioneering Japanese feminist, Yosano Akiko?

Yosano's revolutionary, transgressive poems contained sadness at the loss of life caused by war, but had a certain defiant edge, giving voice to her own story and ideas, to her particular self. Public attention to her boldness and her criticism of the moralistic atmosphere of the time was increased when she had an affair with the editor of a magazine she wrote for, who at the time was still married.

She had started writing poetry aged sixteen in 1894, as Western values were beginning to infiltrate Japanese culture after centuries of isolation, when some said that traditional Japanese poetry was too slight and tender to represent the country globally. She began writing poetry because women's poetry at the time was so disappointing and insipid it might interfere with the possibility of there ever being such a thing as women's poetry, and actually set back the wider political cause of women. She set out to draw attention to the sort of young Japanese women generally invisible in Japanese society, whose voices had been silent for centuries.

Perhaps Wolpe saw in Yoko the migrant something of himself when he arrived in New York: both were chased from home by extraordinary frightening circumstances, subjects of a series of forced displacements, haunted by violence and trauma, finding solace in artistic communities where others exiled in various ways found artistic self-representation as a way to respond to the dehumanising political disasters of the twentieth century.

Perhaps Hilda saw in Yoko something of herself, existing in some special place between the world and seclusion, what she once described, borrowing a line from the Greek poet Cavafy, as like seeing her reflection as being at an angle to the universe, immersed in 'what / the world calls shyness'. It was a way of hiding the kind of strength that was dangerous for a woman to have, even in art settings that superficially seemed open-minded and to celebrate equality and diversity. Yoko, like Hilda, wrote poetry to write herself out of timidity and fragility, and discover the inner strength and self-knowledge that enabled her to deal with the world and its discrete, disturbing and diabolical obstacles.

Here was more informal but powerful education for Yoko, from other parts of the world, as she talked with Wolpe, and Hilda, the New York-born child of Russian émigrés. Hilda taught English literature at Black Mountain College, as well as Hebrew, and her intimate, confessional, shapeshifting Black Mountain poems were eclipsed in the mid-fifties by the dominant male poets, comfortable they alone were custodians of the 'big ideas', presented with the necessary, resistant aggression that didn't seem appropriate coming from women; Wolpe and Morley were another art couple, very much in love but with the wife in this case patiently walking behind the husband, at least in public, as though there could only be one genius in the family.

Yoko relished the way they energetically exchanged ideas and passion in private as though there were no dominant partner, and what she called 'the intellectual, warm and very definitely European atmosphere the two of them created', which seemed to come from another planet. There was not much small talk, or at least the agile conversation was about art, aesthetics, paintings, structure, analytics, until temporarily all possibilities were exhausted, and there was time for a certain amount of less taxing talk.

Wolpe shared with Cage a commitment to composition as a 'proportioning of proportions', but also strongly disagreed with him on a number of issues, especially his unstoppable relish for chance – to Wolpe, an outspoken radical humanist, a committed socialist, an exile from Germany wounded by memories of the Nazis who'd written numerous anti-fascist protest songs, Cage's precious surrendering of free and individual choice in pursuit of a gentle new world was a betrayal of the human freedom that had been so dangerously threatened by the rise of Hitler. Wolpe wasn't averse to the accidental, the random unexpected moment emerging in the process of composition, but resisted sacrificing his creative imagination as Cage seemed happy to do in case 'the mechanics of arbitration caused the possibility of a false choice'.

He was inspired by the Dada methods, the energy they supplied, their openness to new material and form, but he also liked to be in control. Wolpe had been present at Cage's pre-happening at Black Mountain College, as director of music relishing the college's Bauhaus-like freedom, but he walked out, considering it too gimmicky and slapdash, or maybe just tame and derivative next to the original uncanny Kurt Schwitters performances he had witnessed.

He was as experimentally minded and conceptually restless as Cage, had enthusiastically investigated atonality, post-serialism, improvisation,

191

electronics, montage, concrete, appropriation years before Cage and other intrepid composers. They were both on some kind of quest, but Wolpe wasn't as generous as Cage in allowing the universe to take its own course – at least initially, when his moral belief system and ideological integrity was at its fiercest.

As a teacher – which he regarded post-Bauhaus as a mission, not merely a livelihood – he was more unequivocal than Cage, in some ways a complete opposite – closer, in fact, to leading into a new world from Schoenberg than reacting against him and racing away.

For Wolpe, there was no Cage-like adaptation of a Buddhist framework taking Dada's chance techniques into pure apolitical sound. He was as fascinated by the transitions between sound and silence as Cage, agreeing this was where the essence of music resided, but had no interest in playing around with sound to such an extent that it was emptied of actual sound, or was sound made without musical instruments.

He thought that Cage's approach meant a collapse of music into nothing but noise, which he thought lacked soul, and human spirit. Nothing in Wolpe's life, however brutal and brutalising, however lonely and adrift he might feel, crushed his love for the sensuality of sound, the enticement of putting certain instruments together to produce uplifting sonic glory. All of this, for him, was threatened by how far Cage would go, how free he would become, in order to avoid too much interference through preparation and consideration.

Dada as history-tampering, reality-shadowing collage, because everything is permitted in the ruins of war, meant that in the early 1920s, imprinted by Schwitters' dance with meaning, Wolpe could play Beethoven's Fifth Symphony at different speeds from very slow to very quick and mix it with a waltz, a funeral march, using eight record players, with no idea how it would sound.

It was an assault on the deliberate establishment assimilation of Beethoven's mystery, the worship of his music as an example of national might by corrupt and even evil Germanic forces looking to soften their image. It was also a way of regenerating Beethoven, throwing his sounds into a new time and space, engaging them with new technology and its assistance in taking sound beyond traditional systems and chasing infinite possibilities. Wolpe loved the miraculous mystical power of Beethoven, hated the cultural domestication, which undermined the music.

Wolpe rejected classical dogmas, recommended awareness of contemporary experiments and materials, involving style and technique from other art forms, and even imagined different kinds of scores, ones that were literary, poetic and visual as much as traditional, but, tutored by Busoni, he also encouraged the studying of scores, moving back through the great modernists Schoenberg, Stravinsky, Debussy and Bartók in order to appreciate the original breakthroughs of Bach, Haydn, Mozart, Beethoven and Brahms. He saw definite historical antecedents in contemporary music, even as the composers resisted admitting it, and identified the modernity lurking in the older music.

He had spent a few years in British Mandatory Palestine in the 1930s, as a Jewish refugee from Germany searching for a new life and an uncertain future in a new, strange land gripped by ancient but always modern conflict between Arabs and Jews, seeking solace and place and ultimate harmony in music. In Jerusalem, he naturally absorbed Middle Eastern spirit and non-European sounds, building close collaborative relationships with Jewish musicians.

He arrived in the United States in 1938 after a short detour in Vienna, and a meeting with one of his heroes, Anton Webern. Always keen to soak up local atmosphere and the musics of his new homelands, he was immediately fascinated by jazz, which took his music somewhere else again.

With a relentless curiosity, and a knack passed on from Busoni for finding unexpected musical and cultural allies, he was soon in the same circle as the American expressionists and teaching post-bop jazz musicians like George Russell – a rare example of a Black musician studying with a white teacher – Bill Finegan and Gil Evans. These young jazz composers pursuing ideas about music, finding links between Ravel and Gershwin, circulating from there through to Miles Davis – bringing Europe with him, and its recent volatile art adventures, its anti-commercial radicalism – were transmitting new signals direct from a Dada source to the imaginatively anarchic and other obscure fellow travellers gathering in downtown New York.

Only Wolpe had been and seen places that meant by the mid-1940s he had moved from the emotional intensity of Brahms through the transcendent delicacy of Webern through the logical dislodging nonsense of Dada through charged Brechtian protest – all that cascading European action – to Hebrew folk and art songs to the pure American music that was called jazz and then all its vital variants and subdivisions.

Gil Evans, a keen, quick-witted aficionado of Wolpe's worldly methods, remarked how his musical ideas would stretch you without changing you – 'I'd go into lessons as a jazz arranger, and I'd come out a jazz arranger' – but somehow with his basic ideas changed and improved. 'People would say where have your crazy ideas come from. They came from Wolpe. From a classical composer.'

It was a time when musicians were taking their ideas from any place they found them, whether pop or classical, jazz or Broadway, French Impressionism or Stravinsky expressionism. It was a perfect free-for-all environment for Wolpe, whose intense, cerebral, non-dogmatic music representing freedom of movement existed in a space between composition and improvisation, which made him a perfect mentor for a jazz arranger, inspiring Evans to reach for the impossible.

It was his Bauhaus background, the crossbreeding of technique and fantasy, and also a desire to articulate an affinity between Cubist painting and music, that gave his lectures and theories about music a fresh modernist perspective that attracted the new jazz musicians looking towards European concert music to add different styles of depth and daring to their experiments with the relatively young worlds of jazz.

Even as bebop was in the frantic throes of becoming bebop, a set of jazz musicians fancying themselves as composers were guided and directed by Stefan Wolpe and his perspective on twelve-tone origins. They turned nervy bebop intensity into a slower, moodier form, its delirium transformed into a slow-motion grace. Wolpe had a sober, considered European musical background, even if it had been subtly distorted by the haywire disordering of serialism, but his contact with Dada's mocking of coherence and order infected him with a craving for constantly adapting experimentation that as he said contained 'extreme innovations, suddenness, contradictions, shocks, simultaneities and dissociations'. One of his late 1940s studies had the title 'Displaced Spaces, Shocks, Negations, A New Sort of Relationship in Space, Pattern, Tempo, Diversity of Actions, Interactions and Intensities'. He was advocating a new sort of abstract musical space where music as shape, mass and planes of sound could move freely and independently, where sound, as Gil Evans said, 'hung like a cloud'.

Wolpe was effectively describing how, with his assistance, Evans was hanging a Parisian cloud over New York, introducing the original derailing spirit of serialism that begat the heat of bebop – a way for jazz to storm outside the box it had placed itself inside by the early 1940s – which begat the cooler, more considered, chamberlike improvised modal jazz, which begat free jazz. He was also describing how serialism begat *musique concrète* – which broke up the box serialism had locked itself into – which begat electronics, drone and minimalism.

Wolpe's cosmopolitan personality, his illuminating soul, his ability to elegantly combine musical styles smuggled its way into the *Birth of the Cool* tracks rehearsed, recorded and released on 78s between 1947 and 1951 and collected as an album in 1957, and marketed as a historic breakthrough.

When *Kind of Blue* was released in 1958, the logical Miles Davis development of the hybrid of classical theory and jazz improvisation, Miles himself, pianist Bill Evans, Gil Evans and John Coltrane had worked with George Russell, whose ideas on how to transmit a composer's thinking to improvisers had been influenced by Wolpe.

The *Birth of the Cool* discs were released under the cool Miles Davis name – he was twenty-one when he started work on the music, originally known as the squarer, less cool *Impressions in Modern Music* – but featured a collection of these serious new composers – a 'composer conclave' – imagining a modernist orchestral jazz, including Mulligan, Russell, Evans and John Lewis, as well as another Wolpe student, the trumpeter and arranger Johnny Carisi.

Carisi had been part of Glenn Miller's US Air Force Band, and uncomfortable with the regimental swing of Miller's big band would join manic, noisy early-morning jam sessions at Minton's in Harlem where Dizzy Gillespie, Kenny Clarke, Thelonious Monk and Charlie Christian dug into the flesh and bones of bebop, a music which ultimately inspired him, like his peers, to wonder – after the relief, the release, the riotous, side-splitting momentum of bebop – what and where next? The answer in part, for unorthodox new nourishment, involved a detour into classical music, into the sound if not the structure of Ravel, Milhaud, Stravinsky, Copland and Gershwin, a sound already in the works via the heady orchestral jazz of Duke Ellington and Stan Kenton.

Wolpe never made direct contact with Miles, but he had direct contact with Gil Evans, the ideological and idealistic centre of the Cool, the wise man who co-ordinated personnel, planned the direction, marshalled music's greatest innovators of the time, shared and debated ideas through the night in his small basement apartment on 55th Street, taking his collaborators to Juilliard to listen to the latest music by Hindemith and Stravinsky.

Wolpe also had contact with the modern/cool composers and arrangers through his other students, including Carisi, whom he took through scores by Bartók, Mozart and Beethoven, four notes at a time. 'Your ear progressed doing this,' Carisi said, and after combing through the methods and motives of Berg, Webern, Schoenberg, then you'd take them back into the jazz field. 'That's where the crazy ideas started to come from.'

While Carisi was working on a sophisticated minor blues piece that ended up as part of the *Birth of the Cool* collection, he would play it to Wolpe, who would have thoughts about it, as an old master and a new type of musical thinker, and suggest changes, which Carisi kept in. 'What

I had was pretty nice, but once I incorporated his suggestions, it became startlingly beautiful. In that sense, it was partly Stefan's piece.' If it was a collage, shapes and colours moving through and around shapes and colours to locate new meaning and new dynamism, there were a few pieces in the assemblage lifted from the mind of Stefan Wolpe.

Carisi casually titled the piece 'Israel', in honour of the establishment in 1948 of a new independent state, reflecting Wolpe's contribution. By the time he settled in New York, escaping tension caused by the post-war plans for the partition of Palestine and the creation of the State of Israel, and independent Jewish and Arab states – accepted by the Jewish Agency, rejected by Arab leaders – the idea of naming a track 'Israel', for God's people, as a celebration of the biblically told redemption of humanity, seemed an innocent act of paying homage to some kind of hopeful-seeming new dawn.

It may be a coincidence that *Birth of the Cool*, consciously inheriting chamber-music tones and textures, with Wolpe as a furtive secret agent who loved Mahler and Mingus, Varèse and Ellington advising some of the composers, featured nine instruments, with all that possibility for creating a music that mixed liquids into a solid, or solids into a liquid.

The nine instruments of *Birth of the Cool* matched Wolpe's 1937 'Concerto for Nine Instruments', a construction of different sonorities itself inheriting Webern's 1934 Concerto, Op. 24, for nine instruments – piano, six brass and woodwinds, violin and viola – a symmetrical masterpiece of concision, variety and hallucinated perpetual motion that can sound like Brahms played like a jazz band making a move through time from bop to free improvisation, as though cool Miles existed at the same time as *Dark Magus* Miles. Both concertos advanced into the jazz age Schoenberg's theory of sound–colour movement, which Wolpe passed on to his jazz students keen to learn how to connect preparation and spontaneity, how their idea of modern could be even more modern.

The 'Israel' piece, which most specifically captured Wolpe's elusive influence over 'cool' proceedings, became a dream-jazz standard; it was later associated with Bill Evans, and the resonant, experimentally minded 'cool' music of 1950, which would be elaborated on in Miles Davis's Gil Evans-arranged *Porgy and Bess* and *Sketches of Spain* a decade later. It was an anomalous spectral glimmer of a classical music emerging from Black musical roots, or a Black American music riffing on European classical music.

Wolpe made himself at home in New York to the extent he found himself at the centre of its art and music activity even if it was a secret, an unknown community, as though he had found a new Bauhaus, more ragged and scattered but just as fruitful: a Bauhaus where there was a Charlie Parker, whom he would meet when he was with another of his jazz students, the innovative clarinettist and arranger Tony Scott, who would take Wolpe to jazz clubs like the Half Note and the Five Spot.

The clarinet of Scott seemed out of date by 1950 or overshadowed by Benny Goodman, even as he was influenced by Parker and Ben Webster, and he worked hard to keep up with the bebop speed of thought. He studied with Wolpe between 1950 and 1954 to extend his understanding of music beyond jazz, to help his jazz, and as Wolpe took him from the rules of Bach to the rules of twelve-tone music, he relished excursions into the atonal, realising how much traditional musical experience it required to make it work as coherent music with its own internal integrity, and hinting at the 1960s free jazz to come on 1955's septet 'Scott's Fling'.

It was Wolpe who had taught him how to play 'free' but not chaotically, with a lot of soul and certainty, often by improvising together, Wolpe on piano, happy to improvise in the style of Mozart and Debussy, now with close-up knowledge of Thelonious Monk and Bud Powell, Scott marvelling as they played how the swing of jazz could head off at the same time in so many new directions.

Towards the end of his life, seeing Wolpe's impact on his friend Scott, Charlie Parker was desperate to develop his music into new areas. He became interested in being taught by Wolpe, for his energy and inspirational life force as much as his musical mind. Wolpe loved Parker and his music, and loved hanging out with him, even if Parker would come and go without any ceremony, and often fall asleep when they were together.

When Wolpe wrote his 'Quartet for Trumpet, Tenor Saxophone, Percussion and Piano' in 1950, New York jazz as though it was a European invention emerging out of Debussy and Satie, he asked Scott if Parker would play the tenor sax part eventually played by Al Cohn.

Wolpe called him Birdie, and here was the one composer who knew Kurt Schwitters and knew Charlie Parker, and understood how, worlds of time, space and mind apart, they shared the same spirit.

When Wolpe met Yoko Ono, something and someone yet again new to him, she had a light, energetically questing, homeless spirit he recognised. It was Wolpe who introduced Yoko to Cage, who had been introduced to Wolpe, Wolpe's first wife Irma, and a lively community of young composers, musicians and artists in the late forties, by the endlessly ambitious pianist David Tudor.

Irma was Tudor's piano teacher, and Stefan his composition teacher, with the view that the best musicians and interpreters were those who understood the fundamentals of composition. It was hearing Irma's mesmerising performance of Wolpe's 'Dance in the Form of a Chaconne' that inspired Tudor to switch from organ to piano, and he would become one of the great players of Wolpe's pieces, culminating in his playing the premiere of Wolpe's fiercely complex and turbulent 'Battle Piece', in 1950, playing from memory after months of practice the difficult, overwhelming humanist protest against war.

Having tackled with such force and flair Wolpe's monumental five-part piano panorama celebrating freedom of expression and the abstracting of abstraction itself, he was recommended by Cage to play the American premiere of the 'Second Sonata' by Cage's new friend and pen pal Pierre Boulez.

The prime post-war European classical rebel still in his twenties had impatiently jumped in a few years from acclaiming Schoenberg as the new messiah to announcing Schoenberg as musically dead, and there was much to do to keep up artistically with a world out of control. His manic, volcanic 'Second Sonata', flamboyantly taking apart the sonata form and piercing the edges of a new strain of total serialism, was even more technically intimidating than 'Battle Piece', with some highly skilled pianists reduced to tears at the thought of having to play it.

With the desperate, determined post-war theatre of 'Second Sonata' and 'Battle Piece', the twenty-four-year-old Tudor had climbed the most extreme peaks of serially triggered post-war solo piano virtuosity, where each one was as tricky to navigate as the other.

He immediately went in a new direction by becoming Cage's pianist of choice, utterly at home with the unusual and unpredictable, where the music was transcending being music, and post-Romantic twentieth-century systems were replaced by philosophically framed empty spaces, prepared piano strings and cryptic open-ended riddles.

For a while, in the early 1950s, Tudor functioned in between the rigour and ideology of Wolpe and Boulez, needing to move things forward but still using what in New York was an unfashionable, highly organised musical vocabulary, and the experimental movement and angles of Cage and the New School of Earle Brown, Morton Feldman and Christian Wolff. Wolpe and Boulez were joined to the past even as they championed moving far beyond it; Cage and the New School had decided to switch off the past, or condense it into a guiding, instructional thought or two, and build a new civilisation.

Wolpe's immovable attachment to the musical score also set him back. Yoko would note Wolpe's frustrating, expensive and time-consuming attempts to get his complicated, beautifully conceived scores copied and printed. For the contemporary New School, said Yoko, Wolpe's struggle with making and reproducing his scores was 'like talking about the time we all travelled in carriages. He fell in between two schools – the "modern" music of Stravinsky, Bartók and Copland, and the post-war composers such as Cowell, Cage and Feldman, and those beginning to experiment with electronic music like Varèse, Stockhausen and Kagel.'

As Tudor moved closer to Cage, and Feldman, he took with him some of Wolpe's meticulous precision and musical exploration, shading some of the new experimental music with echoes of Wolpe's processes that Wolpe himself would not have taken as far as they went with the New School. Tudor was the perfect pianist for Cage, being so ready to respond to his dreams and schemes with scrupulous musical planning. He added the disciplined preparation learned during his time with Wolpe to the indeterminate frameworks and unorthodox scores Cage was beginning to develop.

The detailed, ideological Wolpe musical event sounded very different from the open-ended, abstract Cage musical event, but they were both radical, reforming events, and Tudor could see what connected them, and how both the complex erudite assault on the senses of 'Battle Piece' and the wily advanced retreat of '4'33''' were in very different ways – one perhaps in disguise – major twentieth-century compositions for the piano.

Within two years, Tudor was at the other extreme to the notes, speed and fury of Wolpe, performing the premiere of John Cage's noteless, toneless, motionless silent piece, made more real, more resonant, actually more emotional because of the way Tudor approached its empty intricacies with the same transcendent concentration and of-the-moment application he applied to his performances of Wolpe and Boulez.

Yoko met Cage for the first time in the Russian Tea Room on West 57th Street after a concert she'd gone to with the Wolpes at nearby Carnegie Hall featuring pieces by Wolpe, Cage and Varèse. Yoko didn't know she was going to meet Cage, and hadn't asked to, wary of what she might find, knowing of him only as a near-myth, a soft, querulous voice in a small lecture room strolling to the end of his thoughts, peering beyond.

As if it had to happen, Wolpe effectively opened the door for Yoko to his genially disruptive, slightly devious friend and aesthetic opponent Cage, and to some extent Wolpe as a kind of teacher who wasn't really her teacher ruefully lost her to the 'noise maker', a new teacher who wasn't really her teacher, where Yoko found ways to make herself more than a poet, more than a musician, more than a dreamer, ultimately more than herself.

Both men were described as teachers who saw teaching as being as much a creative act as composition. They both encouraged a constructive looseness, breaking away from the rigid and drily theoretical, encouraging fluidity of thought, an enhancement of what you already believed, a creation of a new slate even as you still kept hold of what you believed in. They loosened something in the people they taught, mentored, inspired.

Cage was much looser and freer than Wolpe, who as much as he was committed to progress and whose concerns took in a range of other arts, as well as a social and political activism that never bothered Cage, still seemed to have Beethoven, Brahms, Webern and Varèse, and the new Miles cohort, over his shoulder.

As much as Yoko loved Wolpe – not least for his fierce optimism – in the end, for him, it was all music, every aspect of his life was devoted to music, and for Yoko, music wasn't everything. It was something and part of something. There was something else over John Cage's shoulder, something or nothing, sound or silence, present or future, art and beyond, and Wolpe had as a teacher and friend taken her so far, and connected her with so much history and experience, so much twentieth-century energy, but Cage was what was next, where you could spend your time in the twentieth century but at the same time be completely outside it. The 1960s were approaching, but time, for Cage, didn't have to trap you. There was more to life than the time you found yourself alive in.

Yoko responded positively to the Cage school talks and adventurous concert experiences while still remaining cautious, wondering whether Cage's anarchic, non-intentional art, the way he got out of the way of creating art, was too elusive and neutral and self-consciously purposeless. What did he stand for?

It didn't seem to bother Toshi, swept along by Cage's constant, provocative ideas about ways of making music, finding them useful to the development of his own music, but Yoko, interested in the intoxicating novelties of new music and the wild noise of exploratory vocal technique but not in pursuing music alone, wasn't immediately convinced Cage's art was as helpful to her less channelled approach to art and text.

Toshi would visit Cage at the Land commune at Stony Point, a radical anti-capitalist art colony in the woods of Rockland County forty miles out of New York City, where Cage had moved after losing his spacious New York loft in the mid-1950s. The commune had been founded by the philanthropist Paul Williams, the 'Williams Mix' architect friend of Cage's from Black Mountain, hoping to recreate some of that school's collaborative spirit. Numerous avant-garde exponents would make the move, and Cage along with Merce Cunningham and David Tudor were among the first to join the project.

Cage said he moved to the country because he had decided that there was much to learn about music by devoting himself to collecting wild mushrooms; he was letting his composing run free via chance and disharmony, but mushrooms had strict rules in terms of those that were deadly and those that were edible. 'I take the attitude that in music no sounds are deadly.'

In 1959, after a trip to Europe where he refined the lectures he gave on indeterminacy as a series of stories followed by a recital for two pianos by Cage with David Tudor, he was invited to give a talk at Columbia Teachers College. He decided that he would deliver the lecture, an even greater accumulation of short anecdotes, quotations, memories, thoughts and observations, in an unplanned order, one story a minute whatever their length, the shorter ones read slower, each reflecting purposelessness, chaos, emptiness, serendipity, with David Tudor's musical accompaniment playing the piano part of Cage's disruptive and determined indeterminate classic 'Concert for Piano and Orchestra' – sixty-four pages of detailed parts and instructions presenting eighty-four types of composition which could be played in whole or part for any length of time with any number of musicians from solo, duet, trio up to orchestra, with added noise from several radios.

The two orchestras that played the madcap world premiere, in New York, and the tumultuous European premiere, in Cologne a year later, were on a knife edge between interpreting Cage's wishes as meaning they could play what they wanted when they wanted to and actually responding to the precise methods; they followed the rules which implied they should break all the rules; they combined improvisation and personal discovery with a certain strict exactness, obedience and imagination. It came across as a combination of a conceptualised free jazz and a deconstructed concerto, of controlled mayhem and disorganised delicacy.

204

Tudor played at both premieres, knowing what Cage expected of him, with a grace and elegance, and occasional wildness, combining faithful interpretation and his own individual contribution that the American orchestra, not used to the ways and means of Cage, wasn't ready to equal. For the orchestra it was more a comedy routine than any serious investigation of the relationship between chance and composition.

The lecture itself, while saying nothing about 'Concert for Piano and Orchestra' or explaining its endless variety and its existence as the ultimate example of instrumental indeterminacy, is in itself a mirror of the work. It explains the work without seeming to have anything to do with the work, apart from the fact Tudor was playing a carefully worked out solo piano distillation as Cage delivered his lecture, which was more a theatre venture, a sequel to his multi-sensory Black Mountain 'Theatre Piece No. 1' happening and a prequel to how art was beginning to cross the boundaries of different media.

As Toshi got closer to Cage and Tudor, and Stony Point's rural inner sanctum, he was writing music that suggested where Wolpe might have gone if he had been more convinced by Cage's interfusion of music, sound, art, dance, drama, philosophy and chance. Yoko remained less 'officially' aligned to Cage's growing influence, diligently making up her own ever-shifting response to his ever-shifting ideas, realising he wasn't too concerned with forcing his definitions on others.

Just as Tudor brought with him to ever-evolving Cageland some of Wolpe's poetic technique, meticulous historicity and compassionate power, Yoko brought with her a sense of Wolpe's post-war conscientious outrage, his activist sensibility and his disorienting experience as an exile. Like Tudor, she contained both the romantic, perfectionist Wolpe and the anarchic, inscrutable Cage, one wounded and set adrift by war and the other innocently seeking out the wonderful, connecting through them to where the violent, tumultuous energies of the twentieth-century American and European avant-garde interacted, but mostly herself, made more so because she knew and engaged with both ways of making the world new.

She became a floating female, an opaque drifter, an unfixed element – uncompromising, defiant, tender, overcoming pains and wounds, conquering apprehensions and fears – in how the theatre, nature, processes and experimental actions of Cage transmuted into impudent first flickerings of Fluxus, where thinking just seemed to happen.

As Cage would say, he had nothing to say, and he was saying it, and that is poetry, and meanwhile was becoming an eccentric kind of celebrity, a spokesman for something if only his own credo, which Yoko admitted initially made her a little suspicious, even cynical. Later, she would understand more about his methods, to a point, which was the point.

Slowly, as she watched, and waited, the wife of one of his favourite students, spending a little more time in his company, and the company of those he felt comfortable with, she began to notice how Cage had found a way, even as he lived through the years he lived through, to be on the outside of everything. He'd found an entirely new space, separated from where most people were, and she in her own way wanted to know how he had done it, and how he thought about doing it.

Yoko carefully processed the information of what at times could seem like an all-male club, with Cage as the mild-mannered but opinionated leader of a clique of outsiders perversely leaving little room for other forms of outsiderness, unlike Wolpe, with his history of escaping real danger and horror and needing to find a safe space as a matter of life and death. Initially she identified more with Wolpe and the social and aesthetic consequences of his migrancy.

She took a little time to deal with Cage's accepted authority among the various avant-garde schools, even as she loved the experience of watching provocative performances of Cage's music, and seeing him present his fastidious, impressionistic lectures, striking out into a completely new form of teaching and communicating mood and thought.

In one way he was in charge, in control of events, but mostly he was encouraging his students, who were really in a larger sense freelance collaborators, to take charge of their own destiny, generate their own events and have confidence to be themselves, however opaque and disorienting their ideas.

Meeting and talking with him, letting him wash over her, outside of the clubby classroom or Cage's out-of-bounds private retreat, she began to understand how after spending time with him, or remembering something he had said, or music he had made happen, how he trusted change, the world itself seemed clearer, brighter, newer, and she seemed more awake and alert. He seemed to exist in a world of spirits, exploring other worlds that fed back into this one, unashamed in how he intended to fill it with peace and love. He was in his own way crossing borders and settling down in a series of new places.

She responded to him as a fearless adventurer seeking a spiritual transformation that was psychological rather than religious. She already felt the same way as he did, that she was not interested in necessarily making solid, permanent art objects, but in creating the space for art and sound to exist, for the new to appear, in a variety of forms, able to constantly rearrange itself. He was always asking questions. He always had an answer that satisfied his own needs, even if no one else's, at least not immediately. Everything is an experiment. Everything can be pushed to the limit until there is no limit and then you start again.

She also noticed that both Cage and Wolpe always wanted to find new ways of creating new artistic activity, whatever their temperament, as one trusted randomness and contingency and one remained faithful to the conventions of 'opus music' and was unconvinced about giving up control and allowing musicians playing his music to effectively be co-composers, or even themselves give up control.

Both composers were constantly in action, creating collaborative communities and scenes as curators and educators, mobilising the imagination and finding hope through discussion, theory and a chain of events. They were looking to make things happen and move things forward, creating a demand that would only be satisfied later, looking for new routes and spaces to test their ideas and refine their own work. It was this sense of being active and a part of new communities finding their own networks and spaces to perform that led to her early enigmatic appearance as an artist working herself out.

The passions of both bordered on chaos, and their ways of collecting this chaos, of organising their memories, their aesthetic progress, helped her understand what she wanted and needed to do next. She was their student, but never did anything they had to grade or judge. They were her teachers, but they never demanded anything of her. They never indoctrinated her, only pointed her in various directions, including places she was heading anyway but now with added fearlessness.

The Yoko Ono who was committed to developing a female image made by women that did not yet exist.

The Yoko Ono where tenderness stood alongside aggression, lasciviousness alongside asceticism, the feminine alongside the masculine, and the dead serious and profound alongside a revealing and occasionally biting humour. At times, the one switches into, or merges with, the other.

The Yoko Ono who, at times when she saw nothing but emptiness and the dead closed in and she felt watched and judged and no one kept their promises and no one knew how she felt, felt like taking her own life. Art would help her fight her demons, even her deep depression, and art seemed to offer better solutions to the problems she faced than suicide. She never talked about it outside of her art, and art was the question and the answer; art made you well. Art itself became the dangerous addiction, which didn't necessarily consume you as long as your energy never ran out.

Yoko had an affinity with the kinds of mischievous, conceptual activity ushered into place by Cage and his bohemian acolytes that didn't belong in formal concert halls, nightclubs, jazz clubs, dance halls, bars, cafes, galleries or festivals, in any of the usual self-organised ad hoc spaces however underground where new art and outsider entertainment tended to locate.

She needed to find a place to display her thinking about sound, art and language, her attraction to the imaginative subversion of performative and compositional norms. She thought about a different sort of venue to present her interactive ethereal pieces, notes and invisible paintings that were an embryonic, translucent synthesis of poetry, theatre, painting, play, choreography, magic, ritualistic actions and sound. The arrival of difference required a different setting, premises that hadn't yet been imprinted with expectation and habit. The new practitioners with their challenging non-traditional mode of performance, which apart from playing esoteric new music and other less extreme activities would involve setting things on fire and banging their heads against walls, needed something of their own.

Toshi and Yoko were living above a liquor store in 125th Street by Amsterdam at the time, past the place on the Upper West Side where Tenth Avenue took a turn for the less salubrious. As an experimental pianist playing modern pieces, Toshi's only option for a performance was the Carnegie Recital Hall, and once you'd played there, that was it, even if you were John Cage or Edgard Varèse. Walking one day down Broadway, a few blocks from home, they passed a large ballet studio with the evening light shining in. Yoko said to Toshi, that's the kind of place that would be great for you and your musician friends to play, and artists could do their thing as well.

They mentioned the large dance space they had seen to a Japanese artist friend, the abstract sculptor and future collaborator Minoru

209

Niizuma, who told them about artist friends of his who were working in lofts downtown. 'Loft' was a new word to Yoko and Toshi, and Niizuma explained they were neglected and unused old warehouse spaces and took them to the Lower East Side south of Canal Street, what would now be Tribeca, a City Planning Commission label that came into use in the early 1970s; at the time residents called it LoCal, Washington Market or SoSo. In 1950, the population of these streets was nearly eight hundred; by the time Yoko ventured there, it was less than four hundred, with no real sign it was ever going to increase.

Then it was an old neighbourhood in decline, its local population and industry shrinking, with business and the city's centre shifting into midtown, leaving behind predominantly warehouses and industrial buildings, many of them often set on fire by bored vandals. There was some light industrial activity, a few sweatshops, stores and food importers operating during the day, but at night the streets would be largely deserted and silent, the looming derelict warehouses and tall ageing houses seemingly of no use to anyone.

The industrial spaces, offices and stores the manufacturers and traders left behind had high ceilings and good light. They were raw spaces that attracted artists who were also drawn by the cheap rents, making them places where they could both live and work without drawing much attention from the more populated parts of the city, or from officials noticing that they were illegally making their homes in what were categorised as workplaces. You could be in the city, but also on the edge, of history, and somehow the future, a little lost in ways that suited the temperamentally nomadic and enterprising.

Living there seemed more connected to the city of the past, when the United States of America was not much more than a hundred years old, with its busy bustling industrial culture, than to the fast-growing, more impersonal rest of the city. Artists living and working in abandoned, primitively fitted commercial spaces reflected the activities of the pre-industrial craftspeople and artisanal specialists of the eighteenth and nineteenth century. In the long run, the artists' insular outsider adventures in the crumbling middle of nowhere were opening up a fashionable and desirable Lower Manhattan that was like a luxurious boom town, by the early twentieth century the most expensive zip code in New York City.

On their loft hunting in a Manhattan wilderness so far south that Yoko had never been there before, the dark, mysterious and secluded other end of the island to where she lived, home to a scattering of early art pioneers and outsiders, they came across a space for let at 112 Chambers Street owned by the guy who ran the store on the ground floor.

A dingy fifth floor walk-up, it felt even higher than that, as though each floor went up more steps than the one below. It seemed larger on the inside than the outside. When Yoko made it to the top of the endless-seeming final set of stairs, on the other side of a heavy iron door was a long, empty, grey, low-ceilinged room, heated only during the day, with no hot water and rotten windows at the back black with decades of soot and dirt. The windows at the front were reinforced with wire, but they did let some light in, and the thing that made Yoko fall for this unprom-ising bare room was a skylight that let the sky in. It was as though New York was nothing but sky. Above her only sky.

Number 112 was part of a once-proud terrace of buildings with facades built in the 1920s that had housed a variety of businesses, stores and firms – electricians, engravers, printers; cutlery, automobile, dry goods, hardware, paint and shoe shops. It had been developed on land leased from Trinity Church, founded in the late seventeenth century as the first Anglican church on the island of Manhattan and an integral part of New York's history for three hundred years, since the takeover of New Amsterdam by the British. At the end of the nineteenth century Trinity Church was the second-largest landowner in the city, owning most of the area between Wall Street and Chelsea.

Yoko was so excited about the room that she couldn't sleep that night, worried that another artist she was told was interested would take it. There were plenty of other choices nearby, sad, empty, unused rooms hanging on to history and needing some love, but she felt a connection to this particular address, as if it was fate that she made it a home, sensing important things would happen there. She spent a restless night worrying she wasn't going to get the place, that someone else was going to beat her to it, that by not getting it all her building hopes and dreams would come to nothing.

Nest morning, she raced a hundred streets down Tenth Avenue from her home on foot to stake her claim, finding out when she got there that the other artist had decided not to take the room. The rent was $50.50 a month, and she managed to scrape together the $25 she needed for a deposit from tips waiting tables and doing scrappy odd jobs.

She got her loft and all that sky above, signing a crudely worded lease that suggested there would be artistic use of the studio using canvas and associated materials, but no mention of any performance or live music.

Within weeks, in December 1960, with the addition of a baby grand piano hauled up the stairs on a rope and hook and some orange crates that served as chairs and at night as her bed, she opened her precious room to performances, the venue barely dealing with the New York cold using a noisy heater lent to her by her landlord.

Musical friends of Toshi and classical musicians she knew told her she was mad to think anyone would venture so far south of what was then the city centre of musical activity, places around the Lincoln Center and the Carnegie Hall. No one was going to make their way to a place lacking home comforts and any facilities, more or less an industrial slum. Yoko, though, stubbornly sensed a deliciously forbidden place that suited the mix of extremes she was imagining, and didn't care when she was told trying to put on performances in this dark corner of a shut, shattered part of the city would be a waste of time and money.

She felt like a pirate, a smuggler, an explorer, and if her eccentric plan was unrealistic, that seemed like a good thing. She had imagined a beautiful, magical place, a place to dream, to encourage new kinds of artistic exchange, and there it was. It didn't matter what it looked like, only what went on inside.

This was where the first downtown stirrings of alternative performance spaces in New York began, a new kind of artistic and musical setting separating new music with the attached energies of happenings, imagination exercises and conceptual art from the more formal, established concerts on proper stages with at the very least functioning chairs that happened in the elite rarefied spaces uptown.

Yoko's endless stairs that led to Yoko's endless sky would lead to Lower Manhattan avant-garde venues such as the Knitting Factory and the Kitchen and even Andy Warhol's Exploding Plastic Inevitable, and tantalising new kinds of covert dance clubs, and the specific idea of a downtown versus an uptown, of an exploratory downtown music and liberated dance parties that broke free of the deadening customs and habits of musical sound and performance. It was how unpromising parts of a city got reinvented from scratch through the actions and reactions of a few creating for themselves an urban bohemia.

Yoko found a place for herself, and helped find a provocative collaborative scene she was part of, even as her gender, Japanese background and untraceable personality meant she never entirely belonged to the history and legend of a series of obscure but intensely influential performances she helped make happen. Rumours at the time reflecting the inability even among musicians and artists seriously pursuing hardcore art research portrayed her as a kept woman, housed in the loft doing the bidding of a shadowy, wealthy Chinese man.

This was a wilful mishearing of the surname of former academic and jazz saxophonist turned avant-garde explorer La Monte Young, who was ready to use Yoko's newly found, deliberately isolated space for a stray, unclassifiable, occasionally unperformable post-Cage music he and a few musical peers were developing. Many coming to the loft with no idea about these salacious rumours knew only that it was owned by a mysterious, beautiful Japanese girl with long flowing black hair speaking charming lopsided English named Yoko Ono.

Inside, it would be cold, dark, loud, there were sacks filled with who knows what and blankets and glass bottles hanging from the ceiling, the smells were weird, something's burning, no stage, no curtains to raise, no curtains to come down, no clear division between spectators and performers, both seemed to be getting in on the act, everyone milling about waiting for something to happen, long silences when nothing happens, shadows rushing past you, something twitches in the corner, a sudden rush of activity and sound, of crude shapes and unclear movement, canvases are slashed, food thrown, someone reads something that might be a poem or a safety warning, you don't know whether to laugh or leave, whether what's happening is important or stupid, whether it was right you paid to be there, or whether you should have been paid for being there, because you mingle with the event, moving in and out of its moving parts. Then it would all be over, gone for ever, until the next time, the next collection of bits and pieces and unhinged sound and, possibly, existential commitment.

For uptown music audiences, however adventurous, the music played was not what they considered music, which must be read from a score and directly connected to a formal music history that went back through time, even if only to the revolutionary modernists Stravinsky and Schoenberg, who came out of Brahms, Wagner and Beethoven.

The uptown sensibility was still influenced by centuries of commanding European culture and academic refinement; the amorphous downtown mood building on the disposition of Cage included the non-Western, with ultra-modern New York additions, establishing an intrepid American culture that didn't get swallowed up by American orthodoxy but kept spreading through the twentieth century.

Young could be traced back to Stravinsky, who taught his mentor at UCLA, the musicologist Robert Stevenson, and looped forward to the warped, distorted rock and repetition of the Velvet Underground, the slow, decisive electronic drones of Neu, and from there into the abrasive stasis of noise rock and the space that coalesced around the stop-time in hip-hop. His late 1950s music shared some of the shapeshifting conceptual energy of post-war, post-Duchamp artists, a collaboration between musicians and visual and performance artists both testing the boundaries of art and music from their own perspective. It opened up musical possibilities and pulled Young away from the dried-up dead ends of serialism without having to drift back into jazz.

It was still 'serious' music, tenderly undoing Webern's early twentieth-century compression and letting sound unfold over time, but in other senses, it misbehaved: it played rigorous, restless games with sound, repetition, loops, delay, amplification, long tones and musical motion, the kind of games that meant the music it fell into would eventually be called 'minimalist'. It focused on sound itself, and the space and silence at its centre, the silence and space that surrounded it.

It sometimes seemed to murmur and drone as if feeling its way forward through the liquid of time into unknown places, stripping formal instrumental music of its usual orchestration, ornament, tunings, crescendos and narrative direction, breaking it down to an enthralling, hypnotic essence and tenderly, sometimes a little impatiently, persuading time to stand still.

With La Monte Young, music came to a stop, and then started again, as something else altogether – a music that came out of classical music, Indian modal music, progressive jazz, Stockhausen's vital early electronic music using sine waves, and Cage's silence and his thoughts on sound and spirit, and from there, it could and would go in any direction – from soft to loud, dreamy to precise and punk tough to ambient delicate.

In 1960, Young had moved from Los Angeles after earning a scholarship to study with Cage at New York's New School, a year after Cage's classes in experimental music had ended. He'd been alerted to Cage while studying with Stockhausen in Germany, Stockhausen making Cage seem more in line with Young's thinking than Stockhausen himself was.

Young had played some Cage piano pieces at Berkeley, to the horror of the music faculty, hearing music apparently collapse: they were delighted that the pushy, challenging twenty-four-year-old was moving to New York, out of their hair. Cage's lectures had mostly been inspiring visual artists more than musicians with his talk of chance, multiplicity and indeterminacy, but Young ended up studying at the New School with one of the musicians who had been motivated by Cage, and then became a replacement when Cage moved to Stony End, Richard Maxfield.

Maxfield helped Young see how Cage's floating theories and proposals and his borrowings from Eastern writings that were making more sense to conceptual artists attending the classes could be of great use to composers. You could make music thinking like an artist, a writer, a poet or an inventor. Non-musical acts could be performed in a musical setting, sounds produced need not be traditionally musical and could come from outside accepted musical history, and compositions could be as much about asking a series of questions that may or may not have an answer as much as about the organisation of sound.

For Young, this self-conscious puzzling out of methods and motives enabled him to understand what variety of music he wanted to make, and why. The philosophical questions that triggered his early music and which were a fundamental part of its structure and sound – and absence of sound – became as important as any learnt musical skill and technique, and led him to the revision of musical form that became so influential.

Maxfield is credited as America's first teacher of electronic techniques for his classes teaching composers how to produce electronic music from solely synthetic sources. The fifties saw the tools and techniques of broadcasting, as practically predicted and enacted by Cage's esoteric merging of art and technology, transformed into compositional methods. Novel methods of producing sound needed new compositional ideas.

Maxfield's music formed a missing link between *musique concrète* and Cage's randomness and the electronic music to come; he was among the very first to produce completely electronic music using only electronic input, using pre-recorded tape and electronically manipulated sounds, and although he used Cageian methods of selecting pieces of tape and various sounds by chance and accident, he would reject any choice he made that he didn't like, and kept selecting sources until the piece felt right.

He was scrupulous about finding and adjusting the raw material, but free in how he organised it. The unpredictability was disciplined, the randomness was arranged, the pieces fell into place and the history of electronic music found its groove, eventually taking over commercial pop music itself.

For a while Young was Maxfield's teaching assistant, and then Maxfield helped Young curate the music for the Yoko loft series. Each set of two performances was based around a particular musician. The musicians were all chosen for their fundamental agreement with the La Monte Young observation that 'we must let sounds be what they are', a thought probably picked up from Cage, who picked it up somewhere but had forgotten where or pretended to forget.

217

The loft series was a brief, six-month season spread across the 1960–1 winter, introducing some of the concerns, interactivity and ideas that became Fluxus, and even though Young and Maxfield were not so interested in the more chaotic, haywire elements of the group of artists becoming Fluxus, the alliance with Yoko's downtown dream of artistic freedom, the blurring of research and rehearsal, home and performance space, the provision of an informal, clandestine artistic community, gave them the flexibility to experiment with duration, instrumentation and structure that the uptown rules and regulations would not have permitted.

Yoko's loft was part of her desire to bring art into everyday life, not partition it inside sterile places and spaces: a real-world application of Cage's note that life was endless and art should represent that. For Yoko, rejecting the 'strange false value people place on art', art should be free, like light and water. It should just be what happens around us, raw, unarty, an overall experience, rough and sudden, beautiful and unruly.

The isolation from well-ordered, rigid institutional and conservative establishment interference allowed Young himself to concentrate on his musical research, and try out challenging conceptual pieces in front of a relatively sympathetic, certainly curious audience mostly made up of artists, musicians, poets, dancers, academics and sundry drifting art vagabonds. Most were experimenting themselves with how long or dissonant a piece of music could be, how invisible or nonsensical a work of art, how uncanny – even mystical – a dance, a poem, a non-specific gesture.

This was a world where if something went wrong, the audience wouldn't necessarily know, where the action went wherever it wanted to go, where little seemed to have a beginning, a middle or an end, and was rarely ever reproducible in any accepted way. You lived through the experience, you couldn't take it with you, except maybe a piece of something that got broken.

To uptowners, the performances might have seemed rough sketches, vague proposals, tentative collaborations, idle talk, primitive, incoherent workouts, at best whimsical, heretical attempts to define composition

218

itself, more scientific than musical or artistic. Downtown, each new piece was a whole new world, complete and considered, enigmatic structures reorienting and reinvigorating the listener's relationship to sound, ready to take on, and make better, and different, this world.

The first performances at the Chambers Street loft were announced to a small circle of friends and possible future participants who received invitations with the words – a warning and an incentive – 'The purpose of this series is not entertainment.' A piece of paper with the words scrawled on it was stuck to the heavy door that separated New York as it was then from a fragment of another city, a possible future, inside.

They started the series with no real planning and relied on inviting friends and the friends of friends, with a small charge on the door to cover basic costs.

Some reports suggest the opening performance was attended pretty much only by Marcel Duchamp with Max Ernst and Peggy Guggenheim and John Cage with partner Merce Cunningham and musical partner David Tudor travelling in from their Stony Point commune, an over-coated battalion of extreme avant-garde icons braving the snowy weather and infinite stairs to cross the threshold into what even for them was verging on the unknown. Such an idea about how to have, hold and present ideas and essentially throw pieces of reality at the audience couldn't have happened without Cage and Duchamp and their various associates and affiliates, and there they were, as if they were ceremonially cutting a ribbon and declaring the series open.

As George Brecht remarked, Duchamp is one thing, but Duchamp plus Cage – who had influenced a rediscovery of Duchamp spirit – is something else. This was the beginning of the something else again that was Duchamp plus Cage plus the results and consequences of what became during the loft series a combination of research into various systems and randomisations and a sort of scholarly dinner party of friends and acquaintances whose small talk was more about colour, words and perfume than the weather or a trip to a local shopping market, although they also had their place in the art of life. Yoko hadn't yet worked out how to bring electricity into the room from an outlet in the hall outside, so the loft was lit by candlelight, emphasising how the evening was so fragile in its obscurity it could have been snuffed out in an instant, but also the heady mood of otherness.

Young's partner, the spiky twenty-three-year-old Surrealist poet Diane Wakoski, who'd travelled with him from California and was quickly getting used to the very different New York ways, was in charge of checking tickets at the door and taking entrance money, as well as inviting poets she was meeting in New York's ad hoc poetry venues to become part of the audience. She once stubbornly argued with a nonplussed Max Ernst about whether she had given him his correct change. He said no, she said yes. Even though she was shyly impressed to see the famous Surrealist and realised she might be wrong, she wouldn't give in. In itself it was a perform-ance in line with what was going to happen. For Wakoski, Yoko was a part-time model and brazen social climber with unrealistic ambitions to be a poet and certain rough-and-ready entrepreneurial skills, but everyone always saw Yoko as they wanted to, without ever really seeing her.

The first two nights, a few days before Christmas Day 1960, consisted of a night of piano, cello and saxophone music, the debut performance of the diffident, prescient twenty-year-old Californian composer Terry Jennings, who'd studied Cage's *Sonatas and Interludes* as a twelve-year-old and become friends with his mentor and eventual collaborator Young. Young made a point of saying that he wanted Jennings to begin the series, considering him the most talented musician he knew at the time.

Jennings brought with him nine quiet, spiritually charged pieces moving at their own uncanny pace, which ended up being about half of the known pieces by a composer who became known as the 'lost minimalist', the less remembered, uncelebrated member of a coalition of foundational West Coast minimalists who moved to New York including Young, Dennis Johnson, Terry Riley and Harold Budd.

Jennings's ghostly presence in the first loft performances extended throughout the rest of his life, before an early, violent and lonely death at forty-one. Another ghost in the proceedings was the innovative young

220

jazz bassist Scott LaFaro, who had just helped put together the revolutionary Bill Evans piano trio with Evans and drummer Paul Motian and was due to play on some of the nine pieces.

Jennings had written 'Cello and Saxophone', intuitively tracing the impact of improvised modal jazz on the sustained tones of embryonic minimalism, inspired by the transformative post-Miles and Mingus playing of the Webern-loving LaFaro. LaFaro couldn't make the premiere, and died himself tragically early at twenty-five in July 1961.

That LaFaro from jazz had abstract input on the thinking and composing of Jennings who'd been learning from Cage symbolised the accumulating bursts of genre-resistant energy materialising in New York at the end of the 1950s and beginning of the 1960s. These bursts of hybridised activity would lead to other bursts of hybridised activity, influences rapidly combining and recombining, and emphasising the intoxicating cross-fertilisation of New York at the time.

The Jennings nights also featured an electronic piece by Maxfield, 'Wind', and Terry Riley's 'Envelope for Piano, Soprano Sax, French Horn and Violin'. Four years later, when the idea of making time-altering music out of repeated loops and layered sustained tones was still a marginal, misunderstood concept, it would be Riley's 'In C' that certified the existence of a new form of musical possibility – labelled minimalism, for all the piece's numerous rhythmic patterns and pitches, originally to make a connection to how the word was used to define stripped-back visual arts, although it would be as complex as it was simple, as lush as it was stark, as unlimited as it was strict, and might better have been called 'relativism', resonant or tonal serialism.

Other names proposed include pulse, pattern, trance, modular, meditative and love sound music, and by the time in the late 1970s minimalism became a handy, glamorising household word, at least in the homes of those who knew the Fab Four were Young, Riley, Reich and Glass, it was clear that it was fulfilling a need for certain self-/art-/structure-conscious musicians to be labelled and identified, none of whom would have considered themselves as minimalists.

By the time minimalism was a thing, there was as such no such thing, not unlike by the time punk was a thing, it had changed into something else. But the names stuck, and began to mean something else, and identify new kinds of musicians and musical intentions.

'In C' freely emerged while being entirely itself from the serenity and unfixed rules of Satie, Cage and Young, the open scores of Stockhausen, sombre, solemn Hindustani classical music, the communal improvisational energy of jazz, the joyous, liberating pulse of rock – and also as catalyst in the mix there was the plain love for the strangeness of all things and the insouciant, disruptive mischief materialising in Yoko's loft.

With his own directly credited contribution to Jennings's nights, La Monte Young demonstrated why he, reluctantly, would find himself aligned with the Fluxus nexus, uncomfortable with the attachment more because of the cultish jokers and proto-conceptual pranksters than the participatory anti-commercial anti-establishment elements of Fluxus. Young was no joker, but he didn't lack a sense of humour.

His 'Invisible Poem for Terry Jennings to Perform' was a footnote to the music, or him playing the straight (line) man to Jennings. When Young asked him after the concert why he hadn't performed his poem, Jennings replied, 'I did. Didn't you hear it?' Ultimately its only performance was the printing of the title in the programme.

Young, as with Brecht and his event score and Yoko with her instructions, was beginning to use what he called 'word pieces'. All three aligned in setting up conceptual actions ranging from the actionable and absurd to the probably but not always impossible.

Young's own two nights on 19 and 20 May 1961 followed evenings of protean energy showcasing Maxfield and Toshi with a fluid ensemble of contributors including Yoko, Young, Maxfield and David Tudor; the formidably adventurous performance poet and language artist Jackson Mac Low presenting poetry, music and theatre works with the assistance of what in this short series was becoming the Young-directed 'company' or charmed circle, playing pieces with titles such as 'An Asymmetry for La Monte Young', 'Right Hand Moving', 'F# for Simone Morris', 'Night

Walk (for VBW)', 'Peaks & Lamas', 'Thanks' and 'Verdurous Sanguin-aria'; and freeform philosopher, one-man band, renaissance agitator, eccentric musical hobbyist and cultural tinkerer Henry Flynt, who briefly sat in for John Cale in the Velvet Underground in 1966, invented avant-garde hillbilly music as a self-styled folk creature, and whose two loft performances consisted of a lecture and experimental chamber jazz in a band featuring La Monte Young, 'Flynt-music', and a conceptual com-petition where the prize was a Jew's harp. (Flynt was also responsible for the use of the word 'tweet' in 1960 when defining the rough formula for the event score, word pieces and instructions of Ono, Young and Brecht as 'a title, a tweet and a date'.)

There was also another eclectic Cage apprentice, the electronic com-poser, sound designer and multi-instrumentalist Joseph Byrd, who was also taught by Maxfield and Morton Feldman and conducted pieces by Cage. He would later – as one of the very few avant-gardists to make such a move – form the psychedelic rock group the United States of America, and co-produced and arranged Ry Cooder's impressionistic history of early jazz, *Jazz*.

To Byrd's surprise, the great avant-garde piano virtuoso and imperturb-able Cage sidekick David Tudor, who had just finished recording Stockhausen's intense, demanding Klavierstück 1-XI for piano, enthusias-tically tackled 'Prelude to the Mysterious Cheese Ball'. An exercise in inspiration Byrd had written with no piano in sight, it featured ten or so players scattered around the floor carefully letting air out of rubber bal-loons as slowly as possible to create thin, tiny sounds and occasional silences, with 'static and instatic scenery' provided by Yoko, where the marks made by painting were in the process of becoming letters and words.

It was daft and divine, and it took ten minutes for the members of this surreal wind orchestra to finish making their sound – Yoko was first to finish, enjoying a quick noisy squeak and almost immediately destroying her instrument; Mac Low, Young and Diane Wakoski were somewhere in the middle. Tudor, bringing his musical skill and concentration to even this unlikely task, finished last, carefully controlling to the end the chirps and whines and concluding with a poetic, blissful sigh. He'd learnt working with Cage that nothing is sillier than seriousness and nothing more serious than silliness, and there are all sorts of ways to find out what is out there.

Young's own two evenings featured a variation of one of the pieces he had written the year before that were part of his ten text-based *Compositions 1960*, a suite of word pieces to be performed however – and if – possible. The *Compositions* formed a missing link between detached Cage meditation and wired minimalism, in the way Young's transformative 1958 'Trio for Strings' was the missing link between Webern and minimalism, between the classical string quartet and sonata form and a liminal, fathomless musical state that went beyond form and engaged with formlessness without disintegrating.

If Cage had for some, perhaps benignly even for himself, taken musical history to an end, Young quickly, with very slow music stripped of embellishment emerging from an isolated childhood that nurtured a fascination with evocative natural sounds and the mystery of location, showed that there was more beyond the end.

The creative prompts for the *Compositions* with their droll, teasing brevity were clearly inspired by Cage and his belief that music could be suggested by a non-musical or semi-musical event. Talking about poetry with his girlfriend Wakoski was also an influence, taking the scores for his music-making towards the literary, and also making him consider the relationship between the performer and the audience, taking his music towards the theatrical.

Young's 'Composition Number 1' set the tone for the series. It was somewhere between 'make of this what you will' and 'think for yourself': push a piano up against a wall and through a wall if possible and then through any other objects beyond the wall, stopping when you are exhausted. Number 2 began, 'Build a fire in front of the audience,' and number 5 said, 'Turn a butterfly (or any number of butterflies) loose in the performance area,' asking the audience to listen to what they were seeing: the composition ended either when the performer decided, after which the butterfly was let free, or if doors and windows were open, then it ended when the butterfly had flown off.

Number 7 – the only one featuring traditional staff notation – asked the performer to hold a certain tone 'for a long time', capturing Young's obsession with long tones. Number 13 said to prepare any composition and then play it as well as you could. Number 15 requested 'little whirl-pools in the middle of the ocean'.

The text scores provided a template for other performers to interpret, just think about, have conversations with and/or realise in any number of ways, so that the instructions were not a musical score leading to a single piece of music with subtle, sometimes unnoticeable variations but a terse, descriptive 'score' that led not only to any number of variations but ultimately to new genres.

In one direction, via the mesmerising pulses and patterns of Terry Riley, the *Compositions* led to Philip Glass and Steve Reich, and through to the glam ambience and generative stylings of Brian Eno. In another, via what was going on at the far edges, and at the same time the mysterious still centre of Coltrane, Miles, Sun Ra, it led to Black Exotica. In another direction, via contact with the Welsh electric violist John Cale and media studies professor and minimalist film-maker Tony Conrad, it led to the Velvet Underground's mix of resonant rock propulsion and loud, warped drones, and through to art rock, where there is Brian Eno again, and his cerebral sensuality and philosophies of arousal.

The miniature tour de force 'Composition Number 10' said, 'Draw a straight line and follow it,' and Young's loft concerts took this instruction as a starting point for twenty-nine interpretations, suggesting how the piece was a guideline for possible pieces of music but also for his entire life and work, which took him through the next few years from ambitious, restless rule-breaking *enfant terrible* to assured musical mystic comfortable in his methodical skin.

The twenty-nine 'Straight Lines' were dated as being composed between 1 January and 31 December 1961, which means Young was performing twenty-two pieces of music experimenting with the suspension of time months before they were officially composed. He had noticed that until 1961 he had written twenty-nine pieces a year on average, and decided to write a year's worth of music in one night and then distribute them in advance through the year, thirteen days apart.

The dating, which becomes part of the title of the composition, and part of the composition, is a proto-Fluxus artistic gesture, his last conceptual action before he moved away from being Fluxus more or less before Fluxus began, which if you ever need a definition – which isn't a Fluxus thing to want – was pure Fluxus.

Young's 'straight line' and his 'little whirlpools' and 'for a long time' went through various compositional adaptations by others to become minimalism and ambient, and all the subgenres that followed from there. They proved the potentially unlimited capacities of a few words and a spare extended sound, given the right time and place.

In a late loft performance in the spring of 1961, the dancer and choreographer Simone Forti, who had been influenced by some action art conceived by the Japanese Gutai group, was invited to perform two nights at the loft. After Cage, and Cunningham, dance was also becoming conceptual and improvisational – using chance as a creative factor – and in its own way minimalist and stripped down to the physical equivalent of an extended single sound. Movement became a material for an artwork that formed in the gap between the mysterious and the mundane – dance was approaching the borders of a new kind of performance art.

Forti presented five new works from her transformative dance equivalent of Young's *Compositions 1960*, *Constructions*, also using concise Cageian instructions to dictate action and reaction and create events that would never be repeated the same way, that would always be in flux. At more or less the same time, different artists, musicians and performers were using Cage's clues and taking them to different ends. The *Constructions*, mixing the rough and the smooth, the aggressive and the gentle, the ordinary and the extraordinary, reimagined dance as much as the *Compositions* reimagined music. They included an event involving two men and a rope in a kind of virtual combat, a piece where the physical action of some tightly huddled dancers became a mobile sculpture that moved through the room – 'The dancers mesh together as a strong structure and one dancer detaches and climbs up the outside,' the instruction for this said – and an event where her calm, watchful choreography, a focused figure balancing in a loop of rope, was a collaboration with the screeching, distorted taped music of La Monte Young, as though the music was part of the dance, and the dance part of the music, a fight between human gracefulness and multifarious wildness.

In another piece Forti hid inside a box making noises, moving and not moving at the same time, until the audience forgot there was anyone inside the box and just heard a box making sound.

'Slant Board' featured three people walking up and down a leaning wooden ramp for ten minutes using attached knotted ropes, an example of how the *Constructions* set dancers into an incongruous environment with some guidance about their actions allowing for the freedom to negotiate in their own way the particular object they were encountering. The props were made by Forti's sculptor husband Robert Morris, and he had his own three-night installation in early June at the end of the loft series, building sculptures out of plywood to shape an immersive spatial environment. He created a dark passageway inside the loft called 'Passageway', a dimly lit, seemingly endless, curved corridor which became narrower and narrower until you couldn't go any further. A steady rhythm faintly throbbed like a heartbeat and there was a space where people could write messages. 'Fuck you Bob Morris,' read one.

During the series, artists would be lurking in the audience who were midway between Cage's class in chance generation and non-intentional procedures and the naming and therefore to an extent making of Fluxus, as if Yoko's studio loft as workshop–atelier–happening environment– private party was a tunnel between the two dimensions, bringing them together.

Audiences, a congregation soon well into three figures which seemed larger and more intense as that was 100 per cent of those interested, included theorist, performer, provocateur, writer, composer and happening disciple Dick Higgins. There was Allan Kaprow, who crystallised the concept of the happening as an audience-involved performance fantasy linked to real life which he explained could take place in 'garbage cans, police files, hotel lobbies, seen in the store fronts and on the streets, and sensed in dreams and horrible accidents'.

There was also the composer Dennis Johnson, whose fantastically level, lingering six-hour 1959 'November' piece guided Young towards drone. Christian Wolff, who had recommended the I Ching to Cage. The sound artist, land artist, illustrator and poet-philosopher Walter De Maria and his 'meaningless work' – his 1961 'Boxes for Meaningless Work' consisted of two open boxes, next to which De Maria had written, 'Transfer things from one box to the next box, back and forth, back and forth. Be aware that what you are doing is meaningless.' On an opposite wall he would hang two signs – Sign A said 'Walk to Sign B' and B was 'Walk to Sign A', an impression of infinity. Also present, the watchful ad hoc poet, art scavenger, collagist and sculptor Al Hansen.

Individually and collectively, credited or not, they could all claim to have been the first innovative this or that: the one who thought of the name 'concept art' for works where the materials were concepts and language; the great catalyst in the era of accelerated boundary-crossing new media where art could be made of anything by anyone and history could be constantly questioned and rewritten, connecting the dots between French cabaret, Dada displays, Black Mountain College, beatnik, happenings, Cage, Fluxus, free jazz, installation art, op and pop art, Art & Language, Krautrock, punk, post-punk, no-wave, rave, fan fiction, weblogs, crypto art and YouTube channels.

In 1959, Hansen and Higgins formed the makeshift New York Audio Visual Group as a continuation of Cage's classes exploring experimental notation. Their weekly meetings and free-spirited concerts of avant-garde chamber music with hints of happenings set up to extend Cage's philosophical spirit into the real world took place in Greenwich Village cafes and culture and community centres such as the 92nd Street Y.

The Audio Visual Group performances linked the bookish environment at the Research School, the twilight activities at beatnik Village and Lower East Side cafes, the regular performances of Cage and post-Cage pieces at the Living Theatre on 14th Street and low-key neighbourhood meeting places with the downtown setting of the loft series.

It was the loft series that channelled artists, theories, viewpoints, sounds, propositions, materials, intellectual excitement, pacifist-anarchistic politics and forces beyond human control into the not-yet-named-or-even-real Fluxus.

Hansen's sense of mischief, trickery and warped fun, which Yoko loved as a very American form of authority-dismantling, convention-defying surrealism in the spirit of Buster Keaton, W.C. Fields and pie-in-the-face vaudeville, the comic gods of a centreless universe, made it into the more anarchic anti-professional elements of Fluxus. Hansen once explained that the difference between life and art was that if you turned a flashlight on to find your keys, that wasn't art. If you stood on a stage even if there was no one in the audience and turned your flashlight on and off fifty times, that was art. Duchamp's readymade object had become a readymade action.

Hansen had gone to the New School because friends of his went on a certain night, and feeling left out, attached to them like family, he fancied going along on the same night. He looked for a class that interested him, and liked the word 'experimental' in the description of Cage's class. He took the class even though he was not a musician and had no experience of music, couldn't play an instrument, because he had developed an interest in film – seeing them, talking about them, as a modernist art form as much as anything. He read something Eisenstein had said that 'all the art forms meet in the film frame' and he thought a music class would be useful because if he wanted to make a film he needed to meet a musician who could write the soundtrack. The word 'experimental' suggested he would be able to afford them.

At his first class, when Cage asked this new student why he was there, Cage seemed happier and happier as Hansen made it clear he was not a musician or a composer and knew nothing about rhythm or harmony and wasn't even intending to write the soundtracks to the films he wanted to make. He had no idea what that music would even be, and if it was even music as such.

Hansen thought Cage would think he was wasting his time and ask him to leave, but he laughed as though he had found his ideal student – someone with nothing to unlearn, no technique, no taste, no expectations. Hansen was perfectly primitive, his dream non-musician thinking about music as though it had never existed before.

Hansen realised he had been following Cage's suggestions for fifteen years. Hansen performed what was referred to as an original happening when stationed in Frankfurt at the end of the Second World War: he pushed a piano off the top of a bombed-out four-storey building during an army show, just to see what it sounded like when it hit the ground. He would repeat the action over the next few years in many different locations, drops that would continue after his death in 1995, by which time he was mostly known as Beck's grandfather. In 1959, framing it as a percussion composition with implied links to Cage's raw percussion pieces and even his prepared piano, the sound of wood being smashed to pieces, the final, frenzied noises being made as strings, hammers, keys and pedals smashed to the ground, he gave it the title 'Yoko Ono Piano Drop' in homage to his friend.

The Yoko Ono who when asked why what she did was art would reply, off the top of her head, or someone else's head: well, what else could it be?

If Fluxus was a blueprint for the future – and why not, it was a significant trigger of a canonical decade of cultural change and social upheaval – then the loft was a blueprint for Fluxus, as a transmitter of ideas to other artists and artistic groups with their own blueprints for the future, and for the transmission of their ideas to wider mass culture.

The participants and performers, and those who contributed to the events by watching and listening, including Morton Feldman, Jasper Johns, Robert Rauschenberg, Earle Brown, Claes Oldenburg and Jim Dine, can make the series seem like some apocryphal way of encapsulating the connections, shared values and overlapping interactivity of a closely scattered but intensely varied network of soon-to-be-legendary avant-garde artists and musicians each responding to an intense environment and entering through the door of Dada via the classroom of Cage into a changed world they helped shape.

At the centre of this productive, mood-altering collision of genres, styles, art forms, structures, materials, philosophies, performances and texts, composed, meticulous maverick philanthropist La Monte Young, and off centre, Yoko, fancying something a little wilder and jarring, a little more abrupt and contradictory to complement or compete with Young's hyper-focused prophetic sonic curation, never quite coming out of the shadows in the long-term telling of the story, as though she was at the back of the class photo, stuck behind tall, mostly male conspirators and plotters, out of focus. Not completely belonging even at her own shindig.

Young was very particular about his musical choices, rejecting one Yoko suggestion because the composer still used crescendos. Yoko's own performances tended to be unannounced interventions, nebulous confessions, poetic ruses, melancholy musings, disposable paintings, offbeat party games and spontaneous asides, so that history doesn't record one specific performance of her work. There were just remembered rough fragments and droplets of gossip that suggested her contribution could be seen as an absurdist extension of her responsibilities as host inviting people into her personal space, and her responsibilities as an artist seeking more explicit collisions between the irreverent and the solemn, the transcendent and the stupid, the performance and the artist.

Maybe, feeling crowded out by all the men dominating the loft series, she was following through one of her mission statements at the time that included the observation that 'men have an unusual talent for making a bore of everything they touch'.

'Pea Piece' was a distortion of a Japanese exorcism ritual enacted in the month of February where she threw peas at people while flailing her hair, creating a percussive effect. It was based on the instruction to always carry a bag of peas and leave one wherever you go.

'Kitchen Piece' led in the loft to what would become 'Smoke Painting', both following instructions, starting with a quick dash to the fridge for some eggs and Jell-O, which she threw against loose white canvas and – with the addition of some ink – turned into an action painting. She then used a cigarette to set this on fire, the two pieces ending with the sad slow movement of the smoke, a form of memorial for the artwork and for art history, turning the life cycle of historic paintings that traditionally lasted for centuries into a few frantic seconds and a final, poignant visual sigh.

Some of her early instruction paintings and works in progress were exhibited around the loft, pinned to horizontally hung sheets of canvas, pieces of cryptic, trivial-seeming text that weren't forcing their way on people, and weren't formally part of the evening's art/entertainment. She also used some irregularly shaped leftover pieces of canvas laid on the floor and titled it 'Painting to Be Stepped On', based on an instruction where her lines of text were becoming less specifically about self-therapy and more about imagining an object or action, its beginning and its end, and often its impossibility except in the mind.

The work was still a survival gesture reacting to some childhood trauma or memory. She based the idea on fifteenth-century Japanese paintings of Christ used to distinguish between Christians and non-Christians. The Christians refused to stand on the painting of their Lord, and would be immediately taken away for crucifixion. Hearing the story as a child terrified her, caught between two religions each with its own gothic quality, but she promised herself if somehow the circumstances were ever repeated, she still wouldn't step on the painting, despite the consequences. She made the painting so she could step on it, to release herself from the pain of that scared little girl.

Inevitably, much was made of whether Duchamp on a visit to the loft had stood on the painting and, if he did, whether he was even aware he had, and was that conclusive proof given the Duchamp seal of approval that painting was extinct, or at least something you just threw on the floor, unless there was some kind of twist? If he had seen the canvas and deliberately stepped over it, what did that mean? The mind boggled.

Yoko's background loft pieces and paintings were almost subliminally supporting or enhancing the music, dance, spoken word and art objects that were part of the 'official' programme. It was the first time they would have been seen in public, and they were like pages torn from secret notebooks containing Yoko's hopes, wishes, deep secrets and fears, her need to make and find connections, to directly address and involve an audience, and to deal with problems and anxiety, to both follow the action and be the action. A stream of liberating images was emerging as Yoko began to grapple with the world and mythify it.

Yoko's cues, carousals and abstract incentives were as connected to Cage as Young's and Brecht's, and sometimes they ran in parallel – where Young wanted you to follow a straight line for as long as it took, Yoko wanted you to keep drawing a line that was part of a large circle until you disappeared. Her instructions were filtered through translating Cage's Zen-influenced one-liners and mottos into Japanese, and then back into English, giving them a more haiku-like quality, and elemental hints of *mono no aware*, which influenced her application.

Young's straight line led to significant acknowledgement of his contribution to the loft series, but Yoko's led to a disappearance. Yoko's temperament was to view the loft series as a communal activity with no particular leader, a shapeshifting melee of skills, capabilities and perceptions; Young's temperament was more controlling, and there was a sense that for all the artistic co-operation and social anarchy, he was in charge.

By the end of the run, they had a brief affair, their lines temporarily converging. In the end the early rumours of a man in charge and a compliant woman doing his bidding in an attempt to be noticed were not so far off the mark, or at least, there were certain emotional by-products emerging from a group of intense idealists on shared paths meeting regularly to put on new, mind-blowing performances that were causing something of a scene.

Wakowski left Young, and moved on to Bob Morris, who left Forti, and so on. As couples formed and couples dissolved, artists moved in and artists moved on and art kept coming, as if it was really starting to mean something. Nothing might happen, or something might: they may even take their work out of small underground venues and specialist galleries and around the world.

There was much collective movement and realignment as life and art intertwined and performers, oddballs, beginner artists and audience members combined and recombined, few of them prone to revealing their secrets easily, and something radically cathartic and metamorphic happened almost every day, which ultimately leaves gossip trailing in its wake, or even taking the lead. Everyone had their own version of the history, and some told it, and some didn't, and the histories clashed, overlapped and sometimes coincided and a version of history got told, and other histories disappeared.

A name would clarify this network of social relationships and common approaches to art-making that highlighted, among other things, playfulness, simplicity, internationalism, intermedia, ephemerality, an open forum of community and the unity of art and everyday life. A name could give the unnameable a sense of place even as it never settled down in one place.

Relatively speaking, as a couple Young and Ono lasted about as long as one of his drone works. No magical empire ensued, no meeting of muses. They didn't come up with a name for whatever venture it was they were part of: there was no Elastic Ono Band and no advanced echoes of a fateful union of art and music, of two minds resonating to each other's frequencies. One result was that Young would never acknowledge Ono's role in the story of the loft, which for her was as much a social, communally minded artistic project she shaped as it was a musical breakthrough for Young, taking him outside the Cage enclave and the little Cage groups he left behind into his own dominion, his own history.

They were as uncompromising and driven as each other, but while the loft series was part of Young's self-assured glide to gilded cult status if not riches, Yoko felt like she had to start all over again, battling embedded mid-century sexism, the difficulty of playing the games the men played while approaching the art of the time from an honest, unflinching female perspective. Before she could even be taken seriously as an artist attuned to the times, dealing with a world flying out of control, she had to prove that art was something that a woman could do. Young's determination and sometimes wild, wayward energy were seen as natural, hers as a little suspicious, dubious and unbecoming.

The Yoko Ono who over a decade later, the other side of all sorts of fame and fiasco, is still having to prove herself, that she's here as herself not as appendage, and remind those who were there or thereabouts during the loft series that she deserved some of the credit, that the series in a way was her first major artwork, an artwork in the guise of a series of innovative performances, crazy nights and sly ceremonies that helped her work out what kind of artist she was going to be.

During 1960 and 1961, as the loft series opened up downtown as a real and mythologised location associated with a new mode of artistic and musical behaviour, up and down Manhattan there were an increasing number of concerts, exhibitions, events and situations at various venues, featuring many of the loft's avant-garde cohort.

Loft composers and performers heading out from Cage and his coterie in different directions exchanged ideas and performed with each other around town, and started to head further out into the rest of the country. Together they provided cultural territory for new forms of artistic operators and cultural activists to emerge, artists who were also impresarios and philanthropists, performers who were also poets, painters who were also musicians, dancers who were also sculptors, misfits and outsiders who found their way inside without sacrificing their mutinous mentality.

Cage was the spectral leader and spokesman of this itinerant utopian district of Manhattan which changed position and aspect by the day, but he didn't act like a leader – sometimes more like a misleader. Just in case he was going to be pinned down as a leader, with all that meant, he withdrew from his teaching at the New School and moved away from the city.

He told people what to do and how and why, but imagining and hoping they would make up their own minds about what he meant. He had no intention of leading the society that had formed around him and his carefully cultivated ideological blankness; he saw his role if anything as being to help create settings for exploration and discovery, and encourage encounters with the new, unforeseen and unpredictable. If and when anything like that was established, he would then move on, or move to one side, and throw the dice again, pick a new straw, issue a new manifesto, disappear into the woods.

A leader of sorts, a confident, animated mover and shaker, appeared at the end of 1960. George Maciunas was even to the strangest artists and

236

thinkers a strange guy, a shapeshifting would-be artist and impresario, a showman extremist moving from venue to venue in search of the ridiculous and sublime, one of those characters who seemed to be in any number of different places at the same time, soaking up energy and revelling in the clash of ideas and ideals and the convergence of art and politics, intensity and light-heartedness. He was enthralled by those who defied categories, and New York at the time was the perfect place to pursue this as a mission in life, one that suited his almost maniacal personality, and an obsessive need to create order out of chaos, and chaos out of order.

Lithuanian-born Maciunas lived in Berlin until he was thirteen years old, when in 1944 his family fled to Lithuania to escape potential capture or worse from Allied forces, before migrating to Long Island, New York. He'd been working in the 1950s, not yet quite his decade, getting an interdisciplinary education, obtaining degrees in art, art history, architecture, graphic arts and musicology, and teaching himself a history of Russia and Marxist-Leninist ideology.

His student paintings were dashing, unremarkable abstractions, but a more striking visual sensibility emerged from his fascination with graphs, charts and diagrams, and his visionary talent as a graphic designer. He started mapping out a centuries-long history of artistic movements from Roman circuses and medieval fairs via vaudeville, Dada and Futurism that he idly imagined might culminate in a new movement he could be part of, even instigate.

He'd read the book about Marcel Duchamp's writings published in 1959, a co-operation between Duchamp and the French art critic and historian Robert Lebel. Its revelatory compilation and clarification of Duchamp's heretic thinking and comprehensive cataloguing of his work as patron saint of conceptualism and divine, dubious Dada master revived his reputation, began a period of relative canonisation and reached deep into the Cage milieu, including Yoko. For Maciunas, the book was a kind of Bible, a guide to exploiting the something in the air at the time that offered advice in code about how to get rid of everything annoying and uninspiring about art.

Maciunas savoured Duchamp's anti-institutional, anti-authorial, anti-aesthetic, anti-heroic anti-values, his elevated mastery of self-promotion, his lifelong presentation of art as a performance, his deadpan ability to combine holiness and transcendent originality with swindling, fraud and plagiarism. He studied his methods of using marginalia, boxes, various contraptions, notes, plans, letters and ephemera as artworks in themselves, and how the meaning of a work of art derived as much from what was around and outside it as it did from any of its content.

The book was another piece in a puzzle Maciunas didn't even know at the time he was working on about how to package, present and widely distribute particularly esoteric and scandalous forms of artistic faith and utopian ideology. It contained the essay 'The Creative Act', explaining how art is a dialogue between the artist and the intervention of the spectator – who with their own experience and understanding completes the work of art – and ultimately a dialogue with posterity. Duchamp gave as much importance to the viewer of a work as the maker – the impact of a work of art is not up to the artist; the artist is a sort of conduit for inchoate creativity.

The Duchamp book was part of a self-designed course in teaching Maciunas the spellbinding language of the avant-garde. Maciunas sat in on a couple of Cage classes, famous among those looking for an exit from the obvious, and attended Richard Maxfield's post-Cage electronic music lessons. He was endlessly fascinated with experimental minds and the way they connected with each other, making friends with his favourite extreme artists and composers, getting involved in any way he could to help – fundraiser, itinerary planner, publicist, philanthropist, agent, advisor, bodyguard, ultimately as abstract curator, strategic co-ordinator, information designer, Surrealist collector, hoarding archivist of everything, and entrepreneur with a zealous ideological streak.

He was finding unorthodox roles and necessarily inventing combinations of roles in the middle of New York's early-sixties avant-garde turbulence – promoter, publisher, designer, dilettante, all-round creative prima donna, hustler and visionary keeping up to speed with all manner of serious talents, prolific geniuses, tricky introverts and playful extroverts. He turned artist management, and the management of himself as artistic personality, into a form of practically minded magic realism.

He started to become something other than wishful-thinking observer, campaigning acolyte or enthusiastic audience member and inserted himself more forcibly into the lively underground scene after seeing what Ono and Young were doing at 112 Chambers Street, invited by Young after coming across him in Richard Maxfield's electronic music classes.

He had met Almus Salcius, the art-dealer nephew of the Lithuanian economist Petras Salcius, who founded a farmers' co-operative movement in 1930s Lithuania: its pro-community ethos was an early influence on the eclectically minded Maciunas, who envisaged a way to transfer its spirit into an artistic collective.

Almus ran a gallery out of his Long Island home exhibiting Eastern European artists and other immigrants, and with the irresistible Maciunas he opened the AG Gallery on Madison Avenue. It put on events starting in March 1961 of medieval and contemporary music, *Musica Antiqua et Nova*, but Maciunas the fan of Monteverdi and early music was soon more drawn to what Cage and Young and their associates were doing.

Maciunas hoped the gallery would be the base for his plans to make a name for himself by launching a distinctive equivalent of what was happening in Chambers Street, with dreams of reaching a wider audience and actually altering the world's collective consciousness, but he didn't yet have the contacts or the inside knowledge. As his new gallery faltered within weeks of opening, wishful thinking being ruined by practical considerations, he decided to essentially copy what Young and Ono were doing, pulling various artistic ventures into one place of activity, and see if it would work at the gallery.

Yoko first heard of Maciunas when a friend who had contributed to the loft series mentioned that someone was planning to do a similar thing at a midtown gallery he ran. She had apparently met him at her loft, but didn't remember, and her friends said if she wasn't careful, she'd be

239

finished, her ideas stolen by Maciunas – he's got all your artists, he's quite a character, they're lining up outside his gallery to appear.

She couldn't blame any of them as it wasn't as though they were contracted or had sworn some form of allegiance, and she would make appearances herself at other venues, never totally tied to the loft. She still felt a bit miserable that someone else was blatantly taking over the idea, but she was already feeling the loft series had come to an end, in its own way predictable enough to be kind of establishment even in its relative obscurity.

It had made its point, but many of the participants had already grown too big for it, especially Young. Their short relationship had soured things as well; a separation of interests happened as soon as it ended. The general sense was that Ono and Young's joint venture came to an end because he was frustrated with her choice of artists, which he felt was ruining the purity of his own judgement, and she was unhappy being in his shadow. It was presented as a classic case of 'creative differences'. She tried to stay positive.

The loft had helped release many of the Cage alumni into their own world, and the concerts had helped Yoko work out her ideas about ideas and ways to perform, present and stage them. She just needed to keep going.

As the loft showed its final concerts during June, Maciunas's replicas began with a Festival of Electronic Music starting, naturally, with John Cage, a series of concerts titled New Sounds and Noises and a series of literary evenings featuring Chambers Street regulars including Toshi, Byrd, Forti, Mac Low, De Maria and Young himself.

Young took his *Compositions* into the AG Gallery, which for a few weeks absorbed Chambers Street while Maciunas also fed off the knowledge of Young. He used him as a resource to gain access to an avant-garde coterie that seemed to him like a readymade movement, an appropriated densely packed citywide artwork in itself made up of independent, radically self-contained artists that with his skills as designer and his temperament to classify and dissect things could be turned, almost despite the wishes of the artists themselves, into a singular collective.

He imagined an historic art scene in the fast-moving modern Manhattan, with him motivating his prolific, prodigious artistic troops, existing at the same time as Impressionism, Cubism, Russian Constructivism, Futurism, Dada and Surrealism.

Before Yoko could even feel some resentment that she had somehow been expelled from a club of brave companions and allied misfits she had helped set up, she was contacted by Maciunas, who wanted to show her artwork in his gallery. He had Young in his sights, and he also wanted Ono, even if it didn't suit their own aims. For Yoko, it was great timing, and flattering that Maciunas was interested in her work, even if there was a possible catch.

From the outside, AG Gallery seemed a smart, well-funded midtown operation, but it was on the verge of shutting down: Maciunas had learned the hard way that for all the subversive glamour, there was no easy money in the avant-garde. Mostly, there was no money at all. Their business plan to host artists who would pay the gallery's rent for a month so they could put on events and shows was a non-starter. There was no money coming in, and in a last gasp of activity Maciunas put on a series of shows during July 1961 featuring various loft alumni.

There were two shows with La Monte Young playing a couple of his 1960 *Compositions*, some works by Walter De Maria, and one night with Henry Flynt delivering something like a lecture called 'Exercise-Awareness States', followed the next night by a programme to be decided depending on the reaction to the first show. Funds may have been running out fast, but Maciunas was getting a priceless, exclusive fast-track education in the avant-garde of the day, revealing how unlike previous avant-garde eruptions this one spiralled out from music, or at least music as remade as art object, as movement of the mind, by Cage.

When Yoko visited Maciunas at the gallery to talk about what her show would be, she found 'an obviously European, handsome man' with short hair and glasses that made him look intellectual whispering and giggling with a woman she described as young, beautiful and maybe his girlfriend. She turned out to be his mother, helping Maciunas out as receptionist and secretary.

They were in a room at the back of the dark gallery lit by candlelight, it turned out because Maciunas couldn't afford to pay the electricity bill. There were phones everywhere, because every time he got cut off for not paying the bill, he would use another name to order a new phone. A relatively cheap but to Yoko expensive-looking IBM Composer executive-model typewriter and typesetting system – Maciunas's instrument of choice as virtuoso typographer and graphic designer for hire – suggested a hint of money but turned out to be rented.

The tableau was almost like a performance piece, real enough, but also an illusion, staged to make Yoko feel at home in the kind of sterile art gallery she wasn't naturally drawn to. It was also the action of someone already writing the history of something that didn't yet exist, and maybe never would, but was more likely to if he was already writing the history.

The complicated, ambitious Maciunas was happy to allow Yoko to do what she wanted, and like her he belonged to the new Manhattan, but was also displaced, a first-generation American different from the Americans she was surrounded by. They both regarded America with an outsider's eye, and both saw it as a place where they could escape countries being taken over by unsympathetic, dominant outside forces, and create elaborate, insulated worlds of their own.

Maciunas from the beginning wanted his invented anti-capitalist, anti-elitist, non-competitive movement to have elements that came from outside America, and had seen how D.T. Suzuki's philosophy of the East had been distributed through various avant-garde media and disciples by John Cage. Ono actually was from the East, and she had her own integral methods of fusing the empowering epiphanies of Zen Buddhism and *mono no aware* with the technology, games and performative energy of the cross-pollinating downtown avant-garde.

A self-styled learning machine, Maciunas was quick to spot new trends and new ways of doing things, quick to join in from behind the scenes and adjust, adapt and recontextualise his borrowings, and quick to see that superficially Young, Brecht, Ono and others were doing very similar things with their processing of material, text, sound, concept and image, with their eye on an infinitely expandable universe, but each had their own distinct approach.

Young's was music-based, taking music as a starting point even when his scores took the performer or spectator beyond music. Brecht, originally a chemist who was then taken by Zen, distilled a multifarious happening event into a single line or two of text, or even a single word. His 'Solo for Violin, Viola, Cello or Contrabass' consisted only of the word 'polishing'.

Ono's would experiment impossibly and/or imaginatively with the everyday, a collision of a daydream with a modest everyday function, so her 'Tunafish Sandwich Piece' combines the imagining of a thousand suns in the sky shining for an hour and then gradually melting into the sky with the making and eating of a tuna sandwich.

Ono's approach to scoring was uniquely Japanese, and would become an important part in the early stirrings of his new community of ideas,

243

Maciunas's notional conceptual country, his avant-garde confederacy. Any next stage on from a Cage-directed male-centred collection of collectives needed immediate female, anti-masculinist input, to illuminate the intention that Maciunas's permanently provisional new version of the local niche community was open to everyone. If there was any sort of centre to what by its very nature was centreless, it should be female, the female of Yoko Ono, which only existed in a few minds. His idea of a positive movement certainly wasn't going to make women have to exist in a different cosmology to powerful men. Avant-garde at its truest was a gender in itself, containing all possible genders.

Avant-gardists might all be avant-garde and they might even influence and advise each other, but each individual avant-gardist has their own idea about what it is they do and how it connects or not with other artists and the history of art. They're on their own, even if they help each other be on their own. How to make that into something, effectively a brand, was the task Maciunas set himself, knowing full well that it mustn't appear like a brand, it mustn't appear fixed, somehow it must be named and nameless, a fluctuating community of customs featuring regular contributors trading information and sharing a number of social practices who themselves could be categorised as being keen to float free of categorisation.

Maciunas believed in the people who had the ideas that helped him fulfil his vision. He and Yoko were instantly intimately close friends, and Maciunas who in one way was an extreme control freak but was also a great believer in collaboration gave Yoko the confidence to develop her idea of instruction paintings, her novel application of language, still a half-formed idea.

He seemed to understand what she was doing even as she was working it out for herself, and she in turn understood what he was doing even as he was still working it out – if no one ever worked out what Fluxus was, it's because even those wearing an invisible Fluxus badge were always working it out. If Yoko contributed money for the gallery's rent, no one ever mentioned it, and the gallery was running out of time as a going concern.

244

She gathered thirteen paintings and objects that deconstructed the formality of a standard exhibition of artwork, conceptually consigning Abstract Expressionism, which for all its radicalism still involved politely hung canvases, to the past. She arranged the unframed canvases in various shades of grey as objects that had other functions than just being paintings. The canvas was a portal to the imagination, and Yoko was already exploring how she could create this portal without the obstacle of an artistic object, and all the associations that came with it.

These paintings with their muted colouring, dramatic brushstrokes and limited detail, an effect taken from historical Japanese calligraphy, could easily be seen as a form of American non-representative minimalism, emerging at the time and instigated by Robert Rauschenberg, seeing how far he could pull away from an image and still have an image, and Agnes Martin's geometric embodiment of light and air, atmosphere and expression.

This new painting wasn't yet called minimalism, but there was definitely something in the air, and Yoko didn't want to risk being absorbed, and possibly erased, by a movement or a school with her austere canvases which were more commentaries on the idea of using paint on a surface to communicate complicated spiritual ideas than simply images.

She began thinking she didn't necessarily need the canvases and paintings, but had not yet found a way to make them absent but still somehow exist in the mind of the viewer. Two of these spare paintings with suggestions of minimalism's retreat from solidity, the less expensive ones, did sell, as Maciunas felt they might, encouraging Yoko to make something of her Japanese-ness, exotic to art buyers, and to use the matt sumi ink often employed for calligraphy. The more experimental, rough-seeming unframed work had no takers. What could you do with it? There was nothing to hold on to, nothing to take away.

At first, she would accompany people around the exhibition and explain the function of each piece, but this was too clumsy. As involved as she was, she needed more distance: her shy, halting presence interfered with the imagination of the viewer. Talking over the images added more interference and she wanted less.

245

She asked Toshi to write some brief words on small cards to explain how each painting could be used, what it was based on, and he got around to writing out cards for 'Painting to Be Stepped On' and 'Painting in Three Stanzas', essentially transcribing her wishes for how the pieces could be completed.

'Three Stanzas', with ivy growing through two holes, had an instruction which explained that the painting would be finished when it was covered with leaves, or when the leaves wilted, or when it turned to ashes, and a new vine grew. 'Painting to Be Stepped On' could be completely destroyed by the action of doing what you were told, which was essentially to do what you couldn't do to a Pollock painting, where only Pollock was allowed to stand on the canvas.

For Yoko it was a response to the way Abstract Expressionist pictures and their painters were being reverently worshipped, and at the beginning of the 1960s, paintings in art galleries were still being looked at as though they were untouchable religious pieces. Yoko said, why not step on this painting and see what happens? Painting was turned into a do-it-yourself kit, only coming to life when a person followed the instruction. If they didn't, it was just a dirty canvas left on the floor. If they did, it was a new experience.

Sometimes the title – the long, calligraphic 'Painting until It Becomes Marble', the shadowy 'Shadow Painting' – was enough of a guide to what the painting was, and sometimes more was needed to prompt mental participation, so that 'Painting to Let the Dark in' and 'Painting to Let the Evening Light go through', both consisting only of the title etched into a glass window, were both title and instruction. They described themselves as being paintings, but avoided being paintings, and painting was replaced by imagination.

Later, Yoko would say that even though for some reason Toshi only completed two cards, this was enough proof that this was the first gallery showing of her *Instruction Paintings*. The next step was to take away the canvases and the objects, so that the *Instruction Paintings* were invisible paintings to be constructed in your head. There was nothing there but a

Wrapping. Yoko Ono wraps the composer La Monte Young in gauze, performing a version of 'Wrap Piece' during a Fluxus event in New York on 22 September 1965.
Getty / Fred W. McDarrah

Nothing. 'The Nothingness That Was Prior To The Universe' by the English mystic and physician Robert Fludd from his Ultriusque Cosmi in 1617. 'Et sic in infinitum' is written on each side of the black square – and so on to infinity.
Public domain / Wellcome Collection

Entertaining. Poster advertising the shadow theatre puppet show at the avant-garde cabaret club, The Chat Noir, opening in 1881. Alamy / Lebrecht Authors

Smoking. 'Mona Lisa Smoking a Pipe' by proto-Dadaist Eugène Bataille aka Arthur Sapeck, first published in the illustrated satirical magazine *Le Rire* (Laughter) in 1887. Public domain / Eugène Bataille

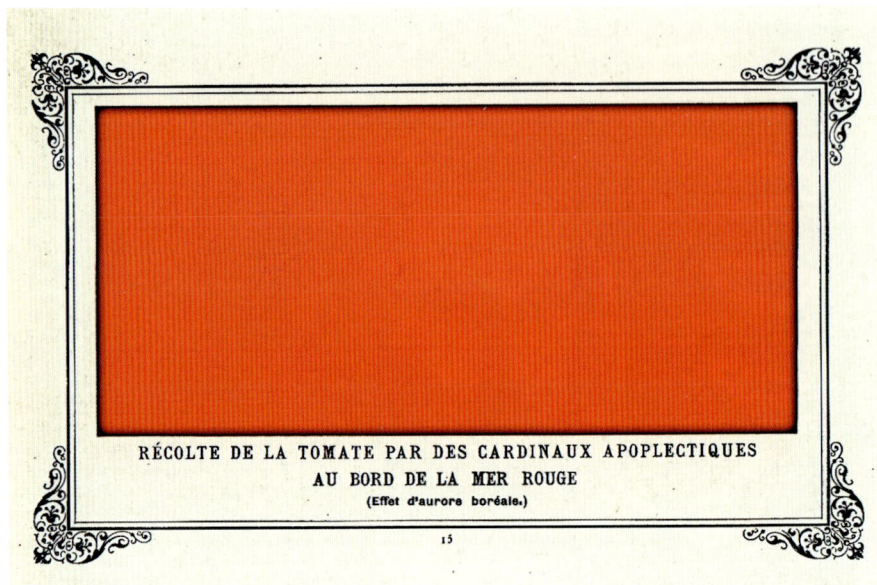

RÉCOLTE DE LA TOMATE PAR DES CARDINAUX APOPLECTIQUES
AU BORD DE LA MER ROUGE
(Effet d'aurore boréale.)

15

Seeing red. 'Apoplectic Cardinals Harvesting Tomatoes on the Shore of the Red Sea (Study of the Aurora Borealis)' by poet, fantasist and humourist Alphonse Allais, 1884, part of the Incoherents shows in Paris. Public domain / Alphonse Allais

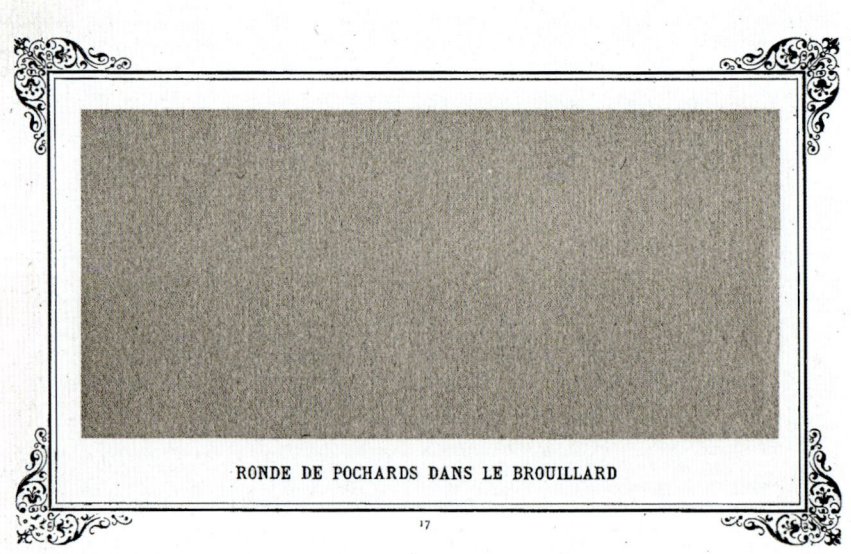

RONDE DE POCHARDS DANS LE BROUILLARD

17

Blanking. Allais' 1884 grey monochromatic painting, 'Band of Greyfriars in in the Fog', also known as 'Band of Dusty Drunks in the Fog'. Public domain / Alphonse Allais

Manifesto:

> **2.** To affect, or bring to a certain state, by subjecting to, or treating with, a flux. *"Fluxed* into another world." *South.*
> **3.** *Med.* To cause a discharge from, as in purging.
>
> **flux** (flŭks), *n.* [OF., fr. L. *fluxus,* fr. *fluere, fluxum,* to flow. See FLUENT; cf. FLUSH, *n.* (of cards).] **1.** *Med.* **a** A flowing or fluid discharge from the bowels or other part; esp., an excessive and morbid discharge; as, the bloody *flux,* or dysentery. **b** The matter thus discharged.

Purge the world of bourgeois sickness, "intellectual", professional & commercialized culture, PURGE the world of dead art, imitation, artificial art, abstract art, illusionistic art, mathematical art, —
PURGE THE WORLD OF "EUROPANISM"!

> **2.** Act of flowing; a continuous moving on or passing by, as of a flowing stream; a continuing succession of changes.
> **3.** A stream; copious flow; flood; outflow.
> **4.** The setting in of the tide toward the shore. Cf. REFLUX.
> **5.** State of being liquid through heat; fusion. *Rare.*

PROMOTE A REVOLUTIONARY FLOOD AND TIDE IN ART,
Promote living art, anti-art, promote NON ART REALITY to be fully grasped by all peoples, not only critics, dilettantes and professionals.

> **7.** *Chem. & Metal.* **a** Any substance or mixture used to promote fusion, esp. the fusion of metals or minerals. Common metallurgical fluxes are silica and silicates (acidic), lime and limestone (basic), and fluorite (neutral). **b** Any substance applied to surfaces to be joined by soldering or welding, just prior to or during the operation, to clean and free them from oxide, thus promoting their union, as rosin.

FUSE the cadres of cultural, social & political revolutionaries into united front & action.

Flowing. Fluxus Manifesto, George Maciunas, 1963. The George Maciunas Foundation

Cleaning. Radical Japanese artistic collective Hi-Red Center's 'Be Clean !', part of their 1964 campaign to Promote Cleanliness and Order in the Tokyo Metropolitan Area. Photo by Minoru Hirata © HM Archive. Courtesy of Taka Ishii Gallery Photography / Film

Freeing. Yoko Ono at work on *Film No.4 (Bottoms)* in art dealer Victor Musgrave's Mayfair townhouse, 1966. 'The 1960s was not only an age of achievements but also of laughter,' explained Yoko. Alamy / KEYSTONE Pictures USA

Hiding. 'Wrapping Event' in London's Trafalgar Square on 3 August 1967. Yoko Ono covered one of the Sir Edwin Landseer bronze lions at the base of Nelson's Column with dust sheets. Alamy / KEYSTONE Pictures USA

Seeing things. Yoko Ono with glass sphere gazing at the universe in her head, at the time of her 'Half-a-wind' exhibition at London's Lisson Gallery in 1967. Photograph © Clay Perry, England & Co / Artwork © Yoko Ono

cryptic piece of text describing what might be there if you wanted it to be. The instructions, the text, had become more important to Yoko than the making of a painting because instructions could generate the impossible, and they could be moved around: they didn't require fixed spaces.

The gallery showing was the point where Yoko decided to show just the instructions, marking her move into pure conceptualism. The canvas wasn't necessary – it was just a place mat, and you didn't need it to experience the idea. You just needed the idea. The idea presented in a certain way made something original and irreplaceable exist.

She was looking for something alive that existed between poetry and painting, between word and image, between place and fantasy. She was inventing herself as an artist who created outlines that produced unique, unrepeatable events, open-ended frameworks intending to generate heightened awareness, unplanned results and entertaining enlightenment.

There was built-in madness as well, because the more defiant experimental artists intentionally acted out madness in order to stop becoming mad. 'The whole world was about to go insane, so I was sure there were other people that needed these instructions that would get you involved in something rather than paintings and sculptures that you're just allowed to look at.' After you'd seen them, all you had left was memories. With her minimalism you still had memories, of something you were involved in creating.

Almost jokingly following gallery etiquette, once the canvases and ink drawings were haphazardly arranged around the gallery, leaning against exposed brick walls or white plastered walls or on the worn floor, Maciunas put a random price next to each artwork. There was nothing to buy, really: they weren't meant to be objects you could own; they were ephemeral gestures that you owned by imagining them, not by buying them. In that sense, they were free, take it or leave it.

Yoko and Maciunas's own imagining was that they might actually sell one of Yoko's pieces, which seemed one way of finishing one of these paintings. What were they going to do then? At the time, Yoko was a starving artist, rejecting her family's banking money to feel free of

247

obligations and their expectations. Four hundred dollars would take them to Europe. Just thinking about it made them believe someone had actually bought one, which made them as happy as though someone had.

It was a hot summer, and very few people came along, just some friends and the occasional bored or curious passer-by, so few Yoko could count them on the fingers of one hand. This meant that giving a personal guided tour to visitors was a practical proposition, including John Cage, who dropped by and listened attentively as Yoko explained 'Smoke Painting' to him – a scrappy section of canvas with a hole in it where you inserted a candle or cigarette and set it alight, letting it smoulder until it burned of its own accord, slowly, peacefully destroying the canvas.

Showing it to Cage, she snuffed out the smoke once the idea was clear. Cage perhaps simplified the concept in his mind by imagining that there was no canvas, no smoke, no Yoko explaining it to him, just a small card with a description of the idea, allowing you to react and interpret it however you wanted. You could envision your own reality, go in whatever direction you wanted.

Perhaps as she watched Cage calmly watching the canvas burn like incense, lost in his own thoughts, she came to the same conclusion. She didn't need to be there. The canvas, the smoke didn't need to be there. The intention was to reduce it to dust anyway. All you needed to do was give an instruction that opened up the possibility of such an idea.

Despite the small audiences, during the run, Yoko and Maciunas used to walk around the city, which was quiet at that time of the year, and feel good, feel in control, in touch with something special that only they could feel, like they owned the city. Or maybe not the city, but something intangible, something happening they couldn't put into words.

The Yoko Ono who worked out, either as charlatan or visionary, a random amount of lazy or ingenious short cuts to transcendence.

As the money ran out, Yoko's daytime show ran on the same days as the evening events with Young, Flynt and De Maria, leading to the final event at the gallery by another Maciunas favourite, Ray Johnson, the mysterious, contrarian pop art pioneer and Black Mountain College student of Bauhaus modernist Josef Albers.

Johnson's obsessive, exquisite collages with roots in Duchamp, the Italian Futurists, Joseph Cornell and Kurt Schwitters set him up as one of the first to sample and remix the beguiling verbal and visual sensations of an emerging popular culture, drawing from a variety of sources including James Dean and Elvis Presley and already mythologising them with explicitly queer relish. He was featured in the first issue of *Village Voice* in October 1955, in a piece that asked what a 'moticos' was. 'Ray Johnson, 27, invented it, and he doesn't know either.' 'Moticos' was his anagram of osmotic, what he called his collages, which he viewed as recombinations that could then be further recombined, so that the images were perpetually in motion.

A book cover he designed for a 1957 New Directions paperback edition of poet Arthur Rimbaud's *Illuminations* poetically stole and remixed a black-and-white photo of ultimate *enfant terrible* Rimbaud as a seventeen-year-old in 1871 into a hallucinatory, sacred combination of ghost, icon, movie star, noble savage, outlaw, teenage dreamer, martyr, avant-garde aboriginal, proto-punk and time traveller.

Cropping and enlarging the original made the grain of Ben Day dots strategically visible years before they appeared in Roy Lichtenstein's pop art explosions. Lichtenstein's dots confirmed what Johnson's dots were doing, representing the mass-produced nature of popular culture and manipulating a technique for gradual shading and block colours in industrial printing first invented in the same decade Étienne Carjat took the Rimbaud portrait.

249

Johnson's respectfully radical treatment of a found, phantom nineteenth-century image, and the lettering he used on the book cover, produced an imagined first ever 1960s rock-and-roll star, a template for mutant countercultural attitude, something that jumped across time and would still burn into a lonely soul in the sixties, the seventies, the eighties and beyond – Rimbaud was newly discovered by a generation who knew just what to do with his words and magic, and was turned into a free-form performance piece as it unravelled across decades, and Johnson came along for the ride.

He transferred Rimbaud's rebel romantic anti-hero image deep into the twentieth century, into the back pocket of Jim Morrison's skin-tight brown leather pants, into the complicated mind of Bob Dylan, into the nervy hands of Patti Smith, stealing a copy at sixteen, seeing the cover in a bookshop near the bus depot in Philadelphia, falling in lust with whoever that was, and thinking, that's where I want to go, some place between bloody murder and damned majesty. The book changed her life and when she moved to New York in 1967 to become an artist, or poet, or star, or all three, she pinned the cover above her writing desk.

As if aware what he had produced was work of art as much as book cover, Johnson discreetly signed it R. Johnson in the top right corner, with hints of Duchamp's R. Mutt.

Johnson's central accomplishment, what made him famous for not being famous, was his creation of what was called, not by him, mail art. Instead of using galleries to show his work, he sent small letters and postcards of his moticos and altered images – and of his translated, continually transformed Rimbaud – through the mail to various recipients with instructions to add something to it and/or forward the piece on or back to him, creating a network of artists, friends and strangers.

He called this chain-letter art the mock-institutional New York Correspondence School as a play on the straight-faced New York School, as if it was both a school of art, as in a movement or an art school, and a correspondence school. He turned his love for the US Postal Service and his fetish for liking things into a conceptual enterprise, an adventure in communication, a form of broadcasting, a social interface.

Johnson was a proto-influencer, a lone social media platform paying close attention to everything that happened around him and distributing his self-curated mail-network identity and the extent of his interests, taste and discoveries, half a century before digital-age cyber-culture emerged. He used public means of communication – the postal system, newspapers, printed material – to reach as wide an audience as possible, although at the time there was no way of discovering how many 'followers' he accumulated.

As an artist in the fifties he was lost in the shadows of his Black Mountain classmates Jasper Johns and Robert Rauschenberg, but was intellectually and emotionally agile enough to find ever-evolving, chaotically creative new roles in the new avant-garde Maciunas was speculating on, even if he was still happy to stay in the shadows, fearful that the haphazard energy of fame and money would spoil his work's dazzling, uncompromising cohesion.

From the margins, as a roving avant-garde investigative journalist, a happy hunter of everyday moments, he could observe as much as participate, finding at every turn a parade of odd and lovely, disturbing and weird, awkward and transcendent, enthralling and annoying experiences, and finding ways to sort, annotate and arrange them.

He was quick to react to Allan Kaprow's messy, exuberant happenings, which came after his own experiments with improvised performance, with his own darker, starker anti-version – nothings, performance art applications of Cage's '4'33"' and the 'nothing to be done', 'nothing is certain', 'all is in flux' absurdism of post-war Samuel Beckett.

He would use various objects – pieces of wood, cardboard boxes and hotdogs – and over a period of time, sometimes just a few seconds, he would make nothing happen, leaving a disoriented audience waiting for something to happen until it dawned on them it wouldn't, or putting obstacles in their way so they couldn't get inside the room where a performance was allegedly taking place.

251

The audience, left to its own devices, coming together to process what hadn't happened, the nothing that took place, was the event: Johnson was finding something, anything, to give the impression that we exist, the illusion of stability. The best answer to anyone who asked what happened during a nothing was 'nothing'. Except something had happened – it just needed thinking about.

Ray Johnson was aesthetic clown, con man, idiot savant, holy fool, needy iconoclast, damnably elusive, discreet show-off, playful antagonist, manically prolific, lonely prophet, obscure celebrity, dancing spirit, mercurial comedy genius, camp Surrealist, counter-logical activist, intense absurdist and ever-more eccentric who was one thing and many things, who did one thing and many things and let his art take on a life of its own. His rarefied, disruptive, non-aligned American energy would range across Andy Warhol, Elaine Sturtevant, the Merry Pranksters, Kenneth Anger, Vija Celmins, Joe Brainard, Faith Ringgold, John Waters, John Cale, Jonathan Richman, Judy Chicago, Cindy Sherman, the Residents, Devo, Andy Kaufman, Thomas Pynchon, David Lynch, Matthew Barney, Beck, Daniel Johnston, Jeff Koons and Childish Gambino.

For Johnson, art was action, it should always be on the move, it should cover and uncover everything, it was a down-to-earth, monumental free-form exchange, finding gender-fluid internationalist safe spaces in a world hostile to otherness. Art was its own punchline. His creation of a self-contained universe that was indirectly connected to the outside world – mirroring his instant understanding of how pop culture and fine art were intrinsically connected – made a big impression on Maciunas and his own ephemeral social art campaigning, especially how Johnson sometimes to a dangerous extreme saw existence as a game with rules made up as you went along and consistently blurred the boundaries of life and art.

Eventually, Johnson decided when to finish his art-as-life on his own terms, defiant to the end, apparently committing suicide in January 1995 in such a way that it could be read all at once as deliberate, an accident, a drowning, a myth, his final performance, a mystery and most of all, nothing.

Appropriately, the AG Gallery ended during the day with Yoko's fallen, disintegrating paintings and haiku-like prompts, her particular undoing of painting and performance, and at night, an audience waited, not sure where to look, before Johnson threw a box of wooden spindles down the gallery's staircase and then . . . nothing. Together, they made an X-ray of what was to come in the eyes, mind, hands and brain of Maciunas.

The whatever, the never known, the always shifting parameters, the sense and nonsense, audacity and diversity of what became known as Fluxus were always threatening to become something in the interstitial spaces of the Manhattan arts. It kept stop-starting, the memory of where it might have begun to begin was always changing, but the month of June 1961 at the AG Gallery, because now Maciunas had arrived, taking control of the uncontrollable, directing a coterie of near-anarchists, even as his first venture ended in failure, in nothing, is, in this paragraph, where art history leapt off the walls ready to run riot, in a cornucopia of hybrid applications.

Perhaps, in this story, Maciunas's dream first entered reality when on a small table near the front of his short-lived gallery, he left a pile of beautiful-looking postcards and small panels with random messages and thoughts that he had designed, and used his architectural training to make a vaulted ceiling for the gallery using translucent stiff paper, an everyday material. His inventive graphic design, schooled in Dada typography, revolutionary socialist thinking and mainstream product design, was unlike anything at the time, and more sophisticated than any expensive commercial branding, giving an immediately distinctive look to his new thing which needed other artists, many in opposition to him but somehow connected, to be truly new.

There was a new-born entity, it was alive, it had parents – quite a few, weirdly, but one in particular, playing the part of midwife, den mother and godfather – it had a personality, and now the difficult part. What to call it? What to call the unnameable?

Nothing, said Ray Johnson. Find out for yourself, said Yoko.

To himself, and a few confidants, Maciunas had thought of it as Neo-Dada, which gave it a historical dimension, which was good, but also bad, because it made it seem like a revival, which implied cultural exhaustion, a sense there was nothing new to be done, which compromised an originality that was emerging because time and place, and technology, were all different. It was inaccurate, a bad label, which was no good for anyone, not even lovers of labels.

Dada was based in 'disgust', Maciunas's Neo-Dada was based in New York, it was an affirmative endeavour, and there were rumours Dada's supreme co-founder and most active propagandist Tristan Tzara didn't approve of this tenuous brand extension. So that was that.

In the end, it was beyond words, it was influenced by life more than any other art movement, Duchamp was ancestor as much as meta-mentor, but a name was found in a list of words, the dictionary, just as Tzara, or Hugo Ball – nothing is certain – randomly and then deliberately had found 'dada' in a French–German dictionary, which brought with it a positive yes, yes, a calming there, there, hobby horse, nursemaid, a foolish naivety, and ultimately, nonsense. Tzara's aggressive celebration and broadcasting of the word alone transformed Dada into an eternal, undiminished emblem of avant-garde reality, and the two Ds and the two As became its most visible representative.

As graphic designer and therefore in some form propagandist, Maciunas was thinking of Dada as a suggestive word that became part of the world through the ingenious artistic and administrative persistence of Tzara. He was desperate for a word, his own word, that would work for something that was an information centre and consciousness raising, a non-group and a collective manifestation, an interaction of independents, a forum that relied on his enthusiasm but could have existed without him. Maciunas came across Fluxus, or Fluxus came across him, even before he knew he needed such a word.

The word worked as a noun, verb and adjective and brought with it a cascade of meanings including purge, tide and flow. It sounded cathartic. Didn't the French philosopher of creativity, change and freedom Henri

Bergson form a concept of lived time, which he saw as a continuous variation and flux, constantly opening doors in the mind?

It was Latin for flowing, representing the fluid and indeterminate, it contained the flux of change, it meant to affect, or bring to a certain state, by subjecting to or treating with flux, or any substance or mixture used to promote fusion. Tzara used 'dada' to create Dada, and Maciunas would use 'fluxus' to create Fluxus. In his dreams . . .

First signs of the word emerged when Maciunas and a group of Lithuanian immigrants planned a Lithuanian cultural journal at the end of 1960 with his AG Gallery partner, and he had the name at the back of his mind during 1961 as he was trying to raise money for a magazine titled *Fluxus* to be produced with Dick Higgins to expose 'the good things being done' in New York. He tentatively mentioned it to Yoko while they were preparing her show.

He was saying to Yoko, we have to think of a name for this movement that is beginning to happen, Higgins's 'good things'. Yoko didn't think of what they were doing as a movement, and the word movement sounded dirty to her, something that at best could lead only to arguments and divisions, at worst to some kind of self-defeating cult. It sounded like a negative company that would require rules, regulations, member numbers and photo ID. A movement meant being part of the establishment, encouraging exactly the sort of privilege they were questioning.

Maciunas giggled when he said he liked 'fluxus' because it also sounded like it meant the flushing of a toilet, and 'flux' rhymed with 'fucks'. Yoko still wasn't impressed. She didn't think a formalised movement was a good idea, even if the name flushed it away as soon as you mentioned it.

This is the name, said Maciunas, flashing some of the authoritarian side of his personality. 'I shrugged my shoulders in my mind,' she remembered, and then never heard the word again for a while.

The Yoko Ono who lived a hard, charmed life.

255

After the gallery shut down, Maciunas wondered how to take forward his loose-knit movement so loose it wasn't a movement and didn't have a name, not even in the only place where whatever it was existed, his mind. He now knew a diverse collection of artists from different disciplines with similar artistic philosophies, and made sure to keep in contact, to see what help they could be to his idea, and what help he could be to theirs.

Cage noticed at the time that the experimental art scene had split into a number of directions, none more or less important than the others. Artists going in different directions doing their own thing were still a part of what was going on. There was a radically open form of community building, but also a number of individuals in their own world with their own interests. Maciunas emerged as the main sponsor and promoter, connecting them all together if only in his head.

As Maciunas made plans to publish an ambitious, elaborate catalogue to present the mobile cultural centre of artists associated with Chambers Street and AG Gallery alongside coverage of the most advanced worldwide art, music, dance, poetry, film and design, La Monte Young and Jackson Mac Low were invited to guest-edit an East Coast edition of the San Francisco-based Beat poet magazine, *Beatitude*. Maciunas heard about their plans when he was taking photographs of them both to publicise the gallery.

Asked to do whatever they wanted, they decided to build on a collection of event scores, instruction-based work, poetry, concrete poetry, dance constructions and essays from America, Europe and Japan that they already had. It would be the loft series given form, a concrete way of co-ordinating decentralised activities, a definitive survey of contemporary avant-garde pursuits and a new generation of experimental artists mapping compositional processes onto all visual arts, with the inclusion

256

of Henry Flynt's theory of concept art and De Maria's 'Meaningless Work', an extension of Cage's purposeful purposelessness, art concerned with process for its own sake.

It was exactly what Maciunas was thinking, recognising the role print culture could achieve in publicising the ineffable and indefinable. When *Beatitude* East failed to materialise, Maciunas opportunistically volunteered to help turn the fastidious collection of avant-garde enterprise into a publication, which he would publish, giving him instant collaborative contact with what he would make the basis for his vision.

Working with Mac Low on the graphically exuberant, multi-coloured and visually sophisticated design for the book, which became its own beautiful utilitarian example of the messages and missions inside, would give Maciunas material for the development of the manifesto and abstract constitution for the movement forming in his mind, that had to represent artists whose instinct was to avoid belonging to a movement and standing behind one particular set of statements and intentions.

The compendium's full title was *An Anthology of chance operations art anti-art indeterminacy improvisation meaningless work natural disasters plans of action stories diagrams music poetry essays dance constructions mathematics compositions*. Yoko was part of the cast list of artists Maciunas was now incorporating into a scene he was beginning to invent, contributing 'To George, Number 18'.

It went under the heading 'Poetry', but was more anti-poetry, or an anti-painting, a poem nearly obliterated by black ink, or a poem emerging from black ink, an example of the kind of dematerialising monochrome paintings or opaque images Yoko was making at the time, existing in a limbo between her written instructions to be finished off possibly in the real world and actual paintings to be finished off in the mind.

Money problems – Maciunas sold his stereo system to Dick Higgins to help raise funds for printing – and various distractions and scheduling problems meant the anthology wasn't published until 1963. Its thousand copies took two and a half years to put together, printed page by page in chaotic slow motion and collated by hand.

257

For movement-builder Maciunas the book, published once the Fluxus name was becoming established, was a pre-Fluxus publication that contained a provisional membership of idea-forming artists who belonged to him, and therefore to everyone. *An Anthology* was for Maciunas as much a guide to the ins and outs, the this and that of Fluxus as it was what it was originally conceived to be.

He made no specific contribution to the content, but he was on every page, channelling a multiplicity of artists and authors through his sensibility, via his IBM typewriter font, Univers, which became the semi-permanent Fluxus font, and the dancing title headings, producing a single consistent artistic vision.

Univers had been designed in 1957 by the influential Swiss typeface designer Adrian Frutiger based on an 1898 typeface, Akzidenz Grotesk, and adapted by Frutiger for IBM. He designed an austere, undecorated modernist typeface for everyday use that would be felt more than perceived, so that you could see it everywhere but not notice it. It was a designer's font, and because of its crisp cleanness it would be used during the sixties and seventies for corporate branding, signage – London's street-name plaques – maps, exams and testing and electronic devices. Apple used it for its keyboards until 2007.

Asked in 2018 what was her favourite typeface, Yoko answered that she loved the one that George Maciunas used all the time. He demonstrated his virtuosity at using type and his love of type in a variety of ways, once advertising a concert with '12! Big Names' which consisted of twelve artists' names displayed on a screen in large type, none of whom were booked to appear.

It became the template for how he would function as leader of a leaderless society, giving it a visual identity through design and typography, and an overall meta-artistic ideological framework and a spirit of play, that both contained and liberated a multitude of artists with their own separate ideological or non-ideological commitments, many of whom had their own issues with Maciunas's methods and personality.

Maciunas took creative control of the Fluxus cause and laid its foundations through his professional experience as a designer tackling a variety of commercial assignments, from the tiniest task like a business card to a complete branding job. Advertising his services as a one-man graphic design business, even as he was directing Fluxus, he would list 'trademarks, logos, letterheads, envelopes, mail-pieces, posters, announcements, 3-D announcements, 3-D displays, exhibits, environments, packaging, labels, box-design, books . . . magazines, newspapers, etc.'.

This summed up how he put Fluxus into the world, treating it as a job, founded on his skills at packaging, collaging, setting type and making decorative products using recycled card and paper. In this case, he didn't charge for his services, always making sure, whatever he worked on and whoever he worked for, that he produced things cheaply, being keen to make things, especially art, affordable for everyone.

Debts and delays in the printing of *An Anthology* forced Maciunas to Germany on military transport in November 1971, working by day in the graphic design office at the United States Army and Air Force Exchange Service based in Wiesbaden, West Germany, and setting up a centre of Fluxus operations by night.

The day job paid for subversive night-time activities, with the army financing his utopian dream – he used its postal system to send communications at reduced rates to artists, and to collect contributions. He earned just enough to afford to pay for him and his mother to live in a room together. She knew little about his night-time pursuits, just as the artists he persuaded to join in with his vision knew next to nothing about his army work.

Back in New York, Young and Mac Low patiently assembled *An Anthology*, with Maciunas, apologising for having to leave, sending via the Army Post Office various materials, visual signals and the cover design from Germany.

While in Germany, on the run, acting as though he was just over a bridge from Manhattan, he organised a series of festivals presenting a mix of avant-garde performers in the spirit of Chambers Street and AG Gallery, still pursuing the idea of an international tendency, a living collage, a constellation of free-thinking artists and ultimately a way of life. Maciunas found in a post-conflict country only a few years after Allied occupation, recovering from possibly terminal cultural disruption, an opening for his ideas, an American import but deflected into something else by his Lithuanian background.

Geographically displaced, which suited him and the artists he identified with, he was still finessing his version of the avant-garde as a kind of anti-avant-garde, a rear-guard energy that resisted being a school or dogma and would dissolve as soon as it became predictable.

He had been thinking about featuring the artists he'd gathered in Germany in a follow-up to *An Anthology*, which Young wasn't interested in, even before that had been published. He was still attached to the word Fluxus, and was going to use it for the new publication, which would become *Fluxus 1*, and for the festival that accompanied it. As with *An Anthology*, *Fluxus 1*, more a collection of pages and two-dimensional and three-dimensional objects, took longer than expected to make, not least to commission artists to produce work specifically for it, and then get them to meet deadlines.

He decided to do a series of concerts and festivals as advance publicity for whatever they were going to produce or publish to sell. The publications were initially intended to be the central core activity of Fluxus, a combination of encyclopedia, anthology, almanac, reference work, index and container for any loose items, objects and envelopes, and a way of spreading the word of Fluxus and co-ordinating an imagined community, first of all consisting of the artists represented in the book, and then of the people who bought the book. The performances and concerts were created to advertise the books and periodicals, which were their own research programmes for possible performances and concerts.

Fearing that if too much time passed he would lose momentum, with both Young's *Anthology* and now his *Fluxus 1* taking time to appear, he started a series of Fluxus newsletters, essentially progress reports, based on memorandum designs he had used in the 1950s for corporate clients. If it turned out all Fluxus consisted of was a series of plans that never came to fruition, a grand non-movement collapsing under its own

260

emotional, dysfunctional weight, then these newsletters, by recording the plans, and other possibilities, some of which might never exist, were in the true Fluxus spirit of making the world a better, more marvellous place by imagining such a place, even if it ended up invisible. They were like Fluxus scores, instructions about what to think, or what might happen if, and what was about to happen, if and when . . .

In May 1962, seven or eight months after he arrived in Germany, Maciunas sent out 'News-Policy-Letter No. 1', which opened with an explanation of its own current position:

> Due to: (1) rapidly changing events, (2) increase in number of FLUXUS Yearbook and festival collaborators, (3) time consumed in typing all there [*sic*] developments to each separately, and (4) high cost of letter postage, it is found necessary from now on to issue 'News-Policy-Letters' printed periodically of which this will be No. 1.

The memorandum listed its recipients on the cover page. At left, a box set off the roster of Fluxus's co-editors, a combination of collaborators from New York – including Toshi Ichiyanagi, who had recently relocated to Japan – and new contacts in Europe, such as Nam June Paik and Wolf Vostell. A much longer column at right included, among others, Anna Halprin, Simone Forti, Robert Morris, György Ligeti, Mauricio Kagel, Karlheinz Stockhausen, Dieter Roth, Piero Manzoni, Robert Filliou, Cornelius Cardew, Williams, Ben Patterson and, of course, Cage. Over the document's fourteen pages, Maciunas laid out his plans for upcoming publications and concerts. He signed off as 'George Maciunas, for Fluxus administration'.

For a few months in 1962, even as artists who would directly or indirectly become Fluxus, or Fluxus by proxy, or by reputation, kept working on their own project, Fluxus was its newsletters, which meant Fluxus was basically Maciunas trying to keep in touch with the fulfilment of a Fluxus dream, and keep it alive by acting as though it already was. If he didn't believe, who else would?

He sent out invitations on Fluxus-headed stationery to potential contributors, requesting their 'esteemed participation in our effort to publish an international periodical dedicated to a new tide in art, music, literature etc.', including some definitions of the word. He organised concerts in Wuppertal and Düsseldorf that continued the music series at his AG Gallery, but the name Fluxus didn't become part of their presentation – he delivered a lecture referring to what was happening in New York as Neo-Dada, and the title of the first concert was 'Après John Cage' and the second 'Neo-Dada in der Musik'. It wasn't Fluxus time quite yet.

He was still believing there would be a Fluxus publication, and announcing it in a newsletter distributed to interested parties made it a possibility, or at least a task to be completed, something to keep the faith. As Maciunas sent out further newsletters, the use of the name Fluxus shifted from the name of a forthcoming periodical to indirectly becoming the name of a concert series.

There were some already experimenting in Germany with the same attitudes and methods Maciunas was developing in Lower Manhattan. Experimental music emerged from the military bases in Wiesbaden and Darmstadt, the latter home to an annual International Summer Course in New Music; experimental artists were earning a living doing creative jobs to order for the army, rebelling in the extreme when off duty, in a depleted post-war setting only seventeen years after the final fall of National Socialism. A pre-Fluxus spirit existed in Darmstadt, and in Cologne, where the German artist Mary Bauermeister ran evenings in her attic studio as an alternative to one held in the city by the International Society for Contemporary Music.

Bauermeister had seen John Cage booed off stage on television playing music that emotionally and intellectually made more sense to her than the more academic contemporary music being played at the ISCM, where modern music was still seen as being Webern and Schoenberg, and premieres of uncompromising, interrogative post-serial work and orchestrated happenings by Pierre Boulez and her future partner, Karlheinz Stockhausen, were presented as though uneasy revolutionary music still belonged in sterile, smothering concert halls.

Stockhausen himself felt more comfortable with the less demure, more unruly atmosphere in Mary's attic, where the latest new music by younger

263

composers emerging from Darmstadt, a lot of it rejected by the purist ISCM jury, found a more suitable venue.

As with Chambers Street and the AG Gallery, experimental music as an educational programme expanded into provisional performance art and vice versa, and led to chancy, hot-headed one-off collaborations between genres. It reflected the same desire that there was in Japan and New York after the war to create something so radically new and indefinable it would escape the clutches of authoritarian forces, and so fluid and mobile it couldn't be shut down and censored or wiped out altogether.

In 1960, as a preview of an art world to come, Bauermeister had put on the Contre-Festival, inviting Stockhausen, Cage and various people who would be associated with Fluxus, including La Monte Young and the Korean future video and multimedia artist Nam June Paik.

Paik had travelled to Germany after graduating from Tokyo University in 1956, where he studied philosophy and music, writing a thesis on Schoenberg. Trained as a classical pianist, which limited his restless ambitions, he wanted to explore the artistic possibilities of sound, and studied at the pioneering, technologically advanced Westdeutsche Rundfunk Studio for Electronic Music, which had become a meeting place and research laboratory for international avant-garde composers, including Stockhausen, György Ligeti, Cornelius Cardew and Mauricio Kagel.

The studio was the first of its kind in the world and the first to make music without conventional instruments. It was founded six years after the end of the Third Reich as part of a public broadcasting institution, WDR, to make a case for how liberal and progressively open-minded post-war Germany was going to be. The studio continued work that experimented with radio, film sound and electronic music abolished by the Nazis as degenerate in the mid-1930s: the manipulating and manufacturing of non-acoustic sound was part of the temporarily paused German twentieth-century musical tradition, a tradition that eventually pulsed into mainstream culture through the conceptual electronic mindset of Kraftwerk.

Work in the studio typified how new music wasn't now a case of writing down notes but of finding and inventing sounds. Composers and technicians using the facility to discover these new sounds found themselves discussing the relationship between technology and the imagination in small rooms that were part science labs, part rehearsal rooms and part smoke-filled bohemian bars.

Paik revelled in what he called 'the court of Mary'; he was prepared for the occasional mayhem and unselfconscious, impromptu actions that came with the new music, having encountered John Cage and David Tudor at Darmstadt in 1958. In an hour or so he went from being bewildered by their anarchic, whimsical-seeming processes and noisy randomness to being a completely liberated convert to how Cage was reflecting on the materials and function of music through music itself. He gleefully covered himself in Cage magic dust.

He said his life began the evening he saw Cage; 1957 to him was 1 BC. Before Cage it had been difficult to imagine combining a speculative trial-and-error sensibility with electronics in any sort of artistic production. After Cage, there was nothing to stop a hybrid of ancient and electronic forms, folk art and high art, East and West, objective and subjective time, light-heartedness and deep thinking, dissolution and change, possibility and impossibility. Paik became more himself by becoming Cageian in the way Cage had become more himself by becoming Duchampian who had become more himself by becoming Duchampian.

Paik had a crash course in perception-altering transdisciplinary performative and permissive post-Cage proposals, as well as being immersed in the technological developments and future-predicting electronic work at WDR. It would lead to his prescient and spiritual use of technology as a canvas and the television as a tactile and multi-sensory object. The television replaced the piano as his instrument, a sculptural object that could also contain endless objects and events and endless ways of combining them. He had an ambition to 'shape the TV screen as precisely as Leonardo, as freely as Picasso, as colourfully as Renoir, as profoundly as Mondrian, as violently as Pollock and as lyrically as Jasper Johns'.

265

While electronic media was in the early stages of development, often seen as a novelty or a cold, alienating product of scientific processes, Paik believed in it as a democratic instrument built for cultural transmission, an extension of nature and what it was to be human. He could see how technology was becoming the body's new membrane of existence, even if at the time the television set was the outer limits, and Google, TikTok and X were as unlikely as immortality.

In the attic of Bauermeister, Paik made it clear he was the kind of intense but playful refugee artist of interest to Maciunas in the middle of an increasingly unstable action recital, 'Étude for Pianoforte', which ended with an assault on the piano and a leap from the makeshift stage to cut off the tie of imperturbable audience member John Cage and pour shampoo over his head. Paik then fled the building, phoning Mary a few minutes later to inform her the concert was over. Other pieces for the fortunately adventurous Bauermeister included epic pieces of audience participation, the apparent attempted asphyxiation of an audience member and sudden embarking on stripteases.

Before Paik had even encountered Maciunas he was already asking the question 'what is Fluxus?' and perhaps already giving a right answer – Fluxus is the constant asking of the question 'what is Fluxus?' He was Fluxus by being simultaneously the adoring and the disobedient child of Cage, and Mary's avant-garde atelier began his transition from orthodox musician and composer to conceptual artist that Fluxus would complete.

Paik and Maciunas were inevitably drawn together, Maciunas finding a local equivalent of Young and Ono to help make plans and find artists for the Fluxus Festivals which were to take place in September 1962 at the sedate Städtisches Museum.

Nine artists and composers including Paik came to join Maciunas in Wiesbaden for a Fluxus Festival of Very New – or Newest – Music; this was another first sighting of the existence of Fluxus, historically its very first, and it was a continuation of the AG Gallery musical performances as a kind of research laboratory.

The Fluxus concerts over four weekends in September were innocently advertised as a series of new music concerts, but those who attended in this quiet city, perhaps expecting something unusual and challenging musically, weren't ready for the physical energy and madcap exuberance of what happened, a parade of art amusements somewhere between carnival and absurdist theatre, between children's party and street fight, now and then spilling into the unspeakable. Even just the fact the musicians also acted as performers and improvised so much was startling, apart from the actual performances that often seemed to be warped, aggressive re-enactments of Marx Brothers routines rather than music recitals. Those on stage, taking part in each other's exploits, all clearly needed to get something out of their system. One or two seemed to be having tantrums or possibly nervous breakdowns.

The audience, sometimes outnumbered by the performers, some walking out almost immediately, were still dressed formally and tidily, with plenty of ties for the men, and modest dresses for the women, as they might have been before the war, before the sixties let people dress for the occasion, and become part of the mood and atmosphere, not separated from it.

Maciunas's own contribution, performed at his 'Après John Cage' concert, adapted the conventional idea of one composer writing a memorial for another by conceiving a solemn slapstick tribute to the recently deceased Italian engineer, entrepreneur, enlightened boss, avant-garde architecture fan and utopian leader of the Community Movement political organisation – his kind of hero – Adriano Olivetti.

Olivetti had become known for his beautifully designed lightweight portable typewriters, loved by post-war artists and writers including John Updike, Bob Dylan and Sylvia Plath. You could trace some of Maciunas's typographical flamboyance and theatrical impertinence back to Marinetti of the Italian Futurists, and his visions for a new type of workplace, a new type of collective, a new type of city, and a new way of living in the city back to Olivetti.

The score of his memorial required around ten performers facing the audience to hold a calculator which released paper strips with various numbers on them. When a number each performer had been given was revealed, they executed a scripted action attached to that number – fold or unfold an umbrella, blow a whistle, jump up and down, bow, salute, point at someone or something, smack lips, clear throat. The scripted element made it seem mechanical and mundane; the randomness made it unpredictable and subtle. Some of the performers smiled, as though watching the performance themselves, unable to keep a straight face, and some stayed still and expressionless, as if inside the performance, a neutral part of its reality.

The jerky, genial and slightly sinister 'In Memoriam to Adriano Olivetti' became a Fluxus standard, and along with the series itself basically described the possibilities of Fluxus, establishing its historic DNA, its combination of smartness and daftness, joy and animus, hope and fears, oddity and obviousness, unity and separateness, its general commitment to making collages using live people and to gleefully head for the unknown, come what may.

There was also 'Variations on Solo for Double Bass' by Ben Patterson, an African American classical musician who faced resistance from conservative American orchestras and ended up in Cologne, working for the US Army, and a regular at Mary Bauermeister's studio, which felt, strangely, like a musical home he'd never known in America. His solo performances there were geographically distant from the AG Gallery series but happening at the same time, part of a series of small groups that materialised in locations around the world that Cage visited, eventually pulled together by Maciunas and therefore unknowingly by the US Army.

The title 'Variations on Solo for Double Bass' was straightforward enough, but as a form of prepared double bass, performed at Maciunas's 'Après Cage', the piece was built to be Fluxus, calling for a solo performer to agitate the instrument's strings using whatever was at hand, in this case a comb, corrugated paper, popcorn, feather dusters and plastic butterflies.

'Dangerous Music Number 2' featured the poet, artist and the sole woman in the series Alison Knowles theatrically shaving the head of her very still husband Dick Higgins, following the score 'Hat. Rags. Paper. Heave. Shave.' 'Four-Directional Song of Doubt for Five Voices' was written by the experimental poet, artist and printmaker Emmett Williams, who had experience linking poetry, theatre and song since the mid-1950s. He also worked for the US Army and had been part of a circle of poets in Darmstadt experimenting with what became concrete poetry, inspired by the compositional methods and processes of Stockhausen, Boulez and Luigi Nono being advanced at the local courses for new music. His first book, *konkretionen*, turned poems into linguistic play and non-literary word sculptures.

For 'Song of Doubt' Williams conducted by banging on a frying pan, keeping a steady rhythm going for forty-five minutes as the five voices, Maciunas, Higgins, Knowles, Paik and Patterson, each assigned a word from the phrase 'you just never quite know', said the word when prompted by coloured dots on a score laid out on a grid, leading to a gradual layering of the words, sometimes leaving silence. Not once did the complete title phrase appear in order. It became simultaneously a theatrical performance, a piece of music and a poetic mantra.

Nam June Paik's 'Zen for Head' was an extravagant interpretation, or absorption – is there a place where an interpretation becomes something else altogether? – of La Monte Young's 1960 'Composition Number 10', the 'draw a straight line and follow it' score. He made the straight line by dipping his head and hair into a bowl of ink and carefully dragging his head like a brush along a long strip of blank paper with the help of his hands and tie. It was both faithful to the spirit of Young's score and sacrilegious, which in itself is not necessarily ignoring the wishes and wisdom of the score.

The straight line, like Young's open score, could take you anywhere, which infuriated, confused or bored some, made others laugh at it or with it, and made some see how it took you as far as you wanted and needed to go away from the inhuman violence of war and towards the future and freedom. Paik, seeing into the future of now like a J.G. Ballard or William Burroughs, followed the straight line all the way into the globally stretching transmissions of his video art; video was his blank paper. The straight line continued into what Paik called the 'information superhighway', into a world overloaded with images, simultaneously too many and not enough, where we can zoom around the world without leaving our homes, into a reality trapped between past and present, between spiritual energy and electronic signal.

Maciunas had written a series of 'homages' in early 1962 including ones to Paik, Jackson Mac Low, Richard Maxfield, Dick Higgins and La Monte Young, almost a possible soundtrack to *An Anthology*, which itself was becoming an aesthetic guidebook for these early concerts even as it was still being prepared, with no publishing date in sight. In the 'Homage to Young' to be preferably played after 'Composition Number 10' Maciunas suggested that any straight line that existed because of 'Composition Number 10' or any other lines encountered should be erased, washed or scraped away as best as possible.

He was already anticipating, or wishing, that a new community, magically dusted by Cage, was forming around him, or at least near him. It contained underground names that were obscure at the time but would become well known, and even legendary for their innovative processes. Here was Maciunas the inspired impresario, the unselfish public-relations maestro with a commitment to advancing the cause for all, spotting important new talents and predicting their future status almost before anyone else.

The homages were also his way of recording how these new artists and musicians were producing pieces, firstly of music, and then the performance art music was becoming, that could be shared and re-authored, based on textual scores constantly implying other textual scores, and this correspondence between artists and musicians was part of their innovation that pointed towards an infinite capacity for continuation. Once things were set in motion – perhaps originally by Marcel Duchamp's 'Bicycle Wheel', sending probing, imaginative discovery forward – they might never stop, and this was true of the artists Maciunas found an allegiance with, who operated underground and then gradually formed in the minds of more and more people – whether that was the unlikely, unintended international fame of Yoko Ono, the musical influence of La Monte Young, the electrifying sound and vision of Nam June Paik, or the scalding notoriety of Joseph Beuys.

If there was such a thing as a hierarchical order of events in this definitively non-hierarchical series, or marks for the performance that achieved the most delighted or cynical media coverage, the experimental minimalist Philip Corner's 'Piano Activities' was top of the bill. For the mainstream media on alert for laughs or obscenity it set alarm bells ringing, and in the story of Fluxus as a release of energy, the turning of danger into a game, as a form of art that was meant to be picked up and handled, not merely looked at or passively listened to, it was an early, very specific announcement of intentions.

It was delirious, scandalous proof of how far avant-garde artists had gone in fifteen years searching for new realities and new forms of expression, leaving behind the Second World War's brutal destruction as far back in history as they could by going as far as they could with what they could get away with in performance. The further out there with their art and music they went, the further they made it into the future, with a greater chance to perpetuate freedom. The performances were about redemption and self-invention, and they were about destruction.

There was destabilising silliness and naive giddiness rooted in relief in many of the performances, and/or anger and frustration rooted in the violence that was now ever-present in their consciousness – the atomic bombs were dropped on Japan when most of them were in their teens, creating the threat of nuclear annihilation in their lives ever since. Life had never seemed so fragile, and the art they were making symbolised this fragility, how everything could break down at any moment. There was no use pretending this wasn't happening even as you were attempting to find safety by finding ways to build a new society and the rituals that came with it.

There were nine possible roles for 'many pianists' which included a stipulation that the piano be played in an orthodox manner, as well as the

272

dropping of objects on the strings, the acting on the strings with a hammer, wires, ropes or drumsticks and acting in any way on the underside of the piano and in using the pedals. You could change roles, but all roles needed to be occupied at all times.

Corner had extended Cage's notion of the prepared piano by pursuing what would happen if the idea of the preparation was extended. The potential sound of the piano wasn't merely altered by using small, everyday objects to distort, muffle and refocus the sounds while still playing it in a mostly conventional manner. The body itself could be used to change the piano's conventional uses and mute and pluck the strings – fingers, knuckles, limbs. All parts of the piano could be used as a source of sound, as if the player(s) was the object used to prepare the instrument and redirect all possible sounds contained inside the object.

Corner wasn't present for the Wiesbaden reading of his carefully worded score for 'Piano Activities' and when he heard what had happened, even he was initially shocked at how far the group had gone in transforming his almost sober exploration of the possible sounds contained inside the piano, treating the piano as an object to be closely examined and ultimately respected. There was always curiosity from those who created an event score at how it would evolve when performed by others, but one thing Corner anticipated, however unexpected a performance, was that the piano would be intact at the end. In the score, performers were asked to show restraint, to be surprising but moderate as well, to ignore or relate to the other performers, and also to enhance, or destroy, or transform their actions.

The Wiesbaden group had a different idea about what to do with Corner's score, or at least, as the performance progressed, they developed different ideas, noticing a number of potential outcomes, and responding a little more directly to the word 'destroy'. They took the score to an extreme, further extending Corner's extension of Cage, spreading the performance throughout the series, reframing the original conceptual framework.

The first night's performance began slowly, with Paik acting like he was beginning a recognisable recital on a lovely, solid grand piano, and other performers gently and then a little roughly interrupting him with single notes and chords of their own choosing. From there, over a few performances, with everyone getting involved, breaking into the piano and then starting to break it up, the piano as object became broken down into a series of objects, some of which would be later auctioned off as sculpture.

The familiar sound of a piano splintered into the sound of banging, scratching, ripping, rubbing, crushing, smashing, small explosions, natural sounds becoming less and less natural. Control cued freedom which cued control and so on, connecting Cage with the free jazz of Ornette Coleman. Eventually, the sound of a piano became an industrial sound, hammering, sawing, tearing, screwing, bedlam; the performers, and some of the audience, were increasingly galvanised by their actions.

The early hints of tentative improvised togetherness become a wilder, less coherent collection of noises – the group was acting together but its members were following their own agenda and decision-making, as if sonically creating the instructions for a new movement which would combine extreme independence with collective socialised properties, freed from the strictures of genre and medium. They were breaking rules to make rules which could then be broken. They were using the opportunity to compose a manifesto; the act of composing, whether composing a score or composing oneself, one's own actions during a performance, is a way of renewing or reinventing relationships between object and subject, and great pleasure can be taken from the process.

At some unplanned point, amid all the play and action creating new internal incidents by chance, the performances found a solution to a problem that the vandalised reshaping of the piano had caused – how to remove the broken, bulky, misshapen piano from the building, because the seriousness of proceedings now became a practical matter, and a script Corner had written for an ensemble of avant-garde musicians became a grotesque comic script for a Laurel and Hardy short. The piano as a shining symbol of civilisation that needed recalibrating so it wasn't taken for granted had become an awkward pile of rubble that somehow needed moving and disposing of.

The audience was either swept up with the taboo-challenging euphoria and cultural vulgarity or alienated by the wanton destruction of a revered musical instrument. The newspaper headlines described it as childish; the artists had already moved on, task completed.

The nine Wiesbaden participants, an elastic ensemble made up of deviant individuals, were nicknamed *die Fluxus Leute* – the Fluxus people – by local press intrigued and bemused by the way-out weird goings on, strange noises and odd performances Maciunas promoted, with Paik and Joseph Beuys as shadowy enthusiasts on the festival planning committee with their own agenda. Yoko Ono was also listed in the second newsletter as being on the planning committee, even though at the time Maciunas and Yoko were on different continents. Their New York walks and her 1961 concerts gave Maciunas enough Yoko idea-input to merit a position.

One newspaper headline became part of their own promotion: 'The lunatics have escaped.' If they had, most of them were rounded up to play their roles on stage, except for Beuys, who was listed as a potential performer, but for some reason didn't directly participate.

The composers and musicians didn't know they were Fluxus, it was just a concert of experimental music they'd been invited to, put together by a magazine called *Fluxus* with vague connections to the artistic schemes of John Cage and his displaced company – the fact that the magazine didn't yet exist might have been a clue that something wasn't quite as it seemed.

The name stuck, grabbed by one local journalist after another, almost as a gimmick, so that Wiesbaden became a holy location in the Fluxus creation myth. The name instantly travelled outside Maciunas's original settings and frameworks. It went from being the possible name of an esoteric magazine to denoting an active avant-garde collective, with each participating artist inspiring the direction of others.

It made sense that Maciunas had thought of it as a name and at the same time not thought of it. He'd set it up, but it landed like an accident, like a chance occurrence. It was an idea he'd had that he didn't finish off;

it was finished off for him. He was possessed by the idea of launching some kind of movement; he knew what he was doing but it was also out of his hands.

In a way the media had labelled his movement, somewhere between affectionately and casually, and his one-man show became the latest instalment in the art-historical avant-garde movements Maciunas had fantasised about, even as all the participants came from different places and headed in different directions. They all had minds of their own and maintained their highly diverse independence while their self-appointed, self-deprecating, self-determined leader, their Walt Disney, their Guy Debord, their Andy Warhol, held them in place inside his designs, publications, newsletters, cheap, packaged souvenirs and emerging efficient alternative distribution systems.

Fluxus was both an increasingly complex going concern and an illusion where nothing happened and everything changed. Maciunas inherited and united a readymade roster of progressively minded artists, a loose network of friends, friends of friends, colleagues, vague alliances, sympathisers and so on, scattered around the world.

The way artists were recruited from places where artists from around the world had settled, its inclusionary ethos and open-minded sense of humanism meant that Fluxus was a rare internationalist movement with protagonists who were Black, white, Asian, Hispanic; male, straight and gay; female, straight and gay. Dick Higgins, gay and married for a long time to Alison Knowles, keen to do away with gender binaries, to find a new language for words that helped maintain boundaries and barriers, used sher/shem/shemself.

They all spoke Fluxus, dreaming they had become fluent overnight, and some even had a Fluxus passport, but they also spoke their own language, and were free-floating agents lacking official paperwork.

This arbitrary Wiesbaden assembly was contributing materials to the publications and books Maciunas was editing and designing along with the Fluxus festival advertisements. Fluxus formed almost accidentally around them as the name for a group of performers, and its imaginary

277

rituals, structure and traditions migrated into the wider world as if it actually stood for something.

The group became a named group and then spent the month talking with each other about what this actually meant and what it could mean. What did they have in common, other than the fact that they had all agreed to take part in Maciunas's festival? How did they know what they were doing was Fluxus? Because it was confounding, confrontational, comic, pretentious, profound, all of that, or something less specific? Had they been doing something accidentally Fluxus all along, some because they worked with Cage, and some because it was coming naturally to them? (Eager new recruit Beuys attributed as Fluxus his pre-1961 art all the way back to 1947.) Did they even want to be identified as a group? Who were they serving? And how? What for?

There were new, different, often exceedingly fussy voices articulating the nature of Fluxus, not just the voice(s) in Maciunas's head. Now there was George Brecht calling it a 'network of active points all equidistant from the centre' and he would write that 'individuals with something unnameable in common have simply naturally coalesced to publish and perform their work'. For him, Fluxus introduced the idea that every object is an event . . . and every event has an object-like quality.

In 1960, when Fluxus was more or less invisible, Walter De Maria thought ahead when writing his 'Meaningless Work' manifesto, which subconsciously seeped into the minds of Fluxus:

Meaningless work is obviously the most important and significant art form today . . . potentially the most abstract, concrete, individual, foolish, indeterminate, exactly determined, varied art-action-experience one can undertake today. It can contain all the old art forms such as painting, writing etc. It can make you feel and think about yourself, the outside world, reality, unconsciousness, nature, history, time, philosophy, nothing at all, politics etc, without the limitations of old art forms.

278

Paik called Fluxus 'the secret' – or at least, the core dynamic was, the constant presentation of enigma and spectacular incomprehensibility, rather than the superficial high jinks, the bait, that attracted the attention of the mainstream media. For the Fluxus historian Ken Friedman it was simply 'a way of doing things'. For the French action philosopher and extreme ironist Robert Filliou it was an Eternal Network of linked poetic gestures, a borderless international laboratory. Fluxus was the essence of his understanding that it was art that made life more interesting than art.

For Philip Corner, Fluxus was about 'throwing pieces of reality at the audience'. Dick Higgins toyed with Arts of the New Mentality, the Going Thing, Exemplificative, and eventually, which it might have been called if Maciunas didn't exist and no one invented him, Intermedia, media falling in the subdivision between other media, generating novel hybrid forms, an array of art forms that shared a certain overlapping structural continuity. Higgins unknowingly reanimated in the plural a term first used by the English Romantic poet and critic Samuel Taylor Coleridge in 1812, intermedium.

Higgins's philosophy of Fluxus, maintaining that its main medium was reality, was as thorough as Maciunas's, his personality as forceful, meticulous and demanding. He was a phantom leader, described as an 'area' editor, using Fluxus to shape a theory of the arts as the world changed around him, articulating his approach through his own activities, charts and ideas and the Something Else Press he created once it became clear that the ever-unreliable, deferring Maciunas was not going to publish the Higgins collection of writings he had promised to.

Higgins didn't publish only himself but also a number of artists orbiting Fluxus one way or another from John Cage to Ray Johnson and Emmett Williams, and republished books that explored and recontextualised the origins of the avant-garde, recovering the elegantly strange modernist and literary anarchist Gertrude Stein as a patron saint, or chief trickster, of the post-war avant-garde, stating in 1945 that her ambition had been to 'kill the nineteenth century'.

Stein's experiments with language, poetic ambiguity and a writing that demands active engagement became a source of fascination for the Cage generation, for the way she preferred metaphor and play to definition and certainty. Her claim that there was no such thing as repetition, 'only insistence', seemed an essential foundation for minimalism. A few years after she died in 1946, she easily became a contemporary of Yoko Ono, George Brecht, Alison Knowles, Ray Johnson and Jackson Mac Low, in the way that Duchamp had been recovered in the 1950s.

In his essay 'Why Do We Publish So Much Gertrude Stein', Higgins wrote, 'Stein was constantly working, thinking, planning the entire cosmology of the arts. She had a fragmented, grandiose concept of theatre – a sort of instant theatre, pageant like but non-narrative, like the more imagistic and disciplined sort of happenings.'

Something Else is also a name for Fluxus in another reality, an outline of an illusionary Fluxus, named because Higgins was told by his wife Alison to think of something else when Dick said he was thinking of calling it Shirtsleeves Press, which she said was terrible. It put books and published objects at the centre of the experience-led, exhibition-avoiding Fluxus system, and acted as a 'container of provocation' refining its intellectual terms and preserving its ephemeral qualities.

Higgins wasn't so obsessed with Dada and any obvious possible precedents, which seemed to instantly brand Fluxus as second hand. For him, Fluxus was a mongrel art with no distinct parentage or pedigree, and if anything, it was returning to the unfinished business of the twentieth-century avant-garde. There was an affiliation with Duchamp's mystical path from art to banality and Cage's sublime route from noise to silence, with paint-flinging Pollock all but freeing himself from the limits of the canvas, confusing everything, but mostly it was atmospheric rather than causal – Fluxus didn't come from Dada even if it did lead back to it, throwing new light on it.

If anything, Dada was remembering Fluxus, and Duchamp was member number one, or maybe member number minus one with Cage as member zero. This made Yoko Ono member number one, cancelling her membership before there was a second member, given an open invitation to interact in whatever way and whenever she fancied, whenever she wanted. (Some internal memos would contain complaints that over time Yoko did nothing to publicise Fluxus but was happy to let Fluxus publicise her.)

The Yoko Ono who didn't set out to be misunderstood but then realised so many great ideas come out of a misunderstanding.

For all the energetic worldbuilding of the many shadow Fluxus leaders or understudies, Maciunas remained the figurehead, determining the group dynamic and dictating terms, even if they were consistently revised, amended or completely ignored. Some artists did come together and do things, as if they agreed with him that Fluxus existed, some loved, hated and feared him but metaphorically attended the meetings, and some had very little to do with him.

As soon as it became clear after Wiesbaden that Fluxus was now the *thing*, not simply a thing, Maciunas the administrator with benign authoritarian tendencies decided to write a manifesto to sort out their group identity, which he had been thinking about for some time.

Let there be Fluxus! And there was Fluxus. Fluxus was absolutely anti-professional. It should become a way of life, not a profession. Fluxus artists were required to obtain their motivation from everyday experiences: eating, working, talking, smelling, travelling, seeing, licking, building, blinking, our bodies, our clothes, our friends, the rooms where we live, the spaces we pass through, the thoughts we have.

He denounced the preciousness and staleness of art institutions, exclaiming that if pseudo-intellectuals, gallery and museum owners and other decadent dilettantes couldn't be converted to Fluxus, they should be destroyed. (Many from the more poetic wing were not impressed by the language, which they saw as verging on the terroristic.) It was an update of Dada's original death-or-glory mission statement, as though consciously preparing for the countercultural ferment of the 1960s, and the arguments, divisions, conflicts and intricate tensions began within the group among those with their own ideas about what Fluxus was and wasn't as a problem-solving, life-enhancing collective intelligence.

They were reluctant to sign the manifesto, as was Maciunas himself, not wanting to be forever what they were during that month. There were other definitions of what Fluxus could be, if only in relationship to the dictionary definition of the word, of how it neatly reflected a reality in constant flux, and discussions about how new members were to be invited, introduced and vetted, and how the group now that it had been 'discovered' would still allow change, so that almost as soon as it existed, it was not pinned down, and effectively ceased to be. And if they admitted they were Fluxus, did they always have to be Fluxus, or did they still exist for themselves, both outside and inside the unit?

Later, when writers and critics improbably searched for the one true Fluxus story, these nine became the core group, a kind of nomadic supergroup, mostly mild-mannered and harmless but not averse to wreaking havoc – with Yoko as OG (original ghost) and confidante of Maciunas, perhaps the earliest comrade in a trusted inner circle, and Beuys already assured as charismatic solemn and/or self-mocking messiah, cult leader rather than co-operative leader, art prophet, so powerful a presence he was invisibly everywhere – everyone able to claim they were there at the beginning, setting the tone and coming up with the skin and bones of a house style.

As soon as Beuys, reaching forty and recovering from depression that hit hard in the mid-1950s, heard Maciunas talk about his ideas for what became Fluxus, as soon as he became involved at just the moment the plans and ideals for a movement of sorts became known as Fluxus, Beuys sensed that it was essentially a virtual communal space where anything went more than an actual, uninspiring everyday movement. He agreed wholeheartedly with one of its core principles – to erase the separation between art, which was imprisoned in history, buildings and catalogues, and life, which was everywhere.

It would be called a movement, and Beuys would take advantage of exactly the kind of limitless, visceral art-historical group consisting of entirely contradictory elements that would suit him, but what attracted him was this almost permanently temporary virtual space where he could find freedom.

He found a place to work and experiment, to make the sort of art as

283

the mood struck him that coincided with the conceptual stirrings and performance rites of Fluxus without having to officially sign up or take part in regular group activities and be in all the group photographs. Where many of the artists being accidentally herded together, or split apart, by Maciunas were post-Cage, Beuys came more from the word worlds of James Joyce – enjoying how their surnames rhymed – but identified similar energies. During his depressive years, reading Joyce helped him deal with the darkness, and this receiving of therapeutic help convinced him that art is therapy. For him Joyce like Cage was East and West, rational and spiritual, and both were creative subversives, which he saw as the key to expanding perceptions of reality.

Beuys was enticed by Fluxus because he saw in himself the sly mischief, grand schemes, nervous energy and socially aware determination of Maciunas. Looking at him, this dissentient modern Renaissance creature, created a lateral self-portrait. He was up to something that was a kind of chaos that meant his plans would always be becoming something, always changing, never settling. Beuys was looking for alternative methods of organising activities and radical means of distributing and making available artworks, many of which didn't exist in any traditional sense.

He was also used to causing and using scandal to audaciously invent himself as myth – he had been a member of the Hitler Youth at fifteen in 1936 before it was compulsory, volunteered for the Luftwaffe in 1941, and claimed he was shot down in the isolated Crimean plain and was rescued by a nomadic tribe of Tatars who gave him shelter and rubbed him in animal fat and wrapped him in felt to keep him warm, which turned out to have happened only in a dream. For Beuys, dreams were as believable as reality, and often the dream experience was more inspirational.

The reality was less wild and ended up with him being a prisoner of war in a British internment camp; the fat and felt came later as elemental art materials, ironically as a symbolic protection from the lies that were told about him. They were also shamanic tools to help heal and regenerate wounds in society, which also made him a member of the Fluxus tribe, rescuing people from all kinds of dilemmas.

Maciunas and his pretensions, promises and contacts, his belief in art as a social process, in humble materials, which became the performances, epiphanies and proposals of the Fluxus personalities, the way they made use of everything, were a kind of found object which Beuys could then insert himself into or alongside, and manipulate and adjust for his own means. He could hide inside Fluxus, use it as a distraction, and also exploit it as a spotlight on his own position and activities, and as a vehicle to outpace those who wanted to pin him down and remove him from view with his dangerous and dangerously special ideologies. It showed him how to make a significant contribution to art, by going beyond so-called art.

Fluxus was a perfect environment for Beuys at the time, because, he said, it contained so many different opinions, and it took in everything from the tearing up of a piece of paper to the formulation of ideas for the changing of society. He saw the group's concerts as completely revolutionary, featuring works sometimes performed simultaneously and sometimes quickly one after the other. Props could simply be a bucket of water, a ladder and a piano. The rest was improvisation, the extraordinary mind at play.

His first named Fluxus concert was at the Galerie Parnass in Wuppertal 1963, participating in concerts by Maciunas, Alison Knowles, the Danish newcomer Addi Köpcke and Dick Higgins, and presenting two of his own works. His first was a twenty-second piece in between two other performances where he rushed on stage, wound up a clockwork toy of two drummers and set it on the piano until it wound down, and then rushed off stage.

The Fluxus co-conspirators enjoyed this confrontationally frivolous interlude, but for Beuys, not so keen on the cute little Fluxus fun and games, his second performance, 'Siberian Symphony No. 1', was genuinely Fluxus because it was Fluxus filtered through his 'animalistic' Fluxus, containing the essence of all his future activities. It was his version of the 'happening' which he called an 'action', which would increasingly become mysterious voodoo ceremonies or exorcisms possibly rooted in long-lost ancient rites of transcendence.

285

'Siberian Symphony' used and abused, shunned and celebrated, scorned and sensationalised a piano, as if it was a variation of Corner's 'Piano Activities' and therefore also an extension of Cage's preparations. Wearing dark grey flannel, a hat, buttoned-up shirt and no tie, he played the piano everywhere but the keys, using many pairs of old shoes to bang it until it started to fall apart. He commented that he wasn't being nihilistic or destructive, that the main intention was to indicate a new beginning, an enlarged understanding of every traditional form of art, or a revolutionary act. It was a description through ritualistic performance of what it was to destroy something so that you would break through into something new.

At around the same time, he interrupted Nam June Paik's first solo show at the same gallery, *Exposition of Music* – which included 'Electronic Television', where a grand piano had been left exposed, without its lid and laid down on the floor so that the audience could walk over it and 'play' it with their feet, another variation of Corner's 'Piano Activities' and Cage's prepared pianos.

Paik would soon be 'preparing' televisions and technology, interfering with their standard uses to enter other dimensions of communication, observing how when we create tools we mould ourselves in their image, and television was a tool. He was following Cage's assertion that art changes because technology changes and Marshall McLuhan's assertion that the invention of electronic technology had led to the whole world sharing one mind.

Paik would credit Cage as the first media artist, and his work would lead to sound art, video art and interactive art with the considerable assistance of Paik and his ecstatic, ingenious collaborations with a humming electric world. John Cage was the only contemporary artist who received a full page of coverage in McLuhan's bestselling *Understanding Media: The Extensions of Man*, with its opening chapter, entitled like an event score, 'The Medium Is the Message'.

On the opening day of Paik's show, Beuys charged towards the piano with an axe and started chopping at it, to astonished applause, before a bucket of water was poured over his head. He had succeeded in destroying expectations and uprooting assumptions. Art was undone. The broken piano remained where it was for the rest of the show. Paik remembered it as Beuys's first piano show.

At a Fluxus show in July 1964, a spectator, furious at what they saw as pointless, self-indulgent chaos, sensing some sort of blasphemy, ran onto the stage and hit Beuys on the nose, drawing blood. Beuys fought back in his own way, ignoring the blood, playing to the crowd and a nearby photographer, and saluting the audience while gleefully flourishing a wooden crucifix.

The image of crazed art martyr fighting for his cause and declaring art on the world as opposed to war made Beuys a little more known and made him realise the importance of establishing a distinctive artistic persona. He would move his performances, his actions, his ideologies from the Fluxus stage to the world stage, defending and explaining his work and thinking on his own terms, which meant exaggerating and mythologising his powers, creating an enigmatic fictional character complete with their own costume and theatrical gestures, making himself new in order to take the first step to making the world new.

When he met Andy Warhol, there was a sense it was like two popes from different bizarro universes meeting, dressed in their usual uniform as though for some state-of-mind occasion, warily circling each other, not daring to catch each other's eyes, not really believing the other existed. They believed in two different gods, in different realities, in different differences; they were in the same space and yet light years apart.

For a few years, Beuys's art was best explained against a backdrop of Fluxus activities and as part of a body of work sometimes seemingly made up of mostly mundane actions, silly gestures and irrelevant moments but that had its own social, political and ethical engagement. This body of work was created by a loosely associated network of artists, musicians and poets while Beuys steered a path between the art world and entertainment, between art and the media, between art and death, or life and art, that was both Fluxus and at the same time fully his own.

287

In 1964 Beuys decided he was no longer immediately Fluxus, excommunicating himself from the organisation, exiling himself from a conceptual country with its own weather system, its own people, even if echoes of his connection would continue making him a member even when he was not. He would continue to use Fluxus terminology, and in 1967 renamed his German Student Party 'Fluxus Zone West', part of an increasing commitment to political and economic reform and to art as a force for social change, what he called 'social sculpture', a profound, almost cosmic campaign that seemed incompatible with Fluxus do-it-yourself standards, however loose and non-conformist they were.

By suddenly ceasing to be Fluxus, or only intermittently being Fluxus, he was in a pure sense being Fluxus: it was a Fluxus gesture, without meaning and loaded with intention, so he could exist as Fluxus being and non-being at the same time, at least as seen from the outside. Fluxus had helped him realise that art was the primary factor governing our existence and our lives, and now it was like he had graduated from an idiosyncratic educational space and was heading out into the world, ready to create new forms of existence. In his own mind, he had moved on. He had left to go solo, with all that meant in terms of ego and one-upmanship. His art had moved on, and it could not be contained by Fluxus even as it remained in flux. Beuys had also outgrown the fundamental Fluxus essence of the event score, which compared to the traditional written music score was incredibly freeing, taking music in a multitude of new directions, but as a direction for a work of art was ultimately severely limiting.

He had become a landscape of his own, just like La Monte Young and soon Yoko Ono, and the squabbles that had developed within Fluxus, over territory, values, ownership, context, definitions, were beneath him. He had become, thanks to Fluxus, The Enchanter, The Healer, The Reformer, The Authority, The Simulacrum, The Phenomenon, a whole seething, hectic host of art saviours, art intellectuals, heroes, anti-heroes, snake charmers and shamans in one body, communing with wild animals alive and dead, bridging the earthly and the spiritual, encouraging us to love the abnormal in order to save our souls.

Everyone could be an artist, he once said, or it was said he said it, and he said it because he felt that to maintain democracy and freedom, everyone must perform, participate, protest, take responsibility for the health and sustainability of society. Everyone could be an artist, but not everyone could be an artist like Joseph Beuys: standing in one spot for hours, living with a coyote, claiming he could think with his knee, bandaging a knife after he has cut his finger, placing a lump of fat on an old wooden chair, which becomes sculptural philosophical enquiry into the nature of sitting and therefore the human body.

Fluxus had taught him well. In a couple of years, he moved from whimsically requesting the Berlin Wall be raised by five centimetres for the sake of proportion to the uncanny 'How to Explain Pictures to a Dead Hare', which for some was the *Mona Lisa* of its time and for others . . . wasn't. For three hours, with his head disturbingly covered with dripping honey and gold leaf as an audience watched through a window, he showed pictures to the carcass of a dead hare while whispering inaudibly as though in a trance. The only sound came from the steel attached to Beuys's right foot, ringing around the room with gothic monster menace; felt was attached to his left foot. Occasionally he would return to the centre of the gallery and stand over a dead fir tree on the floor, calmly dwelling on the nature of his psychic existence, or just adding to the suspense.

At the end the public could come inside while Beuys stood dead still, protectively holding the hare. A transfixed audience completed the action by so thoroughly believing in what Beuys was believing, as though they were inside one of his dreams, or a mysterious reality only he had access to, one of many mysterious realities that we can't usually see and have no idea about. He offered a chance to glimpse it, even reach out and touch it.

On one level the hare represented incarnation, the sacredness of the natural world; the gold represented the sun and his powers as a life-giving artist; the honey represented human thinking, and life itself. There were at least a hundred other levels resonating simultaneously – sometimes terrifyingly, and sometimes reassuringly.

This wasn't the work of someone who needed to worry about what Fluxus meant, or whether George Maciunas stood for American good or communist evil or vice versa. It suggested that if he was arguing with anyone or anything, he was arguing with God, with history, with art, with Germany's recent hollowed-out history, with humanity, with himself, with death, and he was moving so quickly as an artist thinking about art that even the liberating, endless openness of Fluxus was too closed.

He hadn't become an artist to argue with other artists over petty internal problems and engage in constant bureaucratic wrangles; his central interest was transformation, the alchemy of turning one thing into another, and he changed himself as artist into another artist again and again. He had his own mystique to attend to, his own rituals and prospectus, his impassioned transactions. He took seriously his responsibility as an artist to facilitate the emergence of historical awareness. He was inviting people to look at what fascinated, draw their own conclusions, and respond. Fluxus had taken him there, and Fluxus had taken him away.

The arguing, aesthetic difference, political disputes and interpersonal conflicts that began as soon as it became apparent art history would now include a Fluxus faction were inevitable and part of the Fluxus paradox – it argued against fixed notions and therefore naturally argued against itself; it promoted confusion as part of its operational tactics and caused confusion among the group.

It supported itself, opposed itself, agreed and disagreed with itself, and changed its mind according to taste. There would never be a time of ideological unity. It accepted that the many misunderstandings about Fluxus would inevitably contain an element of truth. Some rebelled against the lordly, happily erratic Maciunas; others gave him the benefit of the doubt. He was loved by some and hated by others, but even for those who hated him it was more love/hate. Sometimes he seemed to have been expelled from Fluxus for being so difficult and cantankerous, but by carrying on as though such a thing was impossible, he was never expelled from Fluxus as such.

Ken Friedman would say Fluxus without Maciunas would never have coalesced as it did, but Fluxus under another name would have coalesced in some form without him. The one consistent factor remained, for as long as he was alive, until 1978, the way Maciunas as a ghost in the art-producing machine, as pedantic office manager, as head of human resources, as Fluxus fanatic, its number one fan, packaged, designed and visually rationalised it, making design an integral element of the group's project. It was the one area where he could present the mirage of a united front.

He was essentially generating and archiving the correspondence, the ephemeral material, the posters, periodicals, newsletters, articles, catalogues, photographs, contracts, subpoenas, manifestos, postcards, souvenirs, merchandise, general paperwork and paraphernalia that are used to create the history of artistic movements even more than the art

291

itself. Which was lucky, as not much of the art ever survived being per-formed, or was never actually made.

Books, journals and publications were a main way that the dominant Fluxus ideas were held in place and sold at a reasonable price. Books were where the extreme experimental methods, research, drawings, recipes, games, happenings, events, accidental commodities, gadgets, artefacts and poking of fun could be best transferred and transmitted, making it into shops, represented through graphic design and typographical extravagance so that the text and the instructions seemed to dance on, and off, the page. A bookshop could become an exhibition space.

As The Publisher and The Designer, Maciunas was Mr Fluxus, even if the art was nothing to do with him, and carried on merrily and matter-of-factly after his death, although for some, Fluxus finished when he died. It closed down. At his Fluxus funeral, there were four coffins, each of them empty, and Fluxus lived on, a new forum and a new life cycle emerging.

It was in fact only his Fluxus that finished, and everyone involved one way or another had their own Fluxus, which was a product of all the participants. It would continue until they died, and so on, until there would be no participant/contributor/spectator left, and it was taken over by history, where anything truly goes, which is where it was heading all along, after all that.

Even before Fluxus had a name, Maciunas could make promises, as ringleader and advocate, to prospective collaborators that his aesthetic organisation was going to travel around the world, where it belonged. Now it had a name, if not a written constitution, it was ready to pack its bags.

It moved freely from one country to another, a travelling circus high on its new name and the fast and furious escalation of ideas, artists arriv-ing from around the world overcoming great separation to become a tight-knit community. The Fluxus of Maciunas made network situations into artworks and built a world out of ideas. It was fuelled by relentless commissioning and scouting, the regular asking for artworks whether possible or impossible to be followed through in whatever way seemed appropriate or inappropriate.

It quickly materialised at the poet and art dealer Victor Musgrave's pioneering Gallery One in London in November 1962 as the Festival of Misfits, a topsy turvy Fluxus funfair. Inside the gallery, Maciunas and Larry Miller's disorienting blackout maze 'Flux-Labyrinth' epitomised how Fluxus was combining artwork with audience participation; queues formed to have fun inside art. For 'Ben's Window', one of his living sculptures foreshadowing Gilbert and George, the French artist Ben Vautier lived in a shop window for a week, eating, sleeping, washing, watching TV, thinking, lounging around and basically simply existing, with various thoughts written in his cursive script on almost every surface, including the question, 'Does anybody have any idea what art is all about?' He'd based the storefront on a used record store he ran in Nice, the shop window filled with an assortment of junky objects covered with questioning, celebratory, self-conscious and impertinent inscriptions, which, drawing a straight line, would lead to lines of text used by Jenny Holzer and Barbara Kruger.

After the Wiesbaden festival, Maciunas and company organised concerts, now the central method of transmitting their messages, some of them under the banner Fluxus Fluxorum, in Copenhagen, Düsseldorf, Paris, Amsterdam, Oslo, Stockholm and The Hague, ending in the summer of 1963 at a Fluxus and Total Art Festival in Nice.

Reaction was mixed, from knowing sighs and shrugs in Paris to relatively large crowds and prurient TV coverage in Düsseldorf and full houses over five days in Copenhagen, inspiring a form of Fluxmania, as if in Denmark the avant-garde as arranged by Fluxus was as much a sensation as pop music was in Britain. Younger audiences were rapidly changing as a response to popular music as it expanded into the more eclectically challenging and confrontational rock, and the type of audience increasingly used to new sensations made for a different type of setting for Cageian principles. From 1961/2 onwards, the new generation of post-Cage artists had a very different audience in mind than

293

Cage did, which led to differences in approach that Cage was largely separate from.

A performance repertoire of event favourites started to develop: George Brecht's 'Drip for dripping water and empty vessel'; Alison Knowles's mass of massaging hands for five performers – using Nivea cream, a German brand, and if no Nivea was available in other countries, any hand cream as long as it was labelled Nivea; Paik's 'Zen for Head'; Vautier's 'God', a found glass wine bottle with the inscription 'if God is everywhere he is also on this bottle', which he would sometimes take for a walk; and Brecht's 'Word Event', consisting of the word 'exit', mostly used at the end of a concert.

It wasn't so much that everyone could be an artist but everyone could be Fluxus, which essentially meant believing everyone could be an artist. They probably would have made approximately – even exactly – this art without Fluxus, and artists like Vautier, solemnly mixing street action and extreme playfulness, outside world with performance space, had been experimenting since the late 1950s with the idea that intention alone defined a work of art, that everything is possible in art.

Vautier knew the secret password to gain access to Fluxus: art must be new and bring a shock. When he whispered it into Maciunas's ear when they met, he was welcomed inside the hall of mirrors, and given a gift pack containing the thoughts of Duchamp and Cage. At the time Duchamp was still mostly a rumour, a seemingly inactive outmoded artist in exile, and Cage's implacable philosophy of sound and Zen was not yet widely distributed beyond a select few, many of them now Fluxus. Vautier's mind was blown, not least because his own thinking was in some form approved by Duchamp's concept of an artwork that disappears into the idea of itself, and Cage's decision that a piece of music could now also be a performance, or art, or theatre, or philosophy.

As the interchangeable gang of Fluxus toured, as though another possible name for the movement could have been Tourism, Maciunas used for publicity photos the destroyed piano from 'Piano Activities' and a quotation from the manifesto of Maciunas that promised to 'unite the cadres of cultural revolutionaries from all parts of the world'. Just as wherever Cage went, he left behind a definite presence, Fluxus started to influence artists in the cities and countries it visited, many of whom were thinking the same things about art, primed to add their own imprint to this way of doing things.

In his movement-building element, drumming up enthusiasm, con-tributors, energy, Maciunas set up regional outposts in Nice, Prague, San Francisco and Copenhagen to co-ordinate projects. He dearly wanted to extend beyond the Iron Curtain into Poland, Yugoslavia, Czechoslovakia and the Soviet Union itself. In the Cold War battle to organise mass industrial society through either Russian communism or American capitalism, Maciunas felt Fluxus could function on either side as an elusive corrective.

The Iron Curtain proved too rigid, and it was time to retreat, and advance, back to New York in the autumn of 1963, and show off a more fully formed Fluxus, as though that had been his plan all along.

The Yoko Ono who used humour and paradox to trick you into another consciousness.

In April 1961, Yoko took part in 'An Evening of Contemporary Japanese Music and Poetry' at the Village Gate, a large, low basement room on Bleecker Street in Greenwich Village, the classic smoky, atmospheric nightclub where within a few days there could be appearances by John Coltrane, Allen Ginsberg, Nina Simone, Jacques Brel, Lenny Bruce and Mort Sahl.

In the middle of the jazz, comedy and folk booked by owner Art D'Lugoff – and his beloved salsa – there was time for a night of Japanese avant-garde, because its striving for pure possibility fitted right in with how Coltrane and his classic quartet were extending the language of jazz, jumping off 'A Few of My Favourite Things' and heading into the freedom of out there, and with how Bruce was defiantly testing the limits of artistic free speech. By the end of 1961, the arrests for obscenity and drug use had begun that ultimately led to Bruce being hounded to death by relentless police and judicial persecution.

Yoko and Toshi were joined by their friend Toshiro Mayuzumi; all three featured artists were seeing parallels and circling differences between the post-war avant-garde exploration of Japan and America. Toshiro was well known in Japan for his film scores, a like-minded contemporary of Takemitsu, but later stepped back from post-Webern sound filtered through Cage's prepared piano and Boulez's serialism, feeling he had mastered the avant-garde and there was nowhere else to go. Two years before, he had written 'Nirvana Symphony', which used a painting by Yoko on its George Maciunas-designed cover when it was released as an LP in 1962.

His most self-consciously grand work, it emerged out of his eclectic mid-1950s Parisian studies and collaborations that took in serialism,

296

prepared piano and *musique concrète*, combining an orchestra with added wind and brass instruments, prayer bells recreated orchestrally and a twelve-voice male chorus singing fragments of Buddhist chants. His increasingly more traditional, dramatic, post-romantic elements would lead him to write the soundtrack for John Huston's *The Bible* in 1964 and music for the Tokyo Olympics the same year, his music gradually being overshadowed by his political and artistic alliance with the nationalist and militaristic novelist Yukio Mishima, who committed ritual seppuku, suicide by disembowelment, in protest at Japan's creeping Westernisation.

At the Village Gate, Toshiro was still under the spell of Cage's most tender and ruminative music resetting the tone and texture of sound. His enigmatic, precise late-fifties chamber music was performed by musicians including a string quartet and David Tudor, also playing with Toshi and Yoko, with John Cage and La Monte Young deciding at the last minute to join in on Yoko's piece, 'A Grapefruit in the World of Park'.

The Yoko Ono who in a biographical statement in 1966 noted: late adolescence; gave birth to a grapefruit, collected snails, clouds, garbage cans.

At Sarah Lawrence in October 1955 Yoko had published in the 'Perspectives' section of *The Campus*, a student newspaper, a surreal short story, 'Of a Grapefruit in the World of Park', a mysterious conversation or a series of daydreams between a group of friends or work colleagues about a grapefruit left over after a picnic in a park. A strange fruit, greenish yellow with wrinkles all over. It mustn't be thrown away, as they understood food shouldn't be wasted. What to do with it?

The park, under a sky that is 'too high', is due to close in a few minutes. The grapefruit is the object of some fascination: it's touched, rubbed, peeled; a pencil is stuck into it. It gets tasted, not without a little flinching, but there's something irresistible about the skin, the juice, the sweet and sourness, the segments, the fibrous inner tissue, the size of each separated segment. Eventually the fruit is pulled to pieces, somewhere between violently and fastidiously.

When a mother and daughter return to collect it, it's no longer there, just a few bits of leftover peel dried by the wind and a scattering of seeds. Everyone leaves the park, and as the sun goes down, the trees, the clouds, the whole park gets swallowed up by the dark. The last thing that can be seen is a shiny seed, and then that too disappears. There's nothing left.

The grapefruit was important to Yoko, who loved them as a child, and then growing up, believing it was a combination of an orange and a lemon in the way she was a combination of East and West, of art and theatre, music and poetry, idea and performance, and even if she ever found out a grapefruit wasn't a mix of an orange and a lemon, in her mind it was, and she liked it that way.

It was a mystery, where the grapefruit name came from, how it was also known as the forbidden fruit, how it was created accidentally in seventeenth-century Barbados when pomelo plants, the largest citrus fruit, introduced by Europeans, from Asia, were accidentally grazed by the pollen of the sweet orange, also Asian and introduced to Barbados by the Europeans. The grapefruit was even more of a hybrid than Yoko imagined, but she probably sensed it, and she hadn't finished with it as a symbol. The sky and the wind would also reappear in various settings over the next few years.

Over time Yoko turned her story about what to do with a sad, abandoned grapefruit – as though she was the grapefruit – into a narrated self-styled deconstructed opera. The original dreamlike prose became more fractured, ghostly and absurd, a short extract in twelve parts from an imaginary female *Waiting for Godot* featuring a mother and daughter, with the bleak addition of a dead child and the dissonant addition of clams and an arbitrary flushing toilet, using musicians to improvise a response to her text that included occasional laughter. All the performers knew they were communicating something, but weren't quite sure what, and the spontaneous composition became as much trying to find out what was being communicated as simply following pre-planned guidelines.

It was never the same twice. A few months later she performed it at the prestigious five-day Festival de Montréal, which included works by Edgard Varèse, Morton Feldman, György Ligeti, Karlheinz Stockhausen and Earle Brown, the premiere of John Cage's star-gazing 'Atlas Ecliptic-alis' for full orchestra – if desired – followed by his lecture 'Where Are We Going and What Are We Doing', and the premiere of Merce Cunning-ham's 'Aeon', with music by Cage and 'objects, costumes and lighting' by Robert Rauschenberg.

This 'A Grapefruit' was recited on a dark stage with her back to the audience accompanied by David Tudor and Toshi and a recording of her own highly charged, desperate voice and random anxious mutterings, still playing with the emotion of sound, the sound of emotion, but this time experimenting with what the voice can do, and what drama is, the flexibility of recorded sound. It was a piece of musical theatre for the voice, speaking a pseudo-language between alien and conversational, between acting and singing, somewhere Yoko had found that fell, and teetered on the edge, between performance art, not yet completely a thing, and opera, very much completely a thing.

Later, when she found herself getting an unexpected education in rock music from a choice selection of leading players, and adding that to her knowledge of opera, serialism, Japanese vocal traditions, theatrical improvisation, jazz freedoms and Cageian indeterminism, to her inter-est in the explicit presence of process in a performance, it seemed to confirm to rock conservatives the notion she was mad, bad and not someone you wanted to know. Primly appalled at her conniving inso-lence, they couldn't accept that as an experienced, eclectic musical adventurer, she was adding new possibilities to the sound of rock, opening up new sound worlds.

It's a biographical guess – aren't they all? – but Yoko would have been aware of John Cage's 1958 intimately epic 'Aria for Voice (Any Range)', using a combination of graphic notation, occasional traditional notation and real and made-up words, Cage searching as always for liberating moments of complete surprise.

It's a singular composition that could have naturally remained undisturbed on an island of its own, but there was so much interrelated aesthetic travel at the time, so many different methods and mechanisms of creating new sound and form and inspiring other artists and musicians, it would have reached Yoko – either the solo piece, or as part of a planned combination with 'Fontana Mix', a piece for electronically processed magnetic tape, a sort of sequel to 'Williams Mix', or as a simultaneous combination of 'Aria', 'Fontana Mix' and 'Solo for Piano'.

'Aria' was a complex, colourful score, a work of art in its own right – Cage had made his promise to Schoenberg that he would concentrate only on music, and wanted to keep the promise, but many of his scores even if they were rarely performed were visually striking, opening up ways to incorporate poetry, theatre, dance, philosophy, film and sculpture into his music, and sometimes into the graphic scores alone. He found a way to break his promise to Schoenberg while keeping it. It was all music, but he made music from and into everything.

'Aria' was another of Cage's compositions that was more an entire project, a complete self-contained genre, than an adaptation or adjustment of an existing idea. It asked the singer to make a series of decisions about vocal styles – selecting ten in all – and unmusical percussive noises using the voice or other devices, and the duration itself. Using the amount of material Cage imagined and depending on various performer choices it could be anywhere from around four minutes up to twenty-five minutes long.

The original performer of the score, the mezzo-soprano Cathy Berberian, Luciano Berio's wife and collaborator – Cage said her voice, with its three-octave range, was his favourite instrument – set the standard at ten minutes. Her chosen vocal styles, to be used responding to colours in the score, included jazz, alto, Marlene Dietrich, folk, Oriental, baby and nasal; the chosen noises included tsk-tsk, bark, pained inhalation, peaceful inhalation, hoot of disdain, exclamation of disgust, scream (having seen a mouse), ha-ha and expression of sexual pleasure.

It's one of those fantastical, devious Cage preparations that requires a suspension of disbelief from both performer and audience, so that they meet in some agreed space to create an accepted reality among themselves and go along with whatever happens. As the title indicates, it's a reference to the far-fetched radiance and sublime tragicomic otherworldliness of opera, and needs the performer to both sing and act, requiring such physical, vocal and mental commitment, and such vulnerability, they can risk being seen as unprofessionally chaotic and out of control.

Berberian's ability to inhabit such extreme roles and produce such natural, unnatural and at times supernatural noises as though she were a human synthesiser led her to be viewed by non-believers as an unruly circus freak. Yoko suffered similar attacks – also often dismissed merely as a decorative muse or disorganised diva channelling the assumed genius of male creators – and as a singer also experimented with what kind of berserk, incongruous and naturally or unnaturally beautiful sounds the mouth and body could produce.

You can sense the connection between 'Aria' and Yoko's theatrical presentations of 'A Grapefruit in the World of Park' – sometimes with recorded backing, sometimes with live musicians, sometimes with both, using her performance as a form of conducting, drawing all the disparate elements into a mutual connection, trusting the audience would follow her into this unsettling dimension between the macabre and the melancholy.

She would take on 'Aria' herself in Japan in 1962, for a performance where she used her voice, Cage operated the collaged electronics of 'Fontana Mix' and David Tudor played piano with contributions from Toshi – the sound of tuning between a thousand radio stations, some of which didn't seem to belong to this planet, and a thousand languages, some of which didn't seem human, Yoko unwrapping and breaking apart her voice like a grapefruit, revealing its insides, the pulp, juice and seeds.

On Saturday 24 November 1961, Ono presented another version of 'A Grapefruit' at her first solo recital *Works of Yoko Ono* in the 278-seat Carnegie Recital Theatre on the third floor of the esteemed Carnegie

301

Hall, the downtown spirit of her loft and AG Gallery shows moving uptown for an evening.

The seasoned, specialist promoter of smaller, unusual classical music concerts and off-Broadway plays and a keen, early adopter of avant-garde musicians Norman Seaman had been working with Toshi, helping him out landing various midtown recitals. Loving to outwit the establishment, the shrewd, jovial Seaman had since the very different 1950s discovered ingenious ways of setting up important debut performances for talented but obscure musicians at local recital halls, hiring the venues in off-peak hours, handling publicity and ticket sales, inviting reviewers and occasionally making a profit.

He found himself getting excited, and a little unnerved, when Toshi's wild, wonderful wife Yoko in her gentle, sing-song voice told him about 'A Grapefruit'. He kept nervously laughing as the 'beautiful and somewhat insane' Yoko outlined a performance that seemed to involve noise, a dead child, dancers, a certain amount of chaos and improvisation, and fruit. How could he resist? It sounded like it was going to be an energetic evening, and she was the kind of dreamer he always liked to help – as long as he could keep everything to a tight budget. She might be one of the many talented twentysomethings he helped with their debut recitals who would never be heard of again, but you never knew. She seemed to know the right people, and many of them would be on stage with her.

Ten or so years after they first met, when Yoko had become very much heard of, and she was in a spot of trouble with the American authorities treating her as a pain in the system, and needed some witness testaments from those who knew her – now knowing many more of the right arts and entertainment people – Seaman would say she was a person of 'unusually deep humanity'.

A young, brilliant cellist studying at Juilliard whom Seaman had also helped find a place to play, Charlotte Moorman, came with him to help with backstage co-ordination. She and Yoko, born a few months apart, quickly became friends, Yoko introducing a broke, struggling but determined Charlotte to unpredictable new worlds of wildness where music and art, when combined and rearranged, became something else altogether, which suited her more than just making and playing music, most of it written by other composers.

This generally involved following the sort of rules that made no sense to her, especially those that stopped her, as a performing musician, from actually performing and being herself. The classical music she was destined to play went through her to the audience; she wanted to break through music to reach an audience.

Yoko was accompanied by a crack company of avant-garde luminaries including George Brecht, Joe Byrd, Philip Corner, Richard Maxfield, Jackson Mac Low, Terry Jennings and La Monte Young, along with a small troupe of ground-breaking experimental dancers including Trisha Brown, Richard Levine and Jerome Martin credited as 'Movements', choreographed by the fiercely uncompromising dance radical Yvonne Rainer, who'd performed at the Chambers Street loft. She'd grown up in a family of bohemian San Francisco anarchist vegetarians, at ease with a natural mixing of poetry, painting, cinema and politics, and saw Allen Ginsberg's first reading of 'Howl' at the Six Gallery as a twenty-one-year-old in 1955.

Rainer was a significant, early 1960s part of a disordering, revolutionary dance movement running in parallel to the distilled, demystified minimalism in art and music, an active part of the multidisciplinary Judson collective that co-founded the Judson Dance Theater on Washington Square, a key crucible of performance art, applying Cage's compositional methods to ways of conceptually organising movement. Everything becomes a performance if someone is watching, she would say, anticipating a world sixty-five years later where almost everyone strives to be a performer and everyone can watch.

Her dance was cerebral, visceral body art, the body as an art object, combining neutral, everyday movements with random abstract energy and the effortlessly virtuosic – she viewed the body as a strange, imperfect, eventually broken, weakened thing to be moved through space and time, to be thrown into shapes, to be flung neatly and madly, to be dealt with, reckoned with, ridiculed, revealed, relished and transformed in order to clear the mind and expose the soul. Dancing required knowing the body intimately, and also the mind.

Her 1964 'No Manifesto' was written on a whim as an impulsive 'provocation' to challenge her own ideas, an angry strategy of denial, which she almost immediately disavowed and often contradicted. It was a great example of using the manifesto to clear the air, take back power from negative forces, demand the future-finding new and establish your own authority – she was already rejecting post-Cunningham/Martha Graham modern dance as full of clichés.

The force of the thinking helped it become, if only for manifesto fans, an almost mythical postmodern example, more of use to others as an educational tool than herself: for her it was simply a snapshot of some provisional thinking.

It's not in any Fluxus canon, and she's not often named as a Fluxus candidate, although she was there and thereabouts as art activist and hybridist, later like Yoko moving into making films, experimentally fusing choreography and the moving image, seizing moments where poetry, dance and sculpture were the same thing, but it is more than faintly Fluxus.

No to spectacle, she announced, later modifying this when forty-three years older to: avoid if at all possible. No to virtuosity became: acceptable in limited quantity. No to transformation and magic and make-believe; magic is out, the others are sometimes tolerable. No to the glamour and transcendence of the star-image; acceptable only as a quotation. No to the heroic; dancers are *ipso facto* heroic. No to the anti-heroic; don't agree with that one. No trash imagery; don't understand that one. No to involvement of performer or spectator; spectators, stay in your seats. No to style; style is unavoidable. No to camp; a little goes a long way. No seduction of the spectator by the wiles of the performer; unavoidable. No to eccentricity; if you mean unpredictable that's the name of the game. No moving or being moved; unavoidable.

Rainer is a suggestion of where Yoko might have gone as an erudite, challenging and single-minded artist with a certain charisma if there wasn't the later chance – or staged – meeting, and the subsequent fame, murder and monstrous insults and misunderstandings.

She would be busy existing somewhere between perfecting an obscure but riveting and disobedient artistic sensibility and doing nothing, hanging out, hanging around, under stress, suffering, living, loving, increasingly contemplating mortality and lifespan, creating unclassifiable, obscure works of artistic juxtaposition influentially important and significant to a select few, always looking for the conceptually new, winning the odd distinguished prize, decoration or award, enjoying or suffering the occasional retrospective or reappraisal, growing old gracefully with a few worshipping her every move, being simplified as an intriguing, neglected minor figure in a time of great innocence, pretension and failed optimism, with scholars, art historians and interviewers tending to concentrate on just one or two of her works and her early association with Fluxus, weary of her 'greatest hit(s)' but protective of them, while she was thinking about a hundred things and collaborations she did that seemed as interesting, at least to her. Tied to history, and always wanting to go in different directions in a world where it became increasingly difficult to shock and reorientate – which is where, from one angle, she ended up anyway, except with four and a half million X/Twitter followers.

If she hadn't headed into a different, more scandalous history, Yoko's Carnegie Recital Hall performance might oddly now be seen as more important than it is, as a significant dress rehearsal for the initiatory German Fluxus concerts coming in a few months, a primal harbinger of conceptual art principles.

George Maciunas helped Seaman and Moorman to produce it before he fled New York, and got some ideas about new forms from the theatre of events and incidents, and diverse artists, technicians and performers, that Yoko surrounded herself with. He'd fallen in love with being avant-garde, a condition he could never escape, and he'd fallen in love with Yoko, who shared the condition and the love, come what may. Yoko was stepping out beyond categories and genres to include all art, thought and private, intimate experience – everything could enter the art realm, anything however apparently mundane that triggered memories and held interest, and caused small, and even eventually large, convulsions in the minds of an audience – and Maciunas took notes.

At the Carnegie Recital Hall, as well as 'A Grapefruit' there were two other hermetic dramas – and rumours of a 'Hidden Piece' hidden inside one of the pieces ('Hide') – with music, voice electronics and body movement and what was described as movement of properties, a table, chair, toilet bowl and some boxes, cans, crockery and bottles. Seaman had to admit that for someone who didn't seem to know what she was doing, she knew exactly what she was doing.

'A Piece for Strawberries and Violin' featured no violin and no strawberries and was inspired by visits to the calming Palm Court room at the Plaza Hotel near Central Park, where Yoko would listen to an old violinist play with the house orchestra, drinking tea and eating some strawberries. Maybe it's where she first thought of it, mind wandering beyond the quaint, calm room, on her best behaviour but wondering what would happen if she suddenly lost her composure and shattered the calm.

Rainer and Brown playing the role of dancers sat down and stood up and pulled faces in extreme slow motion, ate something unseen, spat out seeds at hidden microphones, the sound of their mysteriously mundane activities gradually increasing, and eventually smashed their plates while male dancers circled them, tearing newspapers.

'AOS – To David Tudor' was another brief, arcane Ono opera(tion), the title referring to the fitful memory of childhood wartime chaos; each individual performer had their instructions, but didn't know the instructions others had, finding ways to come together, with the stage almost completely blacked out. Yoko was there somewhere, her desperate, mournful live voice combining with some recorded whispers and shrieks and single words. At one point she performed for the first time in public her 'Lighting Piece', first thought of in 1955, which makes it one of the very first if not the first 'event' as artwork – light a match and watch it go out.

Maxfield attached contact microphones to the dancers, who were instructed to be as quiet as possible, so that sometimes all you could hear was their tense, suppressed breathing and random scraping as they moved themselves and various objects with beer cans tied to their legs across the stage.

The dancers moved through some kind of void in ways that were all at once ordinary and ethereal, nothing special and otherworldly. At the end, the lights came on, a canvas was unrolled, and the dancers cut holes in the canvas and pushed their arms through, disembodied arms holding various mundane objects. Yoko's wordless vocals sounded like some primal wailing siren, reaching back to the time she was a refugee in her own country after the nightmarish Tokyo fire bombings.

She would talk of that moment in your mind when you are trying to describe something strange, frightening or unusual, and you mentally stutter before you can explain it, and by the time you get the words out, you have cleaned up the raw, original feeling, forgotten exactly what you were trying to say. She was creating the sound of apprehension, of holding your breath, a sound that can't come out, the sound of awe, darkness and fear that she experienced during the war, and occasional nervous giggling, remembering as a child lying in the dark thinking there was someone behind her, lurking in the shadows. She had someone stand behind the audience; no one was sure what he was doing there.

It was art/performance imagining – having come perilously close to – a world where everything had been bombed into ashes, and people were left with nothing; imagining starting from scratch, looking for materials, for new community rituals, for like-minded company, for the light, for laughter, for some kind of hope, for the imagination itself.

Music critics, unwittingly straying into territory outside music, were straight-faced and nonplussed, not sure whether to laugh or cry or both, but sensing something crystallising amid the building tension and visual gags. Alan Rich of the *New York Times* concluded, somewhere between condescending and grudging approval: 'Whether or not time will prove Miss Ono a master of musical expressiveness, there can be no denying her skill at concocting titles.'

Yoko was frustrated with the reviews, but someone pointed out that the key line in one review was that the hall was sold out. It was a sign of how far she had come as a known figure in a thriving, mostly white, male, American scene, but also perhaps a sign this was as far as she could go, the upper limits of audience attention for a delinquent, unplaceable performer unashamedly and furiously testing limits.

The Yoko Ono who gave other pieces the 'AOS' title, because a title could cover many different approaches, and hers often did – one was performed with Ornette Coleman on trumpet, Charlie Haden and David Izenzon on plucked and scratched double bass and Ed Blackwell on drums as her interruption of Coleman's 'Emotional Modulation', where she supplied written instructions for the band to follow, one of which was 'think of the days when you allowed silences in your life for dreaming' – a seven-minute-long rehearsal tape for a 1968 performance at the Royal Albert Hall appeared on Yoko Ono's fearless, cathartic proto-punk/no wave/grunge 1970 Plastic Ono Band album, when she could do no right for most people, as if her sole reason to be on the planet was to drive them up the wall with her lack of talent and decency. The album in all its voice-contorting, sound-rupturing, beat-torturing, nerve-touching glory, the missing link between Stockhausen's 'Kontra-Punkte' and the Velvet Underground of *White Light/White Heat*, didn't help.

308

It was the voice turned into voices, rock going beyond rock, beyond its basic sources, Yoko – however vicious the trolling, however malignant the moaning about her suspicious self-indulgence – following through fundamental avant-garde research principles, seeing what else, where else, introducing a whole set of entangled influences and other sound worlds into the rock paradigm.

Yoko and the Ornette Quartet sound like a dream meeting-of-minds Fluxus house band – imagine what the Ornette Coleman of *Free Jazz* would sound like interpreting John Cage's 'Aria', with Yoko's vocals going from birth to sex and sex to death and back again; imagine a rock group that knew its *musique concrète* that drew a line from John Cage's percussion pieces through a pop drummer as if he was a fan of Can, to Public Image Limited; imagine Ornette Coleman and Yoko Ono as the Sonny and Cher of the avant-garde.

Toshi didn't play any part in the Carnegie Hall recital. During 1961 he and Yoko had become increasingly more artistic colleagues than husband and wife – he performed with her in Montreal – and in August, he returned to Japan. In his work, he was devotedly avant-garde, at home, less extreme and exploratory, but Yoko, mindful of the formation of Fluxus commandments, was increasingly showing that home and work, life and art, were the same thing and should be in the same place. She behaved domestically as unpredictably as she did in her art, making every day a series of performances, dramas, protests and rituals, a pushing of her mind and body to extremes as she searched for inspiration and truth. It was as though day and night she was living in the imagination, the place where she could find logic and security, and it was exhausting for both of them.

Her emotional idea of peace and love enacted every minute was not compatible with Toshi's, which was contained inside his piano playing and writing. He was more comfortable fifty miles out of New York at the forest-surrounded, anti-capitalist Stony Point commune where Cage and Cunningham had settled, far from the cacophony and distractions of the city. He spent an increasing amount of time there, and it made him think of home and taking back what he'd learnt from Cage, some of which had itself taken some sort of route from Japan to New York.

In Tokyo, catching up with the Gutai Art Association, Toshi found energised pockets of post-war avant-garde self-discovery, a creative outburst of subversion and an intellectual restructuring mirroring activities in Manhattan, with overlapping conceptual preoccupations and a desperate, parallel search for identity and cultural continuity.

There were new independent galleries, art spaces and performance venues, including the 370-seat Sogetsu Arts Centre which had opened in 1958 in the basement of a flower-arranging school. Its director, the avant-garde film-maker and artist Hiroshi Teshigahara, established it as a site for what he called transmedia thinking, a nexus of interaction between the arts, promoting jazz, contemporary music, new wave cinema, photography, animation, underground theatre and diverse avant-garde events – what Dick Higgins would later call intermedia. It was also open to artists from overseas, still unusual at the time, part of what was seen as art being central to locating a national but anti-nationalist post-war authenticity – to be 'Japanese' without evoking the dangers of nationalism, where artists could help confront the demons that haunted post-war Japan. Art and music from other countries gave them a perspective on their own history and future, reminding them of useful pre-modern traditions and progressive legacies they might have missed or prematurely angrily dismissed in their determination to rebuild.

Toshi was immediately involved, performing some Cage pieces at the Osaka Contemporary Music Festival, the first time Japanese acolytes heard Cage's music live and experienced close-up the muted trembles and treated tones of a prepared piano. The reaction was either love, and a delighted identification with the sounds, rhythms and especially the silences, or indifference and anger, with some in an audience of hundreds considering it laughable – one musician complained that music being made because the composer thought other music silly was itself truly silly.

A few weeks later Toshi put together a solo performance at the SAC, featuring Takemitsu and members of Group Ongaku, an offshoot of a university musicology class, exploring his ambition to mix Cageian graphic notation, unexpected results and extreme action with traditional Japanese music and electronic music, the first time electronic music had been performed live in Japan.

The audience, calmed by the familiar Japanese structures, preferred Toshi's less ridiculous-seeming, more human-sounding refinement of Cage's experiments with chance, but he became an exploratory emissary preparing the way for Cage and his life and art partners David Tudor and Merce Cunningham, and also, initially, for Yoko.

311

In March 1962, Yoko returned to Japan, after ten years in New York, initially only for a short time to perform at a concert at Sogetsu that Toshi had arranged for her. Her parents were relieved, thinking her erratic, self-enforced starving artist American adventures were over at last, that maybe she had returned because of their urging and would now settle down, but at the time Yoko felt the Japan trip was an extension of her art adventures, not an end.

She would be back in New York, but not for two and a half years. The longer stay was partially forced on her by unplanned events and illness, but time in Tokyo in a different, less competitive setting allowed her to get new perspective, get outside herself, sometimes by plunging even deeper into her fears and hopes. Different audiences with different expectations, and artists and transgressive art collectives pursuing similar proto-Fluxus thinking, freed her from her New York peers, mostly men, many of them crowding her out and being given credit for ideas she was thinking of first in her own way.

She got back in touch, from the outside, with the Japanese elements that had subconsciously given her New York thinking and performances a distinctive, sometimes awkward-seeming aura, neglecting realism and narrative for irrationality, kinetic images, ritual, vulgarity, dream states – religious and folk dances, abstract dramatic pieces, puppet shows, the Noh and kabuki which emerged from the magical carnival chaos of folk art. Her art wasn't 'Japanese' purely because she was Japanese, but it also wasn't not Japanese.

She had been missing Maciunas, her strongest ally in Manhattan, now he was in Germany, unsure of herself without Toshi, and uncertain what she would find in the new Japan. She was still at the centre of the New York scene, participating in the first of two benefits in early 1962 to raise money for Young's *An Anthology* at the Living Theatre – the stalled souvenir of the loft series/abstract manifesto for the not-yet-named Fluxus was still delayed and always in need of funds.

Yoko's 'Touch Poem No. 5' was shown in the lobby – no sign of numbers 1 to 4, which revealed themselves over time sometimes as imaginary or yet to be conceived – a handmade thirty-two-page booklet containing pieces of cut white paper, no words or information and occasional variously sized locks of black (Yoko's) and red (a friend's) hair that were to be touched in order to receive a message via aura.

It was a hybrid of book of spells, a Jungian shadow work journal and a Braille book, defiantly impenetrable, its blank pages to be filled in and followed inside the imagination. The existence of the hair implying any meaning would emerge through touch, through sensation. Over time, Yoko's sequence of *Touch Poems* and *Touch Pieces*, abstract bulletins, announcements and occasional communal performances suggested that one way of understanding her work was by touch – whether being touched mentally, through the senses being awakened, or for real, through touching something or being physically touched.

She said she first thought of an art of touch in 1958, kept up at night by the possibilities. When she did concrete versions of a 'Touch Piece' that consisted of people touching each other a few years later – 'touch each other' – it was seen as flowery, love-in hippie frivolity. In 1958, with the war still present in people's minds, it felt a radical way of piercing the nervy reserve and reticence that was stopping people breaking free of the war and its cold reverberations, and when, as audience-reaching, audience-discomfiting celebrity ten years later, Yoko gained incongruous access to mainstream television, it was performance art, a representation of communication about communication, part of a campaign against conflict, being shown to baffled, frustrated or knowing live audiences in their millions. It proved, though, that there were other ways of thinking and feeling even if you didn't approve of Yoko's ways.

Yoko returned to Japan without the family benefits she had once enjoyed. She wasn't American, but in a way she was now more American than Japanese. Ultimately she was neither, but becoming a resident of a conceptual country she was among the first to explore and map. Tokyo was not the ruined, war-ravaged, demoralised city she had left behind, still in thrall to Japan's so-called American saviours. It was accelerating through a period of rapid manufacturing growth, becoming a modernised industrial power, leading to the 1964 Olympics, which since its announcement in 1959 had been an important influence on the reorganisation of the city, and a chance to show the world its new prosperity and very exportable consumer-oriented growth. The modern Japan went from tiny Sony transistor radios to sleek, fast Shinkansen bullet trains linking distant regions with Tokyo, a city now lighting up the sky on behalf of commerce, not war.

A bold, aggressive techno-utopian spirit had thrust Tokyo into the future. Its urbanised, ever-changing megalopolis sprawl, the city as power, as a leading, innovative centre of mass communication, but also the city as art, filled with exotic locations and cutting-edge architecture, made even New York seem superseded. *Time* magazine labelled it the 'most dynamic city on the face of the earth'. Yoko was home, but also far away, in a Tokyo that had almost completely replaced itself but still retained poignant echoes of her distant, destroyed Tokyo. There was a sense of breakdown, and a sense of renewal, and of cultural energy flowing in different directions.

She found herself isolated, but it was the kind of isolation she had come to terms with in America, the isolation that forced her to get her bearings, and which she would find ways to overcome and artistically exploit, teaming up with local avant-garde artists to introduce a certain lost uncanniness and high spirits into the rational, idealised, official images of Tokyo.

She now possessed a triple identity: she was a migratory stranger wherever she was, slipping incognito between worlds, between herself and reality. Japan, as a place she both knew and didn't know, offered her something else, something foreign and familiar, to add to what she had discovered about her art and herself in New York.

Before her show at Sogetsu Art Centre the media didn't know what to make of this young, enigmatic, unsmiling female New York-based Japanese avant-garde artist from a well-known, well-to-do family returning home after ten years. Where did she belong? What should we do with her? What had she got to say – specifically, what had she got to say to the Japanese?

314

For *Works of Yoko Ono*, she was armed with a considerable amount of increasingly developed material from the loft, AG and her concerts, showing a mind constantly on the move as it gathered experience. The evening was split into four sections – events and music for the stage, and an exhibition space in the lobby containing her object poems and most radically her instructions for paintings, a large selection elegantly hand-printed in Japanese by Toshi, a skilled calligrapher, on plain sheets of paper, so that even the text, turned into a visual object, was not created as an artwork by Yoko. The artist, withdrawing into herself, had not made or signed anything.

The sheets of paper were loosely taped to the gallery wall. That they were still being looked at as though they were words turned into hand-written visual art meant that Yoko would later print the instructions. The instructions were the point, not in what form or on what surface they were presented. Some invited interaction – 'Painting to Shake Hands (Painting for Cowards)' involved a performer situated behind a canvas pushing their arm through a hole to greet visitors. The instruction ended with: 'Shake hands and converse with hands.'

Some pieces approached the notion of turning the mundane into the magical from different directions. Some talked to no one and everyone or even simply herself. Some were elaborate, evocative descriptions that airily skirted sense, as though she was behaving like a character in *Alice's Adventures in Wonderland* advocating a special freedom. 'Painting for a Broken Sewing Machine' said: 'Put a broken sewing machine in a glass water tank that is about ten times or twenty times larger than the sewing machine. Once a year on a snowy day, take it out in an open space, and have everybody throw stones at it.'

The Yoko Ono who first announced that language on its own on a gallery wall is a justifiable form of art.

She wasn't making her homecoming easy. Nothing was direct. Nothing was certain. There were few things to compare her with. She was exploring possibilities and ideas, that the idea itself could be sufficient as an artwork, aiming for a split-second – or more – realisation that anything is possible. A few years later these ideas would have had a context, a connected place – conceptual art – but in Tokyo in 1962, even with a vibrant, politically active avant-garde scene abandoning mid-century modernism, juxtaposing genres and the realities of everyday life with a subversive fusion of existentialism, absurdism and Buddhist nothingness, she was more or less out on her own, putting together concepts floating free of any obvious roots or precedents, theoretically owned by no one.

Paintings, however modern, were still being framed as one-of-a kind pieces embedded in centuries of aura and hung on walls, and sculptures, however abstract, were obediently placed on plinths and you didn't go near and you didn't touch. With Yoko you could get close, you could touch, you could even get close and touch her, you could break on through to the other side. She was not necessarily being consciously conceptual: she was making up her own rules and following them, however foolish it might look, however exposed she was.

The dematerialisation of the object, painting replaced purely by words, paintings to be imagined in the mind, disoriented many. Was it some nefarious trick, an illusion, a jokey gimmick, a strange threat? Did the text refer to something that was shown elsewhere? They were signs that pointed only to themselves and their own ephemerality. There were no obvious answers anywhere, no explanation, except in Yoko's mind, and, she was suggesting, also there in the mind of the audience, if you feel it, if you want it. She was getting them to perform some of the labour involved in the construction and reception, even the existence itself, of an artwork.

316

Her events and music performances took things further, asking the audience to get even more engaged. Toshi had put together a number of experimental artists, writers, dancers and underground musicians to stand in for Yoko's regular New York collaborators – ensuring that what Yoko did went immediately straight into Tokyo's avant-garde scene, where she might have been if she hadn't left, but without several identities colliding in one self.

She performed 'Wind Piece', a one-line distillation – 'make a way for the wind' – of a discussion between Zen monks she'd read about the nature of the wind. When a flag moves, is it the wind moving, or the flag moving? A senior monk ruled that it is neither. It is the mind moving. While she read the line, a large electric fan was on the stage blowing her hair.

'Question Piece' invited questions from the audience, which were answered with questions, without any explanation, provoking the audience, if they noticed, to come back with 'better' questions.

'AOS – To David Tudor' was always something an audience had to fight to understand or even see and hear – battling through darkness, noise, silence, discomfort, chaos, time, toilets, beer cans, flashing lights, boredom, invisible Yoko, backward vocals, deadpan vocals, ancient vocals, frightening vocals, explosive vocals, thought being made in the mouth, the reading of newspapers in different languages, confusion, panic, any sense constantly losing out to unstoppable nonsensical interruptions, the Yoko lighting a match and watching the flame go out.

The Sogetsu performance was even more demanding, featuring a twenty-minute French lesson and recorded speeches by Adolf Hitler and the Japanese emperor, because there was nothing more nonsensical than the atrocities of war, and it actually ended in a fight between a member of the audience and one of the performers.

By the end of the show, which was long past midnight, the audience and performers had almost swapped roles – the concert ended with the performers staring sternly at the audience, flowing into 'Audience Piece for La Monte Young', searching for any difference the audience might feel having witnessed the performance, some vibrational shift in the air.

317

The audience didn't know what was expected of them, and while some accepted the new conditions, some quickly left. That was their experience: leaving, which had its own resonance.

Others had different experiences. An audience member tried to pinch the noses of the performers, causing a brief scuffle. Some of the performers, perhaps still following instructions, or simply exhausted, lay down on the floor of the stage.

It might have still been part of 'AOS', the part that ends with audience and performers collapsing, waiting for the end of something that didn't necessarily have an end. Even the moment officials from the arts centre stopped proceedings and shut down the concert might have been part of the performance. Someone coming on stage and brushing away all the debris and broken props might have been part of the performance. It was all left unfinished, just as Yoko planned, arranging real-life actions in a fictional way.

The Japanese artists she was working with relished the collaboration and hidden messages, and absorbed some of the techniques and tactics into their own work. Yoko would become an important contact between them and the Fluxus being shaped in Germany and New York, enhancing its internationalist feel.

Generally, the critics and media weren't impressed; sarcastically judgemental critics saw a shoddy, amateurish rip-off of John Cage, while the media patronised her as an eccentric woman who should know better, pretending to be the sort of artist women had no right being. Even the way she wore her hair, loose and often unkempt, when the cultural expectation was that it should be tidy and compliantly feminine, made her seem careless and wayward to the point of dangerous. Ultimately, what stung Ono the most was being called 'old-fashioned', at the same time as being accused of being some sort of furtive primitive.

Toshi came to her defence, insisting she was being underestimated, writing that Ono had been motivated by the ideas of Cage but not dominated. Both might require audience participation, leading to many side effects the artist cannot imagine, but her style and actions were independent of his. She definitely didn't use chance in the way he did, but allowed chance events to occur in a less defined way – she was more likely to just let things happen than Cage, who was more likely to create the illusion that things were just happening.

It was problematic, because it was essentially impossible to copy the complexities lurking under the surface of a Cage piece, but you could appear to be copying the detailed processes and open scores – which was like saying Picasso was copying Leonardo because they both used a canvas, and Bartók was copying Schubert because they both wrote their music down as a musical score.

Both Cage and Ono were approaching from inevitably different places, from different experiences, the Duchampian intention of replacing the artist as an all-powerful grand master with special powers with the idea of the artist as someone who invites an audience to create their own version of an artwork, and of reality.

Yoko let more than just incidental sound and accidental noise from the outside world penetrate her performances: sometimes real chaos would be introduced, which took a certain nerve, as did her dedication to rejecting tradition and replacing paintings with an elusive empty space. She was going somewhere else – unlike a lot of her peers, who were more tied to Cage's grooves – not necessarily beyond, but over the top.

Yoko became worried that her work, especially her live art, its perceived directionless unruliness and at the same time a soft-seeming, perhaps unrealistic idealism, was harming the growing reputation of the meticulous, sensitive and increasingly respected Toshi, still committed to her mission, her quiet masterplan, even as their marriage reached its final stage.

They were living separate lives, Toshi more comfortable mixing socially in Tokyo, Yoko feeling increasingly alone and depressed, known to many only as the wife of a famous composer. She was suffering from labour pains as she gave birth to a new concept, feeling herself being painfully twisted into someone she didn't recognise, and in her darkest moments contemplating suicide.

The shameful fallout from the concert Toshi had so carefully organised and the embarrassment it had caused both of them, the intense self-doubt she was feeling about the fragile, outlandish work she had spent two years developing, led her to admit herself into what she was led to believe was a sanatorium that would help her recuperate. She was seeking solitude more than anything, and later said it was never fully explained to her in her dazed state if it was rest home, meditation retreat or psychiatric institute.

This decision extended her stay in Japan, and while she was at the clinic, she couldn't stop working on her ideas, turning her room into a makeshift studio where she could contemplate what she had been doing for the last few years. If she was there for rest, her behaviour in her room made those looking after her suspect that there might be some mental issues. To make herself at home, she used the walls of her room to display her instruction paintings and the pages of a book of poems that didn't have words, just blank pages and some random hair clippings. She scrawled some of her instructions directly onto the wall and doodled shapes and faces, giving structure to her convalescence, a way of steadying herself and tethering her mind and body to the world.

As an emotional stocktaking, she surrounded herself with a haphazard accumulation of her aphorisms, dreams, wishes, hopes, fears, confessions, self-analysis, meditations, fantasies, visual experiments, imaginary ready-mades and poetic, proto-conceptual fantasies.

To the outside, to the doctors checking her state of mind, these seemed troubling signs – what appeared to be fragmented rantings and ravings, stuff about dripping clouds and puddles, stealing moons, bandaged bodies and sharing shadows, piano keys as hardened petals, fractured memories, imaginary languages. It was as though she was directly admitting she was seeing and hearing things. She was trapped inside her own thoughts. She was recording her hallucinations, parading her anxiety, compiling a ghostly memoir of derangement and torment. She was trying to express something that wouldn't let itself be expressed.

She was also apparently revealing morbid tendencies, haunted by loneliness and fear of loss. Hide until everybody forgets about you, hide until everybody dies. Use your blood to paint. Keep painting until you faint. Keep painting until you die. Sleep as long as you can. Stay in a room for a month. Do not speak. Do not see. Whisper at the end of the month.

The presence of the wall seemed to be there so she could map out the disordered patterns of her existence.

Trying to explain what it all was didn't help – that it was her thoughts, I collect them, it was Zen, it was *mono no aware*, it was art, it was magic, moments happening in the now that now go on for ever, she was a hybrid of orange and lemon, sour and sweet, childish wonder and adult, Japan and America, true and false, wish and lament, experience and innocence, there is not here, I can fly in my mind, watch the sun until it becomes square, it's all in the mind, an invisible world where you can make yourself invisible, portals made of words and insight through which you could slip into other dimensions.

It made it all sound even more incoherent, and to medical staff with no knowledge of her life as an artist she seemed to be disappearing into another reality. It was like trying to explain in a different language why a series of jokes was funny, or the details of a complex philosophical treatise on the nature of self-awareness.

Her medication was increased, and she started being monitored for signs her depression was becoming dangerous, spending hours heavily sedated, sinking into exactly the inertia she hated. If she had made some of these texts and signs to help her through strange and difficult times and solve problems, they really had their work cut out now.

The Yoko Ono under stress, twice displaced, boxed in, cut off, 'still groping in a world of stickiness', her mind a blank, surrounded by bits and pieces of herself, a rich density of discrete actions moving between art forms, between worlds that existed and didn't exist, that she could put together in her head and then with a stapler, glue and a needle and thread in the form of a book which contained a chamber exhibition you were invited to destroy once you had experienced the contents.

Back in New York, news spread with the logic of gossip that Yoko had been put into a mental hospital and that she was struggling. Having disappeared from Manhattan, she now seemed to have completely disappeared from faraway Japan, as though she had slipped through one of her imaginary paintings into another dimension.

La Monte Young, painstakingly working on the production of *An Anthology*, showed Tony Cox, an eccentric jazz musician friend, hustler and would-be film-maker, some of the pages, including Yoko's contribution. He mentioned to Cox that he'd heard Yoko was being treated in a clinic, with no apparent sign of her being allowed out.

Learning more about Yoko and her character and recent activities, Cox was intrigued enough to make the long journey to Japan – ostensibly to pursue an interest in calligraphy – and seek her out. He found the hospital where she was being treated, and started to visit her, becoming aware that she was being given a strong dose of a medication he realised was dulling her senses rather than aiding recovery. He later claimed that at times she could barely talk, and that she was being mistreated, and he contrived to help her get out of the facility by claiming he was a journalist and threatening the hospital director with exposure and scandal over how a famous New York artist was being held against her will.

Yoko emerged from her confinement feeling attached to Cox, her saviour, and her last significant artistic collaboration with Toshi was helping arrange, along with Tōru Takemitsu via SAC, for John Cage to visit Japan in October 1962 for a series of seven concerts in Tokyo, Kyoto, Osaka and Sapporo. At the same time, in Germany, Maciunas and company were taking a fresh-faced, full-on Fluxus around Europe. 'Cage' as an attitude, a mobilisation, was starting to exist in many different places at once, and take on different characteristics, which would then blend together.

Cage had wanted to visit Japan since the 1940s, feeling it was 'the country in the whole of the world whose art and thought has most vitality for me'. His subjective Eastern sound and his appreciation of Japanese religion, philosophy and aesthetics, his appropriation and modification of the Japanese concept of *ma* – a pause in time, the sound of silence after sound, an emptiness in space, the fullness of shadows – had been part of his general post-war ambition to recover America's – and the West's – lost spirit.

Japan's oblique, transcendental dimension would survive Japan's warrior instincts and its crushing end-of-days defeat, connecting East and West as the post-feudal Meiji era had before it was truncated in 1911; instead of the modernising Meiji slogan 'Japanese spirit, Western technology' it was now 'Japanese spirit, Western modernism'.

Cage's influence on Japan as music philosopher had grown gradually since the early 1950s, particularly through Toshiro Mayuzumi, Tōru Takemitsu and the Jikken Kōbō avant-garde group of like-minded musicians also paying attention to the iconoclastic activities at Darmstadt in Germany, but the tour of Japan and the specific sighting of John Cage being John Cage, a mix Japan had never seen before of artist and priest, performer and philosopher, nature lover and technology aficionado, was given a handy label – *Jon Keji Shokku*: John Cage Shock. It wasn't as sudden as that, but Japan was another place Cage visited where he left behind lingering signs of his benevolent personality, radical insights and enlightening approach.

Even those who didn't consider Cage's impact a particular shock in a country with its own lively avant-garde sector and disagreed with his unusual, possibly hit-and-miss musical methods were still inspired to create their own musical questions. For others suspicious of Cage's allegedly authoritarian motives, and his belief that his world was the only true world, seeing him in person – serious, gentle, tactful and intensely interested in the people and history of Japan – helped them put his music and methods in context.

There was inevitable balance in what was a cultural exchange; Cage gave to the art and music of Japan, and Japanese art and music continued to

323

give to Cage, who discovered more revelation on visits to Zen temples, monasteries and tranquil rock gardens, meeting his mentor D.T. Suzuki and experiencing ceremonies and rituals that deepened his faith in indeterminacy, chance and silence and set him off in rarefied new directions.

He'd arrived half-expecting a Zen-like, ancient Eastern country, and found a fast-moving, modern society discreetly incorporating Zen Buddhism. Japan was beautiful, he said, suffering from Japan shock, and the rapidly growing Tokyo was as annoying as any great, at times overwhelming city.

Yoko was one of the small welcoming party meeting Cage and Tudor at the airport when they arrived, acting as guide and translator, also hoping to prove to her doubters that she was a collaborator of Cage, not so much a disciple or, worse, assistant. She was mostly now known as Toshi's wife; she didn't want to add to that being talked of as Cage's secretary. Peggy Guggenheim, also part of the entourage, met Yoko for the first time, describing her as 'terribly efficient'.

Yoko's life of art, the art of her life was picking up pace again after pausing for some quiet time, some peace of mind, which backfired but led Cox to her. She had become close to Cox, who was happier than Toshi to commit himself completely to promoting her art and supporting her psychologically, and they started to live together, with Cox as much a manager and artistic accomplice as a romantic partner.

For the loyal Cage, Yoko Ono and Toshi were still a couple, and they joined him on parts of his tour, accompanying him in performances. On Cage's complicated, indeterminate 'Music Walk' for one piano or more, which at its core involves walking around a piano playing parts of the instrument in different positions, as well as producing other sounds, some off stage, using voice, radios, record players, tape recorders and whistles, Yoko lay down on top of the piano, performing a conceptual music walk, while Tudor, Cage and Toshi took their silent, contemplative walks and attended to the piano.

The image of Yoko sprawled across the instrument in black dress, stockings and heels with hair falling to the floor as a pensive, professorial

Cage in suit and tie sat at the piano was the image most used in the press, relegating Yoko to the role of decorative magician's assistant.

Cage was the perfect conductor for Toshi's ghostly, undulating 'Sapporo' for any number of performers up to fifteen, displaying what Toshi had learnt studying in America about Webern's concentrated, meditative intensity, the liberating freedoms of graphic notation and through Cage where East and West, silence and sound, touch and time and painting with sound could intersect. Music was sound waves moving through the atmosphere audible to the human ear, you could organise these sound waves however you wished using whatever tools, musical or not, and 'Sapporo' was one of the most beautiful examples of this new musical philosophy.

There was no fixed start or end, no fixed length or shape; it could last anywhere between a compressed fifteen and a languorous fifty minutes depending on various choices, with the conductor also expected to make sounds; here it was a nine-piece ensemble, a group looking and often sounding more like slow-motion impressionist jazz than politely classical, following a scrupulous score of symbols, lines and dashes, allowing their wandering, halting solitary sound-making to occasionally come together before separating again. Tudor played a *biwa*, a short-necked Japanese lute-like instrument borrowed from eighth-century China with Indian roots, and Yoko, as usual surrounded by men, therefore the only participant risking immediate accusations of dilettantism, contributed voice and soft percussion.

Yoko performed 'Chair Piece', a visual haiku, a mute intervention, where she sat on a chair held on wires above the stage staring at the audience, a whimsical, incongruous theatre piece of her own with no obvious context, more likely to make sense sixty years later on social media. It was attributed to Cage, because Cage was the master, and the assumption was that Yoko as the female member of his small parish was merely doing what she was told. Playing with the mind, with life, was something – she was being told directly and indirectly – she wouldn't understand. The performance was about how she did understand.

325

'Chair Piece', Yoko in a chair high above the stage, performing in exactly the way she wanted to, was possibly a response to a journalist's comment, opening the way for future generations of anti-Yoko trolls, about her show at SAC, that instead of pretending she could be an artist, why didn't she just sit still and look pretty?

It was also a reference to her first time on a stage, as a small four-year-old taking part in the monthly show her school put on for parents. She would say that she grew up small, not necessarily because it was a Japanese trait, but small even for the Japanese, and she was particularly tiny as a child.

She was extremely nervous before it was her time to take part, about to play the piano as best she could, suffering a strange stomach ache and throwing up. She forced herself to face up to what felt like an ordeal, which turned into an even greater one when she tried to climb onto the adult-sized piano stool, which seemed impossibly high, and some people in the audience started to laugh. She wondered what they were laughing at, and never forgot her embarrassment. She was taking seriously the fact that she was to play the piano as well as she could, and she was laughed at. She took it as an offence. The incident accounted for the public strategies and steeliness she later displayed when faced with derision and mockery; in private she would still feel the strange stomach ache that could seem to be taking over her mind and body.

Here she was, twenty-eight years later, getting some delayed revenge, climbing onto a chair held high by wires above an audience, and, sitting pretty, impassively looked out at them – if they laughed at what they saw as embarrassing and idiotic, she was now in control of the laughter. She could do whatever she wanted, even fly above them, and offend their notion of what was expected of a deferential Japanese woman. She was free of their obligations, free to be herself, even if at times it seemed the whole world was against her, years before it actually was.

Cage's '0'0''' was a deviant sequel to the silence and the 'there is no such thing as silence' of '4'33''', which had over ten years become a national anthem for an imaginary, recently named country built around the simple but transformative premisse of changing the world by opening the mind.

A rethinking and a replacing of the original's structured silence, which itself was also a theatre piece to be seen as much as heard, composed in the image of a traditional music piece, the first performance by Cage in Tokyo on 24 October 1962 consisted of writing a polite but firm single-sentence score for the performance, prompting a disciplined action using maximum amplification but no feedback.

In this first performance the 'disciplined action' was the writing of the score in front of an audience, fulfilling an obligation he had made to produce a new piece for the concert. It didn't exist before he walked onto the stage. The 'fulfilling of an obligation' – for it to be a social, responsible action – became part of the score if and when performed by others. It was the ultimate last-minute making of a deadline.

It was to be played solo, to be performed by anyone, 'in a situation' using amplification so that whatever the disciplined action was would create the sound of the piece even though it was essentially silent – in the debut performance, this meant attaching contact microphones to Cage's pen, glasses, pipe, ashtray and paper, which as he touched and moved them supplied most of the sound, loudly enough to transmit unheard-of detail. By spontaneously making up the first performance the implication was that all other performances would also be spontaneous, and required no rehearsal, and therefore no technique, and were as long as they needed to be to complete the chosen action.

For some the measured forty-minute performance was pointless tedium and rustling noises, for others a spiritual training for endurance that could extend into everyday life using objects releasing their spirit through sound. For watching members of the sound-art collective Group Ongaku, with their roots in *musique concrète* and Dada ideas mapping a route towards extreme, implacable noise music, it resonated with their own experiments focusing on sound and performing spontaneous conceptual actions as music.

As Cage would say, there is nothing forbidden in the creation of music; for some Japanese musicians this meant they could engage with the traditional Japanese instruments that once seemed regressive; for others they could use anything as an instrument, from vacuum cleaners to dolls. They could combine ancient Japanese instruments with a vacuum cleaner.

Group Ongaku arrived independently at this blurring of composition and performance and viewing art as play, representing the living that takes part every instant, but recognised a fellow traveller showing them other directions, one of which took them into Fluxus. The group's members weren't shocked, but they were stimulated.

Later, Cage modified the score to suggest it could be performed by two or more people deciding between them roughly how long the piece might be, but not timing it with a stopwatch, and the performance need not be amplified. He also later added that there could, even should, be interruptions, no two performances were to be the same, and the 'action' was not to be musical.

A further note referred to a well-known haiku by revered seventeenth-century poet Bashō, a master at using a few spare words to allow a memory to linger, imperfectly but sublimely. Following D.T. Suzuki's English rendering of the haiku, which can be translated in endless subtly different ways, Cage had assigned a particular current composition to each line – 'Atlas Eclipticalis' for orchestra to the first line, setting the scene of an ancient, silent pond; 'Variations IV' for a group of performers collaging miscellaneous found sound to represent the action of a frog jumping into the pond; and '0'0"' to the sound of the water as the frog jumps in – with the implied deep resonance.

'0'0"' was performed a number of times by Cage, a significant part of his virtual lifelong one man Being Nothing but John Cage show, something that was all at once drama, autobiography, purposeful purposelessness, pantomime, prayer, provocation, absence, presence, maddening, explanation, a wordless lecture about time and timelessness, role-playing, comedy, nothing special, profound, showing off, self-analysis, a practical demonstration of his fascination with the power of technology and the extreme sound-revealing marvels of amplification, ultimately simply an ordinary part of his day, the day it was performed. 'One's daily work', he would say, 'is now coming through loudspeakers.'

It was intended to reject self-expression, self-consciousness and self-promotion – art for Cage was self-alteration, if anything – but it was purely Cage, staging himself at a particular stage of his life, sporadically performing it for the next twenty-five years. He set out to remove the personality of the artist but in this he was a total failure, as in a John Cage composition there is nothing but John Cage, even if sometimes he hides behind himself just being himself.

His later performances included eating raw vegetables and blending them into a smoothie and drinking it amplified with a contact microphone attached to his throat, lighting and smoking a cigarette, cleaning the nib of his fountain pen, taking the opportunity to catch up on some correspondence while the squeak of his chair and the drinking of water would be played through loudspeakers.

Performances by others were farcical, solemn, celebratory, political, involved pianos, ice cream and a bowl of ramen noodles. 'Everything we do is music,' he would explain, 'or can become music through the use of microphones.'

Where '4'33"' relied on accidental ambient environment noises emerging from outside the performance and had a duration dictated by its title, '0'00"' used sound from inside the performance itself, from the usually overlooked, ever-present sounds and internal vibrations made by living, and lasted as long as it lasted. '4'33"' for all its seriousness had become a kind of one-hit wonder, a joke piece, and '0'00"', conceived during a visit to Japan, was a Zen correction, a renovation and a purification, intentionally made to live in the protective shadows of the original's distracting notoriety.

The score, a few words requiring imaginative, oblique interpretation, was more a Yoko-like instruction painting inviting imaginative individual responses than a layered, strikingly visual Cageian score setting up multiple outcomes of choice and chance.

There were thousands of possible variations, but none were arrived at by randomly selecting options from a list. Yoko's instructions were haiku – simple on the outside, but once opened up, so that you could

329

enter by accepting the invitation to see what was inside, astonishingly rich and complex.

'0'00"' was in some ways a response by Cage to Yoko's own version of the Cage-instigated visual score. In her translation, with an unavoidable Eastern element, the whole enterprise was chance – the chance of when and where you were born, and where you ended up, and the chance that you would find yourself in a position to read the instruction and have the desire to act on it.

Yoko herself performed it at the Cage Musiccircus memorial in New York on 1 November 1992, ten weeks after Cage's death aged eighty, with his obituary printed on the front page of the *New York Times*. (Music-circus was a 1967 piece by Cage 'for any number of performers willing to perform in the same space at the same time' in any way they desired.) Yoko slashed a canvas, releasing some red paint which left a mournful trail. She walked to a piano and played some chords, consciously rebelling, in a Cageian way, in her way, against the instruction that the action should not be a musical action.

At the end of his public/private writing session, his debut performance of '0'0"', which created another Cage composition that imagined other genres, he tenderly blew on the ink to dry it, and walked towards Yoko and Toshi in the audience, bowing as he presented the score to them. Yoko in turn kissed Cage on the cheek.

Above the original one sentence Cage wrote for and during its debut performance, he noted that it was 'For Yoko Ono and Toshi Ichiyanagi', dedicating it to them perhaps because of their help on his first visit to Japan and in some of his performances, perhaps because of his fondness for them as a couple and as artist and musician, hoping that they would stay together, and keep inspiring each other and him. A little paternally, he felt Toshi's steadying presence in Yoko's life helped her in her life and in her art, and that she should adapt to his expectations of a marriage.

It was too late. Toshi and Yoko divorced – a functioning art couple, arguing badly in life, Yoko refusing point blank to be submissive and build her life around his, to fall into the trap of being a docile Asian woman eager to serve. After some legal delays, Yoko married Tony Cox in June 1963. Cox believed in Yoko's art and slipped into her headstrong, impulsive lifestyle in a way the more formal Toshi couldn't manage.

She never hid her background, but resisted cultural stereotyping, finding for herself a self-made imaginary place that was both within being Japanese and far away from being Japanese. She was making herself ready for the insurgent countercultural 1960s, seeing it coming for years, the drugs, clothes and overall appearance part of her post-war understanding that to stake out real freedoms in life and art needed an anything-goes philosophy, structured with its own unorthodox disciplines.

Toshi was not making it beyond the much straighter Year 1960, when bohemian could still mean short, clipped hair and a nicely fitting suit and modest tie. Toshi would write to Cage, back in New York, that he was truly sorry he had not found a way to make Yoko happy.

While in Japan setting up home, studio and immediate future with Cox, giving birth to their daughter Kyoko two months after they married, Yoko put together two works that were among her most powerful and significant, one a collection of her 'wishes and hopes' up to that point, the other the reduction of all she had produced to a single, dramatic three-letter word, which could flourish, like a haiku, into an intense experience with its own illuminating vitality.

Both appeared in July 1964, as her stay in Japan came to an end and she was becoming as prolific as she had been in Manhattan. They would have ensured a place as influence and innovator even if they were her only major art achievements, the climax of a brief artistic adventure, and there was no unimaginable transformation into fraught, frightening celebrity which took her name and her art out into another world. They were two powerful representations of her mind that suggested she was something other and deeper than definitive home-wrecking, man-eating parasite and corrupter of art.

They showed how she was negotiating the constant pressure she was feeling, trying to establish herself as an artist at the indistinct beginnings of an emerging conceptualist revolution and the early ripples of a modern feminist uprising, not the wife of a renowned Japanese composer always walking a few steps behind or a minor player in the entourage of an American avant-garde icon, her efforts being absorbed into the reputations of others.

She was on her own fighting the kind of battle all artists fight against scepticism, the constant nagging voice in your head that says what you do as an artist, especially an avant-garde artist, is ridiculous, the sense that what artists do is fundamentally unnecessary and expendable. Art is from another, imaginary world, it has no intrinsic value, and requires imagination to make it real, and fixed, regulated institutional structures to make it professional.

Critics and cynics who made it difficult to remain sincere and committed inside this imaginary setting threatened its provisional, fragile nature. There needs to be some benefit of the doubt given for an experimental artist spending their time getting inside your head and messing with it to continue their exploration, and Yoko worked at a time when that benefit of the doubt was given first of all to men, and mostly white Anglo-American Westerners. The doubt facing her kind of art, which seemed to both mock art and take it too seriously, turning the everyday into the sacred and vice versa, was already considerable, and the fact she was a woman and Asian made it many times more than her male peers. Failure, contempt, hostility were always a breath, a scream, away. Sometimes it felt that the only way to avoid them was to accept the risks and keep going. It was a test of faith.

In the summer of 1963, as was now the way among disparate avant-garde Fluxus people and near neighbours keeping in touch, supporting each other and activating and anticipating action through newsletters and new scores and instructions, Yoko wrote an instruction, originally titled 'Instructions for Poem No. 81', alongside a 'Poem No. 86 – Fly', which announced the birth of Kyoko, written in Yoko's own hand, and the planning of a forthcoming collection of scores and instructions which she was planning to call *Grapefruit*. Maciunas published 'Poem No. 86' in a Fluxus newsletter and it was planned he would help produce the collection.

She had given birth to Kyoko, was giving birth to *Grapefruit*, and you should see the world through their eyes, touching everything they see, leaving a fingerprint in place of a signature; 'Poem No. 81' also included an inked handprint made from Kyoko's tiny hand. There were also some impressionistic examples of what you could see through the eyes of Kyoko, and potentially through *Grapefruit*, such as snow in India, J.C.'s as in John Cage's overcoat, Simone's equilibrium and clouds, for their place in the vastness of the sky, and their transitory state.

She had found a place in and around the Japanese art scene, had started a family, but she still felt like a misfit. *Grapefruit* was a book by her and about her, conceived in New York and Tokyo, that came together while her mind was in limbo, and her life was moving in between a Japanese husband she'd married in New York and an American one she'd married in Tokyo.

The New Yorker in her, the accidental American, decided a good publication date for *Grapefruit* was 4 July 1964, the date a knowing statement of independent intent for something that was outside commercial formalities. The publication date could easily be made up.

Despite Maciunas pressing her to release it as a Fluxus publication, he became too distracted by Fluxus, and as always was lacking funds, and Yoko published it herself in an edition of five hundred copies, possibly less, via an independent publishing house, Wunternaum Press, that she founded for the purpose. This was the result of the sifting and sorting she had been doing while she was in the sanatorium.

It was five and a half inches square, with nearly two hundred unnumbered pages and a fragile binding. The original cover was white, with the single word 'Grapefruit' written by hand on each copy on the left-hand side. The uncompromising, clinical simplicity of the cover was not necessarily a choice; she couldn't afford colour or photography, but the stark white space reflected the minimally presented contents, and it was a book about her by her, and 'Grapefruit' stood for both.

Open *Grapefruit* and there was a series of carefully planted seeds numbering 150 that could grow into a variety of things depending on how they were activated inside the mind or in the outside world.

The cover gave nothing away, so there might be nothing inside, and it could have come from the seventeenth century or the twenty-third. Inside, on pages as basic as the cover, there was a quiet rush of life and living, pages and pages of elliptical relief, messages, existential recipes and revelation organised into five categories, a third of them also printed in Japanese, often not directly reflecting the English versions, underlining how the particular language the texts were written in had migrated back and forth between English and Japanese: instructions for Music (52), Painting (40), Event (42), Poetry (8) and Object (8).

This did not mean the instructions were only intended for the category they came under. The categories and genres were just a starting point, a reference to a book (if it was to be a book) requiring a fixed layout, an accessible organisation of content; they dissolved as quickly as they were made. There was also nothing stopping a Japanese instruction that appeared in the Painting section appearing in English in the Music section.

Yoko started selling the books in advance of publication for $3, and after publication for $6. For a while even printing a limited few hundred copies seemed ambitious, especially the choice to do it herself without the practical help and PR zeal of Maciunas. Reviews and any sort of coverage were negligible.

What to make of it? A random list of prompts, pipe dreams, reveries, apparitions, aphorisms, prayers, impressions, conversation pieces, thought experiments and dream sounds scattered in her room inside a mental institution was a cause for concern for her well-being. Elegantly compiled as a pocket-sized artefact, a culmination of an aesthetic philosophy, an enquiry into form and style, economical and precise, it became something else altogether – a book about itself that kept revealing itself, a glimpse into the inner life of an adventurous artist continually testing reactions at a personally and culturally tense, dramatic time.

You could use *Grapefruit* to send advice on how to cut a painting up and let the pieces be lost in the wind, draw a map and get lost, send the smell of the mood, listen (till dawn) to a group of people snoring, put dripping clouds in a hole in your garden, polish an orange, talk about the death of an imaginary person, make all the clocks in the world go two seconds faster without telling anyone, listen to the earth turning, throw a stone so high into the sky it never comes down, listen to a heartbeat, smoke everything you can, including your pubic hair, send the sound of snow to another person, borrow the *Mona Lisa* and fashion it into a kite, fly it so high it disappears into a dot. The painting had been imprisoned inside a gallery for so long; it should be set free, as something more than just an object to stare at for a few seconds. You could make clothes out of paintings by Leonardo, Raphael and De Kooning and wear them with the outside or inside showing. A blank page was titled a painting to enlarge and see.

On the surface it was a list of odd, poignant, ridiculous, impossible, funny, dreamy, trivial, mysterious, challenging, charming, mischievous, inscrutable words and potential sensory experiences, but going deeper it was a book of aesthetic philosophy exploring the dematerialisation of art after Duchamp and Cage; a book about musical notation after G. Brecht, Cage, Young and Ono; a book experimenting with memory and different layers of consciousness; an art book filled with art made from evoking real and imagined instants in the flow of life; a guide to how to adjust to the contemporary world, of whatever shape and date; a draft of a more comprehensive study on conceptualism; a Fluxus recipe book; a book of poems that exceed the page; an explanation of the universe in a few words.

You could also use it to unblock your mind, refine the senses and psychologically reboot. It was a book about the value of creative experimentation as a personal act of renewal, a book about how to resist tyranny and conventionality.

You could, if you were willing to play along, construct new realities and redefine life and thought, which, during the time the instructions were compiled, to a war child looking for light, learning to think on her feet, surrounded by tense social conflict, seemed an urgent demand. It was an exercise in confidence, that the future would be better than the dismal recent past and a present in increasing turmoil. A small, everyday freedom enacted through the imagination could be a rehearsal for hoped-for freedom on a larger scale.

Look to what the artists are doing, with their 'anti-environments', said Marshall McLuhan, if you want to know how to perceive and address changes happening all around us in a world of rapid technological and scientific advance. Art at its best was prophetic more than simply being self-expression.

Grapefruit was one of the great examples of McLuhan's art as early warning radar system – as he pointed out in his 1964 book *Understanding Media* – which you can always rely on to tell the old culture what is beginning to happen to it. Art enables us to discover emerging social and psychic issues and gives us time to prepare to cope with them.

The Yoko Ono whose hand-lettered sheets and small printed cards presenting her instructions and event scores can seem quaint and innocuous in a world of rapidly distributed digitised social media, but at the time, these strange, enigmatic and mobile missives belonging to no known genre could move quickly between the lines of culture, easily reproduced in broadsheets, fanzines, programmes and books, and, ultimately, realised as language, object and performance, spurring imaginative responses.

She resorted to selling the book in the crowded streets of central Tokyo in a hot, steamy summer, hot enough for the Olympic organisers to schedule the summer games for the late autumn. Few locals coming across what at first seemed like a ragged street peddler understood what it was she was trying to sell them, and any who did glance at it were unsure what to make of what was unlike anything they had come across before.

She was a mirage selling a compendium of mirages, a suspicious-looking young woman wearing black reaching into an old orange crate and pulling out a small, delicately wrapped fragile white thing she claimed could unlock the power of the imagination. It will help you see the invisible! Have faith . . . believe in yourself! Most passers-by scurried past her.

It would eventually be described as a manual for the production of DIY art, an otherworldly book of meditation composed in the spirit of a haiku, a book of sounds never heard outside the mind, a collage of emotions in a conceptual space, a book demonstrating how to replace paint with words in order to paint a picture, an abstract self-help book for an individual or a community. Art in itself confined inside the frame had come to an end, but there were many more potential dimensions, interpretations and meanings.

Yoko wrote 'burn this book after reading', to underline her conviction that art is about creation but not necessarily preservation, or at least the sort that neutralises art and turns it into commodity or dead part of a sealed-off collection.

As a defiantly uncynical manifesto of liberation, it would become as important to a number of female artists and musicians discovering it over the next few decades as Rimbaud's *Illuminations* was to Patti Smith. It was an inherited gift which said you could do anything, and use your imagination to escape a mean world constantly judging, limiting and undermining you. And to fight for freedom you had to be fierce. She wasn't giving concrete advice, just saying that they should learn to think for themselves, and unwrap the tightness they felt was hemming them in.

Sixty years after its publication, after the dreams, desires and protests of the counterculture were systematically drained away through repetition and indifference, when the short epic history of popular culture – an extraordinary, fleeting Renaissance – had been dissected into a select, controlled and compressed archive, everything becoming recyclable data, you could see it as a prescient resource for those looking to instructionalise AI and sustain the mysteries of human civilisation. It could teach how to input out-of-reach, ethereal, spiritual elements of humanity, signs of the soul, that were being neglected as AI indiscriminately sourced and collated its information and its prompters 'trained' it in a more prosaic, functional way.

Grapefruit also imagined the internet: select a subject and write five million pages on the subject.

It also helped dream up the parameters of the psychedelic.

First of all, though, blank stares, shrugs and a few murmurs of polite encouragement or clipped 'leave me alone's. She was reduced to giving copies away, just to feel someone was getting her messages, which she had put so much into.

It was also a publication that was Fluxus and not Fluxus, so that Yoko could always be and not be a Fluxus artist, one who had with *Grapefruit* constructed one of the foundational texts – and elsewhere conceived some of its economical, mobile production processes and set in motion many of its ground rules – and then had to do nothing else to be Fluxus but did things that were inevitably Fluxus, but that were never of Fluxus but were asterisked as Fluxus. She was Fluxus and at the same time she wasn't Fluxus, which confirmed her indisputable Fluxusness. This mixed sense of belonging and not belonging reflected her being Japanese and not Japanese, rooted in its traditions, but transforming them as well.

Yoko sent to Maciunas a work in progress made up of a sample of the typewritten instructions on loose cards. She included a list of thirty-five people she had dedicated individual instructions to, some of whom were aware of the dedication, some of whom weren't. These included – as well as herself – Cage, Tudor, Toshi, Cox, Maciunas, Young, Paik, Mac Low, Feldman, Rauschenberg, Morris, Forti, Brecht, Brown, Jennings, Johnson, Knowles, Guggenheim, Wakowski, Maxfield and Byrd, which in itself was a list of accomplices and co-workers in an unofficial atelier of New Yorker originals she was at the centre of – even in Tokyo – roughly running parallel with Fluxus and *An Anthology*.

Six years later, *Grapefruit* got another life, once she had become a name, had controversially married into a musical family with globe-spanning fame, a woman with so much on her mind seen as having nothing on her mind except a shamelessly cynical plan to steal a husband, steal attention, and steal music itself and music fans' souls.

Grapefruit was published in an expanded and amended form with Film, Dance and Architecture pieces as a lively, goofy popular book, in America by the established mainstream publishers Simon & Schuster, who were unable to resist cashing in on the wife of a beloved rock star with her own transgressive notoriety. It would be published in a number of covers but all of them would retain the book's original size and shape.

The original British edition published by Peter Owen kept the idea of a monochrome cover, inside a minimal maroon art-book slipcase, with the addition of a photo of Yoko as a psychedelic Alice in Wonderland, subtly smiling to herself in quiet pleasure at not having to be a desperate salesperson for her own work.

A cheaper orange and yellow Sphere paperback version featured a cheeky hybrid of bare bum and grapefruit, the art book as novelty, a 'wit and wisdom of Yoko Ono' item and a comedy book by one half of rock's wackiest couple with a thing for bottoms. In America the first cover was accessibly sunny yellow, and the paperback version a close-up photo of Yoko as sultry, inviting pop star in aviator sunglasses.

This was an image of Yoko that made some of her more single-minded former avant-garde comrades think she had surrendered to the dark side, sacrificing her experimental integrity for the sake of commercial comforts even as she wasn't being made welcome on the other side. Yoko was still following *Grapefruit* as her personal manifesto, just putting her latest thinking onto bigger stages in front of larger audiences.

The contents inside the more commercial, cheerful, upbeat-ish covers were still more or less the same, subversively reflective heart-to-hearts, inspirational dictums, made-up customs and seductively secretive sayings. *Grapefruit* had effortlessly passed into another very different, post-hippie psychedelic era, the few years since its original appearance as a speculative special-interest avant-garde investigation seeming a lot longer.

It kept up to date and always a few steps ahead because its mind-bending, freedom-seeking principles making no reference to the fashions of the day had been absorbed almost despite Yoko's perceived villainy into the fashions, attitudes and appearances of the 1960s. Its ancillary prophecies came true as technology, fashions, art scenes, music, countries, media and eras kept changing.

In 1964, regarded as the beginning of the end of Japan's 'official' post-war period heralded by the Summer Olympics, with the organisational and motivational help of Tony Cox, Yoko was picking up the momentum she'd had before she left New York. It was a deeply ambiguous time to be there, a country that had in a few years gone from fascism, militaristic imperialism and ruin, through American occupation and its imposed consumerism by the very people who had dropped the nuclear bombs, to a fresh, conflicted but determined new democracy.

Collaborating with Japanese artists energetically wrestling with their identity, with their own developing connection to the unsettling stunts and events of Fluxus and their heretical investigation of the everyday helped make her feel she was part of something without it threatening her autonomy. She was a loner, but also happy to join others when their work had a close affinity with hers – especially when that meant artworks that didn't seem like artworks, and art with a caustic, playful anti-establishment attitude using the body as material that would influence the counterculture to come.

In January, she participated in an uncanny live event orchestrated by the short-lived, radically satirical post-Gutai collective Hi-Red Center. Formed in 1962, it became an absurdist, dissident specialist in using unexpected, defiantly non-gallery spaces including apartments, department stores, train stations and trains themselves to stage cathartic performance art pieces with a disorienting documentary aura.

The collective scrutinised what impact the war still had, its spirits and ghosts, on an increasingly dynamic, self-consciously Westernised Japan. For Hi-Red, art was linked to revolution: its members had faith in the subversive potential of art, and it drove them onto the streets in serious and nonsensical protest.

One of their first self-styled 'mixers' was 'Dinner Event', where people invited to mark Japan's defeat in the Second World War turned up and found they were there only to watch the artists eat – these included Hi-Red's founders Genpei Akasegawa – also part of the Japanese Neo-Dada group – Natsuyuki Nakanishi and Jiro Takamatsu. 'The Great Panorama Exhibition' involved opening and emptying a can of crab meat, sealing it shut, and announcing that the world was now contained inside the can.

In the run-up to the Olympics their public, deadpan 'Be Clean!' street 'ultra-cleaning event' mocked the government's menacing-seeming, intense cleanliness campaigns intended to highlight the new, modern, economically miraculous Japan and its developing post-war sociocultural identity, carefully constructed to satisfy Western expectations.

There was an inevitable youthful vibrancy to the reborn Japan, with Tokyo a thriving centre of advanced technology and design, and Japan's avant-garde was an extreme, mutinous symbol of this national enterprise, and also a by-product of the urgent need to quickly re-establish stability – in this case, stability through destabilising convention.

Wearing white lab coats, gloves, surgical masks and sunglasses to maintain anonymity, holding signs saying 'Be Clean!', members of Hi-Red meticulously wiped down the busy pavements of the fashionable Ginza shopping district. They used inappropriate tools – toothbrushes, bleach-soaked cotton wool, buckets and small brooms – to examine what was being lost, what was being wasted and hidden, in the state's determination to publicise a hygienically clean, polished, secure and non-toxic Japan and to generate a controlled image of national progress and unified social life. They worked with such concentration that a passing policeman thanked them for their service.

Japan was no longer occupied, but in other ways, it was still being occupied by its own government. Mirroring how local residents had been asked to volunteer in the official cleaning up, they asked passers-by to help them clean the streets.

For 'Shelter Plan', Hi-Red Center co-opted the lobby and room 340 of the hyper-luxury Imperial Hotel, an elaborate, modern version of the original nineteenth-century wooden structure that was designed by the Japan-loving American architect Frank Lloyd Wright and finished in

1923. It was intended to symbolise Japan's civilising modernity, the adoption of Western ideas and techniques motivated by the Meiji era. It survived a massive earthquake that happened three months after it opened, and the Second World War firebombing of Tokyo, which made it – with its iconic sheltering reputation, and the sense that its local and international grandeur was 'the heart of the city' – an ideal location for the interventionist staging of 'Shelter Plan'.

Acting as the imaginary, official-sounding Shelter Plan Conference, Hi-Red sent an invitation containing instructions to a host of specific artists, musicians, designers, photographers, writers, dancers and filmmakers including Yoko Ono, Nam June Paik and his partner Shigeko Kubota. It wasn't its central meaning, but the event was a way of assembling a comprehensive Japanese underground of subversives midway between their understanding of the happening and their preview of performance art.

When their guests arrived, their personal details were taken, they were weighed and measured, effectively scrutinised in intimate, almost biometric detail from interior mouth volume via fingerprints to shoe size, and closely photographed around the body to create highly accurate body data. The measurements would be used to create an expensive, customised one-person bomb shelter, to be produced in four sizes. The fictitious bureaucratic planning for the bomb shelters recalled unwelcome memories of Hiroshima and Nagasaki that were already becoming an obstacle to recovery for some, in the middle of the Cold War, and for a country desperately needing to make the attacks distant, unrealistic abstractions.

Getting on with life, concentrating on building a new society as if the atomic bombs were just some unrepeatable scientific experiment, merely the opening salvos of the Cold War, a necessary show of American strength to actually keep the peace, was seen as helping to get rid of any lingering psychological effects.

'Shelter Plan' was like a committee meeting as performance, the avant-garde talking to artistic allies, planning a revolution of the senses. This

343

shadowy underground club of elite agents provocateurs using art to fight the system and achieve different levels of consciousness naturally drew the attention of the authorities.

A few hours after the private scene in room 340 was dismantled and its mysterious props removed, Genpei Akasegawa was arrested for forging and distributing thousand-yen notes, which had been used in 'Shelter Plan'. His fake money, enacted as interventionist art to interfere with the order of things and propose a new world, was seen as being a form of terrorism. The years of legal problems after he was charged with serious currency fraud would lead to his prosecution and, within months, the dissolution of the collective.

A documentary film made at the time by avant-garde film-maker and on-the-spot witness Motoharu Jonouchi shows Yoko lying on a bed and being measured for her one-person bomb shelter, taking seriously her role as subject and object submitting to disciplinary power. As actor and activist, she had developed a ritualistic understanding of how to participate in this kind of staged, theatrically untheatrical spectacle, simulating and getting inside the everyday, creating vivid, immersive experiences that planted unreal actions inside real settings and evolved in their own manner.

She was also featured in an affectionately made 1964 film about the lively Tokyo experimental art scene and its haunting oppositional presence in the nationalist spectacle of the Olympic Games made by Nippon Television and directed by Chiaki Nagano.

Some Young People followed Yoko Ono and the avant-garde collectives Zero Dimension (Zero Jigen – 'bringing a human being back to zero') and Sightseeing Art Research Institute as their performance art materialised out of rebellion against conventional art institutions and their protests against Japan's hasty, American-encouraged Cold War rearming and the carefully arranged propaganda distraction of the Olympic Games.

The Sightseeing Art Research Institute protest artists and social surrealists Hiroshi Nakamura and Kōichi Tateishi were filmed in front of the Yoyogi National Stadium, the futuristic symbol of Tokyo's Olympic

Games, eating five doughnuts that formed the Olympic rings, interspersed with ominous, fantastical paintings conjuring up images of Second World War air raids, visions of Hiroshima, the ongoing nuclear arms race, Olympic fever and the subordination of Japan to America. Their name came from a play on the Japanese word for sightseeing, which could be literally translated as seeing light.

Zero Dimension's self-styled art terrorist events, known as rituals, mixing the secular and the sacred, showing how traditional national rituals were mutating as Japan modernised, were performed one time only in public locations such as public baths, shrines and cemeteries. 'Ritual of Sleeping Body' in 1963 featured members of the group looking at an erotic print on the ceiling while lying on futons covered with small nipple-shaped stones. A naked man and woman tied together with a rope walked through a subway train. Members streaked through Tokyo streets wearing gas masks, as if escaping both incoming danger and pervasive cultural homogeneity.

For 'Crawling Ritual', group representatives would be strolling along a busy street minding their own business and suddenly all fall to the ground, abruptly breaking the everyday peace, and start crawling, stopping the traffic and putting nearby pedestrians on alert, faced with a bewildering militant flash mob operating in the wrong space and time. They took part in staged nude actions involving fireworks, slogans and hanging from nets.

Art was a battle, and these performances and social experiments were part of a strategy of attack and defence. The participants explained in the film how they were imagining universes beyond ordinary human perception, and thinking of ways to access them, and live there.

That Yoko was portrayed in the film as the symbolic leader shows how she was at the vanguard of this convergence of artistic energy – teaching and learning at the same time. One of Yoko's appearances in *Some Young People* is more in the spirit of *Grapefruit*, using her mind as a weapon, or a shield, with an intention to slow life down by introducing poetic events into daily life so that people had time to consider what was being done

345

by the state on their behalf. Her patrolling of the boundary between the everyday and the non-everyday was more revolution by stealth.

'Flower Event' is a softer, oblique, more peaceful intervention on the Tokyo streets than the collectives mostly made up of more boisterous men, a quiet and reflective but still assertive artistic action, approaching art and anti-art from a less explicitly disruptive direction. 'Any place and anything can become the object of their artistic acts,' explains the documentary narration, introducing the various artists 'resisting the myth of happiness'.

Wearing the neat black dress and modest heels she had worn when performing with John Cage and David Tudor – the at-play equivalent of her Sunday best – she left chrysanthemums one by one in various places on the street, hanging from traffic lights, on cars and motorbikes, in storefronts, seeing if anyone noticed her solo attempt to beautify Tokyo, mocking what the voiceover calls 'the superficial happy atmosphere of contemporary Japan'.

There is little sign in the film that anyone does notice, and if they do they ignore the anomalous interruption to their lives, an incongruous waft of flower power years before hippies. One passing schoolgirl goes out of her way to step on one of the flowers, rebelling against the rebellion.

The performance dissolves into the everyday, caught on camera so that it can now be seen as a comment on how out of place Yoko was in Japan: at home and visibly present in transformative avant-garde reality, wherever and however it occurred, but a little lost and absent in the fabricated reality of the new Tokyo, looking for allies. She's shown in a street busy with office workers racing home trying to sell copies of *Grapefruit* with the assistance of her husband. The voiceover notes, 'There is no audience to participate in their artistic action here.'

For Yoko, the social agitation and atomic-age, anti-war dimension of Hi-Red Center and Zero Dimension, their unprecedented sexual openness, was more evidence that some danger in art, whether gentle and playful or visceral and malevolent, took it further away from the consoling, controlling and complacent safety of tradition and the art institutions, and out into the world, where it would be expanded and changed by its contact with reality, using elusive, challenging live situations. It could even cause a real, unintended disturbance. Art was not placed in opposition to politics, but integrated seamlessly.

The actions of Hi-Red Center and Zero Dimension were more evidence that interactive art using audience reaction to performance as part of its structure could and should be pushed into the larger public arena. Zero Dimension was often featured in popular magazines and newspapers and on primetime television, as a group of very watchable, sensationalist 'urban eccentrics', as well as in art magazines with their limited circulations.

Yoko saw this multimedia transmission of invented rituals, customs and experiences that could only be experienced in person as a conscious strategy. The mass media could be your exhibition space, where your work was displayed and entered wider culture. Troubling, difficult issues, a more authentic reality, the link avant-gardists strived for between imaginative freedom and social liberation, could become part of everyday experience and memory.

Attention was the reward for presenting art as performance and instruction with no discernible end, which didn't exist to be sold after it was finished or experienced. The media could be an appropriately fluid gallery, showing this art as it happened, archiving it – which would make even more sense in the digital age, which helped follow the ghostly trajectory of transient art and understand its social context – and part of the process.

347

Among the venues Yoko used in her final few months in Tokyo, looking for the audience she needed to help make her art exist, was the Naiqua Gallery, the birthplace of Japan's Neo-Dada group and one of the city's unique, locally situated rental galleries giving experimental artists freedom to live, work and play. Naiqua, meaning internal medicine, was set up by a doctor, Kunio Miyata, who had become partial to the potential social therapy of avant-garde actions. While he was waiting for his medical licence, he turned his small rented second-floor office next to a busy road over to artists.

Yoko performed a 'Touch Piece' in which she and future Fluxus allies Takehisa Kosugi, Shigeko Kubota and Mieko Shiomi sat silently in the dark touching each other, with Nam June Paik calling in from home and 'touching' everyone through the ringing of the phone.

In April 1964, Yoko stayed away from a Naiqua performance of 'Fly Piece', because in this case her physical presence was not needed. Her husband Cox, Paik, members of Hi-Red and Neo-Dada among others performed it. The audience as co-author followed the single-word instruction – 'Fly' – by jumping from a stepladder positioned in the gallery, leaping into the air in whatever way they wanted, symbolically or imaginatively, or physically embodied, bravely from up high or less recklessly from only a couple of steps, creating a sense of being aloft, hovering between states, between the floor and the ground, the inside of oneself and the outside.

If you believed in Yoko, and/or like Yoko, you could fly, as if in a dream. 'Fly' stands for freedom, independence, overcoming obstacles, a sense of control, personal growth, a spiritual ascension, breaking free of all earthly limitations, elation at how your life is unfolding, preparing to take a step forward into the unknown.

'Fly' became many forms, representing many forms of life, freedom and action, adopted as a flighty pseudonym, another name for other subliminal identities she used at various stages. She was Grapefruit, she was Fly, she was others, a collection of identities, pieces, reflections and moments in time. She made a series of works that became other series and sub-series: an instruction series, a performance series, an events series, a series of Pieces, a water series, a tape series, a film script/score and film series, a music series, a music and film series, a Plastic Ono Band series, a solo album series, an anti-art and anti-war series, a fame series, a victim series, a post-murder series, a post-recovery series, a post-being rediscovered as an artist in the twenty-first century series, a meticulously curated retrospective series awarding late-life applause and approval to what was previously scattered, ignored and scorned.

Touch was at the centre of many of the series; for Yoko it was the most mysterious of the senses. Touch, immediate and powerful, spanning the whole body, was a fundamental form of perception, a primary source of both pleasure and pain.

Her use of touch from the very beginning and the 'Touch Poems' of 1960 was part an exploration of the relationship between the senses, how individual sensory experiences contribute to people's knowledge of the world. Was the sensory experience total, rather than both visual and tactile? What is the relationship between human consciousness and our external reality?

Without touch, Yoko reasoned her art was missing something. The conceptual pieces were vague suggestions about how to imagine touch and touching in the production of mental images. The performance pieces encouraged actual touching, which could mean encounters, new ways of generating new forms of sensory experience, that were spiritual, sensual, awkward, therapeutic, emotional, challenging, communal.

What made sense of all sensory input, centred on seeing, hearing and feeling, depended on the mind. For Yoko, the mind was the magician at the disposal of everyone.

These interconnected series all spiralled out of her earliest instruction pieces, from the original 'Secret Piece' seed, the lit match and the touching, the sky and the 'flying', building up intensity during the final weeks of the two years she spent in Japan before her life changed beyond recognition. At the time she was getting ready to return to the New York she was increasingly missing, armed with new pieces and performances.

The intensity of those last few months in Japan, soon to become an intense year or so in New York, also helped her get ready for the then-unimaginable change in her circumstances a few years ahead, when she would for better or worse be the subject of attention outside of the usual, limited, self-perpetuating avant-garde niche.

She would admit she then lost a little bit of her edge, in a nice way, going along with ideas that initially seemed a bit Hollywood to her. She was still left with a lot of edge, still one foot in the underground, but with one foot in entertainment, and a vigilant kind of responsibility – not necessarily to an audience, but certainly as one half of a prolific double act presenting marriage as a performance. She took this responsibility as meaning she should encourage the other half of the double act to put one foot in the underground, and the marriage to be itself a self-contained multi-disciplinary art movement in itself with strong links to Fluxus.

'Fly Piece' announced its own birth, and then flew off in different directions. Some versions of it used the same title; some evolved into something else and used other titles. There were other audience performances of the instruction piece in various settings, some containing ladders of different heights. 'Fly' was a twenty-minute black-and-white film based on the instruction 'Let a fly walk on a woman's body from toe to head and fly out of the window.' It was a film about a fly. It was a film about where we look and why when we watch such a film. It was a film about signs of life after a nuclear explosion, the fly a reminder of the imminence of decay.

It was made by someone who at the time was not taken particularly seriously as an artist and musician even by those taking her seriously and appreciating how she had moved art into new dimensions and was moving music into new places.

It began with a close-up of a housefly, and closely follows the fly's unique voyage as it crawls across the sugar-water-and-honey-covered abstracted skinscape of a motionless, seemingly oblivious naked woman named in the credits as Virginia Lust.

The fly slowly meanders, rubbing its knees, pausing to contemplate and savour various body parts, arm, nipples, stomach, lips, vagina, expressing interest in her nostril, considering at length slipping inside the mouth, into another landscape, the heart of darkness, deciding to stay on the surface, journeying across the woman's body, through shadowlands and deserts, valleys and slopes, crevices and plains, encountering other environments and sources of strangeness, other swarming, bristling flies self-cleaning and minding their own business – a little stoned on carbon dioxide, slowing them down so they followed human time.

As an idea, 'Fly' began with Yoko's fondness for the double meaning in the English word 'fly', and a saucy British cartoon Yoko had seen of a man looking at a woman in a low-cut blouse. His wife sees him staring at the woman's breasts and asks him what he is looking at. He says, oh, I'm looking at a fly on her shirt.

Yoko made a definitive fly-on-the-wall film where there is a moving fly and an unmoving naked woman, creature and flesh, and you are never sure what you are watching – the fly, or the woman, the flesh or the creature. And are you watching Yoko Ono as annoying fly despoiling a human being, or Yoko being invaded by something inhuman treating her as object, as insect representing monstrous-feminine bodies that threaten to disrupt masculine order, Yoko wondering what it's like to fly?

Who is doing the inspection – fly investigating woman; woman feeling fly; the artist at work, either in control or making something up as she goes along; or the viewer watching the clash of realities, of real and surreal, nature and naturalness, art and life, which also involves a language specially invented for the occasion?

The film's extraordinary improvised wordless soundtrack – the sound was made first, so the visuals can be seen as the silent soundtrack to the sound – is all Yoko, all Fly, all Voice, all Woman, one becoming the other, inside and out.

There's a phased, grazing electric guitar, a hint of her new world patrolling the rarely crossed borders between multi-track rock-and-roll recording studio and avant-garde art, but even that becomes part of the all Yoko: all her body, softness, power, knowledge, desperation, rawness, pleasure, pain, violation, sensual, memories, delicacy, horror, mood,

351

intensity, extra-terrestrial, grotesque, depression, surprise, love, melancholy, euphoria, violence, disgust, fascination. It is a self-questioning sonic autobiography of a woman's life, a fantastical story about a fly discovering a new world.

At the end, after the woman's motionless body is near-fully revealed, as part of some unclear experiment, the Voice and shadowing electric guitar drop away, leaving stillness and silence, and the camera follows the fly out of the window towards an open blue sky, and we fly with it. A last Yoko wail fades away; credits roll because this, after all that, is a film, and Yoko's Fly voice begins at the beginning, on another journey we don't get to see. The insect 'fly', a model of her own unconventional lifestyle, becomes 'fly' where you defy gravity and leap and swoop above the world.

Perhaps this has been a film about reincarnation, and Yoko's reincarnation, the overlooked, underestimated and marginalised Japanese American artist anticipating an ascendant media culture, becoming a radically conscientious transnational luminary.

If you hated the sound of Yoko screaming, never heard it but just hated the idea of her screaming, whimpering and growling, done just to set your skin crawling and yours alone, then this is the mythical, obnoxious screeching sound you would be thinking of.

This sound of 'Fly', of a free woman in flight, was used to further punish her, as if it confirmed she was mad, and what she had done to the world was part of her madness. The noisy, screeching, hissing woman who didn't belong in pop music, or any music, who deserved to be swatted away.

This didn't stop her producing this hallucinatory, spellbinding non-verbal theatre, the sound of total commitment, of disrupting the shape of everyday life, of someone emotionally involved in their work and convinced of the truth of it – the sound of 'it isn't easy to demand the impossible'.

The 'Fly' sound was also part of a scream series that began nine years earlier in 1961 with the instructions for 'Voice Piece for Soprano': scream against the wind, scream against the wall, scream against the sky. The tremendous scream that comes with the arrival of a new life. The blood-curdling scream that comes with seeing close-up a life or a love violently snatched away from you.

The Yoko Ono asking everyone to scream with her.

The Yoko Ono explaining that the world doesn't want a woman to sound too strong; people prefer a woman known for a pretty voice and pretty songs. The world doesn't like a woman to scream out. 'I thought we have to show what women are. We're the birthgivers of the human race.' Why be ashamed of it?

The Yoko Ono who screamed for freedom.

The Yoko Ono who screamed I am here.

The Yoko Ono who screamed to make you feel how she felt her own body, from deep inside.

The Yoko Ono who screamed at the edge of chaos.

The Yoko Ono who screamed for dear life.

The Yoko who screamed, 'I do these sexual sounds but they could also be the sound of someone being tortured. I was interested in the animalistic side of the human voice, the groans a woman gives when she is having a baby. There is no line, or maybe it's a fine line. I heard people chanting in Morocco and thought that's like what I do. It's rooted in something pre-history.'

The Yoko Ono who screamed as though imagining the cries and sounds a human makes before language is learned.

The Yoko Ono who screamed as if it was a way to enter a different form of existence.

The Yoko Ono who screamed so she could be heard above the amplified electric guitars.

The Yoko Ono who screamed as if to say, do not feel fear or embarrassment whenever you get a glimpse of your ignorance.

The Yoko Ono who screamed as if it was a form of reproduction.

The Yoko Ono who screamed to see where/if the sound she was making tipped over into meaning.

The Yoko Ono who said, I don't think I screamed enough. 'I mean, look at the world.'

The Yoko Ono who said in the big picture, in the whole of the world, an individual scream is just a whisper. When she made a noise she was whispering. When she was silent she was screaming.

The Yoko Ono who makes our muscles jump, our spines tingle, our hair stand on end, as if she's standing right by us.

The Yoko Ono responding to the racism, sexism, loathing, to the vilifying assault on her by a male-centric press, by laughing and screaming at the world.

The Yoko Ono who, reacting to what she saw as the asexual atmosphere in the music of La Monte Young and John Cage, wanted to throw blood with her voice.

The Yoko Ono who said sometimes her scream was a whisper and sometimes her whisper was a scream.

She was voicing pure emotion, articulating the hidden turbulent depths of a woman's world, responding to fear, hate and prejudice, letting it out in one mesmerising twenty-minute vocal improvisation, a supreme one-off spiritual collage of sea shanty, plantation chorus, blues moan, pagan dance, primal drone, animal pulse, abstract opera, ghostly breaths, birth pangs, lullaby, hocus-pocus, tongue in cheek, Nordic herding calls, traditional Japanese *nagauta* singing, vinyl hiss, overtone throat singing. Voice as a pure musical instrument transcending language.

The sound of 'Fly', which needs a book of its own to properly translate and explain, would itself extend to another production called 'Fly', becoming part of the double album *Fly*, self-titled like *Grapefruit* was self-titled, with a George Maciunas portrait of Yoko on the front cover. As a record sampling and reshaping recorded music from the viewpoint of a performance artist and experimental musician ignoring fashions and fads of the time, it's as timeless and alive as the words on the pages of *Grapefruit*. Both take on new meanings depending on time and setting.

The title track is one of the great Krautrock tracks, one of the great avant-rock tracks, and also an avant-classical twentieth-century tour de force connected to the shrieks and groans of Stravinsky's *The Rite of Spring*, Luciano Berio's *Sequenza* – virtuoso works for solo instrument – and the sonic brashness and kinetic sound sculptures of Harrison Birtwistle.

It's a wildly original, jarring, often beautiful sound formed on the other side of familiar fixed points that somehow, because it's made by an outsider who happens to be a woman, is never called a masterwork; the performance is never named as a visionary unlocking of new cultural horizons, as if a woman cannot possess genius, at least not until it's safe to do so, when the world has caught up, and she's no longer a danger.

355

There are few examples of an artist in one medium crossing over so authentically into another, and transferring techniques and perspectives from one to the other so successfully – in this case, Yoko moved from music to conceptual art, the concepts of one emerging from the other, and then moved back into music, the approach to sound – as a location, an unknown space to fill with energy and unexpected encounters – emerging from the conceptual other.

It needed an art critic who was also a music critic – and perhaps also a theatre critic, a film critic and a television critic – to properly follow all the multiple directions, and such a creature didn't then – possibly couldn't – exist, not until the internet. Yoko's albums in the 1970s weren't fully heard and she wasn't fully seen as a musician, and they lived a shunned half-life somewhere between curios and monumental asides fully approved for their agonising originality by very few. If there was any determination directed her way it was to diminish her by diminishing her music and her voice.

'Fly' also became part of a series of street signs she imagined existing in a city she designed, dreaming of a ludic society – fly instead of go, dream instead stop, 'this is not here' placed alongside densely packed cars. There was an exhibition called *Fly*, deep into her strange, oppressive life as artist's widow, after another reincarnation, another need to remake herself, to continue as artist, built around the many pieces that fed into and came out of the word 'Fly'. At the centre of the exhibition were the sounds of Fly flying in from the past, calling people into a room where the film was playing. Viewers could only see the film through a peephole, which they had to bend down to look through.

A plastic box containing fifty artificial flies inside a black lacquer box with a hole on the top and a drawer at the side was a limited edition souvenir in the Fluxus tradition at a *Fly* exhibition in Japan, forty-five years after the first Fly piece. It was a variation of a 'Box of Smile' plastic box that was issued in 1971, which contained nothing but a mirror, an authorised replica of a piece originally produced for the very first Fluxus art book, *Fluxus 1*. If you smile when you see the mirror, it's a box of smile.

The 'Fly' box included fifty notecards and envelopes, with the sentence 'I saw this fly and thought of you' printed in black ink, half of the cards in English, half in Japanese, and a piece of red material to line the drawer. It was a kind of notional vending machine where you could pull out a fly and send it to someone.

Around the city where one of the *Fly* exhibitions was held, there were billboards featuring the word 'Fly' in large black letters – the avant-garde artist was now an unbound independent art company represented through a campaign that continued a fascination she had in another century and another life with the word 'Fly'.

The billboards weren't particularly plugging the exhibition, or her art, or her history. They were a lingering reminder of a world that once seemed possible where artists were in imaginative control of the immediate environment and allowed to be illogical and dreamy, and to turn everyday communications into art forms, turn the street into theatre. There were shapes and words and sounds and symbols and sentences and colours and requests selling you nothing but hope and togetherness. That reality never happened; it never took off.

Towards the end of her life, Yoko, still Fly, still Grapefruit, still Touch, was one of the last witnesses, one of the last survivors of a strange, innocent, elaborate fight for freedom, where you believed in magic – which you could make exist, at the extreme opposite to the manmade existence of dropping atomic bombs and causing carnage – and in the idea that selling 'mornings' due to happen in the future for various prices would lead to a future where buying 'mornings' due to happen in the future would come true.

The Yoko Ono who in 1971 staged and publicised an unofficial one-woman show at the Museum of Modern Art in New York, a fictional show that mostly consisted of pretending that she was being exhibited at the museum and falsely claiming she was releasing perfumed flies around the building.

The Yoko Ono continually making an assault on the commercial art system.

357

There were a number of outdoor 'Morning Piece' mind games or living poems produced in May 1964: it was a performance where people could buy different 'mornings' – before sunrise, after sunrise or all morning – for different prices, real or imaginary. The mornings came in the form of fragments of broken glass bottles, and a price list for the event suggested you wear gloves so you wouldn't hurt your fingers when holding the morning, which you could see the sky through. The pieces of glass were dated decades ahead, as though the sky you could see was in the future; the future was yours, and whatever happened in the meantime, it would be there, ready for you when you arrived.

The piece was originally called '9 a.m. to 11 a.m.', and one of its sites was the roof of the Naiqua Gallery. It was filmed for inclusion in *Some Young People* on the bank of the Tama River, where mornings were sold to the occasional passer-by. Yoko decided to put thirty-five mornings on sale, and a few were sold to those willing to take part in the game, with those left over offered by mail order. (The river had been a site for outdoor performances since the 1950s: a Gutai event in 1955 preferred the banks of the river to a gallery, with random, transformable debris and junk strewn along the river included in *Experimental Outdoor Modern Art Exhibition* as 'Challenge the Burning Midday Sun'.)

Yoko explained in the documentary, the explanation becoming part of the event, that she wanted to insert useless acts or things into everyday life to 'delay culture', effectively to add reflective contemplation into accepted routines, and to emphasise – often among friends, family and colleagues also playing with art and its value – that art, however or especially when it is ephemeral, confounding and non-linear, fundamentally defines humanity. Something can be important and useful because it is useless, existing outside the mundane pressures and expectations of the commercial world. Art's uselessness becomes a source of its usefulness.

The apparently pointless performance was presented as though it was part of some wisdom tradition that needed preserving, the creation of a new brand of commonly observed, shared experience evoking the fleeting quality of life.

It was another exploration of the unworldly uselessness of art that doesn't exist beyond the time it is performed, stopping it from being absorbed and appropriated by the system it is opposing. It was the dramatisation of seemingly futile actions that seem to have no lasting impact, the ideal of art unsullied by usefulness; it was then up to others to discover its usefulness.

She was following her intuition, following trains of thought, pursuing what seemed useless and might always remain useless in order to make moments of revelation and innovation possible. It might lead nowhere, her time in Japan might have been the end of her art, and the freedom that came with it, or it might cause something to happen, which made sense of her life and the places she found herself.

Another 'Morning Event' was staged on the roof of Ono and Cox's apartment, a regular place for the trying out of new ideas, including 'Bag Piece', which would become another of her deceptively simple, mostly taken-for-granted 'hits', an art/protest movement in itself, and another ghostly residue of a previous life, a volatile fragment of a larger, mysterious self-portrait – Yoko remembering being a shy child, wishing she could hide inside a box with small holes to see out when people she didn't know came to visit her parents.

'Bag Piece' could be performed by Ono solo or with a partner, or by other interpreters finding themselves becoming a work of performance art, acting out the original, inhabiting and experiencing another world. It is a temporary living sculpture existing between geometry and gesture, a three-dimensional haiku or a dance movement made of startling, non-human shapes where one or two people climbed into a large black bag made of delicate Japanese cotton and covered themselves, took off their clothes, and then put them back on before getting out of the bag.

Those inside the bag can see outside; those outside cannot see inside. All they can see is the peaceful or restless, beautiful or awkward struggling movement of the body or bodies, and guess what is happening inside, and what experience of themselves and their environment the performer is having. They're floating in a different dimension, losing themselves surrounded by people, showing off in private for an audience who have no idea what you are up to.

Inside the bag, said Yoko, you become something different, and you go beyond race, sex, age; identity is erased, you simply become a spirit or soul, invisible, removed, but able to observe the actions of others who do not realise they are performing for the bag. At times, a performance can seem like the X-ray of a soul.

When Yoko was inside the bag, she could watch people respond to one of her self-conscious artworks, see into their boredom, intrigue, patience, annoyance, amusement, watch how their presence and their decisions, their imagining, completed a particular performance or event. Observing behaviour led to other ideas about how to provoke certain types of behaviour that she would find new ways to observe.

There is no fixed duration: it could be a few seconds, or many minutes, and at some early performances by Yoko and Tony Cox, an audience would come into an auditorium with them already inside a bag. Yoko and Cox would barely move for nearly an hour, and the audience stayed watching the black bags, not sure what was happening inside, imagining all sorts of things, not realising they could be seen. Some would leave, deciding after a few minutes of stillness there was no one inside the bag.

In July 1964, a few days after the publication of *Grapefruit*, there was a three-day Yoko Ono sequence of events as a concert, event night and symposium in various Kyoto venues featuring her Japan-era repertoire including 'Bag Piece', 'Chair Piece' and 'Fly Piece'.

A serene, drawn-out variation of her 'Touch Piece' was held overnight under a full moon in a stately, centuries-old Zen temple, Nanzen-ji. Participants met at its epic gateway, which pays homage to the three gates of spiritual liberation, and were invited to be silent, before making their way through its large, sedate gardens past a nineteenth-century brick aqueduct and an ancient rock garden – which transfixed John Cage during his 1962 visit – before being instructed to touch each other.

Some of Yoko's touch pieces might be over in a nervous, giggly few minutes, and took place in crowded nightclubs featuring blindfolded participants and at messy parties for underground newspapers for a sneering, prurient media to classify as orgies, but this one lasted for hours under the noiseless stars.

Temple monks calmly watched as if it was a natural occurrence that a few ghostly strangers under the discreet instructions of an artist lost track of time and created the kind of illusion, a restrained playing with spiritual energy, that made great use of the setting. They were witnessing something that contemplated the connections between people and the world and between Zen and conceptual – both looking to blow the mind – finding the very simplest of things in everyday life magic.

'Word of Mouth Piece' – later 'Whisper Piece; To Destroy a Word' – was based on 'Telephone', a children's party game, which involved passing a word or sentence through performers and audience, whispering it to each other all the way to the back of the hall. She would later ask what the message had become as it passed along the chain, and what it ended up as, revealing a variety of different words, noises or sentences. She would then admit that she hadn't whispered anything at all. She was both involved, and not involved, in what the message had become. It was everything and nothing to do with her.

Her instruction pieces and her various event and performance series evolved over time depending on context, interpretation and individual perception, the flexibility and fluidity essential to the process as it became part of another reality. Her pieces were one thing that became another in various ways, so that there was audience participation, but often the participation that took the original instruction and took it somewhere else.

'Striptease for Three' consisted of nothing but three chairs under a spotlight for five minutes – other performances feature the chairs being put in place for thirty minutes until they are removed. It was another visual haiku, challenging the critics who said she didn't do what was expected of her as a young Japanese woman, as though it was more expected that as a woman she would perform a striptease and reveal her body than play with art and cultural values and use her body as artistic material.

There was no strip show, no flirting with eroticism, and no obvious reference to striptease, there was just whatever the audience projected onto the chairs, so that the objects were reflecting their minds. This was Yoko stripping for the critics, many of whom expected that the only way a woman could be outrageous was through her sexuality.

A Buddhist monk who saw the piece was confused, as were some of the reviewers, that there was no music. He expected an avant-garde composer to make music, not play with ideas of emptiness and the blankness of the mind that he compared to Zen actions. Was that art? Secular prayer? Playtime?

The 'strip tease', the body reveal, that did occur was through what would become one of the most famous and interpreted of her pieces, and the most dramatic example of what being in Japan and her own altered Japanese-ness had added to her thinking about performance and art.

She had received knowledge and information from being in Tokyo, and amid a hectic, idealistic and media-aware avant-garde – treating her very much as one of their own, and even as a kind of mentor – that she wouldn't have found if she had stayed in New York, as well as the anxiety and estrangement that came with it and contributed to a different sense of purpose.

It all led to the formidably unique 'Cut Piece', which was first staged in Kyoto on 21 July 1964, as another response to the art critic who wondered why she didn't just sit still and look pretty. In its focus and intensity, it even anticipated later critics dismissing her work as the naive and guileless efforts of a hack, hanger-on and hobbyist, at best belonging to a simpler, sweeter time.

Some later American reviewers became part of the piece with their jokey, trivialising comments, their flippant response adding its own detail to the performance, turning it into more of a story about being seen as one thing which made it harder to be seen as what you really were, again anticipating famous Yoko.

Yoko would be called a 'Japanese lovely' as though she were nothing more than a mute, exotic nameless extra – or perhaps a female villain with back-alley allure known as Yellow Peril – straight out of a James Bond film, and readers of men's magazines were told that in this 'striptease', you could take her clothes off, and she would actually let you. Imagine your favourite fantasy. These reviews, cutting pieces off her, causing more suffering, helped the work move closer to being finished.

'Cut Piece' was the most vivid, visceral and poetic demonstration of how Yoko existed as an evolving self, hub and connector between movements and worlds that explored provocative ideas about the essential nature of art as experienced by viewers. It can be described as proto-feminist, proto-conceptual, quietly violent, one of the first artistic events to put a live female body at its centre, a female artist putting their body to use as an active agent of artistic creation at a time when even in the avant-garde, the tendency would be to objectify the body, and expect relative passivity and assumed weakened force from the female artist. 'Cut Piece' begins from the struggle of the unofficial half-American half-Japanese artist to even work out where to put her body.

363

Yoko, as usual, never claimed it as one particular thing, a type of art, a feminist statement, a theatre piece that could be performed by others, a comment on race, consent, vulnerability, remembrance, unconditional giving, something mystical or political. It could be all of that, or something else, and whatever else it became over time, but labels and fixed interpretations limited what was one of her most dramatic pieces about freedom, not least the freedom to make of the piece whatever you wanted.

When she was at her most hated and most misunderstood, after the early 1970s when she became perhaps the most famous Japanese person in the world, she accepted that was how it was, and that was the space people wanted to occupy when it came to dealing with her, the space they wanted to put her into.

She responded to that the hostility and resistance in 'Cut Piece' – not realising at the time she staged it how furious people would soon become about her existence, metaphorically stripping her again and again, wanting to take everything she had, even stab her in the arm, in the eye – and that tension that in her life would eventually become epic and unfathomable was already part of the piece. As much as any other meaning that can be read into it, it's a piece about being assaulted by strangers who feel, rightly or wrongly, that they have been given permission to take something out on someone who by accident and perhaps design has ended up in their lives, in front of them, asking for it.

'Cut Piece' as a philosophical artwork is theatre, protest, performance, it's exposing, dangerous, intimate, requiring deep trust and willing but disciplined audience participation and concentration. The artist passively waits to see what happens; the audience member actively performs, close enough to see into Yoko's eyes, sense her nervousness, agitation or calmness. The artist is placed at the centre of a different level of attention, at their most vulnerable. They don't act. They are acted upon. They don't move. They don't make a sound. It begins with one word.

Cut.

The first score for the earliest renditions of 'Cut Piece' by Yoko herself was for a single performer. As a pure drama of touch, it was perhaps an extension of her touch pieces. The performer sits on stage with a pair of scissors in front of them. An announcement is made inviting members of the audience one at a time onto the stage, where they can cut a small piece of the performer's clothes and take it with them. The performer remains motionless and decides when the piece ends. Another version of the score was more nebulous, announcing that members of the audience could cut each other's clothing, and do so for as long as they wanted.

In a 1971 reissue of *Grapefruit*, after 'Cut Piece' had been generally certified a feminist classic, Yoko set out the parameters of 'Cut Piece', ending with the note that 'the performer, however, does not need to be a woman', turning the piece on its head.

In the debut performance, Yoko wore her familiar sleeveless black dress and stockings, her 'best outfit', and folded her legs beneath her in a traditional, polite Japanese sitting pose – 'Cut Piece' was partly inspired by a story about an incarnation of the Buddha on a spiritual journey, encountering people in need, giving them what they required, even his wife, children and clothing. A tiger appears and says he is hungry and wants to eat him, and Buddha lets him. As soon as the tiger eats the Buddha it becomes enlightened.

At a time when she had little money and relied on her best clothes for the occasional office and teaching jobs she did to earn money, Yoko was sacrificing some of her most important possessions. She explained that the artist tended to give what they wanted to give, but in this case, the viewer could take what they wanted: you can cut all that I have.

At first, after a pause before volunteers emerge, those cutting at Yoko's clothes are tentative, gently cutting small pieces, surprised they are allowed to get so close to the artist, and to use the dangerously sharp scissors which often point in the direction of her eyes and face. As the piece progresses, and it's clear that the cutting is allowed, it's not going to be a quickly curtailed performance action, the cuts become bolder, and there's a clear difference in the ways men and women approach the cuts, how they approach invading her space, and even her inner space. Some in the audience who don't join the queue hold their breath, wondering how long it's going to last. Will it go on until she's naked? Until she's made her point – whatever that is? What is she doing this for? Art? Some form of self-analysis? Should they stop it? Is she calling our bluff?

By the end of the performance, the dress has been shredded, her bra has been cut, a reminder of those whose clothes were blown off at the edge of the Hiroshima and Nagasaki nuclear blast, and the focused, trance-like Yoko has been used as body, canvas, victim, plaything, intimate self, target, benevolent Buddha and unguarded artist voluntarily experimenting with audience engagement and violence itself.

Like many of her events and participatory performances, it moves as though through multiple takes of the same action, a series of auditions, preparations and rehearsals. Something set up and manipulated takes on its own dynamic, becomes its own layered truth, seen from many angles, and then something that becomes a memory, and then a reported memory, occasionally a historical re-enactment, and then a part of her history, and other, associated histories. The performance is usually captured on film, necessary documentary proof that it ever took place.

'Cut Piece' exists in one astonishing and frightening form largely because a performance by Yoko at the Carnegie Recital Hall on 21 March 1965 was filmed by the documentary film-maker brothers David and Albert Maysles – Albert was the handheld cameraman, David the soundman, and their pioneering technique making non-fiction feature films was to just let things happen and avoid narration, their own version of *cinéma-vérité* that they called 'direct cinema'. Yoko's husband and manager Cox paid the brothers, who were just beginning to make headway, $300 to film 'Cut Piece'; years later, Yoko bought it from them for $40,000.

They'd made a film with Marlon Brando, beginning a fascination with exuberant personalities as well as eccentric mavericks, and were there in 1964 as the sixties became the sixties when the Beatles arrived in America from another planet, making a name for themselves, acting up for the world, imaginatively revealing and revelling in the future.

Five years later, the brothers would record the sixties coming to an end when the Rolling Stones played the Altamont concert and a member of the Hells Angels murdered a spectator during 'Sympathy for the Devil'. A decade later, they filmed Muhammad Ali in the build-up to his last fight, against his sparring partner Larry Holmes, as Ali tried to make everyone believe he remained the greatest even as his powers as poet and fighter were failing, a film that became about the end of an era rather than a rebirth of a hero.

A lot could happen in a few years, and a world always on the cusp of change was never going to last very long. It would last for so long, and the rest was pure momentum, myth and manipulation.

The Maysles brothers watched closely as things unfolded in front of them with an emotional detachment, so were perfect to film 'Cut Piece', neutral but involved artistic partners with Yoko and the audience in a spontaneous observational event that staged a reality within reality.

It was an artwork about being right there, and the brothers made an art out of films that were about being right there, come what may. Later, when they made films for thirty years with the boundless environmental sculptors Christo and Jeanne-Claude, they used the experience they had gained working with Yoko, whose work was the response to it as much as if not more the work itself. The film can become the final, or latest, stage of a project that by its very nature only exists for a short while, and sometimes remains unfinished.

Maysles's camera is mostly on Yoko in her best clothes, dark stockings and cardigan over black dress, and occasionally takes in the darkened auditorium as people cough, giggle and randomly applaud. We could be in a Buddhist monastery or a library. Members of the audience walk to the stage and along it towards the metal scissors next

367

to the silent Yoko, silent enough to suggest they too remain silent, building up tension.

Sometimes, someone does speak, nervously or a little cockily, producing an abstract voiceover, or you hear the audience – look at her face, he's gone too far, I'll make a piece for *Playboy* with it. Suddenly, as a cut seems to break open her bra, verging on violating the unwritten rules, Yoko abruptly breaks her pose, a man circles her like she's prey, and you hear someone say, 'Stop being such a creep.' Some of the men, adrenalised and charged up by their proximity to a woman losing her clothes, get back into the queue after they have made their cut, for another go. The transgressive experimental performance artist Carolee Schneemann slaps one of the repeat offenders on the face – 'She could have been stabbed,' she would remember – which only gets him more turned on.

Violence is in the air, the singular only-in-America violence that made the American 'Cut Piece' different from the Japanese 'Cut Piece'.

The violence hung in the air, striking at Altamont, and making its presence felt fifteen years later and a mile or so away around the corner of Central Park, when a stranger, surely just another autograph hunter, got close enough to take control of her reality, and Yoko heard a shot on an otherwise – for her – ordinary day. Comprehension was shattered like a windscreen. She would forever be associated with trauma, becoming the avant-garde Jackie Kennedy.

Without audience participation, the spectator in action, encouraged to make the performance work for them personally, there is nothing to see, nothing to feel, and no meanings to find, so more than anything 'Cut Piece' is, like *Grapefruit*, about art working only because of the physical and mental actions of the audience.

Yoko is in control of the setting and situation, but that involves losing control, and being at the mercy of a stranger allowed to get close enough to be sexual aggressor, artistic collaborator, unpredictable stalker, playful heckler or cruel voyeur.

The experience of the spectators, their arousal or their confusion, is the object and subject of the work, but the genius of the concept behind the art is the true product, the only 'true' thing about a piece that constantly evolves.

Yoko was taking chances in ways that developed the chance of John Cage; she didn't build the chance potential into the work, into any instruction or score, but created a set of circumstances, giving up a measure of control, where chance would take over once an audience accepted its role imaginatively or actively – and even involuntarily or indifferently – and the viewer understood that they were being watched as much as they were watching.

'Cut Piece', a reaction to how she was being disliked and distrusted in Japan for her politics and challenging personal activities by those outside her immediate artistic circle, also becomes an abstract premonition of the public disgust, ridicule and vitriol she was going to suffer as uninvited, opportunistic mixed-media personality.

The Yoko Ono who was being skinned alive, left with nothing but the rags hanging from her body.

The Yoko Ono in a trance.

The Yoko Ono who was revealing as much about the spectator as she was about herself.

The Yoko Ono whose friend and occasional roommate in early 1960s New York, the irrepressible iconoclast Charlotte Moorman, would perform 'Cut Piece' numerous times.

A Juilliard-trained cellist, Moorman been heading for a more conventional orchestra career when, bored with the usual cello repertoire, she was shown one of John Cage's more obscure but compelling chance pieces, '26 Minutes 1.499 Seconds for a String Player', from 1955, which could be turned into hundreds of different solo and ensemble pieces, some of which could involve the cooking and eating of mushrooms.

Suddenly, with the encouragement of Yoko showing her how exciting things could get when staging post-Cage ideas, new music stretched out before her, taking her mind and body with it. She would soon become a deep-thinking avant-garde specialist in reading and interpreting open scores, performing works by the composers who had been featured in *An Anthology*, including La Monte Young, Joseph Byrd and Philip Corner.

Moorman saw Cage as an effectual genius who could release her own genius. Her later performances of Cage's piece, which became a central fixture in her repertoire along with 'Cut Piece', contained imaginative interpretive choices and creative variations that surprised even him, and not necessarily in a pleasant way.

She still considered following the original desire of the composer, as she had been trained at Juilliard, but filtered through elastic Cage logic, whether he saw it that way or not. Eventually, her rendition would become removed enough from Cage's score to become almost her own piece, and she'd take it onto American talk shows hosted by Merv Griffin and Johnny Carson, following Cage as eccentrically beguiling novelty act smuggling avant-garde high jinks onto mainstream television. Moorman, like Yoko, after sometimes performing in front of a handful of people, saw nothing wrong with finding ways, whatever it took, to reach an audience.

However extreme her performances of the Cage piece that originally sent her towards her own piece, which involved later 1960s protests against the Vietnam War and live phone calls to Richard Nixon, the cello in one way or another was always with her – tied to her back as she crawled around the stage in combat gear, training bombs and human beings turned into cellos.

An anonymous orchestral cellist disappearing into the music she plays became restless musical renegade, and radical abstract sculptor and performance artist. She became a long-time risk-taking limit-testing artistic partner of Nam June Paik on provocative works including 'TV Bra for Living', 'Concerto for TV Cello and Videotape', 'Videotapes and Sculpture' and 'Sonata No. 1 for Adults Only', combining cello, televisions and electronic equipment, and collaborated with Joseph Beuys and the corporate graphic designer and performance artist Jim McWilliams. Working with McWilliams meant being covered in coconut and chocolate, stroking a block of ice and floating from balloons while holding on to her cello – willing to take the risk of experimenting with sexualisation and the fetishisation of the female form as though it was all the work of the male artist, and she was merely the hired body.

In 1967, as both cellist and performance artist, following the composer's intentions with her own uncompromising faith, she performed as a collaborator Paik's 'Opera Sextronique' at Jonas Mekas's Filmmakers' Cinematheque close to Times Square, in front of an invited audience, which involved playing the cello topless – wearing the formal long black skirt of the conservatory musician for telling contrast. For the mischievous Paik and Moorman, this was an unabashed act of sacrilege, attacking the sacred spaces of serious music, which the modernist musicians hadn't necessarily wholly rejected. For the authorities, it was an unlicensed titillating sex show.

Even though it was private, she was arrested, tried and convicted – after a night in jail, she received a suspended sentence for indecent exposure. Nam June Paik wasn't, as he hadn't taken off his clothes, and was clearly the artist with certain privileges, whereas she was the one at fault, clearly not the artist. She was also accused in a farcical trial of disgusting behaviour for playing the cello 'between her legs'.

She became known as the Topless Cellist, as if this was her sole achievement in life, along with being a malleable muse for Paik – for some it was the other way round – and his wacky, tabloid-friendly Cage-y larks. Her reputation as risqué performer undermined her reputation as visionary, innovator, disrupter, interpreter, impresario and one of the great facilitating champions of the avant-garde in the 1960s and 1970s, during and after its New York heyday, committed to breaking down the perception of elitism that kept it in the dark for most people.

She had her own tricky relationship with Fluxus – how could she not be connected with it, as vital, unwavering New York artist/musician/self-publicist and regular collaborator with many of its named participants, but how could she also not be made unwelcome, given her energetic self-promotional skills and aesthetic perspective clashing with the big head of Fluxus, George Maciunas?

371

Her re-performance of 'Cut Piece' was the performance of an experimental artist – and ex-1950s beauty queen – with experience of using her body in public in whatever way she wanted – dressed, undressed, traditional, comically, ritualistically or as an integral element in a staged event. She'd also collaborated with Paik on 'Pop Sonata', the predecessor of 'Sonata for Adults Only', where a Bach recital becomes a striptease, the two pushing each other into imagining more extreme ways of putting distracting actions into a stately musical setting, happy for scandal to be a way of reaching an audience unsure of their uneasy sounds and disorienting visuals.

Her fearless rendition of Yoko's uncovering piece is one of the great performance art 'cover versions', both a recognition that it was Yoko that helped direct her towards a world she made her own, and tried so hard to make others, and an inside understanding of what made the piece so powerful as an insight into how a female performer's body through no fault of her own can upstage its inhabitant. She also knew the importance of documenting some of the performances, which were often surrounded by numerous cameras helping complete the performance, forty years before the majority of an audience at such a performance would be filming it through the cameras as much as watching it. It also inherently became a warning of how mainstream attention that might come because of a woman investigating the power and powerlessness of her body, and the complexities of seduction, eroticism and consent, can backfire.

Moorman's 'Cut Piece' takes liberties with Yoko's original as she did with Cage's '26 Minutes 1.499 Seconds for a String Player', making it as much hers as Yoko's. Hers comes from Arkansas more than Japan. Suffering and sacrifice become fun and games. Yoko's unsmiling Buddhist blankness becomes Southern warmth, or at least, there's an easy, knowing smile, a blatant exhibitionistic come hither-ness challenging the cutters, daring them to go further. It adds extra problems to the judgement of where a piece exploring the artistic manipulation of a woman's body and its relationship to male fantasies becomes to most people simply something that is about revealing a woman's body.

She kept a cut piece of her clothing from every performance of 'Cut Piece', hoping one day to give them to Yoko – when she died in 1991 at fifty-seven, she still had them, and just about everything else she had collected as a relic of her life in art, which by its very ephemeral nature often erased itself. Her last words to her husband were, 'Don't throw anything away.'

The Yoko Ono who marvelled how brave and vulnerable the restless and abrasive art-pop performer Peaches was when she performed 'Cut Piece' at the Meltdown Festival in London Yoko curated in 2011, pieces cut away until there was barely any clothing left, seeing a whole universe unfold in front of her.

For Yoko, 'Cut Piece' was almost a training scheme, an exercise in tolerance and self-control: how to be cut to pieces, how to be exposed, scrutinised and humiliated without flinching, without lashing out, without losing your nerve and confidence. She was learning as living being and self-created artist how to control her emotions and benignly accept her position, ultimately because she was presenting something that was greeted by cynics and disbelievers with the ultimate question for such a precarious, volatile, possibly fraudulent activity: is this art? How is it art?

For the avant-garde artist experiencing and articulating mental freedom, embodying the spirit of creation and conjuring up views of the future, the question itself is perfect proof that these sorts of unstable performances, spontaneous rituals, spiritual deliberations and philosophical investigations are art, and at the same time, anti-art, which creates further antagonism among those who can't see it.

As the shadowy, emanant Yoko of 1964 became the historical Yoko of the early twenty-first century, 'Cut Piece' gathered around it, as if reclothing, various interpretations and acknowledgements of potential meanings – in particular the feminist one, which ultimately helped elevate Yoko above the hate, the resentment, and she performed it for the sixth and final time at the age of seventy.

The younger 'Cut Piece' Yoko a little nervously revealing her body had no idea how her life would turn out, the life story, the death, the trauma, the recovery, the public image, the stripping away of who she once was; the older 'Cut Piece' Yoko calmly revealing her body had been through the life, the death, the outrageous fortune, had to deal with the public image, and found a way to place herself, in control of her history, as if her art above all else had protected her. The immediate danger had passed.

Where once she preferred ambiguity about its origins and meaning, to protect it from being prematurely filed away in art history, ultimately shorn of its fluid, confounding energy, now she performed the piece 'against ageism, against racism, against violence and against sexism'. It still wasn't finished, it was never meant to be finished, but there was much more to it by then.

'Cut Piece' was the end piece of her final Japanese concert, *Yoko Ono Sayonara Concert; Strip Tease Show,* held at the Sogetsu Arts Centre on 11 August 1964, where her first show in this stay had taken place two and a half years before.

'Cut Piece' was effectively her goodbye to Japan, having realised her insides didn't belong there even if her ancestors did. In Tokyo, she still lived what her parents would have seen as a squalid, bohemian life, with a husband struggling as much as she was. In New York, it was also a hand-to-mouth existence, as much as there were those who felt her extreme artistic commitment was made easier by the family wealth she rejected. It was always there, even if she didn't claim it.

She was beginning to think there was nowhere she'd fit, but New York was always a good place to start. In some ways, it was outside America, like she was, but existed adjacent to it.

In New York, it was easy to pick up the kind of part-time work that enabled her to keep doing her real work, and to local critics, she wasn't Japanese enough to become a legitimate part of the local avant-garde, or American enough to be where they considered the real action to be. She was, though, Japanese enough to resent the warmongering and hyper-active Americanisation of Japanese culture, and American enough to be seen as a stranger whose life now belonged elsewhere.

An international tribe of artists and activists was taking shape, and sometimes falling apart, around George Maciunas and his febrile company, and that's where she could be more herself. While in Tokyo, she'd discovered a way to mix the particular cultural sensitivities and quiet persistence of the Japanese and the fast-changing, vigilant boldness of the New Yorker, and found an answer to who and what she was, and where home was – a third answer. She crossed over into new cultural territory.

From then on, she'd occasionally visit Japan, but it was just another country she passed through. She was loosely, sentimentally connected, to a somewhere else she knew before she became someone else and it became somewhere else again.

At the end of *Some Young People*, Yoko is preparing to leave Tokyo and return to New York. The city had become, because of Yoko, a favoured destination for Japanese avant-garde colleagues hoping to become part of a more internationally minded art scene and make what one artist described as 'a better use of my Japanese identity'. Yoko and Cox with various art friends dance and party at an arts cafe bar.

'I did various things here in Japan,' Yoko explains, 'but it seemed that what I was doing was not understood and disappeared into thin air. I always felt as if I were talking to a wall. I'm going back to New York soon. For a Japanese to say "going back" may sound funny, but for me New York feels like a place that I return to.'

We see her kissing goodbye to Cox, who stayed behind to wrap up their Tokyo life and would bring Kyoko along later. Cox's responsibilities looking after Yoko extended to being the lead parent – he was house-husband so she would not be reduced to housewife and therefore seen as not obsessive enough to be an artist.

She would admit she wasn't ready to be a mother, didn't feel she wanted to be a mother. The thought of playing a traditional female role was threatening to Yoko, as if the distraction would confirm her only as a mother, never as the artist she was fighting to be. When she was pregnant, she would say she had to concentrate on being pregnant for nine months, fearing it would take her away from her art. The sense she was a different kind of mother to Kyoko would help contribute to some of the reputation she would have as 'cold'.

The female artist, especially in Japan in the early 1960s, was forced to sacrifice family intimacy to maintain her militancy and independence. It was the price of freedom. As an artist, freedom was the most important thing – the chance to do something spontaneously without feeling a young child was stopping her. Cox's dedication allowed her to move as and when she wanted to.

In the film, she doesn't talk about temporarily leaving her child behind with the father, but the move she is making as an artist. 'Because my world here has become so small, I feel like going to a place where I can express myself more easily – where I can communicate with people more easily, and feel my artistic expression more tangibly communicated.'

The documentary ends with her at Haneda airport in September 1964, surrounded by Cox and her friends, waving goodbye and smiling as she climbs the steps up to her plane, about to fly into the sky above the clouds. She's heading home, towards the next thing, following her own instructions . . .

In 1963, many of the artists who had become Fluxus by the accident and design of George Maciunas and who had featured in the tour of European cities had returned to New York, including Dick Higgins, Alison Knowles and Ben Patterson. They took a form of Fluxus back with them: *An Anthology* was published after all the slow, dedicated labour – the intricately presented, esoteric and utilitarian story of what Fluxus was before Fluxus, as Fluxus as anything without a mention of Fluxus. Realising that Fluxus would flourish more if it was located in New York, excited by the systems, contacts, rumours and strategies that were forming around the name, Maciunas started planning his own return.

The April newsletter, no. 6, was titled 'Proposed Propaganda Action for Nov. Fluxus NYC', a strident plan for mischievous, sometimes near-anarchist anti-art disruption and sabotage on the streets of Manhattan which contained the sort of imperious one-man policy decisions he had to clarify and tone down in the next newsletter.

Most Fluxus people advocated studied, even ethereal indifference to commercial art and its institutions, suggesting that to be anti-art was in fact supporting art's status quo, or an admission Fluxus could only exist and act the way it did because the establishment existed – a position that was solely oppositional, contradicting its spirit, as to be truly Fluxus meant only opposing Fluxus.

The original return to New York plan ended up with only one of its planned actions taking place, and one of its most reserved – some guerrilla street performances on Canal Street by Ben Vautier and Alison Knowles, including La Monte Young's draw-a-straight-line 'Composition No. 10', resulting in an early finish being requested by a local policeman. The straight line was met with resistance.

Amid all the back and forth from those assuming they were an integral part of the abstract planning committee shocked at Maciunas's chaotic, even childish declaration of war, the main news was that he was coming back to New York to run things, or rather, to consult with all the equal partners to assure democratic processes were always followed. (When he designed things and edited copy he decided he didn't need to be democratic. He didn't check with anyone if that was acceptable, and as he did it so well, there was little opposition.)

While he was away, other advocates and personalities equally committed to promoting and hosting avant-garde activities had emerged, not least Charlotte Moorman, who had her own tenacious evangelical zeal when it came to letting the world know how sensational and uplifting the avant-garde could be, and how New York was now the hectic, beguiling centre of the avant-garde universe.

While Maciunas and Yoko were away, the driven Moorman, with managerial skills, persuasive charm, natural showmanship and a growing network of artistic friendships that rivalled his, was developing her own plans for giving shape to the post-Cage New York zeitgeist and selflessly supporting the work of others.

In 1963, with the help of the inexhaustible event producer Norman Seaman, another resourceful, passionate, force-of-nature rival for Maciunas to be wary of, Moorman set up a series of six concerts of adventurous new music to be played through the month of August at Judson Hall.

The six shows featured works and performances by herself, John Cage, La Monte Young, Earle Brown, Toshi Ichiyanagi, Morton Feldman, David Tudor, Christian Wolff and George Brecht, and premieres of music by, and played by, Frederic Rzewski, with compositions by Karlheinz Stockhausen and the Italian composer Giuseppe Chiari. An astonishing electronic concert on 28 August included music by Iannis Xenakis, Edgard Varèse, James Tenney, Mauricio Kagel and Luciano Berio.

Moorman was more interested than Maciunas in presenting substantially new music-based events, even if sometimes with the addition of rubber dolls, paper hats and ping-pong bats and balls, and audiences never reached above seventy-five or so, but her concerts included artists Maciunas felt belonged in his camp and thanks to Seaman's press contacts they received intrigued, cautiously positive reviews in the *New York Times*. The headlines indicated what the paper's classical critics were making of the very new: 'musicians using bizarre sounds', 'far out sound', 'avant-garde doings to pepper up the town' and the definitive 'unusual sounds'. Maybe it was something that would be here today, gone tomorrow.

The six concerts evolved into what became known – Moorman felt for want of a better name – as the Annual Avant Garde Festival of New York, an enduring, increasingly ambitious citywide new music celebration that would last for fifteen years, taking avant-garde sounds and actions from Yoko's loft, Maciunas's gallery and Kaprow's happenings into the city's cultural centre.

When Yoko returned from Tokyo after her time away, she was stunned to see that her funny, loveable but often capricious friend had become such an organising force among the avant-garde community, happily co-operating with many of the male avant-garde musicians Yoko used to moan about for their meanness and indifference to what the pair were doing. When Yoko asked her what had happened while she was away, Moorman replied: 'I was lonely.'

The petulant tyrant in Maciunas was quick to respond to Moorman's successful move into festivals and her dreams of creating a progressive cultural community. He saw it as an intentional attack on Fluxus, and he tried to cut off her supply of approved Fluxus art and artists, forbidding the use of 'his' artists or the name Fluxus in any of her ventures. He even withdrew from using the term 'avant-garde', as though this now referred only to Moorman's festival.

He put her on a Fluxus blacklist, and threatened to boycott any artist or musician sharing work with the Avant Garde Festival that he had helped to make, 'which means that I boycott and do not co-operate with any exhibit, gallery, concert hall or individual that ever included her in any programme or show, past or future'.

Moorman would meet Nam June Paik for the first time during the second Avant Garde Festival, which featured the American premiere of Stockhausen's theatrical collage of music, word and action, 'Originale', based on 'Kontakte', written with Mary Bauermeister in 1961, with a star cast of local avant-gardists including Alvin Lucier and performing poets including Allen Ginsberg. Stockhausen had insisted the fierce, unpredictably charismatic Paik take part, as he had done so successfully in the original Cologne performances, upsetting Maciunas, who considered Paik to be exclusively Fluxus.

Maciunas, following the boisterously ideological lead of Henry Flynt, was part of a chaotic protest, or publicity stunt, outside the Judson Hall by a handful of artists, some of whom seemed to be part of the performance, claiming Stockhausen was a 'cultural imperialist' and 'musical racist', and terrorising Paik as a traitor for leaving Fluxus by taking part. Maciunas's unruly obstructive behaviour and the stern response of many of the Wiesbaden Fluxus participants would lead to a partial collapse of Fluxus, and a quick back-flipping recovery as Maciunas accepted his autocratic tendencies had to have limits.

He could still be easily riled. The prolific, notorious partnership that developed between his perceived rival Moorman and grand traitor Paik further aggravated Maciunas, and he would later criticise her for letting male artists and Paik in particular use her body and encourage her to take off her clothes for their own exploitative purpose.

Moorman's festivals continued, inevitably, to include some of the most Maciunas-sanctified Fluxus artists and actions, but would become alternative endeavours, running concurrently with the unmentionable Fluxus, as if there was no such thing.

Which in some ways there wasn't. And if there was, it would be there every year inside Moorman's epic Avant Garde Festival where she pulled together in one extravagant citywide parade avant-garde music from early minimalism and post-serial electronics to free jazz and no-wave. It wasn't stamped Fluxus, but it was another place where Fluxus flowed, directed by the disinherited Moorman, the counter-Maciunas. She founded a movement that never became historic, perhaps because it was never properly named, and had no one like Maciunas in charge of naming rights and image control.

Maciunas had also been worried about an alternative loose collective that had also been picking up momentum in New York while he had been away, with its own name and free-thinking ways. It was also developing ad hoc ways of co-ordinating the work of disparate artists under one banner and producing art outside the gallery system that could not be bought, which effectively neutralised its energy.

George Brecht had been regularly meeting since the late 1950s with the ex-engineer, artist and teacher Robert Watts – who would later fail when trying to take copyright ownership of the words 'pop art', and was the first to produce artistic sheets of postage stamps – and occasionally Watts's colleague and cultivated happening pathfinder Allan Kaprow.

Their meetings slowly led to the formation in May 1963 of an 'ever-expanding universe of events' they called the Yam Festival – 'May' backwards – which was based on Brecht previously mailing out his accumulating event scores – 'private little enlightenments' – printed on small cards to various friends, most of whom were also artists, and also on the mailing list of George Maciunas and featured in *An Anthology*.

Maciunas and Brecht and their colleagues, collaborators and pen pals were using the mail to keep all interested parties, increasingly scattered in different places, up to date with the fast-moving production of scores, notes, plans, arrangements, proposals, mantras and publications.

Fluxus was in the beginning made by mail: the post gave it energy; it was a mail art with its own extension of Ray Johnson's tactics, relying on the international postal system as its distribution network. Yam was part of this circulation of ideas, issuing what its organisers called 'postal happenings'.

The mailed scores were intended to promote their own future post-Cage activities, mirroring Maciunas's Fluxus newsletters and his post-Cage campaign, and also to be their own artistic process by asking the recipients to respond in their own way to the instructions on the cards. Brecht knew the group of people who received the cards 'would know what to do with them'.

Maciunas became alarmed when the Yam Festival shifted from the mail, where to some extent even as a busy virtual structure it barely existed, to more visible outdoor events, with its anonymous cavalcade of misfits showing their faces. Yam started to mail other things than the event cards: objects as well as words, statements, facts, mini-manifestos, even Yam pencils, all leading towards the invention of new forms and methods to deal with new ideas.

Even though this wasn't a competition, Maciunas felt Brecht and Watts were competing for the same space and overtaking him while he was working in Germany on finding new methods to connect artists in a flexible, multi-purposed way. Most of all, they were calling attention to an emergent diverse and prolific cultural community, testing out thoughts and ideas and making radical changes to the traditional concerns of art and artists. Critical reaction or popular acclaim was not important, only the experiences themselves. To Maciunas this seemed and sounded exactly like Fluxus. Fascinated by military history and how military units would defy an enemy, influenced by his family escaping the Russian invasion of Lithuania in 1944 – Fluxus was his war on the cultural status quo – he planned his response to these energetic interlopers with meticulous precision.

He concluded that, for it to become anything significant all, varied signs of amplified post-Cage enterprise needed to be under the control of one entity, which for operational reasons should be Fluxus, which just happened to have him at the controls, disseminating information. It would still be the product of its participants, with wildly separate approaches, aims and values, but it needed to appear joined up, and heading forward in the same way. Maciunas decided he was how it joined up.

More diplomatic and far less dogmatic than he had been with Moorman, Maciunas wrote to Watts, pleading with him not to make Yam a rival to Fluxus. He offered his services and practical skills as graphic designer, product manager and editor to help artists with the production of their publications and the making of their mailable objects. Watts was delighted to have the messy, demanding business of producing a range of postal items and dealing with unhelpful printers taken off his hands, and Yam became effectively proto-Fluxus, and absorbed into Fluxus.

The odd couple relationship between Watts – *New Yorker*/Mike Nichols/stylish type – and Maciunas – *Mad* magazine/*Carry On*/vulgarian type – reflected the vast differences in approach and temperament of those using Fluxus to express their independence from the commercialism, politics and money of the art establishment. They shared enemies, and formed an unlikely partnership until Maciunas's death between Watts's ingenious use of the post office as a non-commercial cultural space and Maciunas's production resourcefulness and community conviction.

In 1962, still preparing the Fluxus magazine and thinking of annual anthologies of individual artists he called 'Fluxus Year Boxes', Maciunas planned to publish some of the scores from the first Fluxus concerts. He borrowed methods already used by John Cage's publishers Peters Editions to handle his highly visual scores, and the next step would be publishing a collection of an artist's individual works.

The coalition between Yam and Fluxus, the peaceful takeover, the polite hijacking was made official with George Brecht's *Water Yam*, a collection of his constantly evolving, enigmatic, useful, poetic event scores and mental exercises, written to make things happen or not, contained in a box designed and produced by Maciunas. It used graphic and typological ideas Maciunas had been working on when designing *An Anthology* and plotting 'Fluxus 1' and the 'Fluxus Year Boxes', and from hearing what Yoko was up to with *Grapefruit*, thinking of something that was both book and container and portable enough to be easily posted.

It was an object, part of a protest against objects, an object that could contain other objects, so impractical as to be almost impossible – by the time of 'Fluxus 1', finally ready in March 1964 and the first of only two 'Year Boxes' actually produced, the object could contain all manner of loose items made of wood, metal and plastic, a compartmentalised repository of games, reflection, clippings and messages which urged the reader, the user, to become a performer, finishing off as they saw fit the tasks, challenges and puzzles. Flux Kits were more mobile diffusions of the 'Year Boxes', produced relatively cheaply so that, in theory, more people could buy them than one-off pieces. They were manufactured in limited editions, for cost reasons, and to give the kits a sense of artistic exclusivity. At the time, though, the idea of them actually selling was a distant dream, which didn't stop their production.

You could follow Brecht's *Water Yam* scores by doing nothing, or contemplating what you might do, or making an action, anywhere you liked. The rigorous English experimentalist Cornelius Cardew, who had studied with Cage and Stockhausen and then rejected both as dispassionate elitists, would describe it as 'a course study, and following on from that, a teaching instrument'. It could teach you how to view conceptual art's relationship to language, proposing access for people who previously felt distant from the production of text, image and meaning, showing how a cheap, agile, cut-and-paste, do-it-yourself ethos, a chance to experiment with typography and visual juxtaposition, reached out into wider countercultural actions in the late twentieth century – fanzines, pamphlets, manifestos, essays, shrieks, tracts, tickets, treatises, catalogues, T-shirts and letters – and from there into social media, made up of millions of messages. It could teach you how to behave in a number of real and unreal situations, how to keep calm, all things considered, and ultimately teach you a history of Fluxus from the inside in the way *Grapefruit* teaches you a history of Fluxus from the elsewhere.

By 1964, completing the benign co-opting of Yam, Maciunas, now back in New York, had taken over the Yam single-sheet newspaper *V TRE*, named after a broken neon sign Brecht had spotted in New Jersey. It became the Fluxus community newspaper, with the code 'cc' before the title signifying Brecht to indicate it was a continuation of Brecht's Yam paper.

For Fluxus it became a local paper with an internationalist outlook covering and publicising a continuing succession of changes for outside eyes, unlike the internally distributed, near-members-only newsletter. It fixed the radical, free-form, enchanted flow of people, events and ideas inside a mock-up of a traditional newspaper, exploiting the familiar format to advertise the unfamiliar. It imagined an extremely unlikely but delightful world where Fluxus was newsworthy, its antics, personalities and actions known the world over, making front pages, mixing photogenic entertainment with avant-garde incitement. Like the newsletters it was published throughout Maciunas's life if and when he could, after an early, impractical ambition to be monthly, with issues ten and eleven covering the news of Maciunas's death in May 1978 with as much depth as a mainstream paper would have treated the death of a president.

Maciunas was the one Fluxus actor who by being responsible for the look, feel and production of the periodicals and publications documenting its progress and various deviations collaborated with more or less every other Fluxus actor. If anyone is counting, and depending what authority you trust, that's about thirty-five core artists, including those like Yoko Ono who didn't count themselves in any such list, and maybe another forty or so in the outer suburbs.

They had all influenced each other, and were given a visually consistent platform by Maciunas, a prediction of a world to come where idiosyncratic cultural influencers and self-style disruptors reigned, possessing their own indefinable powers, reaching minds in unknowable ways. They were located in a space they constructed for themselves, inventing their own rules, causing new kinds of fuss and infection.

The influence of Maciunas extended to creating space for artists and freelance creative workers in New York which eventually spread through the world; one of his legacies as a real-world utopian city planner, experimental architect and outlaw property developer was real estate. For all that Fluxus existed as a forum dealing in the frivolous, peculiar and ephemeral, building things inside the imagination, it also left an impression on the outside world. Maciunas the magical manipulator of an art movement, its self-appointed head of human resources, was also a managerial virtuoso.

After returning to New York from Germany, when he was looking for cheap Fluxus headquarters, his artist film-making friend Jonas Mekas suggested he look at a derelict but large building on Canal Street. He turned the second floor into a base for Fluxus activities, called the Fluxhall and the Fluxshop – originally it was called Factory, a name perhaps loaned, or swapped, or gifted to Warhol – and moved into what had been described in the *New York Times* as 'the neglected field of artists' housing'.

Working with little money, cutting corners, battling authorities, outwitting the Mafia presence and ignoring local laws, he converted some crumbling industrial cast-iron buildings zoned for manufacturing only and destined for demolition in the old rundown textile district south of Houston Street in downtown Manhattan. Ingeniously and illegally, he transformed them into co-operative live-and-work studios to be owned and managed by artists, introducing a beguiling new migrant cachet into the neighbourhood.

These were the sort of poor, experimental artists who found it difficult to find affordable places with enough space to put together their art and life as they wanted to, and to present spontaneous happenings, exhibitions and performances in their own environment.

Maciunas created an artist's haven interconnected with Fluxus for a city with perhaps the greatest number of artists in the world; it was an idealistic, adaptive reusing of buildings, connecting artist communities with the surrounding society that inspired other cities to follow, transforming international cultural and ultimately commercial life. What was known as Hell's Hundred Acres became an artist colony known as SoHo, loft living became legalised, and avant-garde artists got their own place to work and play in New York.

Eventually, as rents increased and real-estate speculators exploited the edgy, cosmopolitan aura and resultant beautification, after two decades where SoHo was seen as a world centre of avant-garde art, the artists were forced out, leaving behind an underground image, an illusion of progress, rather than the original reality. For all he did as catalyst, planner, mentor, evader, romanticist and Fluxus deity, the reshaping of SoHo was Maciunas's masterpiece.

Maciunas died as his dream was losing its Fluxus foundations, taking his particular box of tricks with him, which wasn't the official or unofficial death of Fluxus but was the beginning of a slowing down of activity, which had been slowing anyway since the early 1970s and the end of its boldest golden age, which couldn't really make it past the 1960s, very much its first home.

If there had ever been an essential Fluxus group of non-essential specialists, by the very nature of their concerns, their restlessness, an independent argumentative nature, they had left early, drifted off, walked out, changed positions, went missing, missed appointments, never belonged in the first place, were not allowed in, had come back, had yet to arrive.

By the 1970s, there were plenty of other things to look at and listen to, other ways of protesting, self-publicising and extending the Fluxus extension of Cageian ideas even as the originals drifted into the background. Yoko as a floating non-member didn't bring word of Fluxus with her, even when she was part of a world-famous double act dominating the cultural spotlight by being more actively Fluxus-like than she was on her own. If she did, rumours of its antics, which by then seemed outdated, just added to her assumed cold, witchy weirdness.

Eventually, helped by a new interconnected world of search, after Fluxus had almost gone from the memory, there was a rediscovery, a reconsideration of its dreams of a space beyond art, and an online storage of its dreams, and its dreams of a space beyond itself.

Yoko herself also benefited from this reality-shifting searching and fitful recalibration, and was slowly returned to her rightful place – of, but not of, Fluxus, there, but always somewhere else, with her own special origin story, her direct influence on activist art and feminist advance, not so much ahead of her time, but definitely ahead of her contemporaries.

Fluxus, finding enormous aesthetic potential in the everyday world, has led one way or another to other movements, moments and procedures, from Chicago's African Commune of Bad Relevant Artists to the Guerrilla Girls, from land art to street art, from ambient music to performance art, Keith Haring to Barbara Kruger, Kraftwerk to Throbbing Gristle, Todd Rundgren to Richard Hell, Marina Abramovic's body art to Damien Hirst's self-advertisements, Cindy Sherman to Kim Kardashian, Christo to crypto art, Ai Weiwei to Banksy, TV pranks to reality TV, the dance remix to TikTok, Abbie Hoffman to Ye, Fistfuck to Fleabag, Barbie pink to brat green. Fluxus is still a faith to believe in, a tendency to develop, performances to continue, an archive to re-transmit, even something yet to take place.

Perhaps it was something that finally fully blossomed – without being credited, naturally – during the Covid-19 lockdowns, when logic and reason were turned upside down, and more and more people used the world at hand, what they had left of it, to make art, or just believed that they were, which turned out to be enough. Art became an elevating, restorative way of seeing and interpreting the world, of exploring your own temperament, of being-in-the-world; it was music, philosophy, film, theatre, radio, poetry, dance, meditation, podcasts, exercise, photography, sculpture, therapy, tweets, deliverables, information, film, farce, a mutant, joyous combination of all of that and more of that, and it was something that gave us the chance to enjoy a happy, indefinable fantasy.

We became a world of artists, performers, communicators, art and entertainment consumers, spending more time at home, mirroring the loneliness of the avant-garde artist, leading to creative activities inside our own living space, teaching each other the creative use of leisure, revealing ourselves, noticing and recycling everything. It was the ultimate Fluxus lesson – how we organise ourselves into a more collaborative society, a watchful, interrelated collective, so we might survive a tense, nervous, dangerous world.

And now there is no Fluxus, you see Fluxus everywhere.

Back in New York, Cox and Kyoko joined Yoko and moved from apartment to apartment, eventually into a gloomy five-storey tenement building on Christopher Street in Greenwich Village, where they took on the role of building superintendents as part of their efforts to make a living, so they could make art, which is where they wanted to live. They wanted art to be their home. Visitors recalled visiting their apartment, seeing a motionless Yoko spreadeagled on a pull-down bed, gothic black hair spread over white sheets, baby Kyoko sleeping nearby.

Neighbours in the building could hear Yoko and Cox's often intense arguments through the thin walls, usually climaxing with slamming doors and hours of uneasy silence. Yoko and Cox as art couple got on better than Yoko and Cox as married couple; whereas Toshi's love was most apparent inside the married couple, Cox's love was most apparent inside the art couple. The perfect balance of love in both the marriage and the art was perhaps impossible.

Home life and art life carried on from Japan, with the building's roof soon being used as an early-morning location to sell a collection of her 'Morning Pieces', with their random future dates, for virtual money, by making the imaginary virtually collectible.

Another dawn event on the rooftop for the very few who responded to sparse publicity for the event found Yoko sitting at a table, covered with more or less identical pebbles priced between five cents and five million dollars. The pebbles had no intrinsic value, but if you paid five cents for one, that was its value, and if you paid five million dollars for one, that was then its value. In the end, you could get one for a quarter, whatever the price tag said, walking away in your mind with millions of dollars.

This one-off, never-to-be-repeated sale of items that had no value outside what you were prepared to pay was its own comment on how art took on value according to a mysterious set of inherited and modified rituals. If you were prepared to pay millions for a painting, then it had become something that was worth millions.

Perhaps it was a statement that needed to be made to many people in a larger venue, but by its very nature, it needed to be merely a whisper, a passing thought, nothing to do with real money, something that might be passed on by word of mouth, or inspire another artist to respond to it.

It was a Fluxus-style gesture, an outdoor happening, but it was also very Yoko – mocking a system whereby art became a commodity, even as she was consistently broke and refused to join the system where her art would be bought, and, part of the same obstinacy towards the system, refused to make up with her parents. To earn a secure living from art she had to make objects that could be bought, which increasingly she wasn't, and Cox was beginning to despair.

As a conceptual artist with a niche star profile enhanced by the Tokyo of *Grapefruit* and 'Cut Piece', Yoko returned to a New York busy with multi-purpose extensions of the avant-garde scenes she had left behind.

The Fluxus paradigm, according to Maciunas, was entering its second, most visible and active phase, and Yoko, as a clear progenitor, some of whose pieces were included in the European concerts, easily slipped into the Fluxus magic circle with full access to its privileges.

Without claiming Fluxus rights, she had been granted them by Maciunas, given his self-designed stamp of approval and access to his publications and concerts, even as she was still allowed to take part in events promoted by his established adversaries Moorman and Seaman. She was her own, bloody-minded offshoot of Fluxus, inside her own forcefield, associated but independent, a jester with mysterious impulses.

She had a place where she belonged, but the room she needed in order to remain an outsider, someone who could both take part in the togetherness of art communities and be free to do things on her own, deal with herself, be the writer as loner using words, ephemeral manifestations and fleeting moments to imagine new realities that could emerge from the unreal. She didn't mind being part of something, but only if she was allowed to avoid any suggestion of a membership structure.

'Self-Portrait' – later used in a 'Box of Smile' – was her first clearly labelled Fluxus work, a self-assembled mirror inside an envelope included in the first 3D Fluxus anthology of works compiled by Maciunas. It was an instant personality test; you looked in the mirror and smiled, or you looked, and didn't smile, and worse, you scoffed. A cheap, mass-produced machine for producing your own, temporary self-portrait, it leapt across time and space, collapsing art history into a manila Fluxus envelope, from Hildegard of Bingen's twelfth-century self-portrait, Parmigianino's sixteenth-century self-portrait, Artemisia Gentileschi's *Self-Portrait as a Female Martyr* and Catharina van Hemessen's sixteenth-century *Portrait of a Woman* through Titian, Velázquez, Ducreux, Courbet, Pissarro, Gauguin and Van Gogh, via the twentieth-century self-portraits of Matisse, Malevich, Cahun, Schiele, Serebriakova, Dalí, Kahlo, Rousseau, Carrington, Pavlović-Barili, Maar, Man Ray, Dine and Warhol, opening a channel to the ceaseless, egalitarian selfie of the future.

In March 1965, outside Fluxus, Yoko's second solo concert at the Carnegie Recital Hall brought with it a selection of the psychologically unveiling pieces she had developed in Tokyo, showing how her methods and performances had evolved since her Recital Hall debut concert. She'd moved from the fractious, mystifying extremes of 'A Grapefruit in the World of Park' to the surreptitious, channelled extremes of *Grapefruit*, closing in on the more explicitly conceptual.

After her personal and public experiences in Tokyo, which concentrated the mind as to what and why she was communicating, and her prominent place in a very different, politicised avant-garde setting, Yoko was more clearly encouraging the active involvement of an audience, inviting viewers to complete tasks, act or interpret a concept. The artwork entered the viewer's mind, and they then owned it, severing art completely from an exclusive, commercialised setting.

The solo concert ended with the quiet violence and abstract theatrical force of 'Cut Piece', the violation of spiritual and physical dignity that was filmed by the Maysles brothers, with Yoko kneeling at a new centre of knowing, as a new model artist, stepping beyond the visual, exploring the relationship between the visible and the invisible, the mental and physical realms.

Demonstrating how she could be simultaneously outside and inside Fluxus, she would return to the Recital Hall in September 1965, taking part in a Flux Orchestra concert conducted by La Monte Young, when Fluxus was – two years after its German concerts – a little more established in framing the everyday and all life activities as art and music, in requiring the presence of an audience for their satirical or polemical effect, and a little more absurd, as though Cage had been translated by Ionesco and Harpo Marx.

Ben Vautier's opening 'Audience Piece' had each member of the audience described as they arrived by a hidden observer through the PA system, and Mieko Shiomi's following piece, 'Falling Event', delivered programmes to the audience as either paper planes or scrunched-up balls thrown at them. Vautier's closing 'Secret Room' took the audience row by row into a secret area, which consisted of ushers taking them through a back exit onto the street outside. Concert over.

Yoko's two contributions, one a 'striptease' and the other a wrapping, were tributes to comrades, former or otherwise. 'Four Pieces for Orchestra to La Monte Young' involved the instructions 'Tear, Rub, Peel, Take Off' and involved actual musical instruments: tools were used to rub the holes of violins or cellos, erasers were used to rub wind instruments, and Sellotape was peeled off various instruments. Preparing the instruments, to transform their function, and treating the random, one-off production with total concentration also made it an indirect tribute to John Cage.

'Sky Piece for Jesus Christ' was a direct tribute to Cage, with his initials J.C., and his various sermons and gospels according to, leading many of his friends to refer to him as Jesus Christ. Yoko slowly wrapped the small orchestra in gauze bandages, stopping them from playing, leading to silence – always of interest to Cage. Yoko asked for help from the audience in completing the performance, remembering Cage's conclusion that there is

394

no such thing as silence. The audience were encouraged to supply sound as the music faded by talking through the performance, and applauding at the end.

Cage himself, who had announced to whom it may concern 'who knows what might become a potential relationship and lead to a future order', became the everyday sky above us and within us, a metaphor for human transcendence, a symbol of the tangible and the abstract, inviting contemplation of the vastness of the universe and our place in it, a canvas where emotions, dreams and philosophies can be projected.

The Yoko Ono reading e.e. cummings's line 'love is the sky'.

The Yoko Ono hearing Bob Dylan sing 'the sky hurls its poems in naked wonder'.

The Yoko Ono who dared to claim the sky.

The Yoko Ono reading Emily Dickinson's line 'to see the summer sky is poetry'.

The Yoko Ono reading Emily Dickinson's line 'a cloud withdrew from the sky'.

The Yoko Ono who never knew what the sky of tomorrow would be like, only that it would be there, until it wasn't.

In March 1965, as another solo venture, an early pioneer inspired by Ray Johnson of using advertising and classified ads in newspapers and magazines as a medium for art, Yoko placed a full-page advert in a New York arts magazine for an exhibition at the IsReal Gallery for what were called *Circle Events*. The gallery was open twenty-four hours a day for almost every day in March, and there was no address, only a phone number.

Circle Events – and a couple of months later the promise of *Hole Events* – were offered on a variety of materials including leather, silk and glass, or anything of your choice. It was a fictional exhibition at a fictional gallery, an extension of an idea she'd been circling since an article she'd written in 1962 for the *Sogetsu Art Journal* about her interest in 'a world of fictional rules – the assumption and realisation of a perfect circle and a straight line that we have not encountered except in a conceptual world'.

Yoko's *Circle Events* originated with a Fluxus postcard-based mail-art performance where Yoko asked a number of artists and colleagues in her circle, including Cox, Earle Brown, Carolee Schneemann, Dick Higgins, George Maciunas and Ay-O to answer some questions about their (fictional) history as a circle maker, and to 'draw circle' inside a rectangle on the card. In isolation it was a simple request leading to different responses, none the same, so that the idea of a 'circle' itself became an insight into each contributor's personality. As a small part of the overall sense of what Yoko was doing, it has greater meaning, as an idea that potentially develops its own momentum, and its own surprising turns.

It led to the idea of an exhibition where anyone and everyone could come to a gallery, and 'draw circle'. At first, before it became fictional, Yoko attempted to make it a real exhibition, or consciously played with what she knew from the beginning was impractical, and contacted Ivan Karp. As his gallery manager and cigar-chomping sidekick he introduced to Leo Castelli and his Upper East Side Castelli Gallery new-wave minimalists like Frank Stella and the select pop art operators Jasper Johns, Robert Rauschenberg, Roy Lichtenstein and, at the shiny top of the tree, Andy Warhol. Karp described Warhol on first meeting him as 'a very shy, strange-looking grey haired man'.

With Castelli as suave, silver-tongued European front man, Karp became the 'chief salesman of the pop art movement', inventing new strategies for selling contemporary art, with a mid-sixties reputation for knowing more than anyone about what was happening at the darkest margins of the New York art world.

Tony Cox, always looking for ways to turn Yoko's concepts into money, met Karp with an idea for a Yoko event at the prestigious gallery where visitors would draw circles on blank canvases, and then buy the result. No other Fluxus-attached artist would have been allowed to go near the enemy, and Castelli generally had no desire to court any of the artists engaged with the mocking, would-be-shocking anti-art and anti-object of Fluxus, but Yoko found a way to float between territories.

Karp wasn't sure whether there was any money in it, enough to cover the few thousand dollars it would cost to put the show on. Would people really pay for something that in the end they themselves had made? And didn't Yoko and the Fluxus crew distrust the role of galleries like Castelli – however art-loving, however much it championed unorthodox break-through talent – in making art about money, fashion and social standing? Wasn't Castelli a bit . . . materialistic for Yoko Ono? Wasn't the proof that her art existed only in catalogues or on obscure, grainy film?

Karp perhaps felt he was being played by Cox and Yoko, that they knew as well as he did that she wasn't the right fit for Castelli, and the gallery was being used as a conceptual prop. She didn't belong in the club, and it wasn't a club she wanted to belong to.

After Cox reported Karp's indifference, Yoko wrote to Karp, cheekily suggesting that perhaps a way to make money, with Yoko maintaining necessary conceptual distance, was for the artists he represented – including Max Ernst – to draw the circles on a canvas, after which they could be sold, and the owner could add their own circle, or not. Karp sardonically replied to what he called Yoko's urgent missive, complimenting it for its pungent metaphysics and adventurous aesthetics.

He had to pass, though, as 'The show you have in mind fails to suit our temperament which is essentially restless, driven, fiercely Western and concrete – not materialistic, mind you, perish the thought – but terribly concrete.' He added that Ernst was tired and didn't want to travel, and most of his other artists despised each other and did not want to contribute. It made Castelli seem very men-only, even if the gallery represented a couple of women artists.

Yoko's answer, the punchline that Karp sensed was coming, beyond his concerns, was the fictional, terribly non-concrete IsReal *Circle Events* show. If you want something done right, do it yourself.

Copies of the letters between Yoko and Karp assuming their natural positions in the ongoing art marketplace wars – the carefully cultivated spectacular versus the haphazardly counter-spectacular – were included in an Ono conceptual sales list distributed as a Fluxus flyer. The original Yoko letter to Karp was marked as three hundred dollars, the original letter from Karp to Yoko was priced at two cents. Copies of both were available for fifty cents. Minimalism, pop art and later the conceptual art Yoko had helped set up would be worth millions; Fluxus, precisely because it was Fluxus, escaping itself, was usually worth at best a few dollars.

The sales list mostly offered the chance to buy imaginary experiences and ideas, another rueful side glance at the commodification of creativity, celebrating the creation of an alternative universe where art was magic, not off the shelf. If a painting is worth so much, how much is a piece of the imagination, a generated portion of time, an open mind worth? Those are things that are made in your brain, which ultimately makes everything, the real and the unreal. Yoko, art dealer in the mind, determined their virtual value.

The sales list also functioned as another of Yoko's discreet manifestos, a cryptic summary of her thinking about art, how it can assume its own independent life, take on a personality, become a self-sufficient, spiritually breathing subject. Even if merely described, as an impossible act, a fantasy procedure, it is a being, and like every being, it leads to further, creative active forces. The list was a manifesto championing poetic conceptual art.

For twenty-five cents an inch you could purchase a tape loop of snow falling at dawn in various locations, India, Kyo or Aos. The neatly snipped tape did exist, although it was never clear which snow sound you were receiving even if you managed to play it. This looped back to 'Tape Piece III – Snow Piece', where the instruction was to 'take a tape of the snow falling. This should be done in the evening. Do not listen to the tape. Cut it and use it to tie strings to gifts with. Make a gift wrapper.' The tape wasn't the point; neither necessarily is the passing on, the sharing, of something that doesn't actually exist, ultimately a memory, or a dream.

You could choose from a selection of touch poems and 'buy' them for between $150 and $10,000. It was like a series of vending machines where each one suggested the potential plot of a science-fiction story by J.G. Ballard or Philip K. Dick or a limited Netflix series: a crying machine that cries tears for you at $3,000, a $1,500 word machine producing a single word, a $1,600 disappearing machine that erases an object of your choice at the touch of a button, an $1,100 danger box, somewhere between time machine and vessel to navigate alternative universes, complete with safety warning, a sky machine which gives you nothing for half the price of the tears, and an eternal clock that keeps eternal time, for a bargain $800.

Architectural works on the list included a light house – a house made of light – a wind house where the wind created a different sound in each room and a transparent house, a reverse development of the bag for 'Bag Piece', where people on the outside could see in and those inside couldn't see out. Garden sets allowed the moonlight to make a pond in a shallow hole; there was a deeper hole for clouds to drip into, longer holes to catch fog, and stones arranged to be covered by snow.

There were events you could buy (a score to produce the falling of pink snow on your own was a dollar, the actual fulfilment of the score two thousand dollars), a catalogue of all instructions and pieces made since 1951, defective underwear for men and psychedelic underwear for women. Some of the things listed were possibly available, including a selection of dance and music scores, and the six film scripts Yoko had written in 1964 – instructional scripts, proposing starting points for films that it might be good for someone to make, but that also exist as wishes or hopes.

You could also buy a copy of *Grapefruit*, and *Self-Portrait* for an unspectacular few dollars, and the list would be published in the later, more commercial editions of *Grapefruit*, as a form of appendix to a study of how consciousness fits into our picture of reality, an example of further instructional thinking and, like the book itself, a way of developing her art system. Process demonstrating process was part of the process.

The sales list, a comprehensive exhibition on a typewritten piece of paper, was perhaps a sign, coming quickly after the signs of 'Cut Piece' and 'Bag Piece', the various distillation of essences achieved in her concerts, that through 1965 and 1966, Yoko was at the peak of her powers. Her work was poised between elegant simplicity and resounding transcendence, with an uncanny ability to place works of art that didn't exist or only existed for moments into the memory, and her multi-dimensional, disconcerting mischief was reflected in the irreverent, agile attitudes of the fast-forming multi-positional counterculture.

Maciunas's ironically jaunty Fluxus graphics and the collective's radical audiovisual variety-show energy were also reflected in the graphics and concerts of the rock underground, linking two worlds. The elastic Fluxus avant-garde mix of sound, art, theatre, light, performance, design, technology, art amusements and spontaneous entertainments was helping extend the sonic, theatrical and metaphysical range of pop music, leading to, on the West Coast, Captain Beefheart, Frank Zappa and the Mothers of Invention, and on the East Coast, the Velvet Underground.

Perpetual Fluxfest in June 1965, with Yoko according to Maciunas's poster effectively topping the bill as a Fluxus principal, exists as an ancestor of the pop festival, a multidisciplinary collective carnival of pleasure and provocation, an eclectic celebration of ecstatic ritual – in its original, sixties form, a mass happening, a spiritual awakening, an adult playground, an energising confirmation of possibility, a metaphorical environment built in the image of a better world. Maciunas and Yoko briefly, abstractly conjoined as a Fluxus double act, previewing the more notoriously infectious one to come.

There were jazz festivals and folk festivals preceding it, but the pop festival established itself on the other side of Fluxus spectacle and its particular approach to protest through imagining a world that you want and living it if and when you can.

Fluxfest presented nine artists on separate days, and Yoko performed 'Bag Piece', a resonant symbol of the mid-sixties desire to think differently, to free the mind. It was also a piece she'd perform when, to make some cash after returning from Tokyo, she was working as a waitress, and occasional ninety-five-cent salad maker, at the Paradox restaurant on the Lower East Side, the first macrobiotic restaurant in New York. Occasionally she would climb into a large black hessian sack and roll around inside it as entertainment for customers eating their rice bowls.

Sometimes Andy Warhol would come in and eat on his own, gently asking after Yoko's state of mind and giving her some oblique encouragement. Lou Reed would come in, gracing the place with his practised sour low-life scowl. The Velvet Underground would be rehearsing the songs from their Warhol-directed debut *And Nico* album around the time Yoko worked there, around the corner at John Cale's apartment, best described as a bohemian slum, its seediness seeping into the music. Allen Ginsberg lived a short walk away, the downtown area feeding bits of life, matter and outrageousness into 'Howl' and other poems, making myth out of the people and places making a life at the ragged edges of the city

The almost off-the-map area on 7th Street between First and Second Avenue, once an elegant turn-of-the-twentieth-century home for the well off, was now a rundown enclave for beatniks and bohemians as they became hippies, free thinkers, anarchists, old lefties and new lefties all mixed up with a century or more of local mixed-up immigrants, the

401

scrappy, intellectual punks mentored by William Burroughs and led by Patti Smith and Richard Hell turning up in a few years, inheriting and recasting the East Village light and dark. In 1965, it was the perfect place to eat a sprout salad and watch one of the Paradox wait staff, maybe a couple, climb into a huge sack and do whatever they did inside for extra tips, or simply some attention.

At the Perpetual Fluxfest, Maciunas gave himself so completely to Yoko's 'Wall Piece for Orchestra', and to Yoko herself, that he nearly knocked himself out – hit a wall with your head a/slowly until the wall collapses b/ violently until your head is gone, one of Yoko's most sublimely deranged therapeutic instructions, on the line between self-soothing and self-destruction. He had a lot to get out of his system, and as mad king of Fluxus, it was expected he would fully expose the often hidden vitality of a Yoko piece.

In the February 1966 issue of the Fluxus magazine *cc V TR*, number 7, Yoko proposed a fictional thirteen-day *Do It Yourself Dance Festival*, a conceptual rave, as part of another Fluxfest. The instructions for dances in the mind – communicated to other participants by telepathy – came as part of a twenty-piece collection of cards with fantastical cut-and-paste graphic illustrations switching between silly and sinister, sampled from medical, botanical and erotic textbooks by George Maciunas.

Yoko's text and Maciunas's designs gave clues as to possible dance moves – 'breathe' for the first three days, on the seventh day find a clover, on the tenth day swim in your dreams as fast as you can, on the twelfth boil water and watch until it evaporates.

On the final day of the February Fluxfest, Yoko performed the 'boil water' dance instruction at their apartment for five friends on the day of a subway strike. It was turned into 'Disappearing Piece', an imagination event where, as the water evaporated, the room was to conceptually turn upside down, becoming something else altogether.

There was no great sleight of hand to create the illusion, just a few Yoko sentences written around the living room – this is the floor on the ceiling, this is the ceiling on the floor and this window is two thousand feet wide on the windowsill, this room slowly evaporates every day, this line is part of a very large circle, this room moves at the speed of the clouds. Because of the words, if you think about it, the room changes. It extends infinitely, even if just for a moment.

Placing these sentences around a tiny, claustrophobic off-white room that had always frustrated Yoko led to an installation, 'Blue Room Event', which Yoko would explain was an act of rebellion by a woman living in a small apartment in New York City that had hardly any furniture and views of grim brick walls through two small windows.

Ignoring the confines of time and space – pure Yoko – and imagining the room as a magical living space was an antidote to despair, and the feeling that as artist and self she too was disappearing. This ephemeral manifestation of Yoko's temporary cramped home would go through various incarnations and be remade in various locations for decades, a memory of 1966 Yoko travelling through time and renewing itself as her world – which the tiny New York room became for a few months – was turned upside down again and again.

Some critics suggested her art stalled over the next few decades, for one reason or another, or merely repeated her early breakthroughs, but a lot of those initial breakthroughs were intended to keep travelling, constantly replicating, revealing and modifying themselves as her life became what it became. She needed to leave enough room for the art she invented in her twenties to become something else because of what happened next in her life. The pieces were designed to accompany her as she grew older, changing as she did.

While she was living, ageing, responding to changes in her life, a concentrated psychic patience would become the artistic input adding other dimensions to her original strategies. Her art, made in and for and because of an instant, needed the addition of time, allowing, as Yoko wrote, 'for the infinite transformation of a work of art that the artist cannot see for themselves'.

It was a word she wrote on the 'Blue Event' ceiling – YES – that would send her world spinning once it made it into the future, and onto another ceiling, in another city, in another country. It became the answer to a question she couldn't know was going to be asked by someone a year later with their own understanding of magic and altering consciousness, but maybe in her own way she expected it. Maybe the YES was the question, and someone had the answer.

Someone made their way to Yoko's YES as though it was where he had been heading since he sang 'yeah yeah yeah', it was what he wanted, and Yoko's wish would be granted, it was what she wanted, with certain provisos baked in by fate, part of a world always at war with itself.

One of the lines from what was another of Yoko's fractured, fantastical manifestos – 'this is not here' – would become the title of a 1971 retrospective in Syracuse of her work since the later 1950s. By that time she had become, shockingly, the shunned, high-profile wife of a rock star with hero status, which generated sensational connections firing in all directions between the promiscuously adventurous avant-garde underground and an exploding pop culture.

An audience wasn't necessarily interested in her art, or whatever it was she did, but it was interested in her dysfunctional glamour, with many people hoping John would lose interest in her. The dark star of Fluxus became an international star by proxy now that John and Paul had become Johnandyoko, whose artwork was an always-becoming, intimate, immediate face-to-face communion of augmented identities and realities, or pop music warped by avant-garde concerns. This still wasn't here, though.

The Yoko Ono who in 1965 became, in the kind of fiction that has a way of interfering with the truth, a little more the demonic, cheerless, talentless cultural vandal she was assumed to be when she first made contact with a wider public.

She appeared, as a struggling conceptual artist creating an artistic situation, or just needing the work, in the sexploitation melodrama *Satan's Bed*. She didn't know she was going to appear in the shredded, sleazy *Satan's Bed*, as she had originally filmed something called *Judas City* as the innocent Japanese fiancée of a heroin dealer who moves to New York, dragging along her husband who tries to change his life.

The film was never completed, and parts of it got chopped into *Satan's Bed* when the notorious underground film-maker provocateur Michael Findlay, then a film fanatic desperate to start making films, was hired to try and finish it, with none of the original actors. Later notorious for the kind of violent sex-and-sadism exploitation 'roughies' – early slasher movies – showing in grindhouse theatres and sleazy cinemas around Times Square, he was unable to find a way to make it work. He mixed his own frenetic, explicit footage of a vicious gang of drug addicts, thieves and rapists into the tonally completely different *Judas City* footage. Yoko's fiancé is somehow involved with the gang, even though they never meet.

Yoko's character is a harassed victim, brutally kidnapped by her drug-pusher husband's supplier, labelled 'an Eastern delicacy', and acts like she's got a brief role in a low-budget long-running soap with no idea of the plot. It's the women in Findlay's seedy additions that are stripped and abused, as though 'Cut Piece' has been turned into a sorry, hell-drenched nightmare.

The lusty trailer claimed it was 'a film about the depravity of our society'. It was so obscure no one would have been aware of it when

405

Yoko married four years later, but the general view would be that she was exactly the desperate, incompetent, fame-chasing person who would end up in such haywire, salacious trash, as if the only thing she had ever done as a performer was appear in a lurid rape movie called something like *Satan's Bed*.

Yoko was moving fast into 1966, keeping up to keep ahead, materialising in different places in different forms, just as her art did. Regular events and performances spanned the Recital Hall, the Judson Memorial Church Hall, her apartment and its rooftop, street corners, restaurants, Maciunas's Fluxus publications and his general networking and word of mouth. She started to make films, as though she was subconsciously getting herself ready for a new stage which would allow no time to invent. She was stockpiling ideas, instructions and intentions.

Maciunas had been close since the early 1950s to another displaced Lithuanian immigrant, Jonas Mekas, designing his avant-garde film magazine *Film Culture*, founded in 1955 by Jonas with his brother Adolfas. Mekas became not just film-maker but theoretician, film critic, programmer, archivist and committed advocate of underground and experimental film, with an unbreakable belief that the avant-garde could never die because it was a permanent state of humanity. With Maciunas he encouraged the early film-making of Andy Warhol, the son of Czech immigrants, all three seeing the wild commercialised beauty and berserk TV-shaped reality of America as refugee outsiders, using the outlandish new country as a stimulus for their inventiveness.

Despite Maciunas's friendship with Mekas, film hadn't been a significant element in Fluxus activities, as though image fetishist Warhol's hundreds of films made since 1964's *Sleep* – five and a bit hours of a man sleeping – were in themselves so comprehensively Fluxus, without being Fluxus, that he might as well be left to it.

Warhol constructed a vast, enthralling anti-film universe that rewired and reinvented the potential of the moving image; organised through sociological and anthropological methods, his films covered silent, scripted, random, documentary, *vérité*, minimalist, real time, living studies, underground, non-narrative experimental, conceptual, improvisational, satire, sexploitation and screen tests, celebrating his role-playing superstars and celebrity passers-by from Donovan and Lou Reed to Susan Sontag and Marcel Duchamp.

By 1966, at Warholworld versions of immersive Fluxus concerts, Warhol's ever-present films were projected onto screens under dancing multi-coloured gels and molten oils as the drily raucous Factory house band Velvet Underground played loud, minimalist action drones and sculpted cacophony, establishing how we would see pop music as much as hear it from then on.

Although Yoko was as cinematically inquisitive as Warhol, with her own interest in making art that let the viewer's mind wander, in watching the expressions on people's faces as they looked at her work, in the early sixties she didn't consider making films, as it seemed too expensive and she couldn't even afford canvases.

She made 'films', conceptually, the six instructional film scripts she wrote in the early 1960s. Film 1, 'Walk to the Taj Mahal', consisted of falling snow, and a circular, zigzagging walk the camera and therefore the viewer will take through the snow, before going up into the sky. Film 2, 'Mona Lisa and Her Smile', asked the audience to stare at a figure for a long time and then look at its after-image on a screen. Film 3: Ask the audience to cut part of an image on the screen they don't like. Scissors would be supplied. Film 4 wanted the audience to stare at the screen until it turns black. Film 5 was look at Doris Day not Rock Hudson, only look at square and angled images and if you do look at something round keep looking until it becomes square or angled. Film 6 was to give a film to a number of directors for them to re-edit in such a way the re-edit wouldn't be noticed.

Later, there would be more detailed film fantasies: imaginary films about death, buildings, sleep – not Warhol-like, but something she called a contemporary sexual manual – a room with many different time zones, a poetic and very rare film about pregnancy, a film of smiles to be seen in two thousand years' time, a film about watching the sky, a film about a fly crawling very slowly across a naked body from head to toe – which was made – and a series of travelogues from various implausible points of view.

She was imagining films that you wouldn't view but experience as visual emotions, as half-remembered dreams. She never thought she'd make films like Warhol was doing, with his interest in cameras, film projectors and the mystery of fame. Fame didn't interest her, until she became famous, and mingled with famous people, when for better or worse it became more material to play with.

Out of the blue, on just another day, Maciunas excitedly called Yoko to say he had the temporary use of a camera, so let's make some films. Yoko went round to the address he'd given her on East 36th Street, and there was an excited Maciunas with the camera, asking Yoko for some ideas, quick, give me some ideas.

He had managed to rent an expensive high-speed scientific analysis camera, which filed at a rate of two thousand frames a minute, producing a dreamy slow-motion state when projected at the standard twenty-four frames a minute. It wasn't clear where he had got it, but he only had it for the day, and rounded up as many Fluxus artists as he could track down.

Checking out the activities of a controlling impresario and marketing maestro who was too alien, and weirdly corporate, to ever threaten his own world-building, Maciunas thought, seeing the Warhol-sponsored intermedia extravaganzas, that Fluxus needed some visual, and social, pep. Maybe he was just reminding Warhol, wherever he was, that he'd taken a little Fluxus into the Factory, and he wanted the loan repaid.

Maciunas was at the apartment of the Fluxus photographer and now film cameraman Peter Moore and his wife Barbara. In a way, he was auditioning his artist roster to see who might become the Fluxus Warhol, giving them the opportunity, for one day only, using very little effort, costing very little, to become film-makers. As a consequence, Fluxus would have a film library, an instant archive, and because a few seconds of footage could become many minutes, they could turn a day's shoot into many days. It was also a way to audit Fluxus strategies, and to confirm directly or indirectly their pure avant-garde avoidance of profit motives and commitment to expanding artistic thought in an autonomous creative sphere.

Of all the people who used the camera, it was Yoko with her Japanese-inspired workaholic energy who became the most prolific film-maker, in tune with Maciunas's functional numbering system and love of sight gags, with her own ideas of how film could work for her.

Maciunas himself, as organiser, financer, publicist, marketer and the one-man selection committee of the Fluxus brand, was a kind of Warhol, without the attention and acclaim – one sad and/or funny consequence of the Fluxfilms, barely noticed at the time, was a grant for $40 a month from a company that specialised in giving grants to experimental film-makers. He needed the money. Warhol in his own way was beginning to use art to print money.

As an artist, with an eye on participating in culture, not just displaying your wares, Yoko jumped into popular culture in the way Warhol and Beuys had. As a serious artist, as a sorcerous performer, she was developing concepts from the inside, creating opinions, personality and actions as much as objects, allowing images to migrate across different media and producing social sculptures that treated society as one ever-present collaborative work of art.

Fluxfilms as a do-it-ourselves series began with the almost ceremonial number 1, 'Zen Film', by Naim June Paik, his calmest ever work, dated 1964, so also a beginning of the video art that became his central concern. An installation using projector and blank luminous screen, featuring flickering dust and scratches on a roll of clear leader, it set the template for Fluxfilms, with their own inevitable connection to or sceptical and/or affectionate comment on Warhol's early, fantastically flat films and Stan Brakhage's adventures in perception, his painting and scratching on film, with their connection to the repetition and durational bravado of La Monte Young – moving, and not so moving, images radicalising cinematic time that emerged from the form and expression of music. (Maciunas was convinced that Warhol had not only been influenced by

409

La Monte Young, but had also directly stolen ideas from Jackson Mac Low's 1961 hours-long static film script for *Tree* (which could also be mountain, sea, lake, flower). Mac Low countered by saying there was no room for the 'who-did-it-firstism' of the so-called avant-garde.)

The blank screen of Paik's 'Fluxfilm No. 1' was then filled in with Fluxfilms' minimal actions, snatches of nothing and experiments with visual representation and time. A series of short, mostly unedited silent tests, film diaries, digital clocks, found footage and visual jokes mostly by Maciunas and Fluxists including Higgins, Knowles, Vautier and Brecht, and Fluxist near-neighbours including Robert Watts, Joe Jones and John Cale, consisting of flickering frames, patterns, colours, close-ups of mouths and eating, sometimes using no camera but applying adhesive patterns onto clear film stock, they were Fluxus home movies, as though Fluxus had a home, capturing insignificant quotidian phenomena, sketchy and flippant enough to make even the most inert, instant Warhol film seem an elaborate preparation.

Yoko's contributions to the Maciunas Fluxfilm programme began with an appearance in her friend from Tokyo and Group Ongaku co-founder Mieko Shiomi's 'Fluxfilm 4' – Maciunas invited Shiomi to New York and paid for her flight on the recommendation of Yoko and Toshi, part of his version of Fluxus as a support network for artists.

Shiomi's Fluxus debut at a 1964 Fluxfest event held at the Washington Square Gallery was 'Disappearing Music for Face' with the instruction 'smile and make it disappear gradually'; it was performed by Alison Knowles because Shiomi was shy, fresh from Japan, faced with New York energy.

Yoko's first idea for a short film was to film a smile, and call it 'Smile', but Maciunas didn't want to as he said he was saving that for Mieko, who had a similar idea and had just returned to Japan. Eventually he said to Yoko, do Mieko's 'Smile', which wasn't quite what Yoko had in mind.

Yoko ended up standing in for Mieko on a performance of 'Disappearing Music for Face': the smile that disappears. The filmed eight seconds of the Yoko smile gradually becoming no smile would turn into eleven

410

minutes. She would keep returning to her idea for 'Smile', which she imagined, as an impossible instruction, would be everybody's smile in the world, an early intimation of Instagram. In 1968, she made 'Smile' as a colour film with the other half of the more conspicuous Fluxus double act than the irregular one with Maciunas had been.

Her new star partner was rich enough to afford the high-speed camera necessary to create the abstracted effect achieved with 'Eye Blink', and she used his world-famous smile to represent everybody's smile. She's looking at him, he's looking at her, and beyond that she's looking at an audience looking at him. At the time, they were discovering each other, living and working together, and documenting it happening, revealing how they met, how he looked at her when they met, coming together as though for a short while they would be in control of their lives.

In the first part he smiles slightly in very slow motion, outside himself, in the moment; in the subtly transformed second part there's a little more life, and a hint of the playful and mocking, even self-mocking, with ambient bird and plane noises at their correct speed, helping achieve the sensation Yoko wanted of seeing someone while under the influence of acid, capturing in this case a gently distant vibratory crack in perception.

Later, Maciunas would turn thirty-nine frames of 'Disappearing Music' into a palm-sized flipbook, where the smile would disappear as you flipped the pages. He wanted to turn the whole series into flipbooks, but the only other film to become a flipbook was Dick Higgins's 'Flux-film No. 2: Invocation of Canyons and Boulders (for Stan Brakhage)', a looped close-up of Higgins chewing something that could last for seconds, minutes or hours and hours, and was described by Mekas as 'a Tibetan prayer wheel, a hypnotic device to free your mind'.

For her own single-shot sculptural 'tests', Yoko filmed one of her earliest pieces, the lit match, as Fluxfilm 14 – 'Match' – transferring it from one medium to another to continue its creative evolution. More or less the beginning of her art life was still coming to life a decade later, still being lit and then going out, lit again, and going out, becoming a sublime slow-motion reminder, a documentary memory, of the revelatory moment she discovered the artistic medium that suited her, which wasn't music or poetry or painting, but all of that, and what more it could become when performance, concept and now film were added.

Fluxfilm 9/15 – 'Eye Blink' – made a fixed-frame silent close-up of a split-second Yoko eye blink last a lonely, endless fifteen seconds. It will always be Yoko Ono 1966, in the precious, pressured last few months of another life, thinking about blinking and about filming herself blinking as much as just thinking about blinking, wondering if anyone in the future will ever think of her, ever know who she was.

Yoko began thinking of a more involved, and edited, film that would become part of the Fluxfilm series – another, unconfined represent-ation and celebration of the human body and the passage of time. It was called 'No. 4', but was Fluxfilm number 16. Maciunas's initial deadpan description of it was 'Sequence of buttock movement as various people moved. Filmed at constant distance,' and it would end up being called 'No. 4 (Bottoms)'.

The film started as a five-and-a-half-minute prototype filmed in Yoko's 100th Street apartment for an eighty-minute film completed in London a few months later. Yoko found encouraging instant connections between her experimental instincts and an emerging underground, her art itself becoming a symbol of – being about – how she moved in life from one experience to another, and one state to another. 'No. 4 (Bottoms)' kept moving, her films evolving as her performances did, the same thing becoming something else as she became someone else, and the remake of 'No. 4' helped make her name in London.

'No. 4' became the link between her New York art, which had dev-eloped out of very insular, cross-pollinating New York conditions and her Fluxus alliance, and a London scene which took her into a wider outside world. The New York artist who to some extent was disappearing into an obscure history – her New York apartments were getting smaller and smaller, the views from the window ever sadder – started to reappear.

A new relationship developed via livid, messy pop culture with an audi-ence and media, one that was beginning even before she stepped into the dazzling, cruel maelstrom of fame. 'Bottoms' was the first sign of the rhythm and sensationalism of rock music – the filmed bottoms moving to a regular heartbeat she associated with rock songs – as a factor in her work, the alert, insatiable Yoko responding to the sights and sounds of rock as a new volatile art form in a way few if any of her contemporaries were doing.

413

Her husband Tony Cox and their friend and sometime room-mate Jeff Perkins helped put together the low-budget New York sketch. They'd met Perkins in Tokyo, where he was stationed in the US Air Force to avoid the Vietnam draft, and he became part of Yoko's inner circle, meeting Maciunas, and making his own Fluxfilm, No. 22, 'Shout' – Cox and Perkins shouting at each other, comically cut off in mid-stream, filmed by Yoko.

He returned the favour, and was the cameraman for 'No. 4', and also participated alongside other Yoko and Maciunas confederates including Bici and Geoffrey Hendricks, Ben Patterson, Carolee Schneemann and James Tenney. Yoko asked John Cage if he would take part, but he told her he wasn't interested in her bottom project, in the same way he had told Charlotte Moorman he wasn't interested in her showing her breasts when she played one of his pieces on the cello.

The New York 'No. 4' was part of how Yoko was making a name for herself as an indefinable New York artist among a small, constantly active artistic community. A number of people from this small community appeared in the film, allowing their backsides to be filmed very particularly for a loving, enchanting Yoko examination of a usually hidden and therefore mysterious part of the human body. Everyone's the same, she said, when they take their clothes off, with an innocence they cannot control. It was filming something ordinary people do every day, but without clothes, and never with such freedom.

It was also a silent Yoko documentary on where Fluxus was at the moment, seen only through their buttocks filling the screen and walking on the road to nowhere, one bare bottom after the other, an unlabelled, often indistinguishable march of masculine and feminine, the whole screen constantly moving, naturally divided into equal quarters. 'People's behinds have right and left and top and bottom,' she explained. The framing led to the title 'No. 4', which was both a conceptual number, loved by Maciunas and Yoko, to mislead and confound, and plainly descriptive of the way the screen was split into four sections.

Keen on trying her new pieces and performances in Europe, Yoko made her first trip to London in September 1966. She was invited to participate in the 'Destruction in Art' symposium co-ordinated and founded by Gustav Metzger and the Irish concrete poet John Sharkey that brought together artists, scientists, psychologists, composers and poets for four days of lectures, discussions and events about how artists were interpreting and processing violence, destruction and survival, and the terror that was increasingly out there in the world.

Many of Yoko's pieces involved destroying the work itself as a way of creating an experience: her instructions like 'Blood Piece' used the body, and perhaps a fantasy about the body, to contemplate violence. Without being itself aggressive, in fact at times it was weirdly peaceful, 'Cut Piece' was an immersion in aggression and destructive desire, and her performance at the symposium of 'Shadow Piece's eloquent hybrid of poetry and theatre – 'put together your shadows until they become one' – recalled the eerie nuclear shadows of Hiroshima and Nagasaki.

When a nuclear bomb explodes, releasing its abominable heat and energy in a split second, a plasma ball produces a flash of light as though the sun has dropped to earth. The world is instantly on fire. The quick, intense flash scorches everything. Anything in the way of the light casts a 'shadow', including people, who would be etched in stone. In post-war Japan the shadows, surrounded by what the pavements and buildings looked like before they were bleached by the light, remained for years until rain and time washed them away.

'Shadow Piece' appeared at a time when innocent victims of the Vietnam War were being reduced to shadows by napalm. Art cannot stop the unearthly devastation and suffering, the endless, ferocious fury, but can be a gentle, humble and necessarily peaceful method of drawing attention, of imagining solutions, of provoking thoughts, keeping the

415

dead with us, remembered and to an extent recovered. An artwork never has a discernible end, but as an action, an unexpected interruption, a provocative prompt, it can make emotion, memory and sensation break open a new reality. It's fragile, even as an investigation of ultimate violence, but much stronger than doing or feeling nothing, with the hope that can be stronger than violence. The imagination – rendered by art, music, theatre, literature, film, philosophy – is the exact opposite to war.

Yoko had been invited to the symposium by a member of its committee, the editor of the recently launched *Arts and Artists* magazine, art critic and curator Mario Amaya, who in June 1968 would be in Andy Warhol's office when Warhol was shot by Valerie Solanas, and was grazed by a couple of bullets. Avant-garde risk-taking continually led to real threat.

Yoko thought of travelling to London on her own, needing a break from the family, but Tony and Kyoko came along. Tony was anxious about letting Yoko disappear for a few days that might turn into an extended stay, and as he predicted an intended short stay turned into another long, life-changing stay away from New York, and, not least because of Tony's paranoia, another marriage rocking and rolling.

Amaya had been scouting New York looking for artists who fit the symposium's transnational, transformative theme of auto-destruction, and was finding it difficult to locate women dealing with destruction and violent erasure, whose art was linked to dread and anxiety – of the fifty or so invitees either attending or sending photographs, text, sound, manifestos, only a handful were female, including the sound artist and experimental composer Annea Lockwood, a contemporary of sonic sculptor Pauline Oliveros, weaned on Cage's prepared piano, which led via Ralph Ortiz's punishing dismantling of a piano at the symposium to 'Piano Burning', a sequel of sorts to Philip Corner's 'Piano Activities'. Lockwood took the 'preparing' of the piano into the realm of destruction, making a solid, beautifully made piano a disposable sound maker, or, in another way, celebrating its life in a final burst of creativity.

The destruction was to set an upright, defunct, irreparable piano on fire, and to play whatever pleased you for as long as possible, and the creation was when the sound became the poignant crackling of the wood and the snapping of the piano strings, and the flames died out.

The noise of a piano being destroyed was like nothing else, and inspired an illicit pleasure among those watching the wanton destruction of a once-prized instrument – seemingly out of date in a world of radio, TV and records; as old-fashioned as a corset – for the sake of a few minutes of rare sound.

The German-born artist, interdisciplinary pioneer and anti-nuclear campaigner Gustav Metzger had arrived in England as a twelve-year-old refugee from Nazi Germany and, having witnessed the utterly negative power of the Nazi state, developed auto-destructive art in the early 1960s, based on the idea of destroying to create. 'Auto-destructive art is to do with rejecting the power of authority,' he said.

In the 1950s, he became exposed to inspirational abstract art that in Germany was labelled degenerate, and his avowedly anti-capitalist, anti-consumerist, anti-gallery revolutionary art facing destruction head-on grew out of some cheap but beautifully made cardboard boxes he'd seen outside a shop in Covent Garden, which he exhibited almost untouched. Objects that cost nothing could be special.

He started to make art that triggered its own destruction and confronted various forms of violence, for him following a line back to the protests of Dada and the political energy and aggressive aspect of the Futurists and their response to earlier twentieth-century instability. His first performative paintings in 1961, a reaction to the use of nuclear weapons, employed hydrochloric acid to dissolve a sheet of nylon stretched across glass, revealing him in hiding. Metzger was one of the first in British artists to interact with Fluxus, participating in the Festival of Misfits in 1962, and seeing elements of destruction as a counterpoint to creation in the events and happenings of Fluxus and other artists.

His action paintings would disintegrate, crumble to dust, fade away, create new forms or just completely disappear, symbolically destroying systems of war and warmongers. Like early Fluxus, he was denying the art market the objects it needed to sell, and like Fluxus, he thought

417

events, lectures, happenings, concepts, installation were art as much as any painting or artefact. His manifestos, demonstrations and exhibitions between 1959 and 1961 contained proto-Fluxus elements: destroy a canvas and create new shapes, bring to life the torn, burnt and disposed of, recover the non-existent, revitalise the modern world.

Metzger's theories led into the Who, and Pete Townshend's exultant, emancipated on-stage smashing of his guitar, which lives forever in rock history. Townshend attended an invigorating Metzger lecture at Ealing Art College in 1962 which included a photograph of Yoko cutting up canvases. He fully intended the Who itself to be an auto-destructive action and to collapse in on itself after three months. He might also have seen or heard of British art rebel and Fluxus member Robin Page's 'Guitar Piece' during the Fluxus-laced Festival of Misfits, where Page in silver crash helmet and rubber boots flung his guitar off the stage at the ICA and brutally kicked it down the aisle, through the door and down the street, trailed by a thrilled audience, until it broke apart.

During Metzger's symposium, among artists getting violent for the sake of art, often sacrificing musical instruments and books with loving fury, Page had dug a hole in the concrete floor of the independent book-shop Better Books with axe, drill and shovel, claiming Australia was his destination. After half an hour, he cracked a water main, put aside his tools and drank a bottle of beer.

Townshend wrecked his treasured sculptural Rickenbacker at a Who show in September 1964, accidentally smashing it into the low ceiling of the Railway Tavern in Harrow, and then turning it into a performance he hoped looked planned and yet spontaneously spectacular. He took the playing of the guitar as a weapon to extremes, as though out of his mind on rebellious youthful possibility, trailing fractured pieces of guitar around the stage, feedback mounting, seeing it as a comment on the emergence of rock music as an outlet for violence.

Prosaic singer Roger Daltrey dismissed the fancy link with Metzger, suggesting Townshend was simply showing off to some giggling girls in the audience. 'Gustav who? Bollocks,' he said. Both agreed – meeting in the middle, making up the Who, somewhere between over-thinking, myth-making Townshend and no-nonsense, doing-his-duty Daltrey – that it made a great rabble-rousing noise, the essence of early Who.

Townshend would explain in hindsight that the Who's first hit record, 'I Can't Explain' – answering the question 'What do you sound like?' – interfered with the plan for the group to almost immediately self-destruct in glorious obscurity. The guitar-smashing and its links with control, violence and aggression became a long-running, deliberate pop-cultural echo of Metzger's vision of destruction–creation, far more than just showing off. Over the years, as the Who raged and then aged, Townshend happily refined the link with auto-destruction in interviews and books.

The combination of Page and Townshend's guitar-smashing ritual made it into Michelangelo Antonioni's *Blow-Up*, released in 1966, a fluid, hyper-real celebration of sixties sights and sounds, sex and fashion, thought and action, drugs and parties, the lonely and the queer, set among charming red-brick London streets and early-morning mysteries. Antonioni was shooting the summer of love months before it happened through the eyes of a freelance photographer suffering an existential crisis, and jumping in the film through a hip update of white rabbit to Cheshire cat to hookah-smoking caterpillar to mock turtle to Mad Hatter. Nothing is what it is because everything is what it isn't.

There needed to be a blast of the new changeling British rock in the film, made by serious young men discovering wondrous new powers, which was making a difference to everything. Jeff Beck of the Yardbirds, the brief, prized Jimmy Page–Beck version dressed for pop glory, destroyed his guitar in front of a bored, self-consciously cool, blank-faced audience. The Yardbirds stood in for the Who, who were originally asked but turned down the chance to confirm their links with auto-destruction.

Motionless, acting out alienation as the beat raves on, waiting to be activated, as the Yardbirds effectively break open a new realm of psych-edelic rock directly in front of them, the audience erupts into screams of delight when Beck assaults his amplifier with his guitar, fighting for bits of the wreckage. Avant-garde cinema searching out new emotional chords collides temporarily with pop in the twilight of modernism, on the cusp of the commercial avant-garde of postmodernism.

Blow-Up caught, or helped make up, the intoxicating, iridescent colours of the decade, as did Metzger. His experiments with liquid colour projections, heating and cooling liquid crystals placed between two plates of glass, what he called light fountains, led to the randomly moving psychedelic light shows projected onto the walls of the UFO Club, paralleling the shifting colours of Warhol's *Exploding Plastic Inevitable*. Eventually he disappeared into a lonely, lifelong struggle as revelatory ecological activist, turning his attention to the destructive and transformative power of nature. Combating the gathering environmental destruction he saw coming from the 1960s, his warnings about manmade climate change seemed the ravings of a madman.

The Yoko Ono, in a book about female genius, being quoted before a quotation from Simone de Beauvoir: 'One is not born a genius, one becomes a genius, and the feminine situation has up to the present rendered this becoming practically impossible.'

The Yoko Ono walking onto a stage to ready to perform, in a way that resists, refuses and downplays gendered stereotypes. Her demeanour is neither feminine nor masculine; her authority is not negotiated, forced to prove herself, endlessly demonstrated. She is here. She is ready.

The Yoko Ono who if this was a book about a certain male artist would, at this point in 1966, as she was about to feature in an influential art symposium, be described as one of the most important artists alive in the world.

420

Following the three-day symposium, there was a series of happenings and concerts, and for a few weeks, London became a first-time worldwide meeting place for similar, often isolated minds and strange types approaching the same thing from different directions – another Fluxus-ite invitee, Al Hansen, delighted to be seeing something of the world outside New York, described it as a 'congress of gunslingers'.

There were 'Two Evenings of Yoko Ono' on 28 and 29 September, at the Africa Centre, a hybrid performance space, gallery and educational facility in a tired-looking old vegetable warehouse in Covent Garden. It was mostly used as a home-away-from-home Afro-centric venue championing the cause for an independent Africa at a time when most of its countries were still under colonial control. Here were lively signs of Africa hiding in plain sight in central London. There were occasional outlier events, and the venue being in the centre of London but also psychologically outside seemed perfect for the symposium, and for Yoko's transgressive cabaret.

Yoko performed more than a dozen pieces, most of them incorporating audience involvement, which increasingly made sense at a time when the mutating dynamics of a counterculture and a radical questioning of authority were being created en masse. For a while it seemed as though people could be the collective producers of their own lives, with a determination to act together and fight for rights, whatever the cynics or sceptics might say.

Yoko made the fateful move from the Lower Manhattan avant-garde underground community to an out-of-nowhere, anti-establishment, pro-rock-and-roll avant-garde community, another scene filled with like-minded outcasts and self-confident cultural criminals sharing an agenda to freak out the straights. The freaks Yoko found were Fluxus with a more urgent, captivating soundtrack which rallied support for

421

alternative thinking and supplied a direct route to a popular audience. 'There was a strange kind of shimmer in London,' said Yoko, 'and a very beautiful one. Once I breathed that, I thought, OK, I'm here, and never looked back.'

Yoko's work became part of the general freak-out, a togetherness based on alienation. 'Bag Piece's madcap sculptural shapeshifting came across as a monochrome human version of the late-night life-enhancing underground multi-coloured light shows, a volatile psychedelic experience generated by bodies and a black bag. The rhythms and tensions of 'Cut Piece' as unscripted drama about the violence of reality were now in place. It was still evolving, depending on time and place – the scene of enactment – and eventually performer, but it was now an identifiable, infinitely relatable work.

Yoko's London performance of 'Cut Piece' was a case of different place, same tension between performer and audience, between confrontation and provocation, voyeurism and exhibitionism, wit and despair, creator and co-creators, complex artwork and exposed sexual object, the turned on and the unsettled, between touching and being touched.

In the context of the male-dominated auto-destruction, which as much as anything was a response to the ever-present evil of the post-nuclear age and an investigation into why men historically acted so violently, it was one of the more ethereal, confessional and intimate performances, and therefore subtly one of the strongest.

Word spread about Yoko, enough to reach outside of the art village. She was being talked about as a disruptive, glamorously displaced artist in a city where modernist art and provisional slivers of postmodernism were rapidly becoming psychically entangled with music, theatre, media, film, writing, photography and fashion. It was a city becoming its own kind of happening, with the mysterious clarity that Antonioni captured in *Blow-Up*, with its own internal idiosyncratic star system. The whispers about Yoko were getting louder among the competitive few monitoring and spreading the news about the currently cool. The inexplicable word of mouth was in action and she had faith it would carry her art, defiant feminine consciousness and as yet unformed feminist iconoclasm into new places and help transform them, leading to a thousand implications.

As had happened in Tokyo, other opportunities and collaborations emerged, even a little bit of money, as Tony Cox anticipated, keeping her in London for longer than she planned, moving closer to her destiny, when she was forced to continually work out how to get herself out of the desperate situations she found herself in, through no fault of her own, or exactly because of who she was, and absolutely no one else's fault.

The increasingly known Yoko had been asked by a London businessman intoxicated by underground buzz and interested in the arts with money to invest if she had any ideas for a film, and she thought of making a London version of 'No. 4', longer and more detailed than the original. This was a time when a female film director of any kind, commercial or experimental, was extremely rare – it wasn't until 1967 that the relatively open-minded London Film Festival screened films by women, Shirley Clarke, Agnès Varda and Věra Chytilová.

'No. 4' was a film, and something else, its own happening, a fashionable term introduced into Britain by the Liverpool poet and painter Adrian Henri, originally inspired in the 1950s by the quick-witted, proto-pop artist Richard Hamilton's disarranged collisions of fine art and pop culture, new technology and city life, representation and fabrication. By 1960, Henri was moving from juxtaposing images in poems and paintings to juxtaposing fragments of the everyday in performance, stacking up visuals, songs, dance, poetry, objects, collective collaboration, audience participation and inevitable Liverpool humour. Henri was as quick to respond to rumours and reports of Kaprow's abstract theatre as he had been to Hamilton's formative montages.

First presented in 1962 as part of the Liverpool Mersey Arts Festival, 'as what couldn't be stuck on canvas', the events became known, after Kaprow, as happenings, which Henri saw as a possible re-enchantment of reality, a way of changing how reality feels, a sensibility which would soon tumble into Liverpool pop music, bouncing out of the idea of the happening, and then into the rest of the country, and then everywhere, at least in the memory of a certain commonly established 1960s.

Not being easily placed as artist, woman or personality, Yoko was quickly getting the reputation for being an arcane London representative of the New York happenings, and would soon be known as 'the high priestess of the happenings', which opened doors, so she did little to correct it. And in the film she was proposing, there would be young naked people; if nothing else it would make people laugh, and it was made by an artist in the process of becoming a strange phenomenon. London was making a scene of itself, and this sounded like it would fit right in.

She got the money to make a swinging sixties, flower power 'No. 4', even though there were no flowers, and the sixties were seen from a divergent point of view. This was her personal documentary take on where the city and its fashions and people were at the time.

She initially wanted to make the new, feature-length film using 365 bottoms, one for every day of the year. To recruit them, she put an ad in the *International Times*, which had been launched on 15 October 1966 as a direct challenge to the limited, narrow-minded coverage of the new dissident pop culture in the mainstream media – a month after Yoko first arrived in England – at an All-Night Rave at the Roundhouse, the venue's debut show.

The event had intermedia and transmedia Fluxus, op, pop, performance art and happening leanings, and the top pop groups of the day turned up in fancy dress, at a time when chart music was made by young radicals associating themselves with alternative pursuits. Music was by the recently formed Soft Machine and the year-old Pink Floyd, when they were still the Soft Machine and the Pink Floyd, and rock was mutating from pop's strange mid-sixties sonorities into the loopier psychedelic, splitting minds open.

It was the perfect time for Yoko to appear, amplifying her scope to match the culture's momentum, where everything could happen at once and art galleries and discotheques met somewhere in the middle. Wearing an invisible Fluxus cloak, she crashed into an erupting, stoned-age music and arts scene that was consciously or not psychically connected to the research laboratories and musical happenings of the Warhol crowd and the Fluxus misfits.

Both sides in their own way saw music as a revolutionary, sensationalist force that had the power to affect the environment. Yoko was too

425

Fluxus to become a Warhol superstar or an accomplice in that cultish brood, but not so tied to Fluxus that she couldn't merge with the action she found in London, where art and music were up in the air, and audiences commingled with artists and musicians. The vast majority of British people were unfamiliar with early twentieth-century modernism, let alone the first acts of conceptual art, but Yoko found a small pocket of underground space, and a mainstream media making its own use out of what it viewed as freaks and freakshows.

Her *International Times* ad said, with a sly, saucy sense of humour that made sense in England, where a lack of humour makes you inhuman, 'Intelligent-looking bottoms wanted for filming. Possessors of non-intelligent bottoms need not apply.' In the first few weeks of 1967, Yoko found her way to a new club that had been opened by dashing counter-culture vigilantes, American record producer Joe Boyd and photographer/political activist and *International Times* co-founder John Hopkins. UFO was housed inside an old Irish dancehall, the Barney Club, on Tottenham Court Road, down a steep flight of stairs in the cramped basement of La Continentale Cinema. Following certain rituals, you could make the dark cellar much bigger and more welcoming in your mind.

It had opened a couple of days before Christmas 1966, and the Pink Floyd was the house band at the centre of an askew, incense-laden atmosphere, which was seen as promoting happenings as much as music. The introverted group of twenty-year-olds with Cambridge roots would take to the small three-foot-high stage after midnight, carrying their own equipment, and drift into a hazy, atmospheric sound which seemed related to the sensuous drones of La Monte Young and the rapturous intensity of Stockhausen.

Someone in the group had been listening to the Byrds and the 13th Floor Elevators and following the free-spirited adventures of Ken Kesey and the Merry Pranksters. Time was a major character in their songs, whether in the whipped-dream whimsy of their pop songs or in their indefinite spaced-out improvisations. By 1968, once they dropped the 'The', and co-founder Syd Barrett with other things on his mind left the group, the whimsy and spontaneity started to dissolve, and the music became more focused and monolithic, eventually taking up a permanent space in the mainstream, rock taking in some avant-garde fuel as it cruised into the middle of the road.

After they'd finished one show, and dutifully taken their equipment off stage, Yoko appeared, atomic, wild-haired and nimble, looking like she'd read *Alice's Adventures in Wonderland* as a book about female empowerment, and climbed the scaffolding that had been holding the group's rudimentary but effective light show. She grabbed a microphone and asked the crowd, many of them lying down on cushions, a few happily drowsy, for some volunteers for a film she was making. Many couldn't make out what she was saying – she was a film-maker from New York, something about peace and anuses.

It made sense, though. A lot did at UFO that previously didn't. Something else was always happening, planned or unplanned. You went with the flow. Everyone belonged as much as anyone else, whether out-of-place mod stumbling into the wrong club and coming out converted, needing to instantly grow their hair and change their drug of choice, a Yardbird or a Rolling Stone or two acting like natural leaders of this new gang.

Within a few days, Yoko as avant-garde pied piper carried scores of followers along in her fanciful antics. A small battalion of volunteers, a snapshot of London scenesters, found themselves being shipped in vans from outside UFO to the home of the poet and art dealer Victor Musgrave, who owned the progressive Gallery One, supporting dispossessed and neglected art and which introduced Fluxus energy to Britain in 1962.

In the same year, the gallery presented the debut show of optical artist Bridget Riley's visually rhythmic paintings, producing the illusory patterns, forms, lines and structures that visualised the social and sexual turbulence of the time, captivating descendants of Duchamp's whirling multi-coloured Rotoreliefs from the 1930s soon appearing in clothing, advertising, album covers and graphic design.

427

Debonair bohemian and champion of the underdog since he'd moved from Egypt after the war, Musgrave had become friendly with Maciunas and Yoko. He'd put some money into the film, and he called Yoko to suggest using his four-storey townhouse on Rex Street, Mayfair, near the Dorchester Hotel, as a place to film her bottoms. Yoko was thrilled: the 'incredibly classy location' gave the shoot a certain integrity, considering that the score proposed that the film would 'string bottoms together in place of signatures for petition of peace' and she would later describe it as 'an aimless petition signed by people with their anuses'.

In a calm living room with cosy fire and Japanese screens, Yoko, with Cox in attendance, had set up a 16mm camera on a tripod, a lighting lamp and a large turntable surrounded by a white cloth for the participants to walk on. The trusting performers were asked to strip from the waist down, and then walk on the turntable while she filmed them, still with the same intention as with the New York preview to fill the screen with pure behind in four sections that somehow moved independently of each other, creating a constant array of dancing shapes, of dissected movement, so that the whole screen would move. There was a sense she was acknowledging in her first film of how the stage was set for the first motion pictures in the 1870s through experiments in producing motion from still photographs.

At one point, as she worked towards capturing 365 bottoms, Yoko felt the shoot was losing its spontaneity, as worries about schedule and the cost of the rented camera were taking over. She decided 365 was a conceptual number in the first place, and after ten days filming about twenty bottoms a day, including her own, she felt she'd collected enough specimens for a much longer 'No. 4' film.

There were about twenty seconds of each person's bottom for eighty minutes, with no sense of who the performers were, as any voiceovers talking about why they agreed to be filmed – or not – and how boring the film might be – or not – were never aligned with the person on screen.

The American version was barely noticed outside the circle of friends and friends of friends who were in it. The British, cheeky bum version gave Yoko something she often lacked in New York: it set her pieces and events off on a trip that would see them go through changes, and inspired a response even from people who hadn't seen it, just heard or read about it.

The film was immediately censored for general release, as the British Board of Film Censors considered it obscene and indecent. It was the outraged reaction Yoko approved of, so that the consequences of making the film became part of the film, helping to finish it off, or to get closer to finishing it off, and leading to publicity.

In London, Yoko was able to flirt with newspapers, which – since the arrival of mods and rockers in 1964 – had been constantly on the hunt for deviant teenage behaviour based however loosely around certain circulation-friendly subjects – sex, drugs, violence – that they could sensationalise in order to create their instant, distorted controversies and what in 1972 the sociologist Stanley Cohen would call moral panic.

Her life a part of the work, adopting a character, Yoko was happy to play the miscreant role in the mock-outraged newspaper coverage of the censorship. She announced that along with two thousand protesters she was going to gather in front of the film censors' offices, and turned up with husband and daughter holding a bunch of daffodils and a placard saying, 'War is indecent, not peace.'

There were no protesters, only a few photographers and a handful of reporters asking where the two thousand were. 'They must be asleep,' Yoko joked.

One form of enacting an event in the imagination met another, and the newspapers went along with the stunt – Yoko's ad hoc campaign gave the newspapers the material they needed to run with a story involving nudity and an eccentric foreign character to patronise vaguely or viciously, so the film got the eye-catching publicity as a symbol of subversion or a sign of hippie silliness that the avant-garde rarely did.

The flowers were sent up to the office of Lord Harlech, the distinguished president of the board of censors, and photos of a smiling Yoko with young daughter holding the flowers were published in a few national newspapers. The censors soon dropped their objections and gave it a special rating, agreeing with Yoko and supporters that the film was light-hearted and uplifting more than sleazy and exploitative. If Yoko was any kind of hooligan, she was a polite one, and certainly a peaceful one.

It was the first sign of Yoko the celebrity, the kind that fifty years later would attach itself to a reality TV personality, immediately causing psychic decay. The headlines and stories started to create the provisional idea of a Yoko that would form the basis of her opportunistic hate-figure image. Every day for a few weeks there would be a reference in the papers to naughty, crazy, far-out – and very foreign – Yoko. The BBC even showed a clip from the film, as something to smirk about rather than marvel at, instantly linking the name Yoko Ono with bottoms, hare-brained schemes and attention-seeking novelty.

Yoko was in London at the right time to get the attention she felt was missing in New York and Japan, not yet concerned she might be playing a dangerous game. A new conspicuous version of Yoko started being built, initially with her tacit approval, one that soon became a monster with a life of its own.

At the time, it seemed she had slipped or forced herself into another shapeshifting collaborative movement, belonging and not belonging just as she did with Fluxus. British versions of the San Francisco hippies doing their thing started to emerge, a loose, amorphous alternative collective emerging from the same national and international tensions and austerity that had led to the early-sixties avant-garde social experiments Yoko was part of.

By 1967, branded as the year of revolt and freedom, the year homosexuality was decriminalised, Yoko was already an experienced free-thinking counterculture campaigner, and merged effortlessly with what became the year of flower children and the Summer of Love with its messages of peace and love and its irreverent happenings. Social mobility reached a fast-moving state Yoko recognised from the clash of identities and sensibilities she had experienced in New York, but with a British twist, where pop stars mixed with royalty and style with hedonism.

430

A few different social scenes collided in a very small place in central London, a capital city and a place of exile bringing together members of the aristocracy, musicians, artists, writers, photographers, boutique owners, immigrants, gadflies, entrepreneurs, models, gangsters, designers, actors, satirists, free-floating visionaries, entertainment sensations, Old Etonians, general duckers and divers, chameleons and miscellaneous bohemians of no fixed abode. They came together through drugs and new species of highs, the clothes they wore and their hairstyles, making them all, more or less, hippie, or at least self-consciously groovy, collectively enjoying the rapid, kaleidoscopic collapse of worn-out certainties.

When 'No. 4 (Bottoms)' was shown in London after being 'released' by the censors, it was hippies and would-be hippies queuing up to see it, as an act of solidarity with its tabloid-harassed humanist peace-warrior maker as much as any interest in sophisticated, transformative underground film and experiments with self-reflection and body issues.

Enjoyment, inclusivity and accessibility had always been important to Yoko, however experimental and unknowable her work, but for many of her old avant-garde allies in their closed circle she had crossed over to the dark side – entertainment, even a few mainstream reviews and a little slippery popularity. 'No. 4' began as a controlled Fluxus investigation into various states of mind and being, but her London trip turned it into an uncontrollable Yoko performance.

One day she was walking down the King's Road near the new Granny Takes a Trip boutique where she was starting to buy her clothes, and some teenagers started screaming her name. Her future life flashed before her eyes. She remembers thinking that she didn't want to become any more famous as she would lose all her friends and her credibility as an artist, and her marriage to Tony Cox would disintegrate, 'which was getting a bit shaky anyway'.

It was too late. Yoko could make things happen, had more opportunities to make independent new works without relying on Maciunas and occasional invitations, but it meant her image would become increasingly fixed as a specific rendering of an airy protest artist, and as

431

a film-maker producing a certain commentary on exploitation film. As the bottoms girl, there was a suggestion from a dubious potential financer she next make a breast version, and some film companies assumed she was in the film but not the director, sent by the real, no doubt male director as some kind of enticement.

Getting to know London, she used the attention to spontaneously wrap one of the four large bronze lion statues in Trafalgar Square in a huge piece of cloth, telling the police that she was making a film, which was somehow acceptable and granted her permission to cover the lions.

The disappearing lion was an extension of 'Fog Piece', which itself was an inversion of 'Cut Piece' – instead of having her clothes removed by strangers, she would be wrapped in white bandages while she disappeared inside smoke billowing from a fog machine. Symbolising how the 'danger' and power of women are nullified by concealing and silencing them behind imposed masks and clothing, it was another foreshadowing of her future life as she's erased from existence as others try to take control of her anomalous, vulnerable presence.

A photo taken by Tony Cox of Yoko wearing sunglasses in the August sun, sitting on a strangely altered readymade lion in the world-famous London square, shows her quiet delight in having completed the event. She's inside a small magical moment, while around her the world carries on as though nothing has happened.

Those watching included reporters and photographers, now on call for Yoko events, where she might make some sort of scene. 'Wrap ins will make the city look much nicer,' Yoko told the press in full deadpan artist mode. 'They will make everyone happy.'

A little more of Yoko as kooky celebrity leaked into the mainstream: if not the details of the subversive ceremonial drama of the wrapping action, the evocation of the spiritual act of Japanese wrapping, her discreet, fleeting tribute to London. No one noticed that she was marking the centenary of the lions' installation at the base of Nelson's Column, making invisible part of a war memorial in support of peace. The stage was being set for later, more palpable theatrics.

432

Barry Miles had been part of the honorary committee selected by Metzger for the 'Destruction in Art' symposium. Trained as an art teacher, a pal of pre-Stones Brian Jones, he had been the manager of the paperback section of Better Books on Charing Cross Road, organising readings and various neo-happening presentations, meeting and befriending poets such as the Beat hero Allen Ginsberg, who promised he would read anywhere for free.

Ginsberg's reading at Better Books led to the International Poetry Incarnation, a mass experimental poetry carnival in front of a sold-out crowd of 5,200 at the Royal Albert Hall in June 1965, with many locked outside, confused that so many had turned up for a poetry event. Even Bob Dylan, hearing about the event having played the venue the month before, was amazed that poetry could sell out the Albert Hall, but as Beat and bohemian and sometimes as avant-garde as it was, it was still mostly men, mostly in suits and ties.

In some stories of the time this is where the sixties that within a couple of years would be seen as swinging began, as an underground uprising, as alternative force, a different way of making things happen; the poetry even led directly to the launch of the *International Times* sixteen months later, demonstrating how quickly the sociocultural revolution had spread.

The poetry fiesta opened spaces for restless imaginations like Barry Miles to enter and make things happen, and after publishing magazines, poetry and radical writing – which eventually led to his role in the creation of *International Times* – he formed a company, MAD, with ex-child actor and pop singer Peter Asher, brother of the actress Jane, who was then going out with Paul McCartney, and the twenty-two-year-old artist and Scotsman art critic John Dunbar, then the husband of Marianne Faithfull, but fairly quickly and notoriously cuckolded by Mick Jagger. MAD was like a pop group, but instead of singing songs

433

they wanted to make culture happen, unnerve the establishment and – as a by-product – construct a mythology about what they made happen.

In November 1965, MAD opened the art gallery and bookshop Indica, named after a particularly intoxicating cannabis plant, in Masons Yard, St James, supported by McCartney, who was living nearby at the Asher family home – also living around the corner were William Burroughs, Roman Polanski and Sharon Tate – with Dunbar looking after the art, Miles the books, and Asher behind the scenes. They found the premises visiting a nightclub, the Scotch, favoured by the new London elite as an exclusive after-hours hideaway, which had just opened in the same courtyard, emphasising the sense that this little spot at the edge of Mayfair was the centre of the pop universe.

Jimi Hendrix, arriving in London on 24 September 1966, bringing with him little but his guitar, looking for where the action was, went to the Scotch hours after landing. He joined the house band for a late-night jam, his first British performance, the same week Yoko had arrived, days before she presented 'Cut Piece' at the Africa Centre a mile or so the other side of Piccadilly Circus.

(A few months later, at the debut American performance of the London-formed Jimi Hendrix Experience at the 1967 Monterey Pop Festival, Hendrix followed the Who, whose guitarist Pete Townshend turned his now ritualistic, tumultuous smashing of the guitar into a near-total destruction of the stage, feedback epically shrieking, mad-eyed drummer Keith Moon setting off smoke bombs.

Hendrix didn't want to be outdone on his return to America to show off his already notorious Experience. His delirious showman's response to the Who's spectacular frenzy was setting his guitar on fire. During the last song, 'Wild Thing', he kneeled down, kissed his guitar, covered it in lighter fluid and lit a match. The guitar burst into flames, Hendrix shook the last life out of it as it fell to charred bits, and he threw some of the remains into the crowd. Star became superstar, and as though he'd absorbed some of the auto-destructive aura while finding fame in

London, Hendrix completed his unofficial auto-contribution to the symposium by explaining, 'I decided to destroy my song as a sacrifice. You sacrifice things you love. I love my guitar.')

Indica was a high-flying, art-mad social club with supreme pop music connections for the new would-be London intelligentsia and the rich and famous, some of them art collectors with the money to burn – their artistic statement – and for those craving the hedonistic high life of the rich and famous, who could become part of a scene by association. The invitation to the opening night on 28 January 1966 promised, in the basement gallery, painting and construction, exploiting new techniques and ideas; they knew exactly what they were saying when they noted the night would 'increase the occurrence of communication contributing to the basic structure of sense data and visual experience'. In the bookshop were modern first and limited editions, small underground presses and literary ephemera and exotica of all kinds.

For a few months Indica became, along with the Scotch, the private club of a few insiders and exclusive clients, led by the Beatles, with Paul especially treating the bookshop as a research and development department and a venue for various press interviews.

In April, John and Paul visited the bookshop together, John searching for anything by Nietzsche that someone had recommended to him. While Miles hunted for some Nietzsche, John looked through the shelves and found *The Psychedelic Experience: A Manual Based on the Tibetan Book of the Dead* by three American professors engaged in a series of experiments with LSD at Harvard University, Timothy Leary, Ralph Metzner and Richard Alpert. It was a guide to tripping, a guide to expanding consciousness, approaching the Tibetan Book of the Dead from a psychedelic perspective, helping to understand what happens to the consciousness, and therefore reality, during a psychedelic trip.

John's perspective of Leary's interpretation of esoteric writings about the limbo between death and rebirth the other side of an acid trip or two became what he called the first Beatles' psychedelic song, 'Tomorrow Never Knows'. It's a John song, as an idea, a mood, but transformed by

435

Paul's autodidactic fascination with Stockhausen and in particular the transcendent thirteen-minute 1956 'Gesang der Jünglinge', an articulation of a dialogue between God, humanity and technology. (In 1966/7, Stockhausen was a guest professor at the Davis campus of the University of California, near Sacramento, claiming that members of the Grateful Dead, the Mothers of Invention and Jefferson Airplane would attend his composition classes, discovering different ways to use music to shape time. Stockhausen's relentless spiritual quest helped tune in the summer of love.)

Sweet-faced Paul was seen as the gentle, sensible one, great with ballads and pop corn, John the snarky tough-nut rebel craving the forbidden, but Paul was first to engage with experimental movers and shakers. It would take John a little longer, and some guidance, to let the mind of Stockhausen, the moving of sound in and out of focus and up and down the co-ordinates of hearing, into his mind.

Paul was living the central London metropolitan life, making full use of the city's cultural fermentation, from the bookshops to the galleries to the refined dinner parties, shaking off provincial naivety, hungry for the sort of knowledge that made him the first Beatle to relish the influence of sophisticated, mind-opening avant-garde energies. Esoteric books led to songs, even songs about books, and insurgent new studio technology made them sound like nothing on earth.

The other three were quickly leaping up the property ladder in the direction of the rock-star mansion on a private estate. In 1964, an over-excited, wide-eyed Lennon led the new rock-star aristocracy's move to the country, into a twenty-five-room house on 964 acres twenty miles outside London overlooking the Surrey stockbroker belt, stacking it with random deluxe things only rock-and-roll money could buy, plus five television sets, tape recorders, telephones he didn't know the numbers of and purple velvet on the dining room wall. He was king of the world he was unknowingly cutting himself off from.

Paul was also up to speed with the electronic landscapes of Varèse and Berio's musical research, and alert to *musique concrète*'s use of tape loops, compositional splicing and tape reverse – sound as raw material – as a preview of what it was now possible to do in the recording studio. Paul's liking of these new sound artists reawakened certain latent skills in their producer George Martin and his team at Abbey Road Studio, which had opened in 1931 as a brand-new way to record music with a performance of Elgar's 'Land of Hope and Glory'.

Martin had been a relatively hands-off producer up to that point, tidying, organising and balancing the increasingly complex Beatles sound, using the latest studio equipment to make it as technically modern and musically coherent as possible with minimal artistic intrusion. It was the technologically executed elevation of uplifting light entertainment into a contagious, radical new art form.

Realising what the group was after with this new song, he reactivated some of the sonic ingenuity and experimental playfulness he had been using when he produced various comedy novelty records before working with the Beatles.

The Beatles were in the first place signed in 1962 to the Parlophone label at EMI, specialists in comedy, cast recordings and regional pre-pop British music, which was Martin's department. He had a mild-mannered but Fluxus-like temperament, and for a maestro of frivolously fabulous, oddly technically superior oddball comedy songs to sign the Beatles was a Fluxus act. The group was a little puzzled to have been given the square-looking comedy guy. He dressed in suit and tie, but then at the time so did John Cage and Stockhausen, who were also applying forms of radio drama, a world of interior monologue and recording ingenuity, to the making of music.

Working on records for the absurdist and antic vaudevillian radio comedy troupe and prime Beatles English source the Goons in the 1950s, Martin would build their giddy, raucous mock songs using many of the zany sound effects they used in their shows. He collaborated with the BBC Radiophonic Workshop, essentially the state-sponsored British arm of the experimental French *musique concrète* sound/radiophonic arts explorers making weird music and special sound for TV and radio,

437

especially science fiction and comedy requiring a different perception of events.

In 1962, a few months before he met the Beatles for the first time, Martin had collaborated as Ray Cathode with Maddalena Fagandini of the Radiophonic Workshop on an early, anomalous proto-electronic pop single: the A-side 'Time Beat' sounded like jaunty muzak; the B-side 'Waltz in Orbit' was the missing link between Dave Brubeck and a kitsch Kraftwerk. The workshop was a particularly female unit, with pioneering sound artist Daphne Oram part of its studio management, and Delia Derbyshire created the workshop's most famous production, a startling electronic warping of Ron Grainer's 1963 *Doctor Who* theme.

The Goons needed invented, original radio sound to turn their gags and flights of fancy into theatrical reality, and working with them was the perfect preparation for Martin when a decade or so later his 1960s version of the Goons suddenly went from singing about teen love and started – perhaps John's 'Help' was a warning something was up – writing songs about loneliness, disassociation and the pressure of fame, and one about ego death initially called 'The Void'. (A slip of Ringo's funny tongue, as with 'A Hard Day's Night', gave 'Tomorrow Never Knows' its actual profound and psychedelic, and more Beatled, title, slangily reflecting being caught in an eternal present.) As Bob Dylan remarked when he heard it, they didn't want to be 'cute' any more.

John was telling the *NME* in March 1966 about the electronic music Paul was listening to, suggesting he quite liked it too, but it was still a bit of a mystery to him: 'You make it clinking two glasses together or with bleeps from the radio, then you loop the tape and repeat it at intervals.'

When John imagined 'Tomorrow Never Knows' being sung by thousands of Tibetan monks, for Martin it was just like when Spike Milligan, the most manic, mind-stretching Goon, asked him for a certain sound that was like two lions walking away bumping into each other. And if not lions then hippos. And what does a squashed sockful of custard sound like? Those echoing footsteps heading backwards towards infinity?

Martin wasn't being psychedelic or particularly bothered about Eastern spiritualism when he produced 'Tomorrow Never Knows'; he was being his usual scientific, matter-of-fact self, combining art and craft, endlessly fascinated by sound and the power of recording, working out how to get exactly what was required for the new world of the song. It was the return of Ray Cathode, a fifth Beatle.

It became the first track the Beatles recorded for their seventh studio album *Revolver*, and the last track on side two, the only place it could really fit with its end-of-the-beginning ending, whatever else they wrote for the rest of the album. It was the death of one Beatles, and the birth of another, the one that turned up fully formed on the next album as Sgt Pepper's Lonely Hearts Club Band in all sorts of drag, just in time for the summer of love – or the summer of love turned up in time for it.

'Tomorrow Never Knows' was effectively constructed from a series of event scores, a cascade of instructions. There was no traditional music score until the song was finished.

Leary's instruction taken from the book was 'Whenever in doubt, turn off your mind, relax, float downstream.' John's instruction was 'Make my voice sound like it's on acid with the sound of the song capturing the colours of a dream.' Paul's instruction was 'Produce a pop song inspired by Stockhausen using the intricate overdubbing of tape loops and the blending of sung tones with electronic ones so that amplified rock and synthetic electronic sound meet in a smooth continuum.' Martin's instruction was 'Solve every technical problem that gets in the way of achieving the sound the Beatles hear in their head and make it sound live.' One of the engineers' instructions was 'Feed John's voice through the speaker of a Hammond organ.' George's instruction was 'Play a tamboura drone and sitar for some of the loops.' Ringo's instruction was 'Play the drums following Paul's guidance.'

The Beatles now played a self-governed transitional world music. Martin was perfecting a fledgling radiophonic dramatic art begun in the 1940s and 1950s that radio itself never achieved, where American rock and roll and soul and British pop, comedy and skiffle were being

439

remade and remodelled using techniques taken from Indian drone generators, modernist orchestral music, European electronic music, American proto-minimalism and event scores. Inevitably, there were no live shows by this complicated iteration of the Beatles, which kept getting more complicated and studio-bound until the group started to crack, overtaken by their untutored genius.

A few months after Leary led John, Paul, Martin and Abbey Road towards tomorrow's Beatles, Dunbar and Miles, invited by Mario Amaya, had seen Yoko's 'Cut Piece' at the Africa Centre and arranged with Tony Cox for a solo Yoko exhibition at the Indica starting on 8 November.

Or, in another reality, another story, because there are now only stories and tall tales, the tenacious Yoko wandered in off the street into the likely-looking gallery, and asked Dunbar if she could show her work. He found he couldn't say no to someone so frail and hungry-looking, possessing such bold charm. The gallery wasn't really about selling anything – they saw it as a miracle if they ever did – it was about having a good time, getting people together, partying with purpose. Times were wild, and if you didn't have fun as you searched for meaning, what was the point? Artists were like special guests bringing in some mental outside glamour, sometimes cultural guinea pigs, rare beasts for the aristocratic scenesters and rock stars to include as part of their colourful menagerie.

It was now only an art gallery, with more space on two levels, following the move of the bookshop part to Covent Garden in late summer, where plans were made for the *International Times*. Yoko was given the two floors to show whatever she wanted, and she used this as a way to introduce Britain – or a fantasy world in the centre of London – to the idea of her 'unfinished work' that needed completing in the imagination of others, showing how much she had developed a personal language.

Promoting *Unfinished Paintings and Objects by Yoko Ono*, Yoko told the *Sunday Telegraph* at the time that she thought it was important to have art which is living and changing, hence 'unfinished'. This was no static display, and nothing was as casual as it seemed. The exhibition itself was an installation, consisting of a sequence of connected moving parts creating a certain atmosphere designed to develop as they moved through time.

441

She had brought little art with her from New York so she showed pieces already conceived that were straightforward to mock up, or new pieces she could produce in London, including her first set of sculptures using a series of found objects displayed with a poetic, *mono no aware* attitude. The pieces are simple, especially before any interaction, sometimes satirically so, because Yoko was in on the Yoko joke before the joke was being made.

One piece she had brought from New York was 'Eternal Time', included in her 'Sales List', a battery-run ticking clock with only a second hand, evolving from an instruction in *Grapefruit* to 'steal all the clocks and watches in the world. Destroy them.' Hanging from the plinth on which the clock stood was a stethoscope, so that you could listen to the sound of time, as a kind of illusion: eternity as a mere moment, but long enough to tell a joke.

The artworks reveal their meaning if and when, depending on the attention paid, and the level of the viewer's sympathy for the concept behind the art, and even the idea of conceptual art, getting inside your mind with ideas and insights, which for some was the devil's work.

The exhibition in hindsight was the calm before the storm. It's a sign of the continually sphinx-like, highly regarded but little-known artist who preferred to keep her life quiet, allowing her to concentrate on art making, sometimes just for herself – the artist who would soon be replaced by another, far more visible and noisier artist. This was a more subliminal way of reacting to the times, cutting with a lightness of touch to the minimalist dreamlike stillness at the centre of busy, ornate psychedelia.

As the world rapidly went pop, and frantically full colour, this rendition of Yoko's art was mostly white and transparent, and meditative. Some basic objects were placed on special plexiglas plinths – a perfect green Granny Smith apple, a needle, a crystal sphere – and Yoko registered the sexual revolution by placing a diaphragm, a condom and a contraceptive pill on white plinths, which says what it has to say, nothing at all, or everything, depending on the mind of the viewer, and where they think they are.

Another, more teasing and intransigent Yoko was being built in the media, a far-fetched Yoko creation based on the assumptions of others, on certain rumours already gathering pace – loosely based on a provocative instruction by Yoko – but the exhibition was where and who she was at that moment, knowing her own mind, always in whatever state she was in at whatever time of her life, thinking of how art is a form of individual and social healing, a way of deepening mystery and signalling possibility.

'Add Colour Painting' had first appeared in her Chambers Street loft as a rough piece of long blank canvas over which Yoko had thrown black ink, and was now blank and white and square, waiting for visitors to add a colour – one per person – using pots of paint and a paintbrush laid on a white chair, until the painting was bought, at which point it was considered finished.

Over time, the same piece became more complex. Spectators could add text and messages, so that the blank canvas became a graffitied thread of comments that seemed to have happened at once. Over fifty years later in a large-scale installation, 'Add Colour (Refugee Boat)', a small white rowing boat in a white empty space was the blank canvas for visitors to add to, in this case wishes, hopes, dreams, thoughts, images, beliefs and ideas, only in blue. Slowly the boat turned blue and the white room became a sea of blue made up of traces left behind by those passing through, and the boat seemed to be floating.

This was the Yoko whose work was as the artist who was like a composer, and each artwork was a song, which would be reworked over time in various settings, repeated by other people at different times for different reasons in different settings.

They mostly settled down as becoming uncomplicated pieces for peace, as though the Yoko who emerged more or less since the Indica, the famous Yoko, the beatific Beatle-bride Yoko, the campaigning 'War is over if you want it' Yoko, was throwing a bag over the work, hiding it from further contemplation, and hiding herself and a more complicated conceptual thinking.

443

They're not simply works about peace and changing the world at all, simple entry-level metaphors for the futility of war – or that's not all they are – but letting them become pure peace statements gave them a life, carrying through the times when few trusted the difficult, distant Yoko and her motives.

'Mend Piece' was a gentle consequence of the recent 'Destruction in Art' symposium, about a world always seeming to fall apart and yet surviving, and becoming something else. It came from the Japanese philosophy of *wabi-sabi* – searching for beauty in imperfection, seeking to live a perfectly imperfect life and accepting the natural cycle of growth, decay and death – and the tradition of *kintsugi*, the Japanese art of repairing broken pottery using lacquer mixed with precious metals. The purposely visible cracks add to the pot's history, and the new beauty of its afterlife.

Yoko supplies the tools, the broken china, the string, tape and glue, the space to work, the basic instruction and intrigue – mend carefully, it will mend the world at the same time – and asks visitors to put together the fragments and make a unique new object, not necessarily a new cup or saucer, but a small, scarred abstract sculpture, opening up an entire world.

Another original Indica piece, which would go through its own large and small changes around the world, becoming known as 'Play It by Trust', was 'White Chess Set', made up of all-white pieces on a white board which was placed on a white table with two white chairs for the players – 'for playing as long as you can remember where all the pieces are'. A beautiful, dreamlike disruption of a chess set and the game itself, with its own occult references to the chess and calculating mind of Duchamp, it played its part in the story the original exhibition was telling, where it was at its most resonant and elusive. A harder, blunter meaning coalesced around it as Yoko herself became a well-known and adamant agent of peace, and parts of its cryptic allure got chipped off.

A battle between players – chess was originally a medieval war and strategy game – in competition and opposition immediately becomes a performance, a collaboration, as the two players decide between themselves who goes first, and what happens next, and come to some understanding, playing the game for as long as they can before they lose track of their own pieces, and find peace. Or they decide Yoko is wearing no clothes.

The Indica show was like a new album, with a striking monochrome cover image used for the catalogue showing Yoko and husband Cox and two assistants from Saint Martin's art college with handkerchiefs over their mouths like a holier-than-thou punk group from CBGB ten years on, or a cerebral group making noise with attitude supporting Sonic Youth in 1988.

The Yoko Ono passing into rock via Richard Hell rather than John Lennon.

The photo shows Yoko looking ahead, stepping outside the sixties for a moment of timeless contemplation, adept at making the future now. It's a glimpse of where Yoko might have been if she hadn't been taken somewhere else in the months – and then the years – after the Indica show, stepping lightly and obscurely through new waves, movements and trends, always ready to drop behind enemy lines and represent herself once more as enigmatic free spirit. She was resigned to keeping the faith in the transformative promise of art as the avant-garde she once hoped would take over the future absorbed itself, becoming a history about history, a buzzword, a mere compliant supplier to the enemy of slogans, logos, images, jingles and memes.

The image had been taken by the Scottish photographer Iain McMillan for a book of photographs surveying the new textures and faces of the 1960s called *The Book of London*. He would become friendly with Yoko, and she asked him to photograph the exhibits at Indica. He also took a full-length portrait of Yoko looking like she might well be fucking with your mind for as long as it takes. After that, he photographed her and her work a number of times, solo and then as Johnandyoko, and she would

445

pass him on via John to the Beatles, where he took the photograph used for the indelible zebra-crossing cover of *Abbey Road*.

The Yoko Ono who understood that art is too serious to be taken seriously.

The Yoko Ono taking various chances at various turning points.

The Yoko Ono pressing buttons just to see how people responded.

In early November 1966, John completed work in Almería, Spain, on Richard Lester's acerbic, farcical anti-war film *How I Won the War* – Lester had directed both Beatles films, 1964's *A Hard Day's Night* and 1965's *Help* – and flew into London from Madrid with his wife Cynthia. He had taken on his only non-musical acting role to fill in some rare Beatles downtime after their final ever live shows in August at the end of a stressful American tour, thinking that acting was maybe a way to a new post-pop music life, but it mostly proved he was no actor. When some of your fans considered that you walked on water, and you sometimes believed it yourself, opportunities to try something you'd never done before presented themselves almost every day.

The most constructive thing he did during the six-week filming was finish off a song he'd been thinking about for a while, 'Strawberry Fields Forever', clinging on to fading, fantastical, disconcerting Liverpool memories now that as far as he could see – as ever-anxious madman fearing abandonment or genius living the dream which had nightmare qualities – nobody thought like him, no one was on his wavelength, he'd be alone for ever, it was his destiny. He wrote a song turning a park and some fruit into a whole world of wonder, fear and love, protecting himself from a threatening outside world.

Yoko heard 'Strawberry Fields Forever' at Mario Amaya's house the day it was released in February 1967; it's the first Beatles song she remembers sitting down and consciously listening to, hearing the devout use of the mellotron, triggering fixed lengths of tape and an artificial representation of orchestral instruments. It was a revolutionary-for-the-time sampling machine originally built to replace an expensive orchestra for live light-entertainment cabaret performances – the well-known TV magician David Nixon was an investor in the company that manufactured it – which created sounds slightly out of synch with each other

447

– the fluid, warping base sound of psychedelia, flowing into the progressive rock that it became. Yoko heard a touch of dissonance, which sent her back to the loft, to La Monte Young and Richard Maxfield. John's enraptured self-consciousness carried her away into a virtual world as if the (impossible) instruction was 'Come with me.' She thought it was good. 'For a pop song . . .'

While John was filming – a few days of nourishing anonymity plus twenty-sixth birthday celebrations – George headed for India, Paul went to Africa and then, back in London, went to see Cornelius Cardew and the microtonal improvising adventurers AMM along with twenty or so others at the Royal College of Art and worked on the soundtrack for a film, without John. Ringo was just generally 'busy' being Ringo, visiting family in England, keeping himself to himself as dutifully as he kept time.

At the beginning of September, their manager and essential organising influence Brian Epstein, a few days out of hospital after accidentally overdosing on his anti-depressant medication, was having to deny that the Beatles were splitting. As soon as there were rumours the Beatles were splitting then the Beatles had started to split up and nothing could stop it happening, especially once Epstein finally succumbed to another accidental overdose at the end of August 1967.

John returned from Spain wearing what would become the famous round granny glasses he wore through the rest of his life, supplied by the costume department for his wisecracking, self-centred but minor character, with a new shorter, more 1940s-appropriate haircut, breaking the hearts of his teenybopper fans, and any lingering link with being a mop top – the bleakness of the film would help as well.

On 7 November, he visited the Indica Gallery, having been asked over by Dunbar the night before the preview show to take a look at the Yoko Ono exhibition they were putting together. He vaguely imagined the exhibition by this mad and maddening Japanese artist and her happenings and some stories he'd heard about her would involve orgies and various bits of silliness.

Lagging, and sniggering, behind Paul when it came to the avant-garde – watching the TV stuck out in Surrey and smoking pot while his songwriting partner was redefining his world, switching between seeing Berio conduct at the Italian embassy and seeing Stevie Wonder live at the Scotch – John wasn't expecting much that would interest him. A little bored and irritated when there was nothing to do, now that every day had to be another adventure, piled upon days of adventure, with no recording session to lose himself in and steady the mind, he was mostly thinking of hanging out and catching up with Dunbar, which might or might not have involved taking some acid, seeing some sights and blowing off some steam.

He wasn't yet up to speed with what Allan Kaprow, happener number one-ish, said about the change the happening, the event, the performance, the concept was bringing, all that participatory urgency – it was time not to just look at art but to get inside it. He did it instinctively as a performer and writer, as a natural comedian and constant day and night tripper, but he hadn't yet made it a part of who he was when he thought about what he did. He was put off by the trappings and trimmings and how all the goings on made him feel like a fool, out of his depth, which he hated to be.

When he arrived at the gallery, there was a lot of work going on, a lot of white, and on first sight not so much obvious art. What was for sale?

A delicate, serious-looking, super-petite Yoko in all black, accompanied by quiet and patient helpers in all black in some kind of art trance hanging blank canvases, arranging nails and fussily choosing the most appley-looking apple, seemed to confirm a view attributed to him that it was all artsy-fartsy bullshit with nothing at the centre. Which was OK, it's an energy, but he had better things to do, lives to lead, songs to find, claims to make.

Slightly on the defensive, entering a room of deep concentration and seriousness where everyone had a job to do, he was in the mood to lark about. Yoko wasn't thrilled Dunbar had brought someone in before everything was finished and was showing him around. It felt a bit intrusive.

Thinking it must be a close friend of Dunbar's, she wandered over to be introduced. Her idea of a Beatle if anything – set in stone when she was in Japan – was as a boyish mop top in suit and tie, or maybe lately, someone with English bad pale skin, tentative new moustache and longer hair. This guy was tanned, had short hair, wore cheap glasses, looked a little tired, was not without charm. He mumbled something about what was going on, what was it all about. She handed him a card that said breathe. He loudly panted with a goofy grin. She looked away.

John saw that the apple on a plinth was on sale for £200 and took a quick bite out of it, ruining Yoko's careful plan for it to decay as the exhibition passed, before being replaced, leaving behind a seed that can be planted. It was another piece coming out of the auto-destructive symposium, the making of a work of art that destroyed itself, that couldn't be collected and destroyed that way. Once destroyed, it grows again. She got upset and he felt a little sheepish seeing how upset she got, carefully putting the bitten apple back on its plinth.

'Painting to Hammer a Nail' as an instruction came from 1961, and then Japan and *Grapefruit*: it was one of her original ephemeral, seemingly throwaway ideas that turned out to have their own scattered internal permanence, developing as an idea and heading off to different venues in different directions over the next sixty years.

It was a way of introducing some audible chaos, some random banging, into the traditional quiet, don't-touch, don't-go-there, finished-off formality of a gallery show. At the start of the exhibition, a small canvas on a wooden panel with a hammer hanging from a chain and a container of nails is hanging from the wall. The viewer is asked to hammer a nail into the board, and gradually a unique metal sculpture materialises, an abstract record of the anonymous strangers passing through and collaborating with each other and the original impulse of Yoko Ono, producing a poignant, captivating bouquet of metal.

The original 1961 instruction suggested you hang a lock of hair over your banged-in nail. One direction it took was the ongoing 'Wish Tree' series beginning in 1981, based on the old Japanese tradition Yoko loved where you visited a shrine and attached a small message of goodwill onto a tree, which ended up looking like it was in bloom.

The austere blank canvas, hammer and nails became the branches of a tree around which you would fold a piece of paper after writing down a secret wish or dream. Like the refugee boat, the hammer and nail and the wish tree represent a sustaining belief in the power of community, and were part of Yoko's ongoing search for a community to believe in and be part of, for another version of a slightly risky avant-garde playground.

Over forty years after the Indica show, at an exhibition at the Seattle Art Museum entitled *Target Practice: Under Attack 1949–78*, the original white wood panel and banged-in nails had become lost among a thicket of sweet wrappers, business cards, plastic bags, receipts, notes and tickets, a reaction perhaps to a sign next to the hanging picture with nails already in place that said, 'Do not touch.' The you-can-touch 1960s version, some of the original heady witchcraft, had been recovered in this new contrarian formal museum setting, over-sensitive to the apparent fragility of the materials.

A different spontaneous sculpture emerged from the usual array of nails, an unofficial community board relying on the careful collective positioning of the pieces of paper. When Yoko was told what had happened, she said let it be, as long as she received the new modification at the end of the show's run.

A security guard and amateur artist began stripping away the 'rubbish' that had been added, returning the piece to where it had been on the opening day. She was stopped by the museum after half an hour, and was sacked the next day for altering a work of art, even though it was based on a work of art designed to be altered.

In a way she had unaltered it, and the museum felt she had somehow interfered with the spirit of Yoko's intention, which to an extent was to relinquish control and see what happened. The security guard decided the addition of the waste paper was not in the spirit of the instruction, which was simply to hammer in a nail, and in this museum setting, to be left alone as a piece of remembrance.

451

Yoko watched the episode from afar with quiet delight. Things kept happening to her, said Yoko, 'very much like life itself, with the original instruction being the genesis of it all'.

When John saw the piece at the Indica, ready for action, he immediately wanted to try hammering in a nail, deciding the show was a far out fun fair for grown-ups. Yoko asked him not to, as the point was that the piece should be untouched before the exhibition opening, to ensure the purity of the collaboration. She didn't want him wrecking the intimacy she was trying to achieve. Yoko still wasn't sure who he was, but Dunbar explained to her that he was a Beatle – really – and he had money to buy something. Yoko, even as she needed some money, wasn't convinced.

Another cruder, more manageable Yoko built out of rumour and gossip and media madness was already forming, the contemptuous, impertinent one who wrecked the mythical innocence of the sixties and had the audacity to claim she did not recognise the greatest rock-and-roll hero in the world, pretending she wasn't interested even as she was making plans to stalk him, dig for gold and take away the old, loveable rough-and-ready John and replace him with an emasculated soft-headed millionaire revolutionary.

The audacity to act like she deserved his attention, that her 'art' was the equal of his songs.

After a little persuasion, she reluctantly agreed to let John bang in a nail for five shillings. John replied: I'll give you an imaginary five shillings and I will hammer in an imaginary nail.

For a split second they looked at each other, even into each other, like they'd thought the same thing at the same time, shared a few secrets, mirrored each other's raw, naked self-awareness, slipped outside time, through each other's mind, figured something out, glimpsed a journey they might take together, and no one would ever believe them.

Then she carried on getting her exhibition organised, arranging her cherished objects she'd found in the past and somehow the future, already someone being placed somewhere else without knowing it yet.

The Yoko Ono who was asked fifty years later if she still had the imaginary five shillings and she said, yes, it's still there in my mind, without ever being used.

The Yoko Ono who said she was depressed at the time she made up her mind about 'Ceiling Painting' – staring at the ceiling as she lay in bed, standing in for the sky, realising her marriage to Cox was coming to an end in a litany of furious arguments, not able to afford a ticket back to New York, struggling generally for money, increasingly cursed, making an art that mostly wasn't for sale because it didn't exist, making barely enough to eat – and was looking for a little positivity.

John, already becoming someone and something new more or less by the hour and getting used to it, started to enjoy himself. Maybe this all wasn't as amateurish as it seemed, and if it was, there was a purpose, a reason, some sort of irreverent impatience with high-art standards.

He spotted a stepladder in the middle of the floor. Yoko had borrowed – or stolen – it from outside a neighbour's flat in the block where she was staying. The neighbour wasn't happy that she had taken it and even less happy that she had painted it white, and utterly indifferent to how it became a work of art, 'Ceiling Piece'.

John thought as it was painted white, it must be part of the exhibition, and it seemed to be the way you get to look at a painting that was fixed to the ceiling, where paintings in galleries are never usually put. A magnifying glass hung from the ceiling for the viewer to look at the painting. The stepladder of 'Fly' had a new use: the 'Blue Room' ceiling was now in London, demonstrating Yoko's methods of recycling and rethinking events, performances and instructions. Here, the stepladder involved a certain yearning, for the sky that no one – not even adored, millionaire pop stars – could ever touch.

John gamely climbed up the ladder, trying to stand perfectly still a few steps off the floor, and peered through the magnifying glass. It simply said 'Yes.' The so-called avant-garde for him was anti-art, anti-this, anti-everything, smash a piano, boring, negative shit. The yes cheered him up no end. You couldn't see it from the floor, but there it was, if you made the effort, and did something a little silly in the middle of an art gallery, getting above yourself. The yes hooked him in, focused his attention, got under his skin. He had to agree with the yes.

A negative 'No' would have confirmed his easy prejudices about the avant-garde; it was all a con, there was nothing there, no one there, nothing to see, nothing to feel, and it was as though the yes answered a few questions he had at the time about what and who he was and what happened next and was there any point. A whole history of the avant-garde, of riddles, puzzles, labyrinths, of euphoric sensations and anarchic spirit, the creating of an evolution even a revolution of the mind, as taken and shaken by Yoko, flashed before his eyes.

There are many ways to get to the top of the mountain, but the view is always the same.

He bought into it, but it would take more than money to get it.

He went home, wherever that was, in his chauffeur-driven black windowed Mini Cooper, wondering if it had all been a dream, and whether it was or wasn't, he should leave it and Yoko alone, don't get involved, just in case it spoiled everything.

The Yoko Ono who made an impression on John and then nothing much happened for a few months, followed by an eighteen-month dance of obsession.

The Yoko Ono who hadn't yet become part of John and Yoko, before becoming completely Johnandyoko. Recording the months as they merged in slow motion into a couple as the Beatles peaked and cracked and became a mess of probabilities, possibilities, speculations, reservations, attacks and presumptions. Everything started to get a little personal. Everyone started choosing their psychological weapons.

The Yoko Ono and John bumping into each other for a second – or 'second' – time on 22 November 1966 at the Robert Fraser Gallery on Duke Street at an opening for a Claes Oldenburg show featuring soft pop art sculpture like *Soft Toilet* and *Floor Burger*. Fraser was nicknamed 'Groovy Bob' by the writer Terry Southern, and directed Peter Blake and Jann Haworth towards the Beatles for the *Sgt Pepper* cover and Richard Hamilton for the *White Album*. His Mayfair gallery showing new British and American artists including Bridget Riley and Andy Warhol was one of the social centres of the new sixties scene connecting pop with art, and he'd been fined twenty guineas under a nineteenth-century vagrancy act for putting on a Jim Dine exhibition deemed indecent.

John and Yoko were shy, not at home at what was effectively a cocktail party with a background of art. They swapped nervous small talk. Or John was talking to Yoko and then Paul arrived and John felt threatened that Paul was more avant-garde than he was and was flirting with Yoko. Or Yoko again had trouble recognising John, this time because it looked like he had been up all night, and was much obviously angrier than he was at Indica, less fresh, less funny, the mischief in his eyes having been replaced by sadness, even fear.

455

The Yoko Ono eight years older than him who chased John relentlessly into 1967, wandering around the grounds of his house, climbing into his car after events even if his wife Cynthia was with him, and/or gradually they started to speak on the phone, meet occasionally and write to each other, especially when John and the Beatles made their famous trip to India. Yoko sent him a copy of *Grapefruit* and the kind of mail-art postcards with playful instruction-like messages written on them she would send to her friends. These were seen in the horror story that would wrap around them parallel to the love story as creepy, as though she was somehow programming his mind and laying traps.

The Yoko Ono who did or didn't know or it did or didn't happen that Tony Cox was thinking that maybe John, her new, very rich 'friend', could become a gullible sponsor for her art, or, think about it, maybe a lover, a solution to all their problems as a couple – this became fan non-fiction, where Cox urges Yoko to have an affair with John, conceptually blackmailing him as a means of survival for their family. When the plan actually took off, Cox was worried that he would be cut out of it, just as her art at last was about to come into money, and wrote up a contract for Yoko to sign.

The Yoko Ono who wasn't going to turn down the chance to use her connections with the Beatles as part of her art life, even if it meant she really did break up the Beatles, replacing their uniquely powerful and original pop excitement with the daily art bulletins of a married couple apparently too much in love for it to be true. Yoko turned love – a new discovery for both of them despite their previous marriages and affairs – into a febrile concept, writing out an instruction that when followed involved all-consuming love with an underlying sense that built in was the seeds of its own destruction. Johnandyoko was so vivid an interpretation of the instruction 'a couple in love expressing themselves openly in public come what may' that it seemed too good to last, and the ending, of a love story, a living artwork, an experiment in fame, a celebration of collaboration, was going to be quite something. The afterlife – the recycling, the adaptation, the various variations, the gently maintained sentiment – would be carefully curated and organised like one of her exhibitions.

The Johnandyoko that took acid together at a time when it was his drug of choice – after accidentally taking it for the first time, his drink spiked by a dentist friend, with George – and his personality changed during his prolific, sometimes daily use of the drug between 1965 and 1967, as 'A Hard Day's Night' became 'Tomorrow Never Knows'.

It accounted for many of the differences in his personality and the spiritual growth between being the barbed, cheeky part of the Fab Four and being a newly self-reflective, peace-loving, risk-taking part of Johnandyoko, to the extent that the LSD as much as anything broke up his group, and opened his mind enough to be receptive, and addicted, to the experimental, protean mind of Yoko.

Drugs always drove the story, from frenzied early years to the final months of unrest, addiction and conflict: alcohol and speed to Dylan-delivered marijuana to LSD to heroin and beyond.

The Yoko Ono who mentioned that snorting heroin gave her a 'nice feeling', and John's not one for turning down a nice feeling, which in some stories becomes another part of the origin story of the diabolical, parasitical Yoko.

The Yoko Ono who turned John on to heroin, which according to Miles was in the long run a good thing, as his LSD intake in 1967 was leading him in the direction of Syd Barrett, going so far out into altered states he might not make his way back. Taking heroin as long as you could afford it kept you within yourself, however extremely, but at least it didn't burn your mind, and you could get off heroin, which one way or another led to various screams of pain and anguish, and the sixties itself splitting apart. So John was saved by Yoko, if a little dangerously. John was saved from himself by Yoko, time and time again, as others tried to save him from Yoko. John was eager to try something new after being taken over by the Beatles, on a fast track to endless disagreements and soft-centred nostalgia, even or especially if that meant being taken over by something other than pure music, a search for personal revelation, which could sometimes lead to a lovely song, a generous anthem, a psychedelic nursery rhyme.

The Yoko plotting the world we live in, for real, or only in 'The Ballad of John and Yoko', John turning his love affair into song, as if for him his whole life was becoming a musical.

The Yoko Ono who when she appeared in a studio alongside the most famous pop group in the world, making history as musicians and collaborators, recording what turned out to be their final album, seemed to be there and not there, to be doing nothing and doing something, to be getting in the way and getting out of the way, inappropriately and insidiously clinging close to her husband and occupying her own perfectly plausible space.

The complete footage materialised over fifty years after it was filmed. Of those in the room, performing the actions that are only ever done in an instrument-filled recording studio teasing out songs and textures, an uncanny blend of work and play, boredom and intensity, tomfoolery and inspiration, accidents and pauses, Yoko alone seems to be anticipating what the film from the 1960s would look like in the 2020s and beyond, when two of the people in the room would be dead, and the others in their eighties and nineties, and the world was very different, a little bit because of the legacy and enduring appeal of the pop group. She imagines how it will seem that she had entered some sacred space, once the world is somewhere else.

She seems to understand how her presence in the footage will over time make a certain sense not as a clingy, mooning, unholy blank-faced intrusion shooting manipulating love arrows in one direction but as an enthralling piece of performance art – 'Studio Piece' – where she uses the studio as a stage, the pop group as a found object and also unknowing participants in her event, and demonstrate her presence as supremely experienced and knowledgeable conceptual artist even as she was being treated as pointless embarrassment. She's thinking ahead as all those around her are nowhere else but in the moment.

Do this with your body. Then this. Look this way. Over there. Move slowly. Keep still as though everyone else is a few seconds behind you. Experience this. Think about whatever you feel the need to think about. Look interested. Look away. Gaze nowhere. Knit. Read. Eat. Chew gum. Sort of smile the smile of someone smiling at nothing. Love.

She plays being the mundane in the middle of the magic and becomes the magic in the middle of the mundane, as if she has landed in a dream and found a way to direct herself in the dream – often by doing tedious tasks that look completely out of place as the members of the pop group, each adrift in their own dream, sealed off from their fame in the unreal studio vacuum, search for inspiration, dealing with their own understanding that a few years of attempting new things in the recording studio were coming to an end.

The Yoko Ono who is often the only woman in the room, audaciously entering a men-only space as if she's merely wandering on her way somewhere else, another part of her show, where something unknown will emerge.

The Yoko Ono who always found ingenious ways to let her mind wander.

The Yoko Ono who doesn't seem to be there for a functional reason, unlike Linda, the girlfriend of Paul, who has a more obvious role, that of photographer, recording the action, but keeping her distance, not putting herself right in the centre of things, by attaching herself to Paul, so there was no way she could be cut out of the film or make an occasional appearance as the girlfriend, the support system. The photographer creates more conventionally useful documentary evidence of the occasion; the interloper apparently might as well not be there, but as conceptual artist, is producing myth, and being a part of things.

The Yoko Ono creating a work of art – a *Studio* series, a *Territorial* series – in plain sight that just about no one sees at the time, and may never see; still being the obscure American Asian avant-garde artist

459

reaching audiences you could count on one hand struggling to be seen even as she is now internationally famous.

The Yoko Ono who as an artist in her own right smuggles herself into a live situation that is superficially nothing to do with her and while she hovers and reclines in the margins creates a story within a story that she imagines might one day be discovered, but it doesn't matter if it never is. She thought of it, and performed it, and then chance took over.

The Yoko Ono who found a way to make money from conceptual art.

The Yoko Ono finding the most extraordinary stage to challenge her own place in the universe while under fire.

The Yoko Ono self-consciously playing with her image and fame in the way the Beatles did in their early days when they were alive and excited at the beginning of something no one had come across before, more aware of her place in their story than they were of theirs, mixed up and deflated as they managed the bringing of their time to an end, and prepared for a long afterlife as ex-Beatles. She didn't break them up, but she was a witness to them breaking up, a silent narrator, a new partner, recognising how their life had become a performance and now they had lost the will to actively continue the performance. She helped bring the performance to an end, as if she had become a Beatle for a time, a shadow Beatle, of the Beatles but not of the Beatles like she was and wasn't with Fluxus, giving their late life some last-minute conceptual input, which some might consider more riveting and revealing than a few more historic rock songs fading into or filling time.

The Yoko Ono inventing reality television, glorifying the everyday and ritualising the banal, playing a game among some who think it's unfair and cynical to be playing a game. She was stepping back in time from the distant future, where this resolute behaviour, these proto-selfies and proto-postings, these fleeting glimpses into other staged realities, were the norm.

The Yoko Ono playing let it be and singing with the Beatles.

The Yoko Ono reflecting her surroundings perversely, actually making the pop group more interesting and richer with potential than might otherwise be the case. Imagine if she wasn't there: something would be missing, a whole lot of history, a whole lot of misdirection and invention.

The Yoko Ono who was clearly following instructions. When the footage was first edited into a conventional documentary her disruptive, obsessive presence seemed deliberately annoying, and seemingly supplied conclusive evidence that she alone in her brazen insensitivity was responsible for breaking up the group, and breaking the hearts of what some suggested was the entire world, possibly even breaking up the world. When it was seen at length, allowed to take its time, she seemed to be directing from within a completely different film, her own commentary on an unreal world. It became evidence that she was a significant artist giving a psychic twist to run-of-the-mill, insider studio footage.

The Yoko Ono who was found out, using history as material, when the footage was looked at closely. Her image had mutated – and she is seen, decades before it happened, prepared to be patient, and to wait for a change in mood.

The Yoko Ono who was using the opportunity to try on a new identity as she applied her personal procedures and processes in a new setting. To which the sceptic would say, well, there you go. A cynical ploy. An intentional upsetting of the apple cart. Getting in the way of invention that was none of her business. She was being weird for no apparent or useful reason, getting in the way of the important work, and who knew if anyone would ever see what she was doing, and know that she was doing it as part of some strategy. But this was her new everyday, and her art had always been in the everyday, making it into new shapes.

The Yoko Ono, the artist and film-maker as opposed to the ruthless, scheming femme-fatale villain plotting to kidnap and control John's very soul, who told John, someone she had got to know, about her

461

idea for her second exhibition at the Lisson Gallery, *Half-a-Wind* in October 1967, a collection of environments, imaginary architecture and spaces to be explored in your own time to make your own space, including 'Blue Room' with its sentences bringing the sky to everyone: stay until the room is blue, this room moves at the same speed as the clouds, this room slowly evaporates every day.

A video sculpture shown at Lisson, 'Sky TV', emerged alongside her new interest in film and had also come to her while living in one of her windowless tiny New York apartments. In New York even having a window often didn't lead to a view. She desperately needed the sky, it was a healing presence, the air she breathed, holding her in place, no one could own it, and it was something that also warned her of approaching danger, that reminded her of a childhood where she could see the clouds and their endlessly different shapes that seemed to be telling her stories.

During the war, she said, there weren't many beautiful things in her life, and the sky became entertainment, art, inspiration, hope, spirit, constantly changing, endlessly renewing itself. It was there in all its bigness, and yet it was not there. It was not physical, and at night, when it turned black, it stopped being sky and became space and everything that was.

She imagined a television with different channels showing different skies bringing the sky indoors. What's on? The sky. A closed-circuit TV was set up in the gallery to produce a television that showed only the sky, a live feed of the sky outside.

For one of the rooms, she cut a selection of mostly white domestic objects in half for 'Half-a-Room' – bed, chair, hat, electric fire, cutlery, painting, chest of drawers, radio, a once-cosy haven now rendered useless, unfamiliar and abandoned, a reminder of time and its relentless flight.

John said – instantly now part of Johnandyoko – why don't you put the other half of what you cut in half into small bottles, producing 'Air Bottles', a companion lament for something left behind, a place of hidden stories and not a little fear.

462

She had been feeling 'half' in her marriage to Anthony Cox, half a being, and the other half needed to be filled. 'The other half may be something we see one day, but now we don't see it.' Life is only half a game, she said; molecules are always on the verge of half disappearing and half emerging. She was now – emerging and disappearing – known enough for queues of visitors to stretch down the street.

The Yoko Ono who was still friendly enough with Cox to let him make a documentary charting the beginnings of Johnandyoko. Things soon turned sour.

The Yoko Ono who got a late phone call on 3 May 1968 from John, nervously inviting her over to his house in Surrey while Cynthia was on holiday in Greece. His thinking was that it was now or never. A few weeks earlier he had been at the International Academy of Meditation, the spiritual Butlins according to Ringo, at the foothills of the Himalayas in India, valiantly contributing to the story of the Beatles – and their break-up; India broke up the Beatles what with one thing and another, eight years after they found themselves in Hamburg – and getting regular letters from Yoko while with his wife. For the sake of argument, his artist friend Yoko seemed a safe, nurturing person to turn to when he returned from what turned out to be quite a let-down – maybe not if she had come with him, as the experience of India melted the Beatles down into a new form. Their form of flirting now they were together was to go into his studio and listen to some of his experimental tape loops. They made one of their own, as an artistic collaboration, which segued – as the sun came up, like the opening of a great John song – into the beginning of their romance.

The Yoko who with John now they are Johnandyoko breaker of taboos appears naked with no retouching or attempt to be commercially pop-music sexy on the cover of *Unfinished Music No. 1: Two Virgins*, their first record together, improvised on their first full night spent together. Yoko is now moving into his world of music and recording, John into her world of art disruption, cryptic activism and

463

avant-garde social science, completely freed of irritating pop-star responsibilities, which opened up a whole tangle of obligations. She ritualistically douses him in the oils and aromas of Fluxus and they announce themselves to whom it may concern as complete equals, starting from scratch, clowns and tragedians, gurus and goons, artists and lovers, teachers and pupils, exhibitionists and extremists, the most enigmatically obscure and the most popular in the world, using all of their bodies to see what else is out there. *Two Virgins* is a soundtrack to foreplay, to their love laid bare and the sixties as a time of innocence and spontaneity, cheap thrills and spiritual enlightenment.

It took them six months after recording it in May 1968 to convince Paul, George and Ringo to release it on the Beatles' Apple label. By then their life had also been laid bare, become property of the media – she had a miscarriage, the two 'virgins' were raided by the drug squad, which for some might have been a sign to reduce the public displays of privacy, the using of their intimate coupling as artistic and documentary material, but for them was all part of their all-the-time live art show.

The Yoko Ono being blamed for the Second World War.

The Johnandyoko whose second album, *Life with the Lions*, was a soundtrack to the harsh reality of their life together as artistic collab-orators, married couple and two of the most famous people in the world. It presented them on side one playing in Cambridge as a Fluxus free jazz unit alongside cerebral British jazz drummer John Stevens and Danish saxophonist John Tchicai, a former student of John Coltrane – Yoko on voice, scream and whisper from heaven and hell, John on cracked, atonal guitar trying to keep up with the noise, nerve and terror, their two guests, both improvising experts, always knowing which way to turn, however violently or calmly Johnandyoko expressed their crazy abstract love for each other and for a music that would only exist there and then. If you demonise us, we'll sound like demons – although in its own far-fetched way it's exquisitely, excruci-atingly human.

Side two bluntly, unashamedly documents on cassette recorder the absurdity and danger they were facing at the time as a singular combination of pop stars and art extremists addicted to confession and to peeling open the privacy the media kept trying to hack and use for its own ends. They invite us deep inside their life as Yoko miscarries their baby; we hear a few seconds of the unborn baby's dying heartbeat looped for five minutes followed by two minutes of terrible silence – somewhere between a tribute to John Cage and a tribute to their lost child – and they sarcastically read press clippings attacking and mocking them over random radio noise, throwing off all outside attempts to stall and neutralise them into further confusion. The response to hatred, press hounding and exhausting personal tragedy is art that, only in their hands, only for a short while, goes beyond music, beyond performance art, even beyond conceptual art. There is no need for it to exist, so for John-andyoko there is every need for it to exist.

The Johnandyoko putting a wall around their lives and then knocking it down for everyone to see inside.

The Yoko Ono whose family when they heard she was marrying a working-class guy from Liverpool issued an announcement saying they were not proud of their daughter.

The Yoko Ono who married John Lennon in the British Overseas Territory of Gibraltar on 20 March 1969, a few weeks after her divorce from Tony Cox was finalised, three years and two weeks after he told an interviewer that his group were more popular than Jesus, a year before he sang about a Lucy in the sky with diamonds. Yoko, dressed somewhere between 'that woman' and a modest, notorious avant-garde performance artist who liked clothes, wore a white crepe minidress, large sunglasses, a large, floppy white sunhat, knee-length socks and white tennis shoes. John wore an all-white suit and turtleneck. It was private and in the middle of nowhere and in full view of the world.

The Johnandyoko that had a long honeymoon making Fluxus films, a series of visual poems reflecting their unlikely historical

465

togetherness, as if somehow acknowledging they were the first of their kind – provisionally anticipating a world fifty years later that naturally shared all its moments forever, plastering self-exposure over everyone's phone screens. As genre-shuffling avant-garde schemers intimately meditating on love and peace they were the last of their kind.

They made a forty-two-minute film of a long shot studying John's semi-erect penis – idiotic self-regard or defying notions of shame, an exercise in flesh-and-blood vulnerability or rich man's indulgent arrogance – that was called *Self-Portrait* – a variation watching an audience's reaction to the film didn't work due to a faulty camera – and a nineteen-minute film called *Erection* that watched John watching a hotel being built in Kensington from stills taken by Iain McMillan over an eighteen-month period.

Apotheosis was a seventeen-minute film of the view from a hot air balloon drifting up into the sky on a snowy December day in Suffolk, leaving a white landscape behind as it disappears into the clouds before rising above them. It was 'Blue Room' or imaginary snowy walk to the Taj Mahal given flight. They dressed in cloaks and hoods and filmed it to pretend they were still in the balloon taking them towards infinity, escaping various predicaments and down-to-earth problems. A local witness at the time said John seemed like he was on another cloud from the rest of us, and Yoko was very much a mystic figure, the mysterious lady from a long way away who had stolen a Beatle.

'Rape' was an extreme and implacable sequel to 'Cut Piece', which was now impossible for famous Yoko to enact as a performance, and which was perhaps the work that took John furthest away from his role as Fab Four mop top. There was also 'Back Piece' in *Grapefruit*, where the seeds for future enterprise could always be found: 'Follow someone for four hours.'

'Rape' was 'Cut Piece' transformed through Yoko's experiences with the relentlessly hounding paparazzi now she was a celebrity with added eccentricity. The score read: 'The cameraman will chase a

466

girl persistently until he corners her in an alley and, if possible, until she is in a falling position.'

A male cameraman and crew follow an Austrian female visitor around London for a few days for no apparent reason, stalking her along streets, through an abandoned Highgate Cemetery, following her in a taxi, into her flat. The woman being filmed has not volunteered for what happens, which increases the brutal build-up of tension and unease, the conflict between public and private. The relationship between crew and girl is never clear; initially flattered by their attention, she starts to negotiate with them, but eventually her initial coolness turns to real fear. Trapped in her flat, scared, confused, she makes a desperate phone call to her sister – aware of the filming, if not the harassment – and moves into the corner of the room, slumping into submission. The film ends there after seventy-seven minutes of insistent, unendurable pressure and a girl being effectively assaulted and raped by a camera.

It's another Yoko projection of her future fate, and the fate of other celebrities chased and bullied to the edge, sometimes beyond, by cameramen or fans as predators hunting their prey, craving raw, candid and unguarded photos, stealing moments, challenging control, intoxicated by the thrill of the chase, and the fetishisation of fame.

The Yoko Ono who made a one-minute film called *Freedom* with sound by John where she tried to take off her purple bra and failed.

The Yoko Ono who as soon as it was Johnandyoko didn't exactly stop making radical art. She was at her most radical, activist and bravely or insanely confrontational when suddenly faced with an audience and all those magical minds. Attention compelled her to experiment more with sensory experience and the nature and impact of art, testing the limits of an audience's tolerance. Johnandyoko in the first rush of their artlove couldn't care less about public perception. Yoko didn't move into the public sphere with the intention of altering her sensibility and becoming easy on the eye, ear, mind; she wasn't going to soften herself and meekly stand beside John the star.

467

The music she made with John was not an attempt to get into the charts, more to wrench him out of them, show him some new sights and sounds. Eventually, having dived into the post-tonal, he returned to melody, just as in the history of classical music, after the serial revolution, harmony reasserted itself. Without the revolution, though, the musical map wasn't complete.

The Yoko Ono who is mistakenly never listed as a major musical influence in the standard rock histories and biographies.

The Yoko Ono who resigned herself to the lifelong sadness of never being satisfied.

The Yoko Ono who said, 'Ask me anything you like, any question, and I will endeavour to answer it.' She said, 'If I can't, or don't want to answer it, I will make it up.'

The Yoko who knew that once the compensatory love and respect came, the massive, flattering, reputation-repairing exhibitions, the asking for forgiveness, the hate and darkness would return, or at least the deep suspicion, the belief she was in it for the money, fame and power that she never earned, deserved or used well.

The Yoko Ono who understood that truth is a dangerous commodity.

The Yoko Ono who said, 'It wasn't falling in love that interrupted my career as an artist. It was how society dealt with it that was disruptive.'

The Yoko Ono who said she woke up one morning and noticed that the whole world had become one big mother-in-law disappointed that she wasn't anywhere good enough or pretty enough for her son.

The Yoko Ono who had trained herself since the 1940s in the arts of taking oppositional negative energy and transforming it into creative energy.

The Yoko Ono whose art became more hidden and unknowable the more famous she became, with her seeming retreat into passive self-parody, and even when she was granted eventual approximate honour and attention as artist more than black widow, castrating bitch idiot

468

savant, figure of fun, wicked enchantress, insincere dilettante, deadpan parasite, her art and life somehow remained out of touch, built ultimately to resist commodification and the deadly if affectionate well-intentioned embrace of acceptance.

The Yoko Ono dealing with the problems that conceptual art was beginning to have even before it was fully called conceptual art, when it was a few stray intelligences claiming they could inject mundane utilitarian objects with artistic intent – the doubts that emerged about its legitimacy and whether it was worthy of being taken seriously that were largely dispelled in the late 1960s soon returned. A lot of those doubts were hanging over Yoko, who was blamed for most things, and over her early experiments with art as a purely linguistic form, as art working with meaning and memory as its material – concretely with nails and chairs and rooms, abstractly with art and space and language – even as she was moving into post-conceptual modifications of old forms such as sculpture, performance, music, environmental art, body art, film, as well as a preview of reality television, a 'marriage art'. The confusions of conceptual art never left her alone; they were loaded in with the confusions of her relationship with John, which never left her alone.

The Yoko Ono who some thought was about to bring the Beatles back together again at the *This Is Not Here* retrospective exhibition in Syracuse, New York, in 1971 which was also an anti-Vietnam War demonstration, advertised with a loving poster designed by the exhibition producer Maciunas of John and Yoko blended together. It attracted a peace camp of five thousand people; celebrities including Bob Dylan, Ringo Starr, Andy Warhol, John Cage and Jack Nicholson came along; and John was a guest artist. No Beatles, though, but plenty of Fluxus, as Yoko and Maciunas fell out after she felt he had claimed too much credit and made a mess of the show's finances. He didn't speak to her for five years.

The Yoko Ono who gently took to the anecdotes, sharing and advice of pre-X Twitter as though that was one place she was always destined

469

to be – alone and embedded into a worldwide community – once her life had become more of a life.

The Yoko Ono who lived to see a time when to be avant-garde – the last refuge of the rebellious – was to be completely obscure, hidden, to keep quiet, unseen, to achieve total mystery, to not make yourself a brand, to not be on stage, to be in fact inside a bag. You can see out but no one can see in.

The Yoko Ono who lived to see a time in the 1960s when it seemed the consequences of the avant-garde collective and its input into the counterculture were taking control of truth, and Fluxus mapped an early version of an internet mindset. She lived to see a time fifty years later when information and all roads to truth were being controlled and distributed through worldwide network culture by the single bullying owner of a reality-warping social media company whose ersatz futurist sensibility was ultimately a throwback to the 1950s and who seemed committed to bringing darkness to the world and closing off all exits, turning the world into a room of his own. Avant-garde was no longer shocking; the world itself was.

The Yoko Ono who lived to see a time when the dark, unethical overlords with their own self-serving form of disruption, performance art, myth-making and provocation – a world where you could get away with anything; the world as they find it is their found object – were prepared to wipe out the history of the avant-garde, along with a world made better by dreaming, imagining, loving, caring, composing, sharing, experimenting. The authoritarians, the controllers, the soulless, the digital rulers want to take all but the palest, softest, prettiest art away because the radical art encourages independence, and resistance. The art they like the least is the art that opens up the world and opens the mind.

The Yoko Ono who was there in the sixties when the ambition was to reach outer space and there fifty years later when the obsession was virtual worlds. Her art made sense and protected and celebrated the human in both eras.

470

The Yoko Ono who never wanted to make sense of it all. She committed sacrilege against herself when, sometime in the late eighties, a few years after Johnandyoko had been violently separated, she turned some of her weightless, transparent, temporary, mundane objects which she said belonged to 'the sixties sky' into bronze, representing a post-countercultural new age of commodity and solidity. Commercially driven common sense replaced a time when she made art that assumed and articulated how the world is not the world as manifest to humans; to think of a reality beyond our thinking is not nonsense but obligatory. In 'Sense Piece', she said: Common sense prevents you from thinking. Have less sense and you will make more sense.

The bronzing of her pieces, many of which were so transient they were brief whispers in time, recordings of sounds that were never heard, was Yoko accepting her fate, or denying it. There was a little reminder of the mistrust and hostility she had earned for being so difficult now that she had so blandly memorialised her dream works, turning the gloriously intangible and immaterial into solid lumps of shiny, marketable, price-tagged seriousness. 'Painting to Hammer a Nail', 'Painting to Be Stepped On', the pill, used condom and diaphragm of 'Revolution: Object in Three Parts', 'Disappearing Piece', her glass keys, the Indica apple with (John's) bite taken out of it, her most basic otherworldly forms, which in other ways had turned to dust as though they never were, had now been turned into bronze.

It started when someone suggested she make a bronze cast of her ethereal all-white chess set, a thought so objectionable to her she cried in frustration. She realised she was staying stuck in the sixties, in another life, and like it or not, there was a world where her ephemeral pieces had been what they were meant to be, and two decades later, they could be something else. The sixties were shimmering, she said, and the eighties are bronze and more materialistic, a time the consumerist treadmill speeds up and there seems less territory for art to explore for the first time.

471

The art world had become sober again, as though Fluxus had never happened, the sixties were a fixed, fallen history, and the avant-garde was just another genre, a career choice. 'The freedom, hope and wishes are in some ways petrified.' She had to come to terms with how times change, as uncomfortable as it made her feel. She had helped make the permanent impermanent and now she made the impermanent permanent. It was neither a failure nor a success. It was what it was, in a world going round in circles, and for a while the circles she was within seemed like straight lines, and time went where it went.

The decades were different kinds of fairy tales, the avant-garde had become merely something else to be nostalgic about, its own material to add to art to taste, and she wanted to apply the flexibility she always gave her artworks to exploring this change. Her art was never meant to be precious, so why be angry that it became some- thing real and more definitively for sale? The bronzes didn't trap her in the past: they set her free. She found impermanence and the ephemeral that's good for the soul elsewhere.

Critics were alarmed at her betrayal, at Yoko turning her pieces into a relatively indestructible material, in direct opposition to *mono no aware*, but then they had been resistant when she first presented the scavenged and abstract objects. The bronze recasts, the secure souvenirs of a shadowy past, were not for them. They were a small part, temporary in her mind, of what she had created while passing through a life that never stopped coming and going. She was still playing with an audience response, the real point of her Bronze Age editions, and you either accepted her calm justification for the seeming sellout, or refused to accept the slippery sincerity.

The Yoko Ono who was often onto something that would become apparent later. Three years after her bronze works, the artist and photographer Sherrie Levine, known for examining the notion of originality, creativity and authorship in art and the process of appro- priation, and for exactly reproducing the work of major male artists, created a series of six cast-bronze replicas of Duchamp's *Fountain*, one of his original readymades. A urinal which in its cheap, off-the-shelf state, if upturned, had been presented as a questionable yet unquestionable work of art was now presented in expensive polished bronze as a sensual, collectible sculpture, simultaneously clarifying and subverting the reputation of a masterwork that was itself both unoriginal and supremely original.

The Yoko Ono mixing spooky sincerity with an exceedingly dry, spectacularly self-aware humour.

The Yoko Ono who loved love and once said: It's very difficult to explain love. Do you want to explain water?

The Yoko Ono who saw the signs but always knew her heart would be broken.

The Yoko Ono who until 1967 would have been performing in front of at most hundreds, suddenly appearing on television, in front of millions, using experience she'd learnt in Japan about inserting herself as art, as construct, into mass media, throwing her voice – her scream – and herself – an installation – right into the middle of wor-shipped famous male rock, members of the Stones Cream Beatles, tearing apart the usual blues jamming and comfy riffing with some-thing female and momentous, a disquieting exuberance, splashing imaginary paint and the force of her fantasy over this new canvas, urging the audience to look somewhere else, and to think something else beyond our reality. They were doing their jobs, and so was she, both keeping a straight face.

The Yoko Ono who was obscured by fame.

The Yoko Ono spanning different political moments and geograph-ical and cultural contexts.

The Yoko Ono who knew more than anyone how people's imagina-tions can run wild.

The Yoko Ono who returned with John to New York after her time in London, carrying on life in the East Village, but with a new man in her life, imagining New York as their home, barring political or chaotic interference. She'd take John to the Paradox restaurant, and introduce him to the macrobiotic food, just as she had done with John Cage, as if life could always be this simple.

The Yoko Ono who talked on camera with John Cage and John Lennon, all three of them relaxed and smoking, as if it was a kind of spiritual small talk – the two Johns with a tendency to talk over Yoko – about vocal technique and breathing, singing, microphones and performance. Cage did a small piece of gruff, cranky throat singing and said he could do it for hours. Yoko said: That was beautiful. Lennon said: That went right through me.

The Yoko Ono implying that if art was completely democratised, to the extent that everyone in their own way made art – more their life as art, representing the mysterious aura of art, as inherited from the twentieth-century avant-garde, rather than conventional art forms requiring certain formal skills – then everyone would be an artist and art would disappear. What was once art would now be an ever-present element, a presented thought, an aside, a gesture, a performance in the flow of life, and Yoko anticipated a time once the twenty-first century was well under way where art seemed mostly something from the past, and what came after featured artistic processes and materials, but was beyond art, in the realm of the ephemeral and digitally interconnected.

The Johnandyoko declaring themselves another country in 1971 when it seemed as though they were about to be expelled from New York, kicked out of America, as agitators, as addicts, as anarchists, as amoral. They called it Nutopia and they opened the conceptual country's embassy on the corner of White Street and Broadway, a few blocks away from her Chambers Street loft. Everyone in the world was an ambassador, and at a press conference to launch their new country they waved a white handkerchief, explaining this was their flag, and this was them surrendering to peace. The national anthem was 'Imagine', the national dance 'Bag Piece'. Perhaps this was the epicentre of a reality that lasted more or less between the 1950s and the 1980s: the perfect storm of pop counterculture and avant-garde play, when it looked like the world was always going to progress in the direction of idealism and optimism, and a shared sense of reality and truth, before a backlash began. Anti-democratic forces started using avant-garde techniques to rip apart truth and send the world backwards.

The Yoko Ono who lived to see the avant-garde become generalised and become second nature not only in all modern art but also in popular and digital culture. Avant-garde art died of its success and the experimental became normalised.

The Yoko Ono who in a song called her third husband, a hero to many, you good for nothing, you scum of the earth.

The Yoko Ono about whom John sang, 'In the middle of the night, I call your name.'

The Yoko Ono who could be the gentle wind rustling through the trees in an empty forest and a great thunderstorm making itself noticed.

The Yoko Ono who said: 'In the mind world, things spread out and go beyond time. There is a wind that never dies out.'

The Yoko Ono who was there when the avant-garde ended, as if it had ever been something.

The Yoko Ono who saw for herself how thoroughly the past becomes the past.

The Yoko Ono who sang, 'I may cry someday,' like she always knew it was coming.

The Yoko Ono who threw the dice in the air and paid the price.

The Yoko Ono who reached for the sky.

The Yoko Ono who had time for one last wish.

The Yoko Ono who has only just started.

The Yoko Ono lighting a match and watching it go out.

1.   Make something happen . . .

2.   Acknowledge

Insight: Elizabeth Levy for being there at all times and seeing the way ahead
Assembly: Alex Bowler, Hannah Knowles, Joanna Harwood and Dan Papps at Faber & Faber
Freelance: Robert Davies, Anne Rieley and Anna Lord
Patience: Alexa von Hirschberg for the original commission
Mediation: Jo Dingley for structural editing
Agency: David Godwin, Aparna Kumar and Bianca Rasmussen at David Godwin Associates
Exchange: Madeleine Morley, Max Boersma and Carol Morley for ideas

Chair, MacBook, Air, Window, Tree, Breathe, Idagio, Internet, Spell, Sleep, Walk, Minutes, Heartbeat, Deadline, Night, Day, Dream, Remember, Process, This, Outcome